PENNSYLVANIA DUTCH COUNTRY

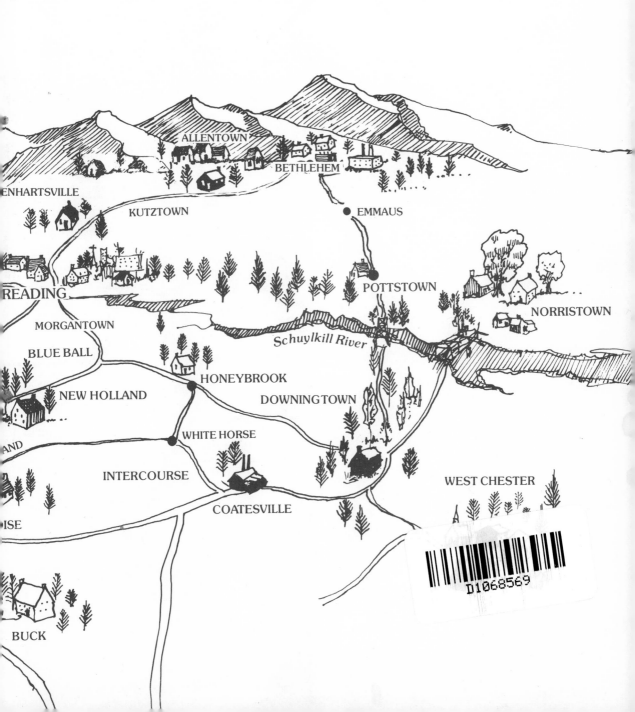

ALLENTOWN

BETHLEHEM

ENHARTSVILLE

KUTZTOWN

EMMAUS

READING

POTTSTOWN

NORRISTOWN

MORGANTOWN

Schuylkill River

BLUE BALL

HONEYBROOK

NEW HOLLAND

DOWNINGTOWN

AND

WHITE HORSE

INTERCOURSE

WEST CHESTER

ISE

COATESVILLE

BUCK

The Distelfink Country of the Pennsylvania Dutch

The Distelfink Country of the Pennsylvania Dutch

MILDRED JORDAN

Illustrated by
HOWARD BERELSON

Crown Publishers, Inc.   New York

Printed in the United States of America

Published simultaneously in Canada by
General Publishing Company Limited

Library of Congress Cataloging in Publication Data

Jordan, Mildred A., 1901-
The distelfink country of the Pennsylvania Dutch.

Includes index.
1. Pennsylvania Germans—Social life and customs.
2. Christian sects—Pennsylvania. I. Title.
F160.G3J67 1978   974.8′004′31   77-25960
ISBN 0-517-53260-3

Book Design: Shari de Miskey

Contents

In memory of
J. Lee Bausher, my husband,
and
Elaine Bausher Post, our daughter,
with gratitude for the deep love
we were privileged to share
over the years

Acknowledgments

ONE NEVER WRITES THIS KIND OF BOOK WITHOUT HELP FROM MANY OTHER persons. Millen Brand, my editor, has worked meticulously with me to give shape to this volume and has been patiently understanding. I am deeply indebted to Noël Bausher Szundy, my daughter, who has written the fine and comprehensive introduction. George M. Meiser, IX, has been most helpful. Fred deP. Rothermel and Dr. F. Wilbur Gingrich generously assisted me too. My precious privacy during writing hours was carefully guarded by Anna Mull. George Bender, my typist, not only unraveled pages of hieroglyphics but supplied many little bits of human interest. Family and friends have been constantly encouraging in many ways.

Whenever I sought help, I found the most gracious cooperation from the staffs of historical societies, libraries, museums, and historical sites I visited. Articles in Pennsylvania German periodicals have been invaluable, as have anecdotes from individuals. Over the years, an impressive number of scholars have written about our folk life and I have made extensive use of their publications.

For a reader who wants to delve further into various aspects of our way of life and thinking, there is a rich reserve of material. Most helpful to me has been the work of other writers mentioned in my book. But I have gleaned much too from the following folklorists, besides those I may have inadvertently overlooked, and to whom I apologize. For history: Thomas J. Wertenbaker, Ralph Wood, Russell W. Gilbert, Walter C. Klein, and Bennett Nolan. For the arts: Frances Lichten, Preston A. Barba, W. J. Seifert, and Claude Rosenberry. For folk life: Elmer L. Smith, Edwin Fogle, Monroe Aurand, Jr., and Edwin V. Mitchell. My list could go on and on, including writers of cookbooks, and books on industry or farming—Walter M. Kollmorgen, for instance.

Many times the fields of these writers overlap, of course. Some are deceased and others are still making discoveries about our background. There is a growing number of books and articles to choose from. But if you read one, beware of a chain reaction, like that of eating the first pretzel from a bag. You'll want to keep on nibbling, as I did.

To the many people who, in some big or little way, have made this book possible, I can only say, "I am truly grateful."

The Distelfink

THE SYMBOL OF THE DUTCH COUNTRYSIDE IS THE DISTELFINK, A FANCIFUL goldfinch or "salad bird" that loves our tiny lettuce. In high German, distelfink means "thistle-finch." The European goldfinch had red in its plumage and is likely the source of our multicolored creations, usually of red, yellow, black, white, and blue. Not green, though, for then you might think it a parrot. And even so, it's sometimes hard to tell the difference.

According to legend: "When God was painting the birds, the distelfink was the last to be painted and God used all the little leftovers." It's the spirit of the distelfink that our artists try to catch—with the same freedom as does a portrait painter in what to him is a "likeness."

Our own version of the distelfink has been beloved since the earliest German settlements. In their early ABC primers with their illustrations were the Adler (eagle) for A; Baer (bear) for B; and so on through the alphabet, with the distelfink, of course, for D. In due time it even appeared in a "gob's" outfit, along with an anchor at the inauguration of the United States Navy's Pennsylvania Dutch unit.

Dr. Alfred Shoemaker said, "Just as the eagle has come to symbolize America . . . so has the distelfink come to symbolize . . . the Pennsylvania Dutch."

And long may both of them live!

Introduction

"Who Are the Dutch?"

A RHENISH REALM OF RICH FIELDS AND HILLS, OUR DUTCH COUNTRY WAS CARVED out of an Indian sea of virgin forests in the English colony called Penn's Woods. Probably that is why a town in northwest Berks County is called Virginville, a name my straightlaced Victorian Dutch father, eyes twinkling, always called "Virgin'sville." Our southeastern quarter of Pennsylvania now constitutes one of the nation's most ardent Bible belts, though it is known more secularly as the Pretzel Belt of the state.

The most common misconception about the Dutch is that we originated in Holland. Of course, many of the original German and French Huguenot settlers did pass through the Dutch Lowlands en route to the New World. Also, one group of Germans settled temporarily in the Holland Dutch colony of New York, thus giving other colonists the impression that they too were of Holland Dutch origin. More correctly called Pennsylvania Germans, these early settlers called themselves generically "Deutsch" because they shared a common Germanic culture and dialect. *Deutsch* is the Saxon and German word for "German," but also is an old word meaning "folk."

The Palatinate, or South German, dialect still heard among the Dutch is locally referred to as Deitsch. Today Deitsch is no longer the exclusive property of those with Swiss and Germanic ancestry, for it is also spoken by those descended from early Swedish, Welsh, English, Irish, Scottish, and French Huguenot settlers who have been assimilated and are now considered Pennsylvania Dutch. Contrary to popular belief, Deitsch is not so much an English corruption of Low German as it is a legitimate South German dialect, specifically Pfalz (the modern name for the Palatine), with English elements added later. To this day it is easily intelligible to Rhinelanders. There is a story about a group of local soldiers fighting in the Rhineland in World War II who, speaking Dutch among themselves, were, fortunately for them, mistaken by German soldiers for German. My father was always a little nervous about traveling, especially across international boundaries, and was advised upon his first trip to Europe, to "play dumb" to any language but English. Though his Deitsch was totally adequate, and though he had studied German at college, he carefully "forgot" these while crossing the border into Germany. Studying his passport, one austere customs official remarked, in German, "You were born in Hamburg, and you don't speak German?" Falling right into the trap, my father quickly replied, "Oh, that's Hamburg, Pennsylvania!"

Another popular misconception among auslanders (outsiders) is that the Dutch are all Amish, Mennonite, or other Plain folk. Actually only about 10 percent of the Dutch belong to the various Plain sects. The rest of us are "gay Dutch," a label that we hasten to clarify only as due to our (relative) worldliness, and to our hearty appetites for life, food, and all the good things of the earth. Nevertheless, the gay Dutch are perhaps as deeply religious as their Plain brothers, though their religious expression is different. Of course, the Plain Dutch are highly obvious with their austere seventeenth-century clergy-inspired dress and their concordant customs. The rest of us are just as Dutch, though we look like everyone else in the area, except there seems to be "more of" each one of us.

Modern psychologists notwithstanding, fat people are traditionally jolly people and the Dutch humor is as earthy and stolid as its perpetrators. A favorite story of mine is about the Dutch farmer who went out duck shooting with his city cousin who was anxious to show off his fancy hunting dog. When the first duck was downed, the city cousin ordered his dog out of the boat to retrieve it. The dog stepped out, walked across the water, delicately gripped the duck, and returned it unblemished. The farmer paid no attention, and after several more miraculous performances, the city cousin blurted out, "Well, don't you notice anything unusual about my dog?" His unimpressed Dutch cousin replied, "Yah, he can't swim."

The Dutch area of Pennsylvania represents one of America's first great cultural and religious melting pots, for it included settlers from Sweden, Finland, England, Wales, Scotland, Ireland, France, Switzerland, the Lowlands, and parts of what are now Germany and Czechoslovakia. The Finns and Czechs came relatively late and did not integrate as easily as the others. But for the most part, all these people, whose cultures and languages differed, had in common their quest for religious liberty. Economic reasons and freedom from war were also motivating factors, but seemed secondary to their great determination to practice their faith unmolested.

The first settlers to inhabit Pennsylvania were the Swedes, who lived along the Delaware in what is now called Amity. They came as early as 1638 at the behest of their king who wished to establish trade in the New World. Theirs was a small peaceable group that started with about fifty and increased slowly. Their descendants are now classed as Dutch, having been assimilated by waves of German-speaking immigrants. The later English immigrants, many of them Quakers, did not penetrate the wilderness, preferring mercantile activities in the greater Philadelphia area and Chester County.

Originally, who were these tough, devout, indefatigable "Dutch" who carved America's richest farmland from a virgin wilderness? Descended from the Hermunduri tribes of Roman times, they were later called Allamanni, meaning "all men." (*Allemagne* means "Germany" in French.) Their home territory was concentrated in the Palatinate, the middle Rhine valley of southwest Germany, whose people for centuries farmed some of Europe's richest soil. When these Palatinates arrived in the New World they were quick to seek out and claim the sweet lime soil, indicated by the presence of black walnut trees, in the southeastern rolling hills section of Penn's Woods. So it is that the "Dumb Dutch" (who are mostly dumb like a fox) now own and till some of the richest farmland in the nation where they can grow almost anything that grew in the Rhineland. There were even extensive vineyards before the turn of the century.

The who-when-whence-why and how of any mass migration are inextricably bound together, as any sociologist will agree. The religious Thirty Years' War ending in 1648 had devastated the Palatinate, reducing the population from a half million to fifty thousand! It was nevertheless followed by pillaging raids ordered by Louis XIV of France, and then by the War of the Palatinate that lasted from 1688 to 1697. During that period the castle of Heidelberg, seat of the electors of the Palatinate state, was ruined along with the surrounding towns of Mainz, Worms, Mannheim, Speyer, and areas of Alsace and Württemberg. To add homemade insult to foreign injury, four consecutive electors of the Palatinate changed the state religion there in four successive reigns—this in a still feudal period when all were expected to adopt their leader's religion. Thus, the people were forced to change faiths as readily as a model changes clothes in a fashion show. How God must have shaken his head over that century! To headstrong Palatinates, such bandying with one's religion was intolerable. Furthermore, eighty years of suffering the ravages of war had left these God-fearing souls desperate for economic and political relief as well as for religious independence.

Their savior came in the form of the English Quaker Willam Penn who sympathized with the plight of his German brothers, as his mother was Low German. In order to satisfy a royal debt owed to Penn's father, the English king granted Penn a huge tract of wilderness in the New World. Though

Penn's Woods would have to be inhabited and developed, and its natural resources exploited to be profitable, Penn recognized a moral obligation to the natives and was scrupulously fair in his treaties with the Indians.

Having visited the Palatinate twice in the 1670s, Penn was impressed with the peoples' knowledge of agriculture and husbandry, as well as with their religious and moral views. He extended invitations to potential settlers, selling them land at ten cents an acre, an enticing bargain even in those days. Dubbing his wilderness a more euphonious "Pennsylvania," Penn envisioned and ensured that his piece of the New World would provide a tolerant haven for all religions. His vision, perhaps divinely inspired, became reality as Pennsylvania became the only colony with a diversity of religious beliefs. Yet each sect respected the right of its neighbor. Nor were all these sects Christian, for Jews came to Pennsylvania as early as 1657, as did a few gypsies. So it was that the "cradle of liberty" grew over the years into a genuine tolerance of religions, surely to the immense satisfaction of its founder.

About the Mennonites, Penn wrote to a confidant, "They are very near the Truth." Undoubtedly it was due to his partiality to his Plain spiritual cousins that the first band of Germans to migrate to Pennsylvania was a handpicked group of Mennonites from the Crefeld area near the Holland border. They were led by Francis Daniel Pastorius, an erudite and multitalented law professor from the University of Frankfurt, and a Catholic dissident who later wrote the first school textbook in America. Thirteen Mennonite and Crefelder families disembarked from the *Concord* at Philadelphia in 1683. They promptly founded their own community called Germantown where their gardens furnished the Philadelphia English with edible novelties unknown in England. As early as 1688, this small group, in conjunction with local Quakers, wrote the first American protest against slavery, while the rest of the world was still taking slavery for granted. By 1708 they had built their first Mennonite meetinghouse at Germantown.

Though differing in language and ethnic background, the Mennonites and the neighboring Quakers had much in common: their emphasis on simplicity and nonresistance, their ethical system, their rejection of infant baptism, and their belief in an "inner light" as the guide for each individual. Both groups were more concerned with individual piety than with theological questions. These tenets were shared with the Anabaptists, and the medieval Waldenses from whom the Mennonites were philosophically descended. Their name is derived from that of Menno Symons (Simon), a renegade Roman Catholic priest who, in the mid-sixteenth century, became disenchanted with the Church and formed a small pietistic group of followers who soon became known as Mennonites.

Most of the Mennonites were originally Swiss-German, some coming here after migrating to the Palatinate, and some coming directly. All left Switzerland to escape religious persecution by both Catholics and Protestants. To this day, most Mennonite homes have a copy of *The Martyr's Mirror* (Martyr Book), published in 1660, and documenting the long bitter persecution of the Anabaptists and their spiritual heirs, the Mennonites and the Amish.

Like the other Plain sects, which did not depend on an educated ministry, the Mennonites were at an advantage over the Lutheran and Reformed churches in colonial days when there was such a dearth of ministers that many congregations had to share one among them or do without any for long periods. The Mennonites choose their ministers by lot, as an expression of God's will, from among their own ranks. They are chosen to serve for life, without pay, and this work is in addition to their long hours of labor on their farms.

The Mennonites assiduously avoid legal and political matters as well as life insurance, and bankruptcy laws are considered irresponsible and evil. No Mennonite orphan or old person is ever allowed to go on public assistance, for the extended family always takes care of its own or, when that is not possible, the congregation provides shelter and necessities. They are truly their brothers' keepers.

All the Plain sects try to keep themselves carefully separate from the evils of the world, and dress in their distinctive manner to witness this fact to others. Their homes and meetinghouses are utterly simple, as decoration is allowed only on certain functional items such as quilts or pottery. Yet despite the apparent austerity of their lives, these Plain farming people are free to enjoy the pleasures of the marriage bed and of an always laden table. Their moral values emphasize integrity, honesty, hard work, simplicity, and pacifism, and deemphasize materialism, pride, luxuries, smoking, drinking, movies, television, and other detriments to the human body, mind, and spirit. Their entertainment consists mainly of visiting Plain friends and relatives on other farms, and of participating in games and songs.

Prior to the Second World War the Mennonites were occasionally criticized along with the Amish for hypocrisy in that they did not concern themselves with their brothers' suffering in other parts of the world. The criticism must have hit home, for by the late 1940s they had become generous war relief workers, sending homemade food and clothing to war-torn Holland and France. Representing one-tenth of 1 percent of the total United States population, they provided 40 percent of all nongovernment relief supplies to foreign countries. They remain not only ardent pacifists, but are among the growing ranks of "healers" in the world who bind up the wounds of their fellowmen, in one fashion or another, and are a vanguard of peace for the New Age, which is now beginning.

Mennonites are the largest of the Plain sects, but among them there are now many subdivisions. One family head will own a horse and buggy, another a plain green Ford, and the third a black Chevrolet with all the chrome painted flat black. Today many Mennonites dress in simple ordinary sportswear, the men looking like everyone else, and the women dressing much like a modern nun who has relinquished her nun's habit. But the women are always identifiable by their absence of fancy hairdos and makeup, and by their distinctive white net prayer caps, neatly set into rich natural waves of brown or chestnut hair. These are worn for modesty (to cover up a woman's "crowning glory" according to some) and also so that one's head is covered and ready for prayer at any time during the day, even when one's hands are wrist deep in sourdough. (Perhaps especially for then!)

When I was fourteen we had a Mennonite girl my age living with us for the summer to help with housework. How I envied Rachel's trim strong figure and her clear complexion unblemished by junk foods and cosmetics! That summer we shared many adolescent secrets, and used to enjoy window shopping together. One day Rachel had been authorized by her parents to spend some of her earnings on school shoes. After much deliberation (and perhaps a little goading from me) she chose a conservative pair of dark green leather shoes. We both wondered if she would be allowed to keep them, as her father was a Mennonite minister, and her family dressed a bit more "plain" than some. Returning to us from her day off, Rachel was dejected but resigned as she reported that her parents had insisted she return the green for brown or black shoes. As a gay Dutch who thrived on mixing and matching bright colors, I felt sorry for her, yet even at fourteen my pity was tempered by a deep admiration of her way of life, and of her serene acceptance of her parents' verdict. (I gathered, however, that her submission wasn't easy, as she had tried her best to persuade her parents to allow her to keep the forbidden shoes.) On other occasions Rachel would successfully indulge her normal adolescent vanity in choosing tiny patterned gingham yard goods from which her mother would make the regulation bib-topped midcalf uniform worn by Mennonite females of all ages. Once Rachel took me to a Mennonite Church picnic where I was cordially, if curiously, accepted, though I felt quite undressed without a prayer cap. Though from a family of eight children, Rachel was sent to the Eastern Mennonite College at Harrisonburg, Virginia, and for a few years we corresponded faithfully, sharing college girl gossip about boys and studies. The inside education one gains from having a "Plain" pal is far different from that gleaned from books! The Mennonites, like all Plain folk, are a gentle, joyful, and delightfully spiritual people whose mere presence is somehow calming in this frenetic world of ours.

From the seventeenth-century Mennonites sprang an even more purist sect, the Amish (pronounced *Ah*-mish) or "hook-and-eye Mennonites," so dubbed because they refused to wear buttons. Buttons were not only decorative but reminiscent of their military oppressors whose grand uniforms were heavily decorated with worldly brass or silver buttons. As early as 1693 the Mennonite preacher Jacob Amman living near Bern, Switzerland, began to emphasize stricter enforcement of Mennonite customs. He especially stressed the doctrine of shunning errant members of the sect. *Meidung,* as it is called, may be one of the earliest ritualized community-wide forms of passive aggressive control over a member's behavior. When an Amishman is "put under the ban" for transgressions, it means total social, business, domestic, and religious ostracism, a most effective form of discipline in a closed society! Amman's followers, like their Mennonite cousins, followed the rituals of foot washing and of giving the holy kiss as an expression of brotherly love. However, these rites are still shared by the Brethren (Dunkards) and other sects.

Like the Mennonites before them, the Amish fled to the promised land of Penn's Woods to escape the bloodbaths inflicted upon them in Switzerland. Though a few settlers came earlier, the first major group of Amish arrived at Philadelphia in October 1737. These quickly moved northwest to the unoccupied land at the foot of the Blue Mountains. There they soon became easy targets for raiding Indians who did not pause to ask a man's religion before using their tomahawks. Most of these first Amish were slaughtered like lambs, though some were kidnapped and taken along with the Indians like other frontier settlers.

The Amish are all descended from about five hundred eighteenth-century immigrants, and share about thirty surnames, and also some genetic problems. It is true that almost all Amish children look like others' siblings. Nowadays the densest settlements of Amish are in Lancaster County, with small colonies in surrounding counties and in parts of Delaware, Virginia, Maryland, Ohio, Indiana, Iowa, and Illinois. In Lancaster County one can find groups both of Church Amish (those who have separate meetinghouses) and House Amish, those whose worship services take place on a rotating basis in their farmhouses or barns. The custom of the latter group seems to derive from the days when the Amish were hunted and persecuted, and were forced to meet in secrecy in each other's homes. Amish meetinghouses have no organs, musical instruments, or choirs, though the congregation does sing in unison; to harmonize would be worldly. The whitewashed meetinghouses are simple as they can be, having only long wooden backless benches where the congregation sits for three to four hours biweekly to hear a sermon that itself may last an hour and a half! Evidently a strong spine is a prerequisite for being Amish. But if one should have any weakness in that area, the farm chores will soon cure the problem!

Homes are as austere as the meetinghouses, for the Amish consistently eschew such creature comforts as electricity, bathrooms, telephones, and central heating. A visit to such a home is truly like stepping briefly into the eighteenth century, with only one's own clothing to remind one of modern times. Family life revolves around the kitchen where it is warm and the odors tempting. Cleanliness is next to godliness, and though all the Dutch are known to be "crazy clean," the Amish rate first despite the fact that water has to be hand pumped at the kitchen sink. One of many contradictions is their use of (public) telephones, flashlights, and radios. A transistor radio might be found in the barn (a farmer has to know what weather to expect) or in the courting buggy (the young blades have to cheat a little) but never in the house. The young men, having sown their wild oats and tested out life with carousing and perhaps a little drinking, soon realize that what is at home is more worthwhile and enduring. With the growth of the marital beard, they seem to sober up. Attendance at the county fairs is taboo, not only because of the worldly atmosphere, but perhaps also because vanity and pride might be encouraged by competitions for the best produce and livestock. Socially far more strict than any of the other Plain sects, the Amish have no cars, and their faith forbids the use of machinery powered by electricity. Though a natural source, it should not be leashed by man, they believe. Nor do the Amish use lightning rods, and will remove them along with modern plumbing in a house they have bought. (They have plumbing, however. A windmill raises the water to a high tank and with piping furnishes water by gravity to faucets and sinks.) Amish fire insurance is their community. If a barn burns, literally hundreds of neighbors from far and wide, gay and Plain, turn out for the "barn raising." This is a famous local phenomenon in which a new barn is raised in a single day. The atmosphere is one of a fair as the women and girls cook and serve food to the many workers. It is truly a miraculous sight that brings a lump to the throat as one feels the brotherly love and responsibility around him.

Most travelers are curious about the Amish dress, now unfortunately commercialized in dreadful little wrought-iron effigies found in every gift shop from Maine to Florida. How they must make the Amish shudder, for they take literally the Fourth Commandment to the extent that they will not pose for photographs. (This is why the rare stolen snapshots usually show glaring disapproving faces!) The Amish uniform, with rare variations, consists of black flat broadbrimmed hats (straw in summer), black "barn-door" trousers, and collarless coats for the men and boys. I once asked an Amishman of the Renno sect why he only wore one suspender. He answered that only one was needed to keep his pants up, and that formerly it had to be of leather instead of the more modern elastic. Women and girls always wear black bonnets, aprons, hose, and shoes. The children, and often the adults, are barefooted when weather and occasion permit. But peeking out from all this black sobriety are shirts and dresses that are almost explosive in their colors: lime greens, royal blues, brilliant purples, and rich cherry reds. Contrary to popular opinion, these styles were not brought intact from seventeenth-century Switzerland, but evolved in the mid-eighteenth century. After the Civil War styles "froze" into the ones we see now, of which there are five or six main groups. Modesty and meekness of spirit are the main criteria for dress.

Since they work so hard and spend so little, most Amish are far from impoverished. They can, and do, afford the best in livestock, for which they have a canny eye. When I went off to college my father was delighted to sell my cantankerous thoroughbred, pedigree and all, to an Amishman for use as a driving horse. Father had carefully warned the Amishman that the big chestnut gelding was a bit *doppich* (awkward) from inactivity, for he had total respect for the Plain people, and was scrupulous in his dealing with them. My Virginia-bred racetrack dropout had been a handful in the hunt field and Father was delighted that this four-footed hellion would now have to do some honest farm work, earning his keep by pulling an Amish buggy! Father predicted that five days behind the plow would straighten out all the horse's neuroses. As we never heard of further mayhem committed by that horse, we believe that he was successfully assimilated into the Amish way of life. And we all felt assured that he would be totally appreciated, and disciplined, as well as superbly fed and groomed.

Though not strictly speaking a communal people, the Amish do cluster in settlements large enough to form independent religious and socioeconomic units. Obviously they need the mutual support of their own kind. There are no loafers, gamblers, or drunkards among them, and dissenters don't last long, for they are shunned, and thus either repent or are driven from the area. Old people stay on the farms in separate Grossdawdi apartments, so no old folks' homes are necessary. While most Dutch farms are tidy, the super-clean Amish farms are scrubbed from pillar to post, literally, and even the manure piles are neatly squared off and covered with straw for the Sabbath services of the House Amish.

Farm cooperatives and other groups may be joined only when all members are Amish, for the Amishman becomes uneasy at being "yoked" with worldly people. This attitude of "unequal yoke" also extends to insurance companies and government agencies.

Amish farms are the most fertile in the nation because their owners regard the soil as God's possession, which they work, in trust, during their lifetime. Misuse of the soil can be a matter for church discipline. It is every Amishman's pride that he turns the soil over to his sons in at least as good condition as when he received it from his father, and this is no mean trick when tobacco is raised year after year! His hard-earned cash is saved up to invest in more land for his sons to farm when they marry.

The Amish ban on education beyond the three R's is one of their practices most commonly criticized by outsiders. Some Amishmen have even gone to Washington, or to jail, over their right to curtail their children's education at age fourteen. From then on, they believe, the young must learn their life's work, farming. Of course this ban on higher education means that the Amishman must turn to worldly people for medical, dental, and veterinary services. The one-room schoolhouse, ideal for the Amish, has given way in many areas to the modern consolidated schools which present all sorts of problems for the Amish such as busing, tabooed social activities, television, and ostracism by other children. But in the Lancaster area, one-room schoolhouses are still being built.

Perhaps unfortunately for the rest of the nation, the Amishman is an apolitical soul, except when problems come too close to home. If there is a critical issue on road repair or school board matters, the Amish may turn out in droves to tip the vote to their advantage. For protection, an Amishman might serve briefly on a school board, or as road supervisor, but that is the extent of his political interest and involvement. He is dictated to not by the laws of the land, but by a much stricter authority, his own assiduous conscience. Despite their "backward" ways, the Amish exemplify one of the strongest moral fibers running through our contemporary American society. Would that our nation had more such sincere and devout people who try to live their religion each waking minute!

Another much smaller Plain sect, the Schwenkfelders, took their name from Kaspar Schwenkfeld von Ossig. He was a noble of the German-Austrian empire, born in the Duchy of Leibnitz in 1490, just seven years after Martin Luther. Like other Reformation leaders, Schwenkfeld did not intend to found a new sect, but rather to reform and purify existing Catholic Church practices. Although both Luther and Schwenkfeld worked and hoped for changes within the Church, they differed on certain doctrinal issues, and Luther soon labeled Schwenkfeld "heretical" (surely the pot calling the kettle black!). Thus Schwenkfeld found himself and his followers persecuted by both Jesuits and Lutherans!

Driven out of Silesia by imperial decree, the Schwenkfelders graciously wrote this parting message: "We hope the enjoyment of our homes and goods left behind will be as profitable to them as the abandoning of them has been to us." And so it is with most political or religious refugees through the ages.

In April 1734 forty Schwenkfelder families sailed from Holland for Philadelphia, on a five months' voyage. More immigrants followed. Nine years later the King of Prussia (for whom a town is named near Philadelphia) issued an edict in favor of freedom of conscience, inviting the exiled Schwenk-felders to return to Lower Silesia, and promising no further persecution. Alas, enlightenment came too late to the Silesians, for the Schwenkfelders had cast their lot irrevocably with the New World.

Like other Reformation sects of the time, the Schwenkfelders did not reach full bloom until two centuries after the death of their founder. It was not until 1782 that the Pennsylvania German Quakers, as they were called, organized a separate congregation called Schwenkfelders. The sect now survives solely in America, the last known European Schwenkfelder having died in 1826.

Like other Anabaptist sects the Schwenkfelders do not subscribe to infant baptism, believing that a person must be an adult, as Jesus was, to decide on baptism of his own free will. The Schwenkfelders were pacifists, but in contrast to their English counterparts, the Quakers, elected preachers (not paid) and used stated prayers. Traditionally they did not accept the spiritual equality of women. Like the Quakers, they did not take oaths or engage in lawsuits, and the interpretation of the Bible was not so important to them as personal revelation. Individual conscience was emphasized as the "guiding light" of each person's life.

Today, the Schwenkfelders have abandoned many of their early characteristics. Though fundamentally pacifist, some have fought in every American war since the Revolution. Their homes and churches may display great wealth, and dress is no longer Plain. Though mixed marriages aren't desirable, some do take place. Members are still known for their generosity to the poor, and their loyalty to the faith that brought them to America.

Probably the most ancient of Protestant sects still in existence is the Moravian Church, which traces back to Jan Hus, who was burned at the stake as a heretic in 1415. By 1501 his followers had published the first Protestant hymnal. Besides the Episcopal Church, it is the only Protestant sect with Apostolic succession, which dates from the mid-fifteenth century. But the Moravian church in Bohemia became a threat to Catholicism by its popularity, numbers, and power, and thus fell victim to the Counter-Reformation movement of the seventeenth century.

Chief benefactor of the persecuted Moravians was Nikolaus Count Zinzendorf, who gave them refuge on his lands. His dream, perhaps several centuries premature, was to unite all the Protestant churches for the common good while preserving their individual and distinctive characteristics.

In the first half of the eighteenth century the Moravians sent missionaries to many countries, including a small colony to Georgia where they attempted to win converts among the Indians. War between England and Spain finally sent them packing in 1740 to Pennsylvania where they were assured asylum. Settling northwest of Philadelphia, they founded Bethlehem in 1741, organizing a congregation there the following year, and also converting many people in the Oley area. Among the Moravians there were no redemptioners, for they arrived here in style in their own ships, which were bought to carry settlers and supplies. Their relatively excellent organization was mainly due to the visionary leadership of Zinzendorf. A Utopian at heart, he began at Bethlehem the "General Economy," a voluntary communistic society where all was owned by the Moravian Church. The community was divided according to age and sex, and lived in several "choirs," each with its own building, hymns, and liturgy. Then, as now, there was much emphasis on music. Chores and even fieldwork were done to the accompaniment of instrumental music and singing! The social-devotional "love feast" was a daily affair in the late afternoon (a frontier version of high tea). Perhaps it was the unusual number of aristocrats among the Moravians that accounts for the great emphasis on arts, education, and manners, even in the wilderness. Birthdays were always observed with special songs and handmade gifts, and with baked goods that were perhaps the earliest forerunners of that great American institution, the birthday cake.

Until the early nineteenth century marriages were arranged by lot and were usually successful. Marriage in general was regarded as preferable to an ascetic life of withdrawal from the world. (In this way the Moravians differed sharply from the members of the Ephrata Society whose communistic cloister was inhabited only by those who had taken the vow of celibacy. The Cloister at Ephrata, between Reading and Lancaster, offers a fascinating trip into the seventeenth century, and may be visited all year round.)

Much to their credit, the Moravians established a unique relationship with the Indians: they treated them with respect and saw them as equal human beings with God-given equal rights. Thus they were successful in converting many to their religion. Moravian hymnals were translated into the Indian languages and Moravians and Indians intermarried and were buried together. At the outbreak of the French and Indian War, Bethlehem became a refuge for Indian converts, for the Moravians were not so pacifist as to see slaughter go undefended.

In the 1770s the Moravians consecrated the first bishop in America. And thanks to the intelligent community planning of the Moravians, Bethlehem is known for other firsts: it boasted the colonies' first public waterworks, built in 1754 and now restored, and it purchased the first fire engine from London in 1762. Today, Bethlehem is still famous for its Christmas celebrations including lights and outstanding music. The Bach Choir concerts are world renowned.

Members of the Church of the Brethren, or "German Baptists," are nicknamed Dunkers or Dunkards (*not* drunkards, please) because of their tenet of trine immersion. Led by Alex Mack, a Palatinate, a small group of Bible scholars baptized each other in a river in Westphalia and thus founded the Church of the Brethren at Schwarzenau. They soon made converts, many from the Reformed Church, and so the latter church began to persecute the new sect. Therefore they too were driven to seek religious freedom in the New World. Twenty families numbering a hundred and twenty souls arrived in Philadelphia in 1719, settling in Germantown. On Christmas Day of 1723 they founded their first American congregation, baptizing six hardy new members after breaking the ice on the creek for the ceremony! On that day was held their first "love feast" and Communion. By 1729 Alex Mack himself came to America with most of the remaining Brethren, thus in effect transferring the whole tiny sect to Pennsylvania.

Like the Quakers, the Brethren are purposely without a creed, for in true humility and modesty their founding fathers believed that the Brethren are continually being enlightened, individually and as a group, and to create a written creed might stifle further growth and illumination. Also Pacifists, they were endeared to the Quakers for their emphasis on plainness and unpretentious living. They did not take oaths, dressed like Mennonites, and disapproved of going to law. A Dunkard could bring suit only with the sanction of his Church. Ministers were elected by ballot, but were neither educated nor paid for the assignment. They differ from other Plain sects mainly by their insistence on baptism by immersion, which is always done face forward in a flowing stream. Despite the occasional winter baptisms, tradition has it that no one has ever caught pneumonia, nor even a cold from this ritual.

Oddly enough their love feast and the accompanying foot-washing ceremony are rare among the Christian churches, even though Jesus emphasized this symbolic act of humbling and purification, advising all men to follow it. The male Brethren washed each other's feet, as did the women on the other side of the church. This symbolic purification was followed by Communion, then by the shaking of hands (with the opposite sex), and the holy kiss on the cheek (with the same sex). Finally there was a congregational supper in which the main dish might be a stew of Paschal lamb. Utensils and plates were reused but not washed between sittings; to ask for clean utensils might reflect on the member who preceded you at table. Their oldest unaltered church, founded in 1777, is at Pricetown, and is cared for today by the Maidenhead congregation.

In the late nineteenth century, the Brethren began to spread westward and southward, always choosing good land, for the majority were experienced farmers. Since 1900 the Brethren have gradually "modernized," now having more ornate churches with organs, and wearing ordinary, if simple, clothing. Their paid ministers are now college educated, and there are colleges run by the church of the Brethren. Joining the military is now a matter for individual conscience, as is divorce. Gambling, smoking, and drinking are still disapproved of, and "quiet moderation in all things" is the rule of thumb.

As a witness to their Christian charity, the Brethren instituted a program of war relief whereby they sent over a thousand pregnant heifers to war-torn European countries in 1945 and 1946. In this project they were joined by many other local sects and also sent huge quantities of food, clothing, and supplies to war victims.

Somewhere between the Mennonites and the Church of the Brethren stand the tiny Mennonite splinter groups called the River Brethren, or Brethren in Christ, founded in the late eighteenth century. They were so named because most lived near the Susquehanna and shared with the Dunkards their ritual of trine immersion. From this group split two other sects, the "Old Order," or "Yorker Brethren" (in York County), and United Zion's Children, all of whom share a strong strain of mysticism and the desire to withdraw from the world. All are pacifists, wear plain dress, and meet in homes and barns rather than in meetinghouses.

The "Church people"—the Lutheran and German Reformed sects— represent 90 percent of the Dutch population, about the same proportion as in Revolutionary days. Though fighting was a matter of individual conscience (even among the Quakers), if the percentage of pacifist Plain people to Church people had been reversed, the outcome of the American

Revolution might have been quite different.

Earliest of churches in Pennsylvania, even before the Quakers, were the Reformed churches founded by early Holland Dutch settlers, and the Lutheran churches, built by early Swedish settlers. The characteristic Dutch arts and customs really belong mainly to the "Church people." Though ingenuous, many were not necessarily plain in their dress. My father told of one country couple who came to a Reading department store where he was working during college vacation. "The Missus" wanted to buy a bow tie for "Pop" for Christmas, and brought him along to try some on. Pop, however, who had a long full beard, couldn't see the ties either when his beard lay flat, or when Mom held it up. Totally frustrated, she finally grunted, "I sink I get him somesing else."

There was little ostensible difference between the Reformed and the Lutheran churches; they often shared the same buildings (and still do), and now intermarry, though likely without the wholehearted blessings of both families. The Reformed Church originated in Switzerland, having been founded by Zwingli who was born there the same year as Luther. (What a great crop of Reformation leaders was produced in those last decades of the fifteenth century!)

Literally re-formed from Catholicism, the Reformed Church is the earliest Protestant archetype. Typically democratic, it is ruled by synods of lay people who share power with the clergy. In contrast to many other sects, the Reformed Church was not so much shaped by any one founder, but evolved from an eclectic combination of Reformation philosophies. It had less emphasis on creed and was more flexible and encompassing than the Lutheran Church. Of all the various Reformation sects, it was perhaps the French Huguenots who suffered most at the hands of their Catholic persecutors in France. Many Huguenots fled to the Palatinate, and thence to Pennsylvania, having joined with the Reformed Church en route. For this reason there are many French names among us, such as Bertolet, Bausher (from Boucher), Boyer, Wotring (Vautrin), etc.

The Lutheran Church was, of course, founded by Martin Luther. Despite his defection from the Catholic priesthood, or perhaps because of it, the Lutheran Church retained more of the Catholic mysticism and ritual than the Reformed Church, which tended toward a more intellectual and rational approach. For example, Luther understood the sacraments as literally transforming into the body and blood of Christ, while the Reformed Church regarded them as symbolic, now the more common view among Protestants. Luther, a "heretic" who managed not to be burned at the stake, boldly stressed an individual's direct access to God, since each man carries within him the Christ spirit. Luther felt that faith, not works, was the way to salvation.

Since the Lutherans were not so persecuted in Reformation Germany as were some of the other sects, they came to America primarily to better themselves economically. For this reason, the Lutheran Church in colonial times was smaller than the Reformed Church, which by 1730 represented half of the Germanic population of Pennsylvania. With the exodus of Reformed Church members from the Palatinate, that area became predominantly Catholic, and remains so today.

Despite all these apparent differences, both churches were influenced by the current Pietism that stressed religion as a way of life, for both were in a state of rebellion against Catholic dogma. Both sects insisted on educated ministers, and thus enjoyed top social standing. Each kept close connection with the European churches, the Lutherans with the Swedes and Germans, and the Reformed with Holland where theirs became the state religion.

Today, the Lutheran and Reformed churches are still the cornerstone of Pennsylvania Dutch religion. But there are many other sects that evolved from overseas churches—Episcopalian, Methodist, Presbyterian, and Baptist, for instance. Especially strong in our area is the Evangelical United Brethren Church (a union in 1947 of the Church of the United Brethren in Christ and the Evangelical Association, a Dutch form of Methodism). The Church of God, founded by a Reformed preacher, resulted from the revival movement of the early nineteenth century.

There were few Jews in the colonial Dutch country but now we have many synagogues, both orthodox and reformed. Catholicism, whose earlier parishioners were mainly German or Irish, has expanded greatly since the influx of Poles, Italians, and, recently, the Puerto Ricans. Among our minority churches are the Christian Science, and the Greek and Russian Orthodox. Others in the telephone book are the Church of Christ, the African Methodist, Church of God in Christ, Evangelical Congregational, Jehovah's Witnesses, Church of the Latter-Day Saints, Seventh-Day Adventist, Unitarian Universalist, Friends Meeting. There is even a nonsectarian service at the Salvation Army. No excuse for anyone not to worship God with his fellowmen!

Ours is a heartwarming and healthy stew of many sects, well balanced and integrated. The Pennsylvania Bible Belt comes honestly by its name. And not only do we have numerous churches of all flavors, but they are thriving, unlike so many contemporary churches elsewhere. The self-respect and resulting respect for others, found among most of our people, is directly attributable, I believe, to our proximity to the earth and therefore to our Creator. When you live in God's palm, it's pretty difficult to be hateful toward your neighbor! The "Dumb Dutchman" has not forgotten his Reformation roots, nor will he ever turn his back on the God who guided his ancestors to these shores.

For the first twenty-five years after the initial shiploads arrived here in 1683, only about a thousand immigrants arrived annually. However, that figure quadrupled in 1709 due to an exceptionally severe winter in the Palatinate, when, it was said, the birds froze in the sky! Most previous immigrants had been wealthy, and many educated. Almost all belonging to Plain sects, those early settlers seemed more industry minded than their followers, and they founded gristmills, a paper mill, iron furnaces, and forges. A more agrarian group, devastated by their losses at home, arrived later as real refugees. Such groups continued to migrate here until the mid-1750s when they were discouraged by the French and Indian War. The peak year for Dutch immigration was 1749 when 47,000 arrived—enough to populate several wilderness counties!

As we have seen, nearly all the immigrants came to escape religious and political persecution that was directly related to the Protestant Reformation and its wars. However, not all were saints, for as with any large immigrant group there was a "mixed nuts" assortment of poets and peasants, scholars and street sweepers, and certainly a few scoundrels. Even Rhenish gypsies joined the migration, undoubtedly due less to a search for religious freedom than to an innate wanderlust. What treasures do you suppose such immigrants might bring?

Although most of them left home with ample provisions and money to begin their new life in a strange land, many were fleeced of their belongings and money by European highwaymen, or by shipowners or captains demanding exorbitant fares to cross the Atlantic. Some had to wait many weeks or months in Holland or England, and used up all their resources awaiting passage, which then averaged two to four months duration. Thus many of these sturdy and independent immigrants became indentured servants to colonial householders or shopkeepers in order to work off their debts and passage. These so-called redemptioners might be apprenticed to serve from four to seven years: a child of five could be bonded until the age of twenty-one! Only children under five were exempt from such servitude, which was just a little better than the slavery beginning to take hold in the colonies. Although ill-treatment could be appealed to a magistrate, many redemptioners like their black brothers in the South ran away. This shipping exploitation system, begun about 1689, started in response to the plight of the Palatinates, but later victimized immigrants from all nationalities. Indenturing became so profitable that commissioned scouts called "newlanders" were sent through the war-ravaged German states and other areas to solicit the unwary, enticing them with promises of the New World's riches.

In contrast, the Quakers and other Plain people were very active in aiding slaves escaping from the South, and sometimes were heavily fined or jailed for their subversion. By 1780 there were more free Negroes than slaves in Pennsylvania, for of course the Plain people did not hold slaves. A century later, the Civil War found the Dutch readily shedding their blood over the issue, perhaps due to the memory of their ancestors' bondage.

Those early ocean voyages, particularly in the first half of the eighteenth century, made the previous crossings of the Puritans and Quakers seem like luxury cruises. Prior to 1738 more than two thousand persons perished en route due to lack of adequate food, water and sanitation, and the terrible overcrowding. Horror tales are recorded of water-starved rats that licked the perspiring faces of sleeping passengers and chewed holes into the water kegs. Certainly nature's seemingly heartless law of survival of the fittest was at work on those early voyages, and those who survived, once recovered, were eminently qualified, both spiritually and physically, to assume the monumental task of taming a vast wilderness.

By the mid-eighteenth century the English-speaking settlers began to feel some alarm at being overrun by these Dutch with their strange customs and odd dialect. By then half the population of Philadelphia was Dutch, and street signs were in English and German. By the time of the Revolution, the Germans numbered nearly three hundred thousand. Consideration should have been given to making German the official language of Pennsylvania!

A stubborn clinging (for political and religious reasons) to their native language kept the Germans backward for most of the eighteenth century. Church services were in German, as were the newspapers of largest circulation. All state reports were available in both German and English into the 1860s. In school and at home the children spoke the dialect that led them to twist syntax in German (or English if they learned it), and to speak with strange intonations as many of us do today. Their reading skills were negligible, some being virtually illiterate, and invited insulting epithets like "dumb Dutch."

To compensate for these lacks, the Dutch turned to crafts, showing their creativity in the design of pottery, glass, ironware, wood, and linen. (These subjects are treated in several chapters of this book.) The Dutch never seemed to share the Puritan's fear that color or fleshly appetites would doom them, and, indeed, the Dutch were generally lacking in complexes and repressions, enjoying a placid and stolid nature in general. Even now there are relatively few psychiatrists in the Dutch country.

Prior to the French and Indian War, Pennsylvania had long enjoyed peace with the red man, thanks to Penn's sense of justice. Later the peace was largely maintained due to the intercession of the Dutchman, Conrad Weiser, the colonies' unofficial ambassador to the Six Nations. Nevertheless, due to French instigation, relations deteriorated to the point of war by 1755, and Pennsylvania paradoxically was the worst sufferer of all the colonies. Nor was it the Quakers and the English at Philadelphia, but the Dutch and the Scotch-Irish on the frontier who suffered most. Gruesome tales abound of Indian attacks, massacres, and kidnappings by the Indians. Yet somehow I can never suppress a smile when I think of the story my father told of our great, great, etc., grandfather in the 1750s. On the banks of the Schuylkill River in Reading he met up with an Indian armed with a tomahawk, and was neatly scalped. Yet, being a thick-headed Dutchman, he somehow survived for another thirty years. Perhaps that is why baldness runs in our family!

Though Benjamin Franklin termed his Dutch neighbors "boors," he lived to see these "boors" become some of the heroes of the American Revolution. It seemed their fate to be involved again in a rebellion against tyranny, and the Dutch quickly rose to the challenge to defend their new homeland. Memories of military oppression in Europe still haunted them, but flight had cost them dearly, and they stubbornly refused to repeat their forefathers' plights. As early as 1739, following the death of Penn, the Dutch were grumbling about the arrogant British rule, and were banding together for independence. Their oaths of allegiance notwithstanding, they felt no loyalty to the British Crown and therefore did not suffer the conflict of loyalties that both Whigs and Tories experienced. (Tories in Pennsylvania were rare.) While New England colonists were more concerned about the colonies' business and financial relationship with Great Britain, the Dutch were more anxious at the threat to their hard-won independence. Fittingly, the first tea tax rebellion took place, not in Boston, but in Philadelphia in October and November 1773. It is no coincidence that liberty first rang out in Philadelphia, and that our first flag was created within hearing of that Liberty Bell.

It is no surprise either that the Dutch were the fastest of all colonials to respond to Washington's call to arms. The Plain Dutch, nearly all conscientious objectors, nevertheless cooperated by donating and handling supplies, aiding the injured, and perhaps by spying a little. About two-thirds of Pennsylvania's Revolutionary troops were Dutchmen, with Berks County sending a larger proportion of its men—nearly half its total population—than any other area of similar size in all the colonies. Of the thirty-five thousand soldiers in the entire Continental Army, more than one-quarter were from Berks County alone! Yet Paul Revere's group gets all the glory in the textbooks!

Though not brilliant in battle, the deliberate Dutch persisted out of sheer German stubbornness after many others gave up. Familiar to all is the story of Molly Pitcher (née Mary Ludwig) who, in the heat of battle, took over her fallen husband's task of loading and firing cannon. Those early Dutch pioneer women had no need of women's liberation movements, being too busy fending off red men and Redcoats!

The voluntary response and the loyalty and tenacity of the famous Pennsylvania Riflemen was so heartening to Washington that, having rid himself of a bodyguard that had plotted his murder, he chose a chef and bodyguard consisting entirely of Dutchmen. (With such a chef, he is fortunate to have fitted into his uniform by war's end!) It was this faithful band that had the honor of escorting him back to Mount Vernon at the close of the war. And it was the Dutch who dubbed him "Das Landes Vater," Father of His Country.

Nor was the Dutch contribution to the Revolution limited to enthusiastic manpower: it also included food and military supplies to the impoverished Continental Army. Priceless at that time were the products of Pennsylvania's flour mills, her forges, and her iron furnaces that fed both men and muskets. The frugal Dutch fed the Continental Army at Valley Forge as best they could, willingly accepting worthless Continental paper money while some of their Quaker neighbors were selling their supplies for the more solid British currency. Reading was one of the Continental Army's provision centers, where stores were kept in better supply than in any other region. Here too originated the Kentucky rifle, so called because Berks County native Daniel Boone later carried it to the Kentucky wilderness and there made it famous. But this superior hand-forged flintlock rifle was so lightweight and so accurately sighted that the British were demoralized when their cumbersome muskets could not compete.

Transportation of provisions and arms to the armies was accomplished largely by Conestoga wagons, made in the Lancaster County area, and named for the Conestoga horses that drew them. (The Conestogas were a local Indian tribe.) First used by General Braddock in the French and Indian War to transport provisions, these wagons were again to be so employed in the War of 1812. The rugged oaken prairie schooners (a later adaptation of the Conestoga wagon) were distinguished by their boatlike curves that prevented slippage of contents on rough terrain, and also allowed them to float while fording streams. They could carry six to eight tons over untracked wilds, and they early helped to beat out the path from Lancaster to Philadelphia, which is now part of the nation's oldest turnpike. These sixteen-foot-long, twelve-foot-high Conestoga wagons might measure up to sixty feet long when drawn by six horses. They were designed after medieval European covered wagons, but were to the pioneers what jets are to us today. Until the advent of railroads they were the settlers' only means of transportation and were often their means of protection against Indian raids, as any cowboy-movie addict knows. At the height of the westward trek in the mid-eighteenth century, as many as three thousand Conestoga wagons might pass a given point in a single day! It "wonders us" that there are any oak trees left in Pennsylvania.

Traveling can always bring the unpredictable. A weary pedestrian once asked a Dutchman driving his farm wagon how far it was to Lancaster. "Sree [three] miles," replied the Dutchman. "Could I have a ride?" asked the stranger. "Vy sure." So the stranger climbed into the wagon. An hour, then two, passed, and the traveler asked the farmer, "Now how far is it to Lancaster?" Shifting his cud of tobacco, the farmer replied, "Sirteen miles."

How do you step back from your native culture sufficiently to describe it to others? There is so much we take for granted, so much we assume is universal, like the childhood *rutchie,* the steep icy patch we slid down with studied expertise on a winter's afternoon. I was twenty before I realized that children in other parts of the country are ignorant of such delightful traditions. The deprivation existing outside the distelfink country often astonishes us!

This is a bounteous, happy place in which to live. The people are generally open, friendly, and polite. Visiting here from New York, I usually embarrass myself with my acquired city crustiness and my automatically aggressive New Yorker driving. My rudeness is inevitably met with polite resignation, the ultimate put-down.

Father was a seventh-generation Dutchman who was fluent in Deitsch, though he spoke it only when necessary, as on our visits to Chon, our tenant farmer. A typical Dutchman in so many ways, my father's deep faith and his dry humor were his very essence. He was to have written this introduction, which he had begun, but he passed into spirit before he could finish it. Somehow, though, he seems to have helped me in its completion. And as in life, he never let me down.

During college, Father found my-mother-the-author, an auslander (albeit of German-Swedish stock) from Chicago. As such, she has the objectivity and perception needed to write such a comprehensive book as this one, as well as her other books on the Dutch: *One Red Rose Forever, Apple in the Attic, Echo of the Flute, The Shoo-Fly Pie,* and *Proud to Be Amish.* The latter two are children's books that delight all adults who share them with a child. Mother can see best what we cannot see in ourselves. Nor is she an auslander after fifty-five years of living among the Dutch and observing, enjoying, and incorporating our ways. She is as Dutch as any of us, yet little traces of a Victorian Chicago upbringing creep through, for example, in her proclivity to wear gloves to town on the beastliest summer day, "to keep my hands clean."

Despite the last few years of increasing sadness, Mother has somehow managed to retain her vigor throughout the book. This and the rich vein of humor in her work, like the rich red veins of iron ore throughout our counties, are what make *The Distelfink Country of the Pennsylvania Dutch* so delightful. It is surely one of the most painlessly readable and informative volumes on the Dutch to be published in many decades.

The author's warmth and love for her adopted home pour from every page, and will, I trust, endear to her readers our land, our people, their customs, and their life.

Noël Bausher Szundy

Foreword

To start writing is like being faced with a bewilderment of riches at a holiday farm table. Where to begin? How to do justice to the needful vitamins when my eyes are only devouring the calories?

At a recent illustrated lecture on Holland, the speaker began by saying that the average person's mental picture of it was limited to wooden shoes, dikes, and windmills. I'm sure the average American thinks the Pennsylvania Dutch are of Holland Dutch descent (erroneous, of course), and a people who dress "Plain," travel in wagons, paint gates blue for unmarried daughters, constantly eat pretzels, and say "Bump—the bell don't make." What do *you* know about the Pennsylvania Dutch?

Though not born in this area, I have lived here most of my life. As a bride I came with the great advantages of curiosity, a fresh perspective, and happy anticipation, learning to know the Dutch by living with them and loving them. And now I am one of them. This is my rebuttal to critics who have said that since I was born an auslander I couldn't possibly understand the Dutch and their customs and beliefs. We are all human beings, after all, and share certain fundamental instincts. As Burns said, "A man's a man for a' that!"

I'd like to give my readers a well-balanced diet like that of the holiday farm table. It may not be highly seasoned cuisine but will be satisfying and nourishing, I hope. For those who want to learn more details about the history, religion, or art of the Dutch, for instance, there are many fine scholarly works available. Books, theses, and articles have been written about specific aspects of Dutch life that I am including here only in essence. I aim to be comprehensive like the farm meal, so you can eat a little of this and that and yet feel as full as if you'd sat down to a bowl of Lizzie Yoder's vegetable soup "vis schtuff in it."

I have included much material from the past, as you can't truly appreciate a meal unless you know the hard work that went into its preparation. But there is one important thing I feel writers have neglected or minimized in treating of the Dutch. Where are we headed in this fast melting pot of America? Though our contributions to the past and the present have been impressive, what of the future? How dynamic or long-lasting will be our cultural influence on others? And how will we be affected by them in years to come? Our community is changing in many ways. We're not as quaint or colorful as in "the olden days" but neither are our neighbors.

Since the meal is waiting on the table, perhaps the answers will come to you as you try the various dishes. So now "eat yourself full" as your Dutch farm host will generously invite you to do. Or, according to the philosophy of a farm woman I knew, "eat as much as you want and live as long as you can."

Seven Days a Week

"THE PENNSYLVANIA DUTCH?" I CAN HEAR A WESTERNER SAY, "SURE, I'VE heard all about them. Penny pinchers, workhorses—ornery as a rusty lock. And love their groceries."

It's easy—and lazy—to make blanket statements. Who isn't guilty of it now and then? We call the French erotic; the British, humorless; the Russians, deceitful. Naturally, many French, British, and Russians have these traits—enough to make them proverbial. But not all Italians carry a stiletto, and not every Dutchman eats pie three times a day.

There is no "typical Pennsylvania Dutchman." We're individuals here as people are around the globe. Another name for human nature is inconsistency. I have a Dutch friend who gives liberally to charities or a neighbor in need, yet saves the backs of wedding announcements for shopping lists. Another, considered generous, keeps a box labeled "pieces of string too short to use." However, some Dutch characteristics are so common that every Dutchman is credited with all of them.

Thrift is one. I had a friend who brought me such a windfall of vegetables from her farm that I was lyrical in my thanks. "Ach," she said, "it's better you use them than leave them rot." If thrift is second nature to many a Dutchman it's understandable among a people whose immigrant ancestors struggled for survival. Great ravage and deprivation in the old country had made them wary of waste. Each calorie was put to use for family or farm animals. Inedible fat was cooked with caustic soda and hardened into soap. The kitchen was the only heated room, and still is today in many a

1

farmhouse. And sometimes, paradoxically, it's hot as blazes! (I have visited farms in winter and thought I must be taking cold—my nose running from the sudden shift from twenty to seventy-five degrees.) In the old days, clothes (unless they disintegrated first) were handed down from the first child to the tenth. Muslin flour and feed bags were converted to towels or women's underwear—and not so long ago. Unfortunately, the dye of ads was tenacious, but if "Winner" were blazoned on the seat of the pants, they could be hung out of sight on the wash line.

A Dutchman may be so thrifty that he doesn't "feel" to use something nice or fancy that he owns. Many a treasure is kept in a cupboard or chest only to be brought out "for show" on rare occasions, or for semiannual housecleaning. The average Dutchman's needs are modest. When we dismantled the house of my husband's uncle after his death, we found Christmas gifts he had never even opened!

A more comprehensible type of thrift is that of timesaving: over a century ago, farmers of certain areas set their clocks ahead in summer. (Who started daylight saving time?) April 1 has long been their traditional moving day, so that adjustment can be made to new environs before plowing. Waste of time, like boredom, is an insult to God, and so is misuse of one's belongings.

My husband, in his youth, lived in a small town in his grandparents' good-sized house. The parlor, rarely entered, had three floor coverings. The Brussels carpet at the bottom was tacked down at the baseboards but only showed at the edges as it was protected by an allover rug on which the furniture stood. This in turn had runners of rag carpet on the walking areas, mainly from door to door. There was a "best" dining room for the preacher or someone of equal prestige (anything done for the church is justifiable), and another off the kitchen for daily use. Though the house boasted a bathroom, it was only for escaping a blizzard or for "quick calls" or the Saturday night bath. Otherwise, one went to the privy. Some scorned the bathroom as being an extravagance, though not outbuildings for horses, tools, and chickens—all part of practical living.

We're not "so" for frills. "Need" is our ideal criterion in spending. (I'm still considering the descendants of the early settlers and not a cross section of our present miscegenation.) There's an anecdote about a village collecting money for a fence around the churchyard and an old-timer refusing to contribute. He argued, "We don't need no fence. Them that's in there can't get out, and them that's out here sure don't want to get in." Logical? The average Dutchman wants his money's worth, either buying or selling. Well-earned profit through labor is preferable to speculation. However, I once asked a dealer in secondhand books to find me first editions of an early novel of mine, which was out of print. He found two in mint condition for which I paid $3.50 each. Soon he phoned again to say he had a third, but this one would "come me" five dollars. When I asked him why it was higher, he answered, "This one's autographed."

Stinginess, at the bottom end of the thrift spectrum, generally is heartily despised (the theme of my *Apple in the Attic*). My father-in-law met a young Macungie friend who had just returned from his "honeymoon." Their conversation went like this: "Well, Amos, did you like Niagara Falls?" ... "Yep." ... "How did your wife like it?" ... "She didn't go." ... "Didn't *go?*" ... "Nope. She'd been there."

There are several stories about a Johnny Weitzel and his two maiden sisters who lived near Fritztown many years ago. They went to every burial in the vicinity, and sometimes ate at all three sittings of the funeral dinner. The girls wore long black mourning veils and carried black-edged handkerchiefs. They had an efficient system of caching food in their many big petticoat pockets; while one hand showily mopped up tears of grief, the other added to the loot. A man who knew them said they always left looking pregnant. None of the three wore shoes, and the girls often tied a black ribbon on their big toes—in respect for the dead.

Johnny too scrounged food by hook or crook from neighbors, and trekked to market with baskets of it to sell. He did do some farming, however, and at one time sold home-cured chewing tobacco. As customers found it very strong and cheap for the price, why notice that it had no government stamp? And yet, knowing Johnny well, they were curious. Johnny was eventually shadowed to the railroad at dusk, and was seen gathering all the cigar butts along the tracks as well as every chewed cud he could find en route. Further investigation proved that he had cut off the burned cigar ends, crumpled the tobacco, mixed it with the cuds, and moistened and bagged the whole. Johnny was a hard worker, but not the kind we respect.

If the Dutchmen work hard, it's because they like to, and enjoy foreseeing the rewards of labor. Their ancestors, when settling, chose the most heavily wooded tracts (except for evergreens), knowing these to be more fertile, and arduously felled the giant trees to make room for crops and cattle. The family was a unit, struggling to bring a vision to reality. The same is true today. Every good farmer, no matter how prosperous, is visionary—he feels his farm can be still more productive, although not along the old lines perhaps. Even the young men who have defected and work in factories know that with greater effort greater success is ahead. They have all been taught diligence, even the city housewife who tackles housecleaning with delirium.

An offshoot who is lazy is anathema. Several centuries old is a cure for Lazie Fevre, using a concoction even a skunk would shrink from. For "fevre with wich many yonge ... persons be sorely infected now-a-days ... take a stick or wand of a yard of length ore more, & lett itt bee so grate as a man's fynger; and with it annoynt ye back and shoulders well, mornings and evenings, and thys doe twenty-one days."

Family pride is innate. Many a Dutchman bears the name of an antecedent who has rested in "God's Acre" for two centuries or more and whose honor must be sustained. To be forced to give up the original homestead is an agonizing wrench; often a man buys another bit of land or house as near it as possible. Even the last dweller in a city ancestral home may cling to it until forced to sell by debt or need for care at a nursing home. Houses are seldom closed for the summer ("there's no place like home") though today people may make a seaside sortie or have a small cabin in the country or along a creek for torrid weather.

Even in the cities, life is rural in spirit. Most of the inhabitants have only been urbanites for a generation or two, and the Dutchman likes the old way of doing things. He is strongly conscious of his tradition, and knows it is a good one.

If some of the city rich take inordinate pride in precious heirlooms and family trees, most of them are simple in habits and have a homespun philosophy. Keeping up with the Joneses or the jet set is for the nouveau riche or invading auslanders who have no signer of the Declaration of Independence or other historical celebrity in the family.

Occasionally a writer will get what I call "pan mail" as well as fan mail. I once was severely panned for writing that the Rev. M— fawned before Stiegel, the eighteenth-century glass manufacturer. "I am a descendant of the famous M— family," wrote the caustic critic, "and I want you to know that no M— has ever fawned." And yet, with all their pride, these old families are "common" (unpretentious), respecting the rights of newer ethnic groups, and active in social work. Keeping up the standard of the community is a vital tradition too.

With or without illustrious heritage or wealth through education or industry, our old families take great pride in their antiques. They may not have a priceless highboy, but they treasure the ancient family Bible or ancestral slipware platter never to be sold but handed down from parent to child. We love gay honest color in all our arts. The distelfink is highly stylized and as falsely bright-hued as a parrot. Color spills from painted toleware, quilts, and "Gaudy Dutch" china. And where else do you find a snowy field brightened by a rich red barn with multicolored hex signs? (Even the Plain people crave color in spite of, or perhaps because of, their drab, simple clothing.)

Our household arts are inspired by religion too. Old stove plates depict Bible stories. A favorite hymn or bit of Scripture in fraktur hangs on the wall. On pie plates, dower chests, book illustrations, and many other things, we find the three tulips representing the Trinity.

We have equal veneration for our ancestors' things and the religion they bequeathed us. In colonial days when both New England and the South were intolerant of other faiths, our settlers welcomed all sects and beliefs, grateful for the peace they'd found here themselves. Today our area is filled with churches of various sects, old and new, and on the whole we're tolerant of all. A door-to-door salesman may be turned away, but not the missionary pair of Latter-Day Saints. (The exception again: a friend's grandmother, a Seventh-Day Adventist, insisted that if he ever saw a heathen Episcopalian's playing card on the street, he must tear it to shreds.) The Plain sects (Amish, Mennonites, and others) seem to have little in common with the gay Dutch, all of us others; however, when the Amish for religious reasons rejected Social Security and state education, the gay Dutch helped them sustain their views against the laws. We respect each other's right to freedom.

Yet we strictly attend our own church services, in many cases inheriting the pew of our forebears. For many a Dutchman his church is the social center of his life, the varied functions keeping him involved throughout the year. His children are expected to follow his example, and usually do in some church or other. However, if one happens to prove ungodly, there can be a fiery eruption.

An illiterate but shrewd and wealthy man in my husband's boyhood town proudly sent his daughter to a big eastern college. During her first vacation, he raged, "All she's learned is how to play bridge and the *Bible ain't so.*" He refused to send her back. Convulsed with tears, she came to my father-in-law for advice. He told her to go home and pray for guidance, and in the evening to see her preacher who by then had "mysteriously" received the money for her train fare. When she made the dean's list the second term, her mother's pleas and family pride had reconciled her father.

Our towns have little of the mental chill factor of the average metropolis, for we're usually good neighbors, taking others' problems to heart. This is instinctive in the farmer or villager especially. When neighbors need help they get it wholeheartedly—money, food, advice, or solace in time of bereavement. Racial prejudice is practically unknown if a family is deserving and meets the village standards of decency. No community is Devil-proof, however, as is proven by the ranting of a farmer in an 1838 newspaper: "I haf the worst neighbors that ever was—my pigs and hens come home from Hans Wagoner's with their tails cropped and today, mein Gott, two of 'em come home missing."

Most of the Dutch look on man as "the son of Adam and born in sin." (Doesn't Holy Communion teach us that we're unfit to gather the crumbs from beneath His table?) And we Dutch are earthy, no doubt about that! I like Cornelius Weygandt's statement: "We accept human nature as it is, and we rejoice in all the instincts that it gives us." Quite logical too in a farming country. The facts of life don't have to be explained with the aid of birds and bees and blushes to a farm child who's seen cattle mating and has helped Pop with a birthing ewe. The swain acourting prefers action to words. To tell Annie "I love you" is redundant. The bride whose waistline bulges with her "engagement gift" is no rarity. If Annie doesn't make the altar, however, everyone knows there are worse sins, and treats her accordingly.

In the market aisles or on the bus you hear the frankest details of mister's "prostrate" operation, Mom's piles, or Minnie's change of life. We call a spade a spade. On a farm one Saturday I talked to a small girl with hair in curlers. "Are you going to a party tonight?" I asked her. She shook her head.

"Then where are you going all dressed up?" . . . "To see an old man." . . . "Oh, I bet he'll think you look pretty with all those curls." . . . "He's dett."

The Dutch disdain hypocrisy. When my first novel was published my butcher announced, "I read your book." I said hopefully, "Oh?" But he only added, "How much sausage?" There is a dread of not being honest and this makes understatement general. "I don't mind" instead of "Yes, thanks" when something is offered may conceal a Dutchman's enthusiasm. His reaction isn't simple to analyze. He doesn't want to deprecate your gift, for instinctively he's humble. If you praise him for his handiwork he may mumble, "Ach, it's dumb." Russell Gilbert thinks it's "not so much a sense of modesty . . . as of having satisfied his conscience and his moral obligation by volunteering his best that prompts indifference to praise or blame."

His being undemonstrative gives you faith in his reliability. I've heard more than one businessman say he likes to deal with the Dutch because they pay their bills promptly and are dependable in their dealings. Amos Cope, founder of the company whose dried corn is shipped around the country, and across the seas, is a good example. He had an order from Admiral Richard E. Byrd for several barrels of corn for his Third Antarctic Expedition in 1939, but was only able to send two barrels. His regular customers had priority.

The Dutch are the most natural of people. Years ago I hired a helper and when I asked her first name, she said, "Carrie, what's yours?" For several days I answered to "Mildred." I didn't relish the many little intimacies, though now I know they were flattering. But the household sparkled. Then I made my mistake. I had company to lunch and told Carrie to garnish the butter plates with sprigs of parsley. She stared at me in contemptuous disbelief. The next time I called her she had evaporated, never to be seen again. And without three days of wages. Only then did I realize that I'd been privileged with Carrie's original feeling that I was "common."

For the Dutch as a whole instinctively put a stranger on probation until he has proven he has no airs. (Aren't all men created equal?) Families transferred here by firms are often lonely at first, shut out by our innate reserve, even prevalent among the prosperous and better educated. Anyone falling short of a Dutchman's principles may have to endure his judgment too, and we have a strong ethical inheritance. Not speaking to people, thereby showing scorn of their behavior, is not an uncommon practice, unless some tainted training has led you to be deceitful. If an Amishman sins, family and brethren will ignore him till he repents and publicly confesses. This is called shunning, or *meidung,* which can even lead to banishment from the sect.

The Dutchman's attitude may seem insular at times, but from the earliest days he was berated by strangers. In the 1777 travel diary of Dr. Johann Schopf we find: "The Dutch are thrifty and industrious but stingy, ignorant and lacking in social amenities. Also speak bastard jargon." Similar criticism was common even among distant neighbors like the Philadelphians who called us "the dumb Dutch" (thanks to Benjamin Franklin). Yet those farmers and their descendants have always been quick to adopt new fertilizing methods, grains, grasses, fruits, breeds of stock, and agricultural machinery. They have created the richest farm country in the nation with their wits. Unfortunately, book learning is the common criterion of education.

The Dutch don't venture into new fields without deliberation, however. During the Second World War, I wrote newspaper articles for the Red Cross to recruit nurses for overseas duty. Results were frustrating, though I used all my wiles in describing exotic countries where troops were hospitalized. I had yet to learn that though the Dutch enjoy challenge they want it to be familiar. As a farmer's almanac says, "Neck is something which if you don't stick out you won't get in trouble up to."

Yet love of freedom is a strong Dutch characteristic following a history of Old World invasions. Many of our forebears were indentured. As the bondage incurred for passage money sometimes bordered on slavery, they knew the misery of the black man. Before 1700 they had protested against bondage and two centuries later conducted the Underground Railroad throughout southeastern Pennsylvania. Many thousands of Negroes were harbored here and helped to escape to Canada and freedom. Still earlier an instinctive sense of justice usually made the Dutch honorable and generous in their dealings with Indians.

In 1776 the Dutch were ardent patriots, their many forges producing cannon, rifles, sabers, and ammunition. Moreover, our farm wagons of food perilously driven to campsites curbed starvation. Each Dutchman fought for freedom in his particular way. The Baron Heinrich Wilhelm Stiegel began a trend among manufacturers when he advertised—the word "American" always preceded "Flint glass." All loyal Americans were urged to reject foreign goods that could be made domestically.

At first we may show hesitancy in espousing a cause, but once committed to it, we're devoted. There's an old joke about the soldier who fell asleep on guard duty, and, court-martialed, was told he'd be shot at sunrise. "Yes, well," he said sadly, "if them's the rules." We have a keen respect for discipline. This is also illustrated by a Dutchman's spending the night around 1900 in a city hotel with newfangled lights. He was warned that above all he musn't blow out the gas in his bedroom when going to bed. Being ingenious as well as cooperative, he "outened" the light with a flood of water from his washbowl.

Self-discipline may involve anything from getting the cows milked at a certain time to regular appearance at church. It even is evident in pleasure-seeking habits, and may smack of masochism at times. A friend of ours, as a boy, received a weekly allowance of fifteen cents, a fortune. No matter how tempted to spend it from Sunday through Friday, he saved the whole for the Saturday night spree of fried oysters and the nickel show (movies). His hard-working parents had taught him the value of reward through restraint. When small he had begged for two years for the little red wagon in the Sears catalog for his birthday or Christmas. He was always bitterly disappointed. "The bike costs much more," he wailed at last, "so why don't I get what I want?" His mother answered, "You must learn that there are things in life you want and will never get." Many years later a church class who heard his story presented him with a tiny red wagon with "Jim" on the side, confirming another lesson of life. If you do get what you want eventually, it may come too late!

Stubbornness can be an offshoot of discipline, which preaches responsibility to ourselves or someone else. As adults, the Dutch have learned to think for their own best good. Self-reliant in trade or farming, they want cooperation rather than assistance, and dislike government interference. Experience has taught them what to plant and when to plant it, and has given them strong political tenets.

Much of our stubbornness stems from childhood training. In "the good old days" an action was either right or wrong and must be treated accordingly. As we all know, the man wore the pants. I like the joke about the woman bitterly dunning her thrifty husband because he hadn't bought her clothes for years. Finally she threatened to go out naked. He promptly handed her a quarter. "What's this for?" she huffed. He answered, "Nose drops. Naked in winter, you'll take your death of cold."

Packed away in mothballs we have a luxurious lynx robe, and you can derive any moral you like from its story. For several days my husband's grandmother had shunned her spouse for being extravagant again, buying the new buggy blanket that he refused to return. Knowing he planned to go to his farm to collect a mortgage payment, she hid both blanket and harness. (He was proud of his equipment, always keeping the harness well saddle-soaped and the buggy spotless.) Nonchalant, however, he hitched up the mare with old shabby gear and drove off whistling. When he returned for supper he had bought a new harness and the lush lynx robe.

This is the ultimate in obstinacy, of course. But it also shows one kind of shenanigan, based on independence, that appeals to a Dutchman's funny bone. The Dutch have a great capacity for humor, ranging from the bawdy to the whimsical. It may or may not amuse you, depending on your understanding of the Dutch and your receptivity. For instance, a city slicker sat down at a country diner beside a yokel consuming sauerkraut and pigs' feet. "Good Lord," said the dandy, "how can you eat that stuff?" . . . "It goes down easy." . . . "I'd as lief eat a plate of manure!" . . . "Yes, well, that depends on how you was raised." There is a sort of gentle humor too. The other day when we suddenly had North Pole weather in April, I asked my farmer in market for rhubarb. "It was up yesterday," he mused, "but now it's gone back again."

He went on to tell me how bad the missus felt about her frostbitten tulips. I felt a pang for Mrs. Machemer who proudly sells her blooms at market.

"She certainly has a green thumb," I sympathized.

He grinned. "She has a whole green arm."

The Dutch women love their gardens and are happiest when working the earth, oblivious of grimy fingernails, tumbling hair, or backache. The farm wife won't know the botanical names of her flowers like the wife of the gentleman farmer up the road, but soul mates, they exchange slips of plants and tend them lovingly as children. Recently Mrs. Machemer refused to sell me an African violet she'd raised from a leaf of Mrs. Eberle's "Ophelia," but she did promise me one of its babies. In winter, plants in tin cans crowd her deep windowsills and grow lush with steam and happy family vibrations. By summer there is a brilliant confusion of blooms indoors and out that dazzle the eye with their boldness of color.

One of the Dutchman's most dominant traits is his love of cleanliness and order, outside as well as inside. The "crazy clean" housewife is common as dandelion, and her dominion extends into the yard. Mrs. Schmucker is said to rush out and clean up the bird droppings on the grass, or a leaf that has fallen since she raked. Her city sister sweeps the pavement daily and often washes it down (even in the rain), including the gutter. There's an old Dutch saying: *Sie fange alle wuerst aw wann sie narische warre,* which means, "They all start differently when they go crazy."

As a bride coming from Chicago to Reading, I was dumbfounded to know I was expected to houseclean thoroughly both spring and fall. But when in Rome, do as the Romans do. A month before the bucket stage (just when woods were most alluring with tiny burgeoning sprouts), I dutifully began the onslaught by washing out and repapering every drawer and cupboard, and straightening the contents. No one was going to pity my husband for marrying a lazy auslander.

As a matter of course, the campaign proper began in the attic. Spider webs, dead flies, wasps, and mouse dirt were swept up and the floor scrubbed clean as a gnawed dog bone, though my hands were punctured by splinters. Household discards were dusted and covered again with newspapers; stored clothing was heaved into the sun and wind, and every inch examined for moth holes.

Next, the bedrooms were bludgeoned, walls being wiped down with a broom swathed in cloths (like my dizzy head). Woodwork was scoured and windows polished. One needed sunglasses for the blinding sheen of furniture and metal. Rebellious by then, I sent rugs to be cleaned instead of beating them outside like our country cousins who also spread borax along the baseboards for invading moths and silverfish. Everything washable (whether used or soiled or not) was laundered. If exhaustion permitted me to escape for a social hour with my friends, the one topic of conversation was "how far we had gotten."

When (five pounds lighter), I "got to" the kitchen, a brawny hired girl helped to wash china and glassware. One midmorning I had a dentist's appointment, and I warned her emphatically not to touch the precious crystal goblets—to save them for my return. My vision of shattered crystal pained more than the dentist's drill, and I rushed home jittery to investigate. But the goblets were waiting. As I carried a tray of them to the sink, a poltergeist tripped me and they broke in fragments on the floor. I went out to pick violets.

The warfare continued right down to the cellar, which got its new coat of whitewash in the bargain. But year by year, I was more enslaved by tradition, though the most beautiful spring and autumn months were enjoyed mainly through windows. After weeks of orgiastic scouring I was in a state of collapse—and revolt. But I would stand on some threshold and say to my husband, "The room really *does* look different, doesn't it?" And he would say politely, "Yes. Yes, it does. But where in the devil did you hide my old fishing boots?"

I never got to the stage, however, of separating frames and pictures to clean the insides like my neighbor who had *de housebutz gichtera*—housecleaning convulsions. Nor did I scrub the broom handles weekly thereafter.

Order goes with cleanliness, like applesauce with sauerkraut. To break the week's routine because of illness, a wedding, or a funeral may be essential, but traumatic. Like dawn following night, Monday brings washing; Tuesday, ironing; Wednesday, mending; Thursday, odd jobs and errands; Friday,

baking; Saturday, cleaning; and Sunday, church, chicken, and visiting. The Dutch farm wife has happily pursued this pattern down through the decades, and the city wife has often caught the contagion.

A family second cousin, Lizzie Yoder, is a good example. She and John, raised on farms, are well along in years now, and live in a small town row house. John works in a battery factory, for he had five older brothers and wasn't needed on the farm. He will soon retire. Four infant Yoders lie in the Lutheran graveyard, but son Sam is a thriving plumber in Leesport. Leah, the daughter, and her numerous offspring live "back a ways" and run in and out like chickens.

When I visit the Yoders I go to the rear door, of course. Lizzie loves company—neighbors, grandchildren, even me—and works right around us with an accompaniment of chatter. On an autumn Monday I found her in the kitchen with suds above her chubby elbows gently "wrenching" John's long, lace-edged christening dress. Normally, it lies in state in tissue paper in the spare-room chest.

"I'm slow with my housebutzing this year," she complained, "down to the spare room only. I've got it so in the legs." She held the dress up smugly. "Ach, you can't think how gray it gets just laying . . . And them pillow shams, too yet. And nobody slept in that spare bed all year."

She limped to the yard with the wash water and dumped it on the cabbage and celery plants to keep the blight and insects away, "like we done it on the farm." The lawn was dotted with spare-room doilies put out to bleach, and guarded by the arthritic old dog, Blackie.

"It spites me to be so slow," she panted, "with everything so easy now. Me and Mom used to start the wash on Sunday night even. Little Mary had to get the corncobs for the washhouse fire." A laugh crinkled her red, perspiring face. "And if they had kernels yet she had to take them back to the chickens. Sundays too I grated and watered spuds to stand overnight for the starch. Once—on *Thursdays!*—my Grandmom sent for me to quick help her wash in the creek. That very day the cistern got low, but it was stuff they'd just wore to a funeral and bad luck to let it lay. Aye, yi, yi, me and Grandmom scrubbed our knuckles raw to get it done before dark . . . You'll eat a piece of my cherry crumb, ain't?"

If I stop on a Tuesday, Lizzie will be ironing in the kitchen, carefully pressing dustcloths and tea towels.

"You make too much work for yourself," I reflected one day.

"Work? Any more there's nobody knows what real work is. A steam iron slides along like a sled. Ach, you got to be old like me to know what work was. I used to heat Mom's iron over the wood fire. And then come the modern irons with live charcoal in the middle. When Mom got fancy after, we had such a gasoline iron." She chuckled. "But I used to get to dreaming about Chon and forgot to fill the little tank; Himmel, once I scorched Mom's best shirtwaist and she had an awful mad on."

"No scorching now with your heat control."

"Ach, shuah—Leah scorches. *Always* you got to think now what you're doing with all the buttons and things. Them flatirons were best. Just changed them when they didn't sizzle with your spit. And we wrapped them in old rags to keep our feet warm in bed too yet, or set them on our chest for a cough. Once I had a wonderful awful toothache, and the old iron cured me quick. Yes, well . . ." She began to press John's Sunday pants—always the sign-off.

On the customary mending day I'll find Lizzie mending a rag rug or darning; she folds John's socks together neatly, tying tops and toes together with a bit of yarn "so they won't get all ferhuddled in his drawer."

The fragrance of good cooking permeates the house all year. But when the garden is producing, Lizzie's work is supplemented—not replaced by—the canning and preserving for the winter. Leah often helps her. "Storing up like the squirrels do," Lizzie says happily, giving me a jar of spicy chowchow.

She winces as she straightens up, clutching her back.

"Lizzie," I said one day, "you and John ought to get some help in the garden—you with your bad back and legs and John with his hernia. There must be a handyman you could get now and then."

"Yah, there's such a vun," she snorted. "He come here only yesterdays and when I asked him what for pay he got, he says, 'Two dollars an hour if you eat me and two-fifty if I eat myself' . . . Aye, yi, yi, such robbery! Chon and me don't have that fancy money."

"But you don't ever rest, Lizzie!"

"Vy shuah, I sleep all night when I don't got to get up. My Mom never got no rest and lived to ninety. How could a body rest when every week brings extra the butter churning and making schmierkase and polishing the stove? Sometime though I seen Mom set down when she scoured the knives and forks with ashes or cleaned the pots and pans with lye when her work was done."

"Thank goodness for Sunday."

"Ach, come Sundays us kids used to near die of resting. No play or running. I cut flowers out of the Sears catalog maybe and pasted them in a scrapbook I made, or Mom played the organ and we sang hymns. When Cousin Zeke come he played along on the harmonica real nice. Come once, I show you something new I got on the organ."

She turned down the "electric" under the kettle and led me to the parlor, which I'd only seen twice. It is a parlor out of the past with horsehair sofa, painted china vases, rag carpet, crinkly crocheted doilies, jar of pampas grass, funeral flowers under glass, and the organ.

Lizzie brushed invisible dust from the top, her fingers caressing it as they do her old homespun spread or her Grandmom's pie plate. The organ is high with much decorative woodwork and a swinging pedestal on either side for a kerosene lamp. There is ample space for bric-a-brac or photographs. Lizzie proudly handed me the picture of Leah's new grandson.

"He's pleasant, ain't? But he looks just like Leah's Myra. I don't hope he'll be so lazy like that girl. Went to Kutztown College and smokes and watches TV now while the dirty dishes set. All sorts of funny pants—and she don't even pay her bills on time!"

"Maybe the baby'll take after your John," I reassured her. "Well, I must be going—it's getting late."

"Yah, soon he comes and after supper takes me in the machine to the graveyard with asters for Mom's death day and to redd up her grave." She sighed. "Rest lasts long enough when it comes, ain't?"

John isn't nearly as compulsive as Lizzie. While she washes dishes he reads his paper, giving her bits of news of local friends and churches, or those in adjacent villages. To himself he reads the headlines about a plane crash or robbery. Otherwise their interests are limited.

They never travel, though once they went to Harrisburg on a bus tour to the farm show. But they were younger then. Now they don't drive beyond Rehrersburg or Fogelsville to visit relatives, or occasionally to Reading where John can still buy flannel nightshirts. They make one exception. Every March they attend the Fersommling banquet in Kutztown where you get fined if you don't speak Dutch. Lizzie doesn't like to get dressed up, though. Her best shoes pinch her bunions. John's excuse for staying home is just as valid. "Nobody cooks like Lizzie," he brags. (And it's bad manners to leave food on the plate.) "I like to eat good." If he has high blood pressure, it's worth it.

He often goes to the firehall to drink beer, discuss local politics, and joke with his cronies. Lizzie helps with church suppers and quilting. Now and then John fishes in a Blue Mountain stream and Lizzie is pleased when his catch saves money. John whittles beautifully too, having made a fine set of spoons and a salad bowl for Lizzie and Noah's arks for the grandchildren. Bedtime is at nine (that's when the clocks say nine-thirty) so he'll be prompt at work in the morning.

He likes the sexy firehall jokes, but I doubt if he's ever thought of adultery. He was taught as a boy that "kissin' wears out—cookin' don't." Anyway, John sowed his wild oats early and Lizzie's there in bed when he needs her, not often now. If she has no more style than a gunnysack of potatoes, neither do their friends or relatives. Maybe John still sees Lizzie as a gay young girl, whirling to "Kiss Your Honey" at the square dance.

John and Lizzie may seem dull to their better educated children who "graduated" (from high school) and stuffy to their grandchildren who are "in" on all the "in things" and will go to college. But not many old folks these days are happy—and John and Lizzie are happy. Farm life, routine, and religion are in their blood and are satisfying.

Dr. Earl F. Robacker said, "The strongest single tradition in the Dutch country is what it always has been—maintaining tradition."

Come, Eat

"KUM ESSA!" CLANGS THE FARM BELL, AND EVERYONE HURRIES HOME TO EAT, FOR their "stomach toads are crying." If the meal is breakfast after early chores, there may be ham and eggs, sausage, scrapple, potato cakes, fritters, or pancakes. Naturally, there will be leftover pies and shoofly to dunk in the coffee. ("Dunk" comes from the German *tunke*—"immerse.") How else to keep up the muscle strength that's needed from sunup to sundown? Since the day of the early settlers this has been primarily a farming country where people need a "stick-to-the-ribs" diet. An old proverb tells us that "he who eats well, churns well" *(Wer gut futtert, gut buttert).*

The midmorning *zehn-uhr-schtick,* the ten o'clock piece, carried to the fields, appeases the stomach toads till dinner at noon. Mom will then have a feast of meat, potatoes, vegetables, sours, fruits, puddings, cakes, and pies. By then Pop needs a snooze on the big old couch in the kitchen before going back to plow.

At the early supper, the "light" meal, there will be soup, cold meats, fried potatoes, maybe apple dumplings (not a dessert), and homemade cheese like ball cheese and cup cheese. No meal is complete without its lottwarrick and schmierkase—apple butter and cottage cheese—or molasses to spread on bread. Bread is part of every meal, of course—but never put it on the table upside down or there will be a family quarrel. No vitamin tablets needed on a farm! Or reducing diets.

Years ago when I was dieting (doctor's orders) and glumly refused ice cream on a torrid August night, my daughter wisely said, "Oh, Mother, if you're always thinking about what's good for a part of you, it isn't good for the whole of you!"

Better by far to be a farm wife heedless of dietetics, at work in one of the old-fashioned kitchens, many of which still remain. In some you will see the cavernous fireplace where cooking was done originally. In others there is also the massive coal range that supplanted it. (Many chilly feet have thawed out in the oven too.) There may be the old Dutch portable sink with the zinc lining in its central tray, now so often flaunting flowers on a terrace. And even if the kitchen has a modern electric or gas stove, you'll still find the big family table, rocker, couch with afghan, and beloved Dutch cupboard; also, the indispensable washbasin with mirror and comb box, the clock on its shelf, pegs for clothes, and calendar. For "fancy" there are plants, fruit pictures, and house blessings. Though linoleum has invaded the farmhouse too, you may even see hooked rugs or rag carpets, and sometimes on an old brick floor.

No wonder such a kitchen has long provided not only for its family but for farmers' markets in cities. Among the Pennsylvania Dutch especially, these markets have been an institution for many generations. Here are sold Mrs. Heffelfinger's homemade lemon sponge pie or coconut custard, cold

boiled mush, fresh ground horseradish and peanut butter, red beet eggs, potato chips, golden paper-thin noodles, and shelled hickory or black walnuts for your Christmas cookies. Everyone has his favorite stall for these and for butter, eggs and fowl, salt mackerel, or the tiny cobs of eight-row corn, a special treat in August. When first married and wet behind the ears, I stopped to price dandelion greens and was told "that'll come you fifteen cents a blade." Too high for my budget. When I indignantly told my husband, he burst out laughing. I hadn't yet learned that "blade" was "plate."

In those early days, the market might have as many as two hundred and fifty stands, and was held on Tuesdays, Thursdays, and Saturdays from five A.M. till noon. Anyone who went after six was just plain lazy and deserved the leavings. Market houses were unheated and lighted by gas, and refrigeration for meats appeared only after World War I. Dressed fowl became the custom then, and the sale of chicken parts, a novelty conceived by a Dutchman. Gradually, flower, bakery, and delicatessen stands appeared, and Italians sold produce. Also there were sundries such as decorated Easter eggs, hooked rugs, antiques, or salable gadgets of any kind. Recently I bought a homemade bib in a Lancaster market.

If you entered the market from the alley, you passed three Salvation Army "girls" singing hymns in mournful cacophony, one playing the tiny portable organ, another passing the tambourine. Dowagers were trailed from stall to stall by chauffeurs carrying market baskets. But for the plebes, there was a chorus of small boys at the entrance, crying, "Haul your basket, missus?" and who were content—imagine!—if you paid them a nickel. Today, dowager and plebe use their own power "to haul," maybe using a shopping cart as wedge.

With the influx of Food Fairs, market houses are being demolished, one by one. It's a case of which comes first, however, the chicken or the egg, for many a farm youth, even among the Plain people, has deserted farming for a factory job, leaving his father short of help. Also, a mid-city market house may not be easily available today because of parking or the exodus to the suburbs. Though market hours and days have changed, a working woman may find it more convenient to shop at night. Sara Lee cheesecake and frozen vegetables are running the farmers of the few remaining markets a race. But no self-service can equal the warm exchange of news with farmers and friends in "the good old days."

The earliest markets were not under cover; farmers sold their produce from wagons along the curb. As early as 1730, the Andrew Hamiltons who founded Lancaster set aside a few thousand square feet for market space. Today, several blocks of the downtown city are still given over to farmers' markets, which draw gourmets from all about our countryside.

Is there a typical Dutch cookery today? Dr. Yoder, an authority on our folk life, says, "Yes," that it derived from an eighteenth-century acculturation of southeastern Pennsylvania immigrants—Germans, other Europeans, and British Isle neighbors. By the end of the next century the Germans and most of the neighboring ethnic groups shared a common farm cuisine, but as the Germans were a majority there was a strong tradition of soups (mostly flour and potato), noodle and dumpling dishes, smoked and other sausages, and pork products.

It would be unthinkable for the Dutchman to live without his soup. We have rivvel soup (milk and flaky noodles), onion soup, various potato soups, bean or split pea soup (with ham broth as the base), pepper pots, the beloved chicken corn soup, and legion others—even pretzel soup. Just to think of Lizzie Yoder's calf's head soup makes me drool.

The early settlers said "the poor must eat what they have" and their poverty engendered lasting thrift. At one time, my husband and I, who had been reading about vitamin waste, saved all the water in which vegetables had been boiled. About once a week we'd add small scraps of meat, fish, vegetables, usually a dash of Worcestershire sauce and other seasoning, and sometimes milk. The whole would go into the blender. Once we turned out such a perfect replica of lobster bisque—minus lobster—that we were desperate, because naturally we could never repeat it.

Soups were one of the mainstays before the stove replaced open hearth cooking. Other "pot cookery" included stews of fish or game. We're still fond of our frugal "pot" dinners, or a combination like beef boiled with turnips, and green beans and often potatoes with ham. Squares of dough too are often dropped into the boiling broth of meat or fowl. Here is the recipe for one of our favorites:

SCHNITZ UN KNEPP

2 *cups dried sweet apple*	2 *tablespoons sugar*
slices, unpeeled	1 *teaspoon salt*
1 *small piece smoked pork*	

KNEPP

1 *cup flour*	1 *egg, beaten*
1 *level teaspoon baking powder*	*a little water*
pinch of salt	

Soak the apples in water overnight. Boil the pork until tender, add the apples and the water in which they have been soaked. Simmer together until apples are soft, add the sugar and salt. Make the knepp by sifting the flour, baking powder, and salt together, mixing with the beaten egg and just enough water to make a batter that can scarcely be stirred with a spoon. Drop the knepp in small spoonfuls between the apples in the stew. Cover and boil briskly for 10 minutes. Serves 4.

Other old-time meat dishes are boova shenkel (beef and dumpling dish), sourbraten (sour beef roast), hasenpfeffer, fowl, seafood (notably oysters), and various by-products of butchering. We are devotees of pork. What is more appetizing on a cold winter's day than pork and sauerkraut, with its inevitable mashed potatoes and applesauce? Because of its popularity with farmers at plowing time, there is an old saying: "sauerkraut and speck pushes the earth away." Totally Germanic is the feast of sauerkraut on New Year's Day, and in certain sections it's even a "must" to eat it with turkey on other occasions; it "cuts the grease." Addicts claim it's best when reheated. I like the silly little riddle: Q: If I sent you to the butcher for a yard of pork, what would you bring me? A: Three feet.

Lamb is low on the popularity poll, though there is more sheep raising now. Years ago when my husband and I rented a country place, a butcher drove up to the door one day. I said I'd take four lamb chops. Believe it or not, Mr. Ripley, he didn't know what they were. Pork, of course—and beef, yes—but lamb? Aye, yi, yi, such a crazy woman!

Our Lebanon bologna is a worldwide traveler and has often warmed the hearts as well as the stomachs of our far-off soldiers. This is a large, hard sausage highly flavored. Scrapple, or *pannhaus,* is literally "pan rabbit," though no one knows why. Its base is the scraps of pork from butchering—even snouts and skin—cut fine in meat broth to which cornmeal and spices are added. The early Dutch, Swedish, and other settlers brought recipes for a similar pork or "hash" dish, but Dr. Yoder says that scrapple, per se, is "the wedding of German skills to American Indian cornmeal." At the end of the nineteenth century, farmers carted scrapple into Philadelphia and other cities for our farm deserters who craved it. Philadelphia is now famous for its commercial product, though various packers make it, even shipping it west. Since it has so little definable meat, it was sold without food stamps in World War II. I've never eaten commercial scrapple, but I shudder at thought of any recipe compared with that of my country butcher. Each farmer has his own formula varying in the kind of flour used—cornmeal, buckwheat, soybean—and in choice and amount of spices.

Since we don't eat meat for its protein value we enjoy it, both fat and lean. We like our eggs, too, better just plain fried than in fancy omelets. Also, we're devoted to hard-boiled eggs steeped in red beet juice, though sometimes we must sacrifice them for economy's sake.

In a country store Annie asked the price of eggs.

"Seventy-five cents a dozen," Ezra told her.

"Ach, still so dear!" she sighed.

"I got cracked ones at thirty-five."

Annie beamed. "Crack me a dozen, Ezra. I'll mix'em vis my fried potatoes."

The potato, of course, is king of the vegetables, appearing in many guises, the most popular being potato filling for fowl, the classic potato salad, and Dutch fries. In the days of cast-iron stoves children loved to slice potatoes thin and fry them on the hot stove plates for winter snacks. These only whetted the appetite for Mom's potato dumpling dinner. There are various kinds of potato dumplings, all important enough to deserve a fancy name. "Pigeons" consist of grated raw potato, hard-cooked egg, onion, and parsley made into turnovers and steamed. Maybe you prefer other kinds like "Old Shoes" and "Pants Pockets." Love of spuds likely produced another old riddle: Q: Where are bellies the fattest? A: In the front—you don't have any in the back.

We are fond of all kinds of vegetables. No turkey dinner is tolerable without its dried corn and tiny fresh creamed onions. Sugar peas are picked as the peas are forming and are eaten pods and all. Green beans are never tastier than when cooked "to" ham. Our baked lima beans are a specialty, perhaps too sweet for foreign taste, but all our cookery suggests a sweet tooth. We relish everything from the first asparagus sprouts to the autumn pumpkin. There are few vegetables in the dictionary that don't appear in a farm garden, and at summer's close the odds and ends go into a spicy pepper hash or chowchow.

If potato is king, then corn is queen. We revel in corn pie, corn pudding, fritters, corn relish, mush, and even waffles made of corn mix. The following recipe for corn pie will make it become a habit:

CORN PIE

Line a 2-quart casserole with easy-to-make piecrust, then prepare the following filling:

2 cans corn (12 oz.) (frozen or fresh corn can be used)	¼ teaspoon salt
	dash of pepper
2 cups milk	6 saltines
3 tablespoons butter	2 hard-cooked eggs

Place corn in casserole and cover with milk. Add butter, salt and pepper and crumble crackers over mixture. (Do not overfill.) Slice the eggs across the top, then seal with crust. Bake at 375 degrees for 1 hour or until brown. Serve hot. (I might add that mention of "boughten" pie dough or canned corn is only for the lazy auslander!)

Dried corn, too, is as Dutch as the Dutch. Its origin is another case of economy in the days when food had to be preserved by smoking, salting, or drying. The corn crop was large and the peak flavor short-lived, but with drying no corn was wasted. Once all dried corn had to be soaked before cooking, but today you can get a frozen variety for quick use.

Cornmeal mush deserves a fervent eulogy. Of all the corn dishes inherited from the Indians it was the first and most common in the colonies. It was eaten throughout the east, though known by different names—in New England, for instance, being "hasty pudding." The frontier Scotch-Irish often ate mush three times a day. Johnny Appleseed's hat is said to have been the large tin dipper in which he cooked his mush while traveling. At the Quaker Westtown School, it was served five nights a week. The luckless Methodist circuit-rider was usually offered mush or nothing by his host of a night's lodging. Even in the late 1800s in our own area, mush parties were held: quilting bees, husking frolics, and other get-togethers.

Though a staple on all rural tables till 1900, mush can still be called typically Dutch because our fondness for it lingers. You can eat it boiled with or without milk and sugar (smooth or lumpy, alas), or in crisp fried slices, swimming in syrup or molasses. But there is still no better sweet-dream-producing dish in the evening than fresh cooked mush.

Salads are anything but the conventional ones you find in the average cookbook. Dandelion salad with hot bacon dressing goes hand-to-mouth with springtime shad. Just "salad" (tiny new garden lettuce no bigger than flower petals) is smothered with either a hot bacon or sweet-sour cream dressing and hard-cooked egg. A tender young cabbage becomes coleslaw or pepper cabbage. (We are generous with vinegar as well as our sugar in cooking.) And oh, those sun-ripened tomatoes sliced with bits of onion and sweet vinegar dressing!

As to our "seven sweets and sours," they aren't all obligatory at every meal as hearsay would have you think. But they are always plentiful on the table: pickled vegetables ad infinitum, jams (even tomato), stewed fruits and sauces (use smokehouse apples for sauce), and the inimitable brandied peaches. Have you ever made them by jarring the fruit, covering with sugar syrup, and burying it in the ground to be "kicked" by early frost?

Mentioning fruit recalls our first months of marriage when we lived with my husband's parents. I was asked to take over some household chores, one being planning and cooking a meal now and then. Thinking I'd impress the family with a special bridal treat I once fried bananas for dessert. They were met with dead silence. Friday was pie day. And besides, this was no dessert for a Dutchman, except for my loyal bridegroom who mumbled, "Delicious."

Like our German-Swiss ancestors we eat an abundance of fruit most of which we raise. Schnitz (dried apple slices) have been part of our farm diet for two hundred years.

When Johnny was having trouble with fractions, his teacher asked:
"If you cut an apple into two parts what would you call each piece?"
"A half."
"Good. If you cut each half in two, what would you have then?"
"Four quarters," was Johnny's quick reply.
"Correct. And if you cut each quarter into halves, what would you call each slice?"
"Apple schnitz," said Johnny, triumphant.

Sometimes schnitz were used in the early days for bartering at country stores, or even served as a pastor's wedding fee. There are sweet and sour schnitz, depending on the kind of apples used. Sweet schnitz are stewed for a side dish, or, like the pretzel, are munched by a country schoolchild in moments of starvation or boredom. Sour schnitz (ideally from Paradise apples) are for pie and other dishes.

Apple butter boiling is a custom brought from the Palatinate where all kinds of fruit were cooked for long hours in great kettles over open fires. All Dutchmen delight in lottwarrick (apple butter) from the cradle to the grave. Depending on the brand of apple used, and the content of spices, it may vary greatly.

Much preserving is still done in the country. Even the city hausfrau, feeling the pinch of inflation, is doing her share of "putting up" these days. All kinds of vegetables, fruit, and wild berries are canned or frozen for the winter. If you have an overabundance of tomatoes, as most ardent gardeners do, and you can't give them away "for love or money," try the following simple Dutch recipe:

SUMMER MINCEMEAT

8 large green tomatoes	*1 teaspoon salt*
8 large sour apples	*1 pound seedless raisins*
1 cup vinegar	*1 teaspoon cinnamon*
1 cup molasses	*1 teaspoon cloves*
3 cups brown sugar	*½ teaspoon ginger*
½ cup butter	

Core the tomatoes and apples but do not peel. Put through food chopper and add remaining ingredients. Pour into large kettle and mix thoroughly. Bring to boil and keep boiling for 5 minutes. Immediately put into jars and seal. This yields a gallon. It is now ready to use as pie filling.

Baking day (bock tawg day), traditionally Friday, is a joyful fragrant time when Mom bakes pie, cake, and bread for the coming week. (Sometimes it's hard to tell cake from bread.) A hundred years ago bock tawg day was a necessity and so was the pie cupboard: besides the family to be fed there were many extra hired hands at haymaking and harvesting time. The days are gone when bread was shoved into an outdoor oven to be baked until brown and crusty. Many a child must have begged then to dust off the ashes, cut a thick slice, and gobble it down smeared with fresh churned butter. In recent years, it's been disillusioning to see a bread delivery at a farm, though with the current high prices, many farm wives are baking their own again. A toddler of the old days, prone to eating everything he saw (food or otherwise) was often given bread or schnitz tied in a rag to suck on. Some of today's commercial bread would surely have broken him of the habit!

The earliest German pie was actually kuchen—flat tins of cake dough containing a mixture of fruit slices held firm with custard. I'll never forget my Grossmama's "at home" days in Chicago, the first Thursday of every month. (The "receiving" days of all her friends were engraved on their calling cards.) The table was laden with a dozen such kuchen, soon devoured by her kaffeeklatsch cronies along with the gossip. Needless to say, I wolfed my share.

The Pennsylvania Dutch adopted the round fruit pie from the British, and we are now so addicted that we are indeed "the pie belt." (No pun intended.) Any kind of pie is desirable—meat, vegetable, or dessert pie. If desperate, we use anything available at the moment for a concoction. We even make a vinegar pie with egg, flour, and sugar, and onion pie is a gourmet treat. Have you ever tried potato custard pie?

Shortly after I married, my mother-in-law took me in hand, showing me how to make her delectable piecrust, without recipe, of course. In Berks County, pie, like oxygen, is vital. At one restaurant we go to we greedily order our pie before reading the menu, or by dessert time the famous cherry crumb might be "all."

Crumb pie, with bottom crust only, and sugar flour crumbs atop the fruit, is a specialty of our area. Is it a kissing cousin of the German kuchen or was it devised by a hausfrau who ran short of dough? Raisin crumb, known as funeral pie, has always been indispensable at funeral suppers. The old cherry custard is something of a novelty today. And what are half-moon pies? Small circles of piecrust folded over schnitz, which keep the Amish children from *rutsching* at the long Sunday service. Small bits of leftover pastry dough can be used to make a tiny milk tart, flavored with sugar or cinnamon or at will. (Remember, no waste!)

Shoofly pie, dating from colonial days, has national renown. Actually it is a molasses cake in a lower piecrust with sweet crumbs on top. Preston Barba, the Pennsylvania German scholar, thought the name might be a corruption of the French *chou-fleur* (cauliflower), suggested by the crumbs and so called by our early French Huguenots. At any rate, it's another indispensable of our diet and is usually classified as wet or dry, depending on how gooey you like the molasses mixture just above the crust. Recipes differ from county to county. (Oddly enough, to railroaders, a "shoofly" is a temporary track around a derailment.)

LANCASTER COUNTY SHOOFLY PIE

FILLING	CRUMBS
1½ *cups boiling water*	4 *cups sifted flour*
1 *teaspoon baking soda*	2 *cups brown sugar*
1 *cup molasses*	1 *cup shortening*
	¼ *teaspoon salt*

Pour the boiling water over the baking soda and stir into the molasses. Line two pastry tins with piecrust, pour in mixture equally, to half fill pies. Sprinkle crumbs on top. Bake in 350-degree oven for 30 to 40 minutes. Makes 2 8-inch pies.

Shoofly makes ideal dunking. And by the way, I recently read of a National Dunking Society with over 3 million members, including such celebrities as Bob Hope, Congressman Jennings Randolph, and Carveth Wells. There are simple ways of making the most of life.

Cakes are highly important and lonely without stewed fruits or puddings, for our concept of dessert is plural. We have numerous intriguing cake recipes—even onion cake—but there is no orthodox definition of "cake," which may be a pancake, dunkable coffee cake, or a soft overgrown cookie. In country districts and villages before the Civil War, old women might keep a "cake and beer" or a "cake and mead" shop where one could give and take local gossip. There is a very old "sticky bun" shop in Collegeville that used to serve coffee "with" and is likely a relic of the mead shop; now it caters to the hurry-up trade.

Today, however, Blue Ribbon winners at county fairs are a marble cake, angel food, hickory nut cake, or Devil's food, for chocolate has won the heart of the Dutchman too. If you want a challenge, try making the following (and beware of dental fillings):

POPCORN CAKE MENNONITE

3 quarts popped corn	*2½ cups powdered sugar*
2½ cups chopped nuts	*3 tablespoons butter*

Mix the popped corn and the nuts, and pour over it the following syrup: sugar and butter cooked together until it forms a taffy when you test it in water. Mix the syrup well with the popcorn and nuts, using a large spoon. Butter a cake pan and put in a layer of the mixture, and press together; then another layer and press, until the pan is full. Then you can slice the "cake."

Fruitcake is made in many a home weeks before Christmas (two weeks before Thanksgiving being traditional) along with the holiday cookies. Epics could be written about the latter. It's a shameful housewife indeed who doesn't hide hundreds of them in old pretzel or potato-chip cans in the attic, hoping her young barbarians won't find them. Some cookies with their red and green sugar decoration, or Christmas symbols, may be hung on the tree, strung on walls, or placed on windowsills "just for fancy." The best are saved to serve with wine to callers, or to give in festive boxes to the sick or needy or friends bringing unexpected gifts.

Most popular are spicy gingersnaps, sand tarts (saint hearts), walnut kisses, Michigan rocks, peffer niss, lebkuchen (ginger cakes), crunchy, lacy Scotch cookies, and springerles. The last is a hard Moravian cookie with finely detailed designs (flowers, castles, birds, people) made by a carved board pressed into dough, which is cut into two-inch squares. It is flavored with rose water (get it from your apothecary) and may be decorated with vegetable dyes, colored sugar, and caraway seeds. Anise should be sprinkled into the pan in which you bake it. Since springerles are made without leavening, they keep indefinitely. (They are often reserved for Easter, and collectors have been known to own some aged one hundred!)

A popular sugar cookie is the apee, or apise (there are half a dozen spellings), reportedly like those Ann Page marked with her initials and sold from her basket in Philadelphia about 1830. Another interpretation is that apee derives from the French *pain d'épice,* a kind of gingerbread. Since our apee has no spice, its source is still a mystery.

For other kinds of cookies there are nearly forgotten recipes handed down from mother to daughter. It's no wonder that cookie cutters may be an old and prized inheritance, especially springerle molds made of wood.

Fastnachts, an Easter treat, are made of bread dough enriched by shortening and an egg or two. Genuine fastnachts are made without yeast. It would be sacrilege to both stomach and tradition not to eat them at Shrove Tuesday breakfast. Might they be a survival of the burnt offering our primitive Palatinate ancestors made to the Spring Goddess, Ostara?

We have always loved waffles (claimed to be Dutch in origin) especially with chicken and gravy. Often too they're submerged with molasses or syrup like scrapple, funnel cakes, or the many fried foods like cold mush, egg bread, French toast, and potato cakes. Waffles baked between two pressed irons are most common, but there is also the deep-fried waffle-hex made from one iron plate with design. Few persons know about the latter unless they live in our area or are lucky enough to own a waffle-hex iron handed down through the generations. In the old days no two waffle irons had the same design, for the mold was made by hand. A rarity is heart-shaped, or one with the date, maybe 1760, a heart, and two sets of initials (his and hers).

Fritters are highly popular, especially those with corn or apple. If you want to be adventuresome, try fritters made with parsnips or elderberry blossom. Cherry fritters, like most others, are deep fried. You make them in the late spring cherry season, of course.

Various cheeses are relished, but usually not the exotic brands of New York menus, and little cheese is used in cooking. We prefer eating our cheese "chust so," and most enjoy the homemade varieties like schmierkase. Ball cheese is made from thick sour milk, and is good with rye bread. Cup cheese is made from baked milk curds to which are added cream, butter, baking soda, salt, and beaten eggs. It is poured into cups and cooled, and hence gets its name. You will find it in every farmer's market.

There is one food for which the Dutchman has a passion and for which we are nationally known, the pretzel. On my first Reading visit I was served ice cream with pretzels—at a party! If they'd been rotten Chinese eggs I couldn't have been more astounded. In the Midwest, pretzels were only part of an occasional kalderaufschnit from a delicatessen. I soon learned that here they were a household staple, delivered like bread.

The little town of Lititz claims the first "bretzel" bakery in 1861—and is still in production. The Lititz pretzel is said to be Moravian in origin, from the formula of an itinerant baker. Originally pretzels were made of soft bread dough, which was mixed, rolled, and twisted into shape by hand. The dough was put in a soda solution in the "cooker" to add color and sheen and help the adhesion of salt added later. (At one time the solution was water in which straw had been soaked overnight.) Placed on wooden peels, the pretzels were baked in a kiln above the oven for four hours, and emerged fully dried out and crisp.

Today, all processes are mechanized and nonstop, and a twisting machine can turn out a pretzel a minute. There are numerous pretzel bakeries throughout the distelfink country with worldwide shipments. Nothing but Prohibition has ever slowed down production.

The word "pretzel" is German but comes from the Latin, *pretiola*, meaning little gift. In the Palatinate it was a reward to children for learning their prayers, and the shape suggests folded arms in supplication (though one early local traveler described it as resembling "a snake twisted up with the cramp colic"). We now have various forms and sizes: big beer pretzels, butter thins, soft pretzels, wispy sticks, and nubbles. And oh, how comforting in a biting December wind to buy a fresh hot pretzel from a shivering street vendor!

Babies teethe on pretzels and old men crunch them with toothless gums. You carry a few in your pocket for a snack. They appear at weddings and funerals and all occasions in between. Years ago in a local private school girls would craftily drop a string with a nickel from the window, and the pretzel boy would replace the money with pretzels. Any kind of drink makes you hungry for pretzels, and they in turn make you thirsty. You can't watch TV without pretzels at hand. Dogs sit avidly in wait for a fallen chunk, and mice run off with the crumbs. Next to bread, the pretzel is the Pennsylvania Dutch staff of life, and many prefer it to candy.

The earliest form of Dutch candy was hard, on a stick or string. It was used for the old clear toy candies, rarely found now. Molasses candy (mojhey or moshey) followed, then apples with their chewy mojhey coating. As the French *moyeu* denotes a glazed or sugar plum, likely our Oley Valley French Huguenots contributed this word to our cookery too. Making marzipan (matzebaum) took infinite pains, but patience was one of our ancestors' virtues. The almond paste was molded into tulips or pomegranate flowers perhaps, and, when the Christmas tree became prevalent, was hung on it with a silken string. In the later Civil War days less aesthetic shapes like animals and patriotic symbols were added to hearts and flowers. Other old sweets were horehound, potato candy, and taffy. Contemporary favorites are fudge, peanut brittle, caramels, and Easter eggs of chocolate-coated peanut butter or coconut.

There have always been quite a few home candymaking industries in our area, perhaps inspired by the Luden and Hershey factories, and some of the smaller have developed a thriving trade. Making your own candy can be great fun, however, especially with an ancient recipe. If the children get rambunctious on a stormy day and you'd like "to drown the whole litter," as my neighbor once exclaimed, turn them loose in the kitchen with this simple recipe for our most venerable sweet:

MORAVIAN MINTS

2 cups granulated sugar

¾ cup water

1 teaspoon confectioners' sugar

¼ teaspoon cream of tartar

12 drops of peppermint extract or 3 drops of peppermint

Simmer together the granulated sugar and water until the syrup threads from the spoon. Take from stove, add the pulverized sugar, cream of tartar and peppermint. (An old recipe says that the sugar and water should be brought to a boil first, then "boil hard, long enough to count to twelve slowly.") Beat until creamy, and drop from the spoon on waxed paper. For wintergreen flavor, use wintergreen extract and pink vegetable coloring. Use also mint flavoring and green coloring, lemon flavoring and yellow coloring.

Country people make soft drinks from every kind of berry, and always an excellent sassafras and birch beer. It's hard to find a farm cellar without its shelves of wine—blackberry, grape, dandelion, plum, wild cherry, and even yellow tomato. Debby Shearer, who lived near the old Hinnerschitz Church, soaked raisins in her wine, which was famous or infamous—depending on your power of restraint. Years ago we had two acquaintances who loved to hike, and once trekked out from Reading to Debby's. After too many innocent-tasting raisins, they began to stagger home and were found crawling through the Reading Railroad Underpass on hands and knees. "That damned hole was so small," one of them told us, "we thought we'd never get through it!"

Cider, of course, has always been "the apple of our eye" and is found each fall at every roadside stand as well as at farmers' markets and Food Fairs. (A bit of horseradish, I understand, helps to preserve it.) In the Lancaster market, cider is on tap for thirsty shoppers. (How can anything so delicious be so therapeutic too?)

Herb teas have been made since time immemorial—spearmint, blue balsam, chamomile, Blue Mountain tea brewed from sweet scented goldenrod, and others, curatives or tonics. These too are not only healthful but refreshing.

And the same can be said for beer—within moderation! Reading's beer has been famous since colonial days. Because of the large grain production our area became a distilling center, much whiskey being made by the Scotch-Irish especially. It was commonly used in the eighteenth century at harvesting, community and social gatherings but lost face in the next century due to the Temperance Movement. However, even Dutch abstainers may like a good dose of brandy in their peaches, a wallop of whiskey in the mince pie, or a hidden kick in the party punch.

To produce all the foregoing good things to eat and drink do we depend on cookbooks? Rarely. The average Dutch housewife cooks instinctively, casual about measurements, as recipes in old German almanacs or receipt books will confirm. For example, they advise "butter big as a walnut," or "a few cents' worth of saffron," or coloring matter "the size of an apple kernel." You might be directed to cook the milk until it "sings." Why be more specific? Your daughters watched you from the time they were small, and your friends were as smart as you—anyway, in the kitchen. To include soups or bread with old family receipts was insulting. Everyone knew by osmosis how to make them. Extra pages in great-grandmother's receipt book might be devoted to home remedies, personal formulas for cough syrups, plasters, salves for burns, et cetera. A miniature doctor book.

Among the earliest printed Dutch cookbooks was Miss Leslie's *Directions for Cooking in Its Various Branches.* Few local hardbound cookbooks have been on the market since, and most have reached oblivion. Now there are many booklets and pamphlets published to subsidize granges, clubs, societies, and church sects. Even the Moravians and Mennonites have made their contributions, popular with tourists, for all over the rest of America cookbooks are the rage. Isn't this ironical considering the huge investment in TV dinners, most of them tasting like cardboard? The new *The Troubled Tummy Cookbook* should have great appeal for most of dyspeptic America. We Dutch don't need it.

Many eating places feature Dutch cookery—scrapple, schnitz un knepp, sauerkraut, potpie, potato filling, and chicken corn soup. Some have a profitable take-out business too, with shoofly the leader. The Lancaster Amish area teems with family-style restaurants for the tourists who find our food a novelty and eat up the pseudo-Dutch atmosphere as well. (I think of these as the "wagon-wheel chandelier" places.) The Dutch Pantry, now a restaurant chain, grew out of a market business of homemade noodles, pies, cookies, and so forth, and still sells its specialties to take home. The Graeff farm at Mount Joy serves delicious meals by reservation only. Its chic hausfrau who cooks, is hostess, and plays the trumpet for a "Happy Birthday" invites you to the cellar for an after-dinner nip of her cherry brandy.

Many old country inns serve meals in the rooms where wagoners once slept before the fire. At the bar nearby you see the neighborhood men consuming red beet eggs with their beer or schnapps. The food, mostly fried, is fair to good. (Flies are not discriminating.) The decor often consists of Victorian fixtures, clumps of dusty paper flowers, and cheap ceramics. At the Shartlesville Hotel many years ago I asked the waitress what on earth they did with all the food that wasn't eaten, for our table was loaded. "Ach," she laughed, "the leftovers go to the chickens and soon back it comes to the table again." Since the general conviction is "follow your appetite and live as long as you can," anyone who picks at his food is scornfully called "sneaky."

My father-in-law insisted that "a penny saved is a penny earned." Pennsylvania Dutch thrift is often joked about, but the early settlers were so poor that they boiled dry corncobs to make syrup, used chicken fat for shortening (and any surplus in soapmaking), and seldom bought anything but salt and spices. A loyal descendant is the modern housewife who uses leftover rice in pancake batter, stale crusts for bread crumbs, and adds water to an empty catsup bottle for the pot roast. Many a prosperous family too has the motto, "You can't waste food when there are hungry people in the world."

Isn't this primarily religious, a reverence for the bounty God has given us and that must be shared with others, in spirit at least? A beautiful custom typifying this is our Harvest Home, once a festival of the Gay Dutch (Lutheran and Reformed originally), but now followed by other churches. Held in late summer or early fall, it celebrates God's goodness at harvesttime. For the service, the church is decorated with fruits, flowers, and vegetables—even wreaths and crosses of grasses and grains, or a sickle of flowers. Foods are donated to orphanages, homes for the aged, or a pastor with a dozen hungry offspring.

Today, alas, there are fewer home preserves on the altar than canned goods from the Food Fairs. At any rate, the Dutchman is usually willing to share God's gifts with others: his time, efforts, and sympathy. To be assured of his hospitality too, just drop in near mealtime.

He is basically religious. Not only at a modest farmhouse but in many a prosperous, sophisticated home, the father lowers his head before the food is served. Hands may be joined around the table, and grace may be silent. But silent or spoken, it carries the message, "For all these gifts, Oh Lord, we are truly thankful."

Dialect and the Three R's

A BUSLOAD OF TOURISTS STOPS AT A PENNSYLVANIA DUTCH RESTAURANT. AFTER lunch of chicken potpie and shoofly (menus and place mats hidden in purses and pockets) they invade the gift shop. Hex signs, Amish dolls, booklets about the Plain people, homemade apple butter and jellies, cookbooks, calendar towels, ceramics—there are hundreds of colorful souvenirs. An avid woman with trailing husband gives a squeal of delight. The search is over! Here, among the haus-segen to hang on the kitchen wall, is a plaque that says, "Papa is All" (implying that he's dead).

This is a commercial dialect distortion to amuse the public—and add to sales. Natives may say "the soup is all" (gone) but are rightfully indignant at the popular corruptions of their dialect and customs. The tourist truly interested in our culture will have noticed basic features of our speech: its singsong quality; the voice dropped, not raised, at the end of a question; the tendency to prolong a final syllable ("Oh, dear-ah"); a juxtaposition of words. At our local crystal cave the guide informs us that "stalagmites grow from the down up, and stalactites from the up down." We have oddities in pronunciation too. Down is "don," house is "haas," and flower is "flahr" or "flowah."

When speaking English, the Dutch have great difficulty with J's, G's, and other letters. John and George are Chon and Chorche. A Dutchman who worked a farm we inherited used to phone now and then. My conversations with him were always identical. "Hello, is Lee dere?" he would ask . . . "No, I'm sorry. Is that John Hess?" After a moment of being awestruck at my psychic powers, he would chuckle, "Yah, dis is *Chon!*" V's and W's are tongue twisters. A "virtuous" woman becomes a "wirtuous voman." "Th" usually turns out to be "s," often with a "z" sound or a thickened "d." There's the story of a resourceful couple about to name their baby. As one Grandmom could only say "Lissbess" for Elizabeth and the other "Ruse" for Ruth (their first and second choices), the compromise was "Wiolet." The following are excerpts from a comic Pennsylvania Dutch dictionary:

> chin—alcoholic beverage
>
> chug—an earthen vessel
>
> close—what we wear
>
> cripps—what babies sleep in
>
> mutt—soggy earth
>
> purse—what the cat does

Surprisingly, some with the heaviest Dutch accent can't speak the dialect. "Such a vun" once guided us through the Ephrata Cloisters. At the end of the tour my husband teased her with, "Wouldn't it be easier if you'd lecture in Dutch?" . . . "Ach," she laughed, "I can't efen talk de schtuff."

Most of our idioms are a literal translation from the German, such as "your hair are pretty," or "he walked five mile(s)." When "the paper wants rain," as a rule it "makes don." A day of the week is often pluralized: "He buried her Mondays." A subtle twist of words still carries its message, as when Johnny cries out during a thrashing, "Any more I'll be good, Pop." Adverbs are rampant: "He's been dead long a'ready"; "She wants a house and car too yet." Adjectives are often used as nouns, "the electric," for instance. Common colloquialisms are "I'm going to [the] bank"; "Are you coming with [us]?"; "The cats wants [to come] in"; "What for [kind of] fruit do you have?" Lizzie Yoder's church "makes sale" of quilts. A real puzzler to the stranger is "I guess I'll say sanks" for "no, thanks." The words "leave" and "let" are usually misused. When you leave the dog out, you send him outside. There's the story of a tailor fitting a new pair of trousers, and saying to his customer, "Yah, vell, it's pretty tight across the rump, so I'll chust have to leave the seat out."

In this Dutch country something original is always popping up. We use the most convenient word if the grammatical one doesn't come to mind. Recently my grandson (raised by college parents) introduced me to, "It doesn't care [matter]." In the market aisle I heard one woman say to another, "I sought I knew you—your face is so conwenient." A more than once repeated story is that of a farm girl rushing to Grandpop who had fallen down the stairs, fanning him with her apron and exclaiming, "Shall I make vind for you?"

We may smile at others' peculiarities of speech, but is our own impeccable, and who sets the standard? Have you ever been guilty of asking, "Shall I make you some eggs?" chalking up for yourself two errors in six short words? Or, being a Bostonian, do you say, "I have hat trouble," meaning that your heart and not your bonnet is awry? When a Southerner says, "Come in, yo' all," we "have right" to look behind us for the others. Personally, I think the Englishman's "I have bean" is far more plausible than our "bin." We're all more provincial than we admit.

Though the Dutch may be saving with words as they are with food, they often use double negatives. "Ain't" or "ain't not?" commonly end a question. Dialect words are frequently used in English, even by the well educated, since nothing equally expressive can be found. When water spritzes it doesn't either squirt or splash. "Tut" (the "u" as in "put") is often used for a small paper bag. In German, *tuten* means to toot a long horn. No doubt our modern tut was preceded by a spirally rolled square of paper. For most things, the Dutch have a logical reason. The ponderous word "bushwacker," though not Deitsch, was first applied to Dutch guerrillas around Nazareth in the Revolutionary War.

Words, like food and customs, were adopted from neighboring settlers. The Dutchman says "Bist du hame?" *(hame* being Scottish) instead of "Bist du hause?" (German). "Vendue" (French) is used for sale or auction, though it may come out as "Fendue."

Frequent interjections are "Ach," "Himmel," and "Aye, yi, yi." The last has delightful variations of emphasis—a strong emotion produces "aye, yi, yi, yi, *aye,* yi, yi!" with gathering force and speed, and though spellings vary, the impact is the same. A lingering sigh with "yes, well" indicates "yes, that's life," or "what can one expect?" The Dutchman has effective substitutes for "damn it!" or the Lord's name used in vain. My husband was once on a western fishing trip when a burning log fell at the feet of a stranger before the campfire. "Harrey-yumma!" howled the man. "What part of Pennsylvania do you come from?" my husband asked him. The man looked mystified for a moment, then grinned when he understood the inference. He was from Lancaster, and no longer a stranger.

Worse than any English curse is *heilig dunnerwetter* (holy thunder weather), implying "May God strike you dead!"

Today, the better educated show little trace of their German inheritance, though many are able to speak the dialect, being one up on our Ephrata guide. It's estimated that half a million people speak Pennsylvania Dutch, and that just as many more can understand it. (It's hard to judge the accuracy of this kind of statistic, however.) Basically, Pennsylvania Dutch is the eighteenth-century patois of the Palatinate, altered here by the dialects of North Germans, Alsatians, Swiss, and other Teutons. It was enriched, like all the mores of the settlers, by their other southeastern Pennsylvania neighbors—Scotch-Irish, Welsh, English, French—but after a century, became fairly uniform.

Of the thirteen colonies, Pennsylvania was the only one to be bilingual, for the High German of the eighteenth century was used in all the Reformed Lutheran churches especially. Actually, this made our people trilingual if they spoke English as well. Some remain so today, notably the Old Order Amish. Though many of the Dutch are bewildered by the High German now, they have been loth to discard it in their church service. It had a dignity, like the King James Bible version, or Latin for mass preferred by many Catholics.

Our dialect is pithy and earthy, and being close to the soil like most dialects with simple grammar and limited vocabulary, is adapted to home life and not abstractions. Humor is rampant, unfortunately losing its punch in translation to English. Speaking Dutch was taken for granted before 1900, and one knowing only English might be referred to as an "Irisher" (there were quite a few Scotch-Irish schoolmasters), or if he lived in a rural area he was branded a snob. Since the turn of the century English is generally preferred except in certain rural areas. The dialect's use declined drastically in World War I when it suggested allegiance to Germany. However, migrants, mainly the Plain people, have carried it to other sections such as Virginia's Shenandoah Valley and parts of Delaware, Maryland, North Carolina, Ohio, Indiana, Illinois, Michigan, and Wisconsin. It is also heard as far afield as Oklahoma, Kansas, North Dakota, and Canada, especially around Toronto. Wherever the Amishman settles he takes this birthright along with his household chattels.

The dialect differs in various counties not only in intonation but in word usage and spelling, depending on the settler's origin. You may spell *wunnerfitsich* however you like. For the last hundred years there have been Dutch-English dictionaries of various consequence but no two in perfect accord. Not so strange, perhaps, when it was only at the end of the eighteenth century that English spelling was standardized.

Though there is less than 10 percent of English words in the dialect, their number grows along with scientific progress such as air space travel and new household gadgets. Television is just plain telewision, or "T-We." Is it any wonder we have never had an accepted orthography? Besides, the dialect was always meant to be spoken rather than written. Even in the settler's days we had no unity except of spirit and purpose—no strict political or religious ties, no common fatherland. Why shouldn't the basic dialect grow temperamental? Yet, even today it is understood (albeit with effort) in German-speaking countries, though best in the Rhineland. It is very similar to Yiddish (an early language of the Rhine Valley, as many Jews came there from the Holy Land around A.D. 800). In certain parts of Poland and the Ukraine our Dutchman also can make his wants understood—though he may not be able to discuss Plato with the natives.

As we don't bother with *zie* but use the familiar *du* even for strangers, we must be considered boorish at times. Yet we're always received with civility (tinged with amusement perhaps) as are those attempting their fractured French in France. Bungling visitors or immigrants find empathy in nearly any foreign country.

Hundreds of our family and place names, of course, are literally

German. Spelling of an immigrant's name, though, was often changed on arrival by a clerk who wrote the original list, especially if he were unfamiliar with German, or the immigrant couldn't spell. As the name usually denoted occupation or place of origin, we have many Bachmans (bakers), Kaufmans (merchants), Eisenhowers (ironworkers), Schneiders (tailors), Hesses (from Hesse), Boehms (Bohemians). The phone book teems with variations of these and hundreds of others. Many, of course, have been anglicized, such as Hoover (Huber). There's the story of a silk mill boss interviewing an applicant for work. "Are you a weaver?" asked the boss. "No, did you sink you knew me?" was the answer. "I'm Bagenstose." Surnames were often derived from physical or personal characteristics, such as Hahn (rooster), Kurtz (short), and Guth (good).

Many given names are biblical, especially those of the Plain people. Among the Amish who have a limited number of surnames because of marriage strictly within the sect, there's confusion in the schoolroom when Sammy P. Horst is called on unless he has a nickname. His middle initial is the first letter of his mother's maiden name or his father's given name—from a list obviously small. The only way to distinguish Sammy is to give him a nickname based on an incident, a peculiarity, or any identifying physical trait. When the teacher calls on Big-Ear Sam, Blabber Sam, or Poison Oak Sam, the victim may *rutsch* (squirm) but he's forced to recite.

Descriptive Dutch words and phrases are practical but often delightful. Typical are *blue cough* for whooping cough, and the fanciful *wind fliegel* (on the wings of the wind) for hussy. Familiar terms are also used in metaphors or proverbs. Throughout the dialect, compounds are typically German, like *fingerhut* (finger hat) for thimble and *grundsaudaag* (Groundhog Day). Will this rich, colorful dialect really be extinct in a hundred years?

Though the motive of the Amish has been religious, they persist in fighting education that effaces their tradition. By 1952 consolidation of schools was booming. Amish children had always studied eight grades in the one-room school, then regardless of age, began their life's work on the farm. When the state offered an annual continuing subsidy for closing one-room schools, twenty thousand children were still in attendance there and the Amish had no intention of letting them mingle with the "worldly" and adopting their fancy ways and talk. They ignored the newly enacted law, refusing to send their young to the "consolidated," and were ready to go to jail for their convictions if necessary. Making national headlines, a deputation even went to Washington, though it's against Amish principles to be active in politics. (An elder may be on a township school board now and then to protect his beliefs.) But this was a crisis. The state government finally conceded since the case involved religious freedom, a provision of our Constitution.

A few years later another newly enacted law required schooling till the age of fifteen. The battle began again, for children were usually finished with grade school a year or so earlier. And what was needed beyond the three R's

for a successful farming life—except the fourth "R," religion? Once more the state relented and a type of vocational program was set up enabling the children to farm. Many of them start school without knowing a word of English, and in many farm families it's a struggle to have to use it. I feel empathy for the farmer who saw his new worldly neighbors driving up the lane at dusk for milk, and muttered, "Aye, yi, yi, I work hard all day and at night I have to talk English too yet."

Consequently, in the Amish sections, the little one-room schoolhouse perseveres. Most schools are public, only a few being church owned. The teacher, "worldly" or gay, is a graduate of a teachers college. This may seem paradoxical, but of course no young Amish woman is equipped with similar education. "Teacher" is well respected by parents and pupils who are usually diligent scholars, used to discipline in the home. Haven't they been up since five doing their farm chores? The trail of thirty-odd black-shawled and bonneted girls and boys with wide black hats and suspenders arrives at eight, lunch box in hand. By then teacher has a lively fire in the potbellied stove and begins the mammoth task of handling eight different age groups. Sometimes the brighter older ones coach the smaller, perhaps under an oak tree in warm weather. The lunch hour, with more romping than eating, sustains everyone until the trail home begins at four. Poor bedraggled teacher, who has had to pantomime for beginners who know no English!

day school for girls in 1746, only taking boarders fifty years later. Now, a girls' academy and junior college, it's proud of its venerable age and traditions. Nazareth Hall, founded in 1807, was the first college solely for preparation of teachers. Not all Moravian projects were so ambitious. Their rural school in the Oley Valley was tiny, but lasted till 1930, the trustees giving the sale profits to the Oley Township Consolidated School.

The Schwenkfelders' school system, concurrent with the Moravians', was relatively small and unknown, but it lasted over sixty years and bequeathed some of its principles to the eventual public school system. Schwenkfelder settlements, scattered and often isolated, had a great need for schools. Classes were first held in rented private houses, with pupils paying tuition. Yet the schools were public in that they were open to all community children. Schwenkfelders supported a fund for the education of the poor and also provided administrators and teachers. The outstanding feature was lack of religious indoctrination, for other schools were mainly parochial. The Schwenkfelders, only organized here in 1782 as a Protestant sect, had great respect for freedom of thought, for which they had suffered keenly. To nourish their beliefs among their own, however, they had the first Sunday school (begun in Saxony) in the colonies. (This distinction has been claimed by Methodism too.) Though their education was not so comprehensive as the Moravian, they later had an academy for advanced studies in the Hosensack Valley.

In the meantime, how were other settlers handling education? During the eighteenth century a great effort was made to anglicize the "dumb Dutch," the Germans. The Dutch weren't dumb—merely stubborn about learning English as they had a real fear that the German language might be obliterated and their independence encroached on. (There will always be a few "dumb Dutch" though, for that's the law of nature. John Yoder tells of an illiterate youth of his early days who received a postcard from a girl he was sweet on, and asked a friend to read it aloud but to hold his ears closed so he wouldn't know what it said.)

It wasn't education per se that the Dutch opposed, just certain methods of education. They not only approved of the above-mentioned parochial schools, but those of the Reformed and Lutheran churches, of which there were many.

When eight public schools were established in the Dutch areas the Dutch grew more suspicious and rebellious and the project failed. They bitterly resented domination by the Church of England. Also, as a whole, they were an agricultural people, and like the Amish, felt that the need for education was limited. Plain or Worldly (a teacher being available), they set up their own schools where the dialect was spoken. The schoolmaster in Womelsdorf was Heinrich Wilhelm Stiegel, the famous glass manufacturer who had become a pauper. Pupils paid from one to ten cents daily.

These early schools taught only reading, writing, and spelling. "Ciphering" was an advanced study for older scholars. "Punishment" was a major

But the beginner's trauma is even worse. Coming h
at school, Adam was asked by Mom (in Dutch, of cour
go?" "Not good," mumbled Adam, "I have to go back

The Amish are progressive according to their own
Recently we picnicked on the grounds of a one-room sch
a Saturday afternoon, and were surprised to find a c
regular schoolmarm's brother was teaching agricultural
girls whose copybooks served as diplomas. No hint of w
These girls will have their own farm work to do as well, e\
records helps to bait a husband. Surely the one w
accompanying enigma will win the prize youth of the lot
dollars in a bank and withdrew it as follows:

$20	leaving	$30
15	"	15
9	"	6
6	"	0
$50		$51

Education has struggled for progress ever since ou
Though William Penn made provisions in our Constitution
throughout the state, the legislature ignored them. Quak\
government from 1682 to 1756, and each Meeting maint;
helped a neighboring one financially. By the end of the ei
there were some sixty in the state. Those still surviving are
excellent standards.

Besides the Quaker schools there were private, charity, ;
schools. In the early rural settlements, someone's home suffi
space became available for a group. It was customary for th
tutor for the young and send their youth abroad to the
Philadelphia there were even a kindergarten and night sc\
famous Log Cabin College of Gilbert Tennent near Ha
theology, however, continuing till Princeton began divinity cl

The Moravians, having their own communities, wei
education, promoting it for both sexes. At Bethlehem they (
country's first girls' boarding school, famous during the Revo
Washington sent his wards there from Virginia, and other stat
enrollment. It's interesting to compare the studies prescribed
girls. They both learned the three R's (though the girls had "ar
the boys "mathematics"), history, geography, music, French,
Boys also studied Latin, Greek, and drawing. Girls, of course, v
sew a fine seam—and, oddly enough, astronomy. Are females
stargazers than men?

In Lititz, another Moravian community, Linden Hall was

But the beginner's trauma is even worse. Coming home from his first day at school, Adam was asked by Mom (in Dutch, of course), "Well how did it go?" "Not good," mumbled Adam, "I have to go back again tomorrow."

The Amish are progressive according to their own standards, however. Recently we picnicked on the grounds of a one-room school near Belleville on a Saturday afternoon, and were surprised to find a class in session. The regular schoolmarm's brother was teaching agricultural arithmetic to older girls whose copybooks served as diplomas. No hint of women's lib, though. These girls will have their own farm work to do as well, even if ability to keep records helps to bait a husband. Surely the one who has solved the accompanying enigma will win the prize youth of the lot! A farmer had fifty dollars in a bank and withdrew it as follows:

$20	leaving	$30
15	"	15
9	"	6
6	"	0
$50		$51

Education has struggled for progress ever since our founding days. Though William Penn made provisions in our Constitution for public schools throughout the state, the legislature ignored them. Quakers controlled the government from 1682 to 1756, and each Meeting maintained a school or helped a neighboring one financially. By the end of the eighteenth century there were some sixty in the state. Those still surviving are known for their excellent standards.

Besides the Quaker schools there were private, charity, and other church schools. In the early rural settlements, someone's home sufficed until church space became available for a group. It was customary for the rich to have a tutor for the young and send their youth abroad to the universities. In Philadelphia there were even a kindergarten and night schools. Only the famous Log Cabin College of Gilbert Tennent near Hartsville taught theology, however, continuing till Princeton began divinity classes.

The Moravians, having their own communities, were pioneers in education, promoting it for both sexes. At Bethlehem they established the country's first girls' boarding school, famous during the Revolution. George Washington sent his wards there from Virginia, and other states boosted the enrollment. It's interesting to compare the studies prescribed for boys and girls. They both learned the three R's (though the girls had "arithmetic" and the boys "mathematics"), history, geography, music, French, and German. Boys also studied Latin, Greek, and drawing. Girls, of course, were taught to sew a fine seam—and, oddly enough, astronomy. Are females more ardent stargazers than men?

In Lititz, another Moravian community, Linden Hall was founded as a day school for girls in 1746, only taking boarders fifty years later. Now, a girls' academy and junior college, it's proud of its venerable age and traditions. Nazareth Hall, founded in 1807, was the first college solely for preparation of teachers. Not all Moravian projects were so ambitious. Their rural school in the Oley Valley was tiny, but lasted till 1930, the trustees giving the sale profits to the Oley Township Consolidated School.

The Schwenkfelders' school system, concurrent with the Moravians', was relatively small and unknown, but it lasted over sixty years and bequeathed some of its principles to the eventual public school system. Schwenkfelder settlements, scattered and often isolated, had a great need for schools. Classes were first held in rented private houses, with pupils paying tuition. Yet the schools were public in that they were open to all community children. Schwenkfelders supported a fund for the education of the poor and also provided administrators and teachers. The outstanding feature was lack of religious indoctrination, for other schools were mainly parochial. The Schwenkfelders, only organized here in 1782 as a Protestant sect, had great respect for freedom of thought, for which they had suffered keenly. To nourish their beliefs among their own, however, they had the first Sunday school (begun in Saxony) in the colonies. (This distinction has been claimed by Methodism too.) Though their education was not so comprehensive as the Moravian, they later had an academy for advanced studies in the Hosensack Valley.

In the meantime, how were other settlers handling education? During the eighteenth century a great effort was made to anglicize the "dumb Dutch," the Germans. The Dutch weren't dumb—merely stubborn about learning English as they had a real fear that the German language might be obliterated and their independence encroached on. (There will always be a few "dumb Dutch" though, for that's the law of nature. John Yoder tells of an illiterate youth of his early days who received a postcard from a girl he was sweet on, and asked a friend to read it aloud but to hold his ears closed so he wouldn't know what it said.)

It wasn't education per se that the Dutch opposed, just certain methods of education. They not only approved of the above-mentioned parochial schools, but those of the Reformed and Lutheran churches, of which there were many.

When eight public schools were established in the Dutch areas the Dutch grew more suspicious and rebellious and the project failed. They bitterly resented domination by the Church of England. Also, as a whole, they were an agricultural people, and like the Amish, felt that the need for education was limited. Plain or Worldly (a teacher being available), they set up their own schools where the dialect was spoken. The schoolmaster in Womelsdorf was Heinrich Wilhelm Stiegel, the famous glass manufacturer who had become a pauper. Pupils paid from one to ten cents daily.

These early schools taught only reading, writing, and spelling. "Ciphering" was an advanced study for older scholars. "Punishment" was a major part of the curriculum. Milder forms were wearing the dunce cap, standing in a corner, or stretching arms out horizontally for several minutes. "Keeping in" after school, involving double lessons or heavy tasks, was likely the bitterest fate of all. And especially for the teacher who must have originated the parents' apology, "This hurts me more than it does you." Beating on the nails with a ruler was common practice—and very painful if the child was made to gather thumb and fingers together. The lash of the cat-o'-nine-tails was most effective in "horsing." The culprit was forced to mount the back of a schoolmate, after removing shirt and vest. This made the burn of the leather thongs more painful. The "wooden horse" was a stout triangular log with the sharp edge uppermost, mounted on four legs, and high enough so that the wicked "rider's" feet couldn't reach the floor. One imaginative master employed the service of a pet rooster. The offender had to sit before it while it viciously snapped up a handful of corn from his head. Another master devoted half a day a month to thrashing every child, since some had been bad and "others would be in the course of time."

A famous and unique eighteenth-century school was that of Christopher Dock, a Mennonite, at Skippack. Though "he spared the rod" he didn't spoil the child; yet he gave rewards for effort. Prizes for progress might be *ein vorschrift oder vogel*—a scriptural quotation, or moral precept, or the verse of a hymn—the finely illuminated text embellished with birds, flowers, and other designs. Obviously Dock was greatly advanced for his time, as his curriculum also indicates.

Before the Free School Act of 1834 there was much antiact demonstration in our area, and Liberty Poles with "No Free Schools" were paraded. It was felt, mainly among the farmers, that few poor existed, and, moreover, that public schools would lure their sons to industry. Landowners feared a heavy increase in taxes, along with the dying out of church schools. This is what actually happened when the Public School Law was passed (and under a Dutch governor, ironically). The law proved unpopular and widely ineffective at first. As many persons realized a need for better education, small groups banded together to found private schools such as Stouchsburg Academy, and female seminaries. Among the oldest are Hill School and Mercersburg for boys and Linden Hall and Penn Hall for girls. But on the whole, the Dutch have never favored private schools, and we still have comparatively few.

Because of a brother's long fatal illness, my husband was sent to a New England prep school. He was often teased about his accent and aptly nicknamed "Dutch." In German class he was sometimes asked, "How do you say that in Dutch?" His native humor often prevailed, as when the professor asked him if he'd had a foreign language in high school at home, and he answered, "Yes, sir, three years of English."

Eventually, the Dutch cooperated with the Public School Law and education made great strides. By 1890 nearly all schools instructed in English, and in 1911 reading and writing English was compulsory. As time went on, the school year gradually increased from six months to nine. Mental arithmetic supplanted the old ciphering. More visual aids were used—maps, charts, globes, and skeletons for anatomy. By 1900 textbooks were free. In the mind of the Dutchman, though, education had one appalling lack—religious instruction. (When a reviewer of my first book wrote that "Stiegel skated on the thin ice of the Seventh Commandment," I'm sure most Dutchmen found no need for Bible reference.) The heavy stress on morals in Sanders's *Union Readers* was no compensation for religion. Mitchell's *Geographies* were full of racial and religious bias, declaring that the Caucasian was the most noble of all the races, and Christianity was the one true faith; Mohammed was called a religious impostor. Though the Dutchman might agree wholeheartedly, he resented having his children told what to think. (Today we have a similar problem when we feel the textbooks seem to hint of communism.)

Spencer's penmanship and copybooks, and later the fashionable Palmer Method, all using the forearm and not the fingers, replaced the ornamental "striking" of the seventeenth century, the rage in England and certain parts of Europe. Though of minor import educationally, its history is interesting. Scriveners brought copybooks here as late as 1820, though at the turn of the century when the steel pen was produced, the old art lost its popularity. It was done with "a good quality of ink-powder" and goose quill, and the pros wrote without touching any part of the paper with the hand. A single dashing stroke could also create a peacock or cupid or other embroidery. As it was hardly the method for a German immigrant who couldn't sign his name, Christopher Sauer filled the need from 1756 on with his calendar. He gave carefully printed directions for a simple penmanship, with interlining instruction in script. This sufficed as self-education for an ambitious German farm family.

Literate Dutch farmers had always read the almanac, hymnbook, and a German newspaper, all secondary to their Bible. It's said that one of them refused to have an English Bible in his house, insisting that Jesus only spoke German. Being asked how he knew it, he pointed to the German passage "Kommet hier zu mir alle" ("come unto me"). He died with his conviction intact.

The Germans had printed the Bible three times and the New Testament seven times before the first English Bible was produced in Philadelphia in 1782. The Ephrata Cloister press used handmade types for the Mennonites' 1,512-paged *Martyr Book* in 1745. The cloister was famed for its printing and handsome illumination, and even printed books for Benjamin Franklin. John Peter Müller, a German Reformed clergyman (the Brother Jabez of the cloister), was chosen by the Continental Congress to translate the Declaration of Independence into various European languages. Not a bad record for the "dumb Dutch," is it?

If our early settlers, as a whole, weren't book readers, neither are the Dutchmen today. They do love news, whether garnered from the newspaper, radio, or TV, or picked up at market or over the back fence or phone. Even an occasional "dummy" may feel the need to be "in the know," like Sam in my husband's native village. One day, sitting with a group of men, newspaper in hand, he announced grandly, "Hm, big storm at sea." A friend, glancing over his shoulder, saw the picture of a freighter, standing on its funnels. "You dumkopf," he roared, "you got the paper upside down!"

Lancaster had a subscription library in 1759, and Reading, four years later. But there are few public libraries in small Dutch towns, just books on loan in a drugstore or Sunday school. The consolidated schools, of course, have very impressive libraries, catering to the tastes of the young. Bookmobiles have gained popularity since 1900 when Hagerstown, Maryland, which has Dutch settlers, began sending two-horse wagons with open shelves into the countryside. Naturally, as education progresses, interest in reading is growing.

And all types of education are progressing. We have the standard nursery schools, kindergartens, day care and Head Start, all preparing the wee ones for work as well as cooperative play. One private preschool program has "aesthetic" training, experimenting with light, sound, shape, and movement, proving that reactions differ and each child's point of view is unique and important. Grade schoolers are bused around to an industry, dairy farm, planetarium, or museum. Guest speakers on cultural subjects visit their classrooms. The mentally retarded or physically handicapped get special attention. "Open education" with elective courses for older pupils is becoming more general in secondary schools, private or public, either for college or vocational preparation. Development of self-direction is considered more vital than studying textbook facts. Teachers are guides rather than instructors. However, as the Dutch as a whole are conservative, the progress of open education varies in school communities, depending on their convictions and needs.

A general tendency today is toward practical education. Our various business schools produce the ideal secretary or typist. As early as 1885 the Interstate Commercial College in Reading was not only teaching shorthand and typing but business training as well. Public vocational and technical schools also offer many opportunities for those not going on to college, producing a first-rate secretary, auto mechanic, plumber, or hairdresser. Their adult night classes and those at high school are well attended by young and old, as are courses at Reading Community College. Practical nursing is a popular field for those who can't afford the time or money for hospital training. Choice of careers is so expansive that an irresolute student may feel like Milne's shipwrecked sailor who had so many things he wanted to do he didn't know which to do first, so he simply basked.

Among thriving colleges and universities are Lehigh, Lafayette, Franklin and Marshall, Muhlenberg, Dickinson, Bucknell, and Albright. Many have religious affiliations, which were forced to broaden after the GI bill of World

War II. A large number of our youth attend Pennsylvania State University's extension schools and teachers colleges spread throughout the Dutch area.

Many small private groups, too numerous to mention, offer a wealth of courses for the intellectually curious. Open to the public is one of special value, I think. The Junior League of Reading has an annual series of lectures with discussion on various aspects of Berks County life.

On the more diversional side of education, we have excellent free travel lectures supported by the school system. These are so popular that many people come an hour early, with reading matter, to be sure of a seat. The Christian associations offer many courses for a pittance. Our local YWCA, in addition to instruction on various sports and handicrafts, teaches yoga. The Red Cross, long known for its nutrition and safety classes, has recently added one on "Charm." Senior citizens are taught to make their leisure time constructive with arts and crafts, and have their own cable TV channel for the dissemination of information and ideas. We Dutchmen keep up to date, though often reluctantly, with long-haired hippies, hot rodders, rock 'n' roll, and streakers, like old Granny Kalmbach. One night while milking she went berserk and scuttled naked down the road. Her son and his field hand in the cornfield squinted at her in the dusk. "Mein Gott, what's Mom got on now?" her son exclaimed. "I can't see so good," said his helper, "but it sure needs pressing."

Granny Kalmbach excepted, it's vital for healthy community living that we keep pace with modern ideas and progress, making our personal adjustments and contributions as best we can. The "what's the world coming to?" attitude is fatal.

When Lizzie Yoder learned that Leah's daughter, Sarah, was studying belly dancing, Lizzie shunned her for weeks. "Devil's stuff," she muttered. Being a peacemaker by nature, I tried to coax Lizzie to tolerance. "You always said Sarah was the family klutz—belly dancing will teach her to be graceful. It's healthful too—exercises every muscle in your body." Lizzie glared at me. "So does scrubbing floors! Ach, all this newfangled stuff!" But I persisted. "Look, Lizzie, *you* use a wet mop now, and you know you love your wash machine. Young people have their own way of keeping up with the times." At long last Lizzie relented, but only when Sarah was made leader of the youth group at church.

On the whole, I think the Dutch have kept well in line with both new trends and educational progress throughout the nation. We may not take the initiative—that isn't our nature. But neither do we like to be left behind. Like everyone else we want our young to "be better than we are." Many of our students not only get college degrees but go on to doctorates. (Even the Amishman hopes his son will be a better farmer than Pop, and profit by the latest agricultural findings.)

Considering our early language barrier, perhaps we've made even more progress than any other section of the country. We "have right" to be proud!

To Plow Is to Pray

"JUST FEEL MY MUSCLE!" UNCLE NIBS WOULD DEMAND EACH TIME WE SAW HIM, and tensing his arm, awaited adulation. Those seventy-year-old biceps were worth it—even weekly.

Though a bit of a Beau Brummel, Nibs was a hard-working farmer. His forebears came from Alsace-Lorraine two centuries ago, and doubtless from them and earlier ancestors who farmed to keep alive, he had inherited an instinct to work the land.

The German immigrants liked stability and group settlements and remained on the soil they bought, not roving like the English, Scotch-Irish, and others always hunting greener pastures. The Rhineland, of course, was one of the most fertile sections of Europe and the Germans knew the value of meadow, brook, and virgin forest. (A great asset was black walnut, used for furniture and gunstocks.) In the original grants, three to four hundred acres were often mentioned, and larger farms were not uncommon. Perhaps the phrase "dirt cheap" comes from those days of plentiful land, though clearing it was a mammoth task.

Once settled in his cabin, the thrifty German learned to make the most of what he had. Knowing that sheltered cattle require less forage, he housed them as soon as possible (unlike other settlers) and used the manure for fertilizer. (It was a good omen if the horse manured the furrow while plowing.) As England didn't export farm tools, the plow and sickle were the farmer's main equipment, the grain cradle not being used till the end of the eighteenth century.

The first settlers knew nothing of the value of lime and legumes, and little more about rotation of crops, so the soil was often depleted. But by 1750 the worth of lime was discovered by Lancaster County farmers—the first in the country to use it. Soon there was a kiln on nearly every farm, as buying lime cost three cents a bushel. Because of the great amount of wood needed for burning, usually the kiln was built in or near a forest, and was protected against strong winds and too quick a combustion by its southern exposure. Limestone was brought from a nearby pit or quarry.

Sometimes the venture was cooperative. Neighbors helped with the digging and hauling of stone, the cutting of wood, and in the nineteenth century, with the hauling of coal. Excess lime was sold to other farmers. It was not uncommon for one selling a farm to retain the right for him and his heirs to use limestone from the quarry hole or timber from the woods. It's in the Dutchman's makeup to grab each chance of gain by the horns. But can the perfectionist ever reach perfection? One of our farmers, after a season of ideal weather for all crops, grumbled that it was "damned hard on the land."

By the turn of our century commercial fertilizers were generally used, but there is many a quarry hole still to be seen as you drive through the country. The tired old kiln is now slowly crumbling with disuse and weathering. Yet once it was a thing of beauty—size and shape differing from farm to farm, like the hausfrau's. It had its secrets too, for lime was often used in folk medicine—driving away moles, or even curing a heifer bitten by a dog.

Later, besides the lime, gypsum was used, brought to Philadelphia as ballast on ships from Nova Scotia or North Carolina. The rocks were ground in local mills. But it was hard to obtain and its effectiveness was short-lived.

Irrigation was commonly used to increase the yield of hay in meadows by supplying ditches with water from a dam. It served adjacent farms and each farmer had his share of labor and upkeep as well as a weekly allotment of time for use. Though irrigation was arduous and muskrats were often destructive, meadow grass was used as fodder till timothy and clover were introduced much later. As timothy was said to kill the land and clover seed was very expensive, some farmers continued irrigation even into our present century.

After the Revolution crops often doubled in value within several years, for by then there was rotation of corn, oats, wheat, and hay. Important here too, as in the Palatinate, were rye, barley, flax, hemp, and buckwheat.

An early traveler wrote of "the fragrance from this blooming buckwheat, mingled with the pleasant odor of pennyroyal along the roadside." No mention is made, though, of buckwheat cakes and molasses, so dear to our hearts ever since, and so hard to come by now.

In the orchards were cherries, pears, and apples serving bees as well as man. Sugar maples provided sugar and syrup for the lucky farmer. If the grapes planted for wine didn't thrive, he grew hops for beer, made cider, and mead from plums, peaches, and quinces. (Besides inheriting a love of hard work, he had inherited a love of easing work by imbibing.)

Cows and pigs supplied smoked meat for the winter, and chickens, ducks, and silly geese happily roamed the barnyard, unaware of gruesome fate. (As you know, "the stupidest thing on the farm is a goose, because it bends to get through the barnyard doorway.")

There was little that had to be bought except coffee, salt, pepper, and spices. The spice chest was guarded shrewdly by Mom. Like every housewife, she must have gloried too in discovering new vegetables: sweet potatoes, lima beans, squash, and pumpkins.

This all sounds prosperous and comfortable, though from the time the farmer cleared his land, his work was strenuous. The German, however, born of farming people, was more self-reliant than the English-speaking farmers who either failed or went on to develop plantations, and had indentured servants, slaves, or tenants.

In the New World, Indian corn was the most cherished find of the farmer. (Even now it's one of the Dutchman's treasures, corn flour often supplanting that of wheat, and he'd rather have his corn pie or chicken corn soup than two tickets to Bermuda any day.) Corn seed (bought now from a dealer) once had to be carefully selected for the next year's crop. Only cobs were kept that had straight rows and large deep kernels. If there was too much corn to shell it was threshed with a flail or the horses tramped it off on the barn floor trailed by an alert young man with a scoop. As one historian put it, "Horses don't wear diapers." (The hand-powered mechanical sheller of later days must have been a godsend.) When planting, the superstitious farmer dug three holes in a fence corner and put in three kernels for the birds, three for the worms, and three for the bugs, or perhaps:

> *One for the blackbird,*
> *One for the crow,*
> *One for the cut worm*
> *And two to grow.*

Field corn was planted in last year's hayfield where the soil was rich, but not near the cherished sweet corn or its yield would be meager. Most farmers also planted a few rows of broom corn. (A tea brewed from its seeds is considered a good treatment for dropsy.) Berks County's Hamburg is still known as "the broom capital of the world"—there, at least, if not elsewhere.

When plowing corn, a farmer sometimes hung a small bag of turnip seeds with a tiny hole in it to the hame of his horse, and turnip planting and plowing coincided. Pumpkins, squashes, watermelons, and beans were also grown in the cornfield. German efficiency again.

During the October husking, silk had to be well removed by hand or it made a snug haven for mice in the corncrib. If husks were close and tight, they predicted a heavy winter. After cobs were ground into chop for the farm animals there was cracked corn aplenty for the chickens.

Besides the many delectable dishes corn made for the family, its uses were legion. There were cornhusk mats and corncob dolls; a section of the cornstalk could be cut for a future fiddler who was still childishly delighting in making wigs and moustaches from the silk; bags filled with kernels and warmed in the oven were used for earache or feet that seemed detached in an icy bed. Cobs kindled the kitchen fire, and we've all heard how indispensable they were in the early privies.

I hope everyone can remember playing hide-and-seek on a farm and crouching in an old square corncrib behind corn shellers, shovels, bags, half-bushel measure, and choppers. A good nose could scent the tar-string (for binding fodder shocks) slung over a rod along the roof with its wasp nests and dripping, sticky cobwebs. Yes, the corncrib was a great place for a pair of "Cupid's disciples" to hide in.

In the early nineteenth century when people helped each other harvest on the larger farms, a group of workers included women. All must have attacked the field with their grain cradles like a swarm of hornets. As they started the day at three or four A.M. with a prebreakfast of wheat bread and butter, radishes, whiskey, or cidereil (a mixture of cider and molasses), naturally there was time for five more meals before dark rolled around again. The only break except for food was the hour for rest or devotion after dinner at noon. One envisions the workers dropping into cataleptic sleep at nightfall. But no! Rooms were cleared of furniture and a fiddle squawked hoedowns. Besides games, stories, and singing, there was even wrestling until after midnight. Samson's image pales beside such strength and endurance.

Though there are many ardent corn lovers, I'm sure the season has a unique association for me. Once when I was on a farm in mid-July, a steaming plate of corn was laid before me on the dinner table. "This looks lovely," I said as I sat down with Minnie, Jake, and the hired man. Minnie thought I meant her new oilcloth, and being a trifle in awe of me since I live in the city, said apologetically, "Ach, it's cold on my elbows come vinter, but Chake likes it to vipe his knife on." She was refreshingly natural in everything she said, like most of the farm wives. But at the table we didn't talk—we ate. Such ambrosial corn!

Raising wheat before the Revolution proved slow and tedious, yet Pennsylvania was the nation's granary. Our hard-working Germans not only helped win the war in battle but down on the farm. It was no coincidence that Christopher Ludwig, a Dutchman, was appointed baker-general by George Washington; Pennsylania was known for its superior quality of flour. Even today, that from our winter wheat brings a top price for cake and pastry.

Farming was never meant for the lazy, but the Civil War era had its special problems. Labor was exorbitant: an 1860 account book relates that Mrs. Nary had to be paid *fifty cents* for two days of raking, and Jesse Nary a *quarter* for one day's manure spreading! However, new implements had eased the toil (though when Jethro Wood patented an iron plow in 1819 farmers claimed it poisoned the soil and encouraged weeds, and Wood had to give his

plows away and died in poverty). But by then the cultivators were in use; first the drag; next, the land rollers to crush the clods; then a variety of implements till the combination harrow and roller. (Today, chisel plowing rips up the soil like a large harrow, or even deeper.) The first John Deere steel plow was made in Reading in 1838. The mechanical reaper greatly aided production and farms began to concentrate on grain crops for fattening of cattle. Most of the stock was western, bought from dealers, and old bossy was replaced by good breeds like South Downs, Short Horns, Berkshires, Devons, and others.

Due to mechanization, there was consolidation of farms and consequently a reduction in everyone's work hours. With the farmer's values of hard work and personal success being challenged, he began to lose his sense of security and self-sufficiency. I doubt if his wife complained of the newfangled gas engines, though they varied in types and sizes and could be used for running a cream separator or pumping water. It was estimated that the average farm woman lifted a ton a day in drawing water from a well or cistern and putting it into various containers. Her man's turn came for gloating too with the arrival of the manure spreader in the late nineties.

They say that after a great cultural crisis a new surge of interest in astrology is usual. The farmer's faith in the almanac had always been great, but after the Civil War it was greater. Christopher Sauer had produced one in 1793, and also Benjamin Franklin, though the latter's soon died from "poor circulation." An amusing story tells of a man furiously upbraiding Sauer for a calculation that ruined his crops. Sauer's dry reply was "I only make the almanac, the Almighty makes the weather." In the early nineteenth century, twenty-eight of the seventy-six almanacs were printed in German and were short-lived. The *Farmer's Almanac* was the most popular and still thrives today, in English, of course. It is sponsored, not sold, and is publicized by TV and radio shows. Its comparison with Philadelphia's WCAU-TV weather expert is keenly followed by farmers and other weather addicts. My husband (deaf to my choicest scandal when the weather report came on) claimed that the almanac often triumphs.

Another devotee of the almanac called me soon after I had published a historical novel. "I happen to own a 1781 almanac," she said tartly. "You wrote that the weather was severe, which it was—but you described a blizzard in early March when there was a general thaw."

A recent copy of the *Farmer's Almanac* (distributed by the American Bank) makes lively reading. Paramount among its material, of course, are the general weather predictions for all months of the year in the United States, and the sun and moon phases, eclipses and planetary positions. This has always been the almanac's lure for the farmer. To know the ascendant planet of the year was vital, as it controlled all atmospheric conditions.

Anything planted in the sign of Gemini will be abundant. There is a wrong and right time to build fences. Hair should be cut in Leo, and if you like it curly, in the increase of the moon. Wells or springs should be cleaned when the moon is down or the water will vanish. Apples picked in the dark of the moon won't rot, and hog slaughtering in the waning prevents meat shrinkage.

The plant and garden section has specific dates for sowing all crops and for killing insect pests. Why shouldn't the farm wife's garden be so lush, since she can find her lucky and unlucky days for planting, depending on her zodiac sign?

There are also the Hebrew and Christian calendars, fish and game laws, and a fishing calendar with days marked "good, fair, or poor." After seeing little Amish boys yank fish from their stream one Saturday afternoon, I'm sure the almanac is part of their diet. A wind-equivalent weather chart tells you when you'd better wear your "wammus" (originally a red flannel work blouse or jacket).

The almanac has its lighter side, however, for the farmer's rare hours of leisure. Recipes, tongue twisters, poems, limericks, and jokes are fillers. The girl graduate says, "Four years of college and whom did it get me?" (The Amishman who believes that eight grades are enough must sagely nod his head.) A section called "Capsules of Wisdom" offers the following:

"Air pollution is so bad that if you shot an arrow into the air it would get stuck there."

"Fill your water bed with beer and get a foam mattress."

Miniature articles, many humorous, treat on the pig, cow, or even golf. But the prize is the attack of a women's libber claiming that many jokes that the farmer relishes are insulting to her sex.

The One Hundred Year Calendar, specializing in astrology, appeared in 1800. It gave not only long-range weather forecasts but ailments expected: "There will be galloping consumption, fevers, sore throats . . . most of which result from having cold feet." (The virus was not yet in fashion.)

A unique astrologer was Lorenz Ibach of Newmanstown, also a blacksmith throughout his life. In 1816 at the age of twelve he left school and became his father's apprentice. But he studied astronomy incessantly. After his marriage, living in Reading, he met Carl F. Egelman, a renowned astronomer and almanac maker, who showed Ibach how to make calculations. Ibach, raising a family of twelve, had started his own business as blacksmith and craftsman but, having kept up his astronomical calculations, also succeeded Egelman at his death in 1860 as chief calculator for a Reading almanac.

Through his own efforts he had gained a working knowledge of six languages and soon became calculator for various almanacs in the States, Cuba, South America, and other foreign countries, and continued to correspond with mathematicians and astronomers. His library had many learned works and instruments. In the village in which he later lived, the farmers affectionately called him the stargazer, and loved their chats with him while he shod their horses.

Webster's definition of astrology is "divination that treats of the supposed influences of the stars upon human affairs and of foretelling terrestrial events by their positions and aspects." (Note the "supposed.") Maybe the subject is so alluring and has always created such widespread belief because astral influence can't be disproved.

At any rate it's certain that many of our ancestral farming Dutch had faith in astrology since they felt great pride in their taufscheins (illuminated birth certificates), usually specifying the zodiacal sign under which the child was born. The influence of comets has always been suspected and even recently it's not an uncommon idea that they foretell cataclysmic events like wars, insurrections, or other catastrophes. Meteors of falling stars such as the Leonids in 1833 disturbed some folk so deeply that they feared the end of the world. There is the joke about the farmer coming from the barn one night who suddenly saw hundreds of tumbling stars. "Come quick," he called in panic to his wife in the kitchen. "It's the end! Bring the Bible." Then remembering it was in the parlor and time was of the essence, he shouted, "Bring the almanac instead!"

Shakespeare wrote:

> *Men at some time are masters of their fate:*
> *The fault, dear Brutus, is not in our stars,*
> *But in ourselves that we are underlings.*

True or false? Who is to say? Yet it's surely a comfort at times (especially for the farmer) to blame the stars for failure. And though we may scorn astrology we often use its terminology, saying people are sunny, moony, mercurial, venerable, martial, and so forth.

However our Dutch farmer has gathered his wisdom (from almanac or Department of Agriculture), his contribution to national husbandry has been continuous. No neglected cattle; no neglected land. Today you have only to drive past a field of potatoes (*grumbeera,* groundberries) to know that they're a specialty here. The harvester grins at you and says proudly, "Only two sizes—big vuns and bigger vuns." (In his grandfather's day, the two sizes were big ones and the culls—cooking, planting, and hog-feed potatoes.) Since it's late in the fall and nippy and the farmer is hurrying, he explains, "The spuds are safe so long as the cow plops don't freeze, but once they rattle—get busy with your hoe!" With our love of potatoes it seems strange that eastern German peasants once refused to eat them until Frederick the Great appeared on a balcony in Breslau and proved their worth to the public.

Potato growing was fairly simple until 1843 when "rot" trickled in from Ireland where it had caused a famine. It took us many years to control it. Crops were then affected by the Colorado potato beetle until the use of arsenicals. But up to fifty years ago when growers sprayed thoroughly or planted disease-free seed, there was little progress in producing "the poor man's bread," for one degenerative and parasitic disease after another invaded the crops. The most effective step was planting after a leguminous sod. Potato growing is now a highly specialized commercial industry. On our larger potato farms we raise new varieties with greater disease resistance, and our yield per acre steadily increases. Concerning modern seed cutters, sprayers, and potato diggers, one writer banters, "The machine does practically everything but fry 'em" (and douse them with catsup!).

Until recent years more manual labor was required for potato growing than for any other crop except tobacco, also important here. Pompey, peer of the cigar-store Indian and a hundred years old, is perhaps our best testimony to this long-time prosperous cash crop. The huge bobbing head must have urged many a pedestrian to "buy cigars here." Pompey resides now in the Historical Society of Berks County, delighting all age groups. Who has seen a more ludicrous moonface with popeyes, moustache, and goatee under rakish cap? Or happier hands on a bulbous tummy? When he was given to the historical society his last owner drove him there in an elegant funeral coach.

Tobacco requires highly fertile soil, preferably limestone, heavy manuring, and much commercial fertilizer rich in potash. Since the days when our farmers rolled the leaves into stogies (sold locally at five for a cent), most of our tobacco has been used for cigars. Pennsylvania Broadleaf is sold for filler almost exclusively. During the Civil War the high price of tobacco gave impetus to our output, but in later years cigarette smoking affected it adversely.

Though it's still more profitable than any other crop on their valuable land, Lancaster County farmers seldom grow more than ten acres, and usually less. (It's ironical that nearly all the Plain people raise it, since religion bans its use; some, however, because of their faith, have turned instead to producing milk and selling tomatoes to canneries for cash income.) The Amishman uses more hand labor, required by tobacco, than other farmers, and usually has sons aplenty to help strip the leaves in winter. Production, curing, and marketing take great skill and long experience. As the qualities of tobacco grown in the same area may be quite variable, individual crops are bought by the packers, sometimes after late-summer harvesting but oftener when tobacco has been cured and stripped. Travelers, seeing the big "elephant ears" hanging in their ventilated sheds, often ask excitedly, "What's that?"

For years the Amish have been buying up farmland and now own many of the fertile Lancaster County fields. Though an ignorant stranger passing an Amishman on a city street may think "poor old hick," his income from tobacco, wheat, corn, alfalfa, steer feeding, dairying, and poultry might well pay cash for the Cadillac his critic is buying on installment. As available land is getting scarcer, many Old Order Amish and Mennonites are moving to other states or to Canada. There are not even so many sons to provide land for these days, though families are just as large; since mechanization (even if the Amish use nothing electrical) the farmer may need the help of only one or two sons and the others often find employment elsewhere.

Every marrying son who farms is given land of his own, either a portion of the homestead, or the next best for sale. There is a titillating story about an Amishman's buying a farm for his marrying Ezra. The transaction was with a Lutheran, a "worldly" neighbor. The price agreed on was fifty thousand dollars. All involved gathered in the Amishman's kitchen one night, and when time came for payment, the farmer nodded to his wife, who left to get a crock of money. When it was spread on the table there was only forty-five thousand dollars. The farmer sighed, shook his head at Sarah, and said tersely, "Wrong crock."

Who would guess that he had a windmill operating a pump for watering livestock, and a wheel sending water to the house? Rich by nearly anyone's standards, yet the Amishman adheres to the tenets of his sect.

The Amish carry religion into all phases of daily life. One of their brethren needing help gets it unstintingly. After a neighbor's fire the community will raise a new barn for him in a day. An onlooker once said to an Amishman, "Is this poor farmer one of your group?" The Amishman replied, "No, but when they give the word we'll all be here to help." A "worldly" farmer was once so overwhelmed by the aid of the Amish that he exclaimed to a worker, "I only hope *your* barn burns down sometime so I can be of help to *you!*"

The Amishman is constantly meeting his conscience face to face. When restriction of yield was proposed by the New Deal, he agreed to reduce acreage of certain crops, but refused to take government compensation. Occasionally, of course, there is one who will compromise. Though he will have no electricity within the house, he may cooperate with the "English" and use a motor-driven refrigerator to cool his milk in order to meet state standards.

Once a friend of ours was trying to sell bonds to an Amish farmer. He refused to buy when he learned that interest would cover all 365 days of the year, thus making money on Sundays. Our friend argued, "But your wheat grows on Sundays, doesn't it? And didn't Christ say the Sabbath was made for man, not man for the Sabbath?" The Amishman finally relented but, in agreeing, closed his eyes. When our friend asked him the reason, he sighed, "So my conscience won't see me."

All Pennsylvania Dutch farms have been a perennial joy to the beholder; even the eighteenth-century traveler called them models of neatness and beauty. Sleek cattle, verdant meadows, orchards of heavy-hanging fruit, and thriving crops—all were commended. And so were the fences tidily hemming in the cattle. There's an old saying: "As one tends the fence he also tends the farm."

The earliest fences were of makeshift materials accrued after clearing land for cultivation. The sturdy *steerolle* was merely a low dry-built wall of stones. The *heckefens* of upright stakes and brush was copied from the Indians who used it to protect their maize from hungry forest animals. Sometimes one still sees the zigzag or "worm fence," perhaps the most picturesque, or the "living fence" or hedge effective as a windbreak. If cattle are turned out to pasture now, Bossy shocks her nose on the "electric." But few fences are needed since tractors have replaced mules and horses. In our area, fences have seldom been used just for boundaries.

One of our ghost stories describes the fate of a farmer who sneaked out at night, dug up a line stone separating his land from another's, and moved it into his neighbor's property. When the swindler died his ghost haunted the farms, carrying the line stone on its back and constantly wailing, "Oh, what shall I do?" When he finally followed the advice, "Put it back where you got it!"—his ghost was never seen again.

Early travelers were also impressed with our beehives—which were crude boxes, or even a hollow log or straw *skep* (a basket of rye straw with strips of white oak). The honey bee had been brought here by the colonists and because sugar was scarce, a great many settlers were "skeppists." Great progress was made with the use of the honey-extractor and movable-frame hive. By 1860 our state produced over a million and a half pounds of honey and over fifty thousand pounds of beeswax. Beekeeping gave the farmer a substantial income until after World War I. Even now, many farmers put the bees to work for them, and the bees put those of Mount Hymettis to shame. At farmers' markets or at many a roadside stand you can find your favorite honey flavor, excepting orange blossom. Gentlemen farmers too produce smartly packaged jars with gay Dutch motifs, sold at exclusive shops. (But I doubt if they know the joy of drinking a demijohn of metheglin in the fields.)

In *Down Oley Way*, Alliene De Chant wrote of a skeppist who kept as many as eighty hives, and once when six swept down the Manatawny in an autumn storm, he pursued and finally retrieved them. He told Alliene, "But it took 'em till November to limber up—and then they died on me!" Since ours is a honey land, we have an abundance of bee lore. John Yoder tells me that when a family business has been handed down, some still believe that bees must be informed of the keeper's death by the eldest son's moving the hive slightly to the right. (It's courteous too to tell them of family marriages and births.) Until our present century, during the keeper's funeral, black bunting was draped over the hives to avert swarming. It's common knowledge though that if bees do swarm, you can make them settle by clanking pots and pans.

If any one in your family is addicted to cussing, bees won't work, and will assuage their sense of nicety by stinging. But there's a remedy, of course. Apply to the swelling a paste of homemade soap, tobacco quid, milk of celandine, juice of a red-beet leaf, unsalted butter, and ear wax—if these things are handy!

Never underrate the practical knowledge and ingenuity of the average Dutch farmer. He seems to have a sensible answer to everything. One pious farmer who had given liberally to erect his church rebelled when funds were needed for lightning rods. "I've helped build a house for the Lord," he argued, "but if He sends donder to knock it down, He must do it at His own risk." Eventually he capitulated, but a year later when an expensive weather vane was added, he was adamant. "When the peacock sees its feet," he reminded them with a grin, "its tail falls."

Though our farmers have great respect for tradition and always time for a bit of fun, they concentrate on progress on the land. We still combine crops with cattle raising like the eighteenth-century farmers, but styles in cattle change as they do in dogs or clothes. In favor now are herds of Guernseys, as their milk is low in butterfat, and cholesterol has become a fashionable threat. One sees many Jerseys and Holsteins too, and perhaps some Ayrshires and Black Angus.

We're still growing corn and wheat like the settlers, but not flax. Barley, soybeans, and alfalfa are important today. Harvesting meadow hay is almost a thing of the past, with alfalfa replacing pure clover, alas. (I can still hear my mother say as we drove past a fragrant purple field, "Breathe deeply, Mildred!")

With the increase of insect pests in this century, fruit growing has become specialized, though it would be unthinkable not to have enough apples on a farm for making schnitz. Raising swine and sheep is becoming more profitable.

As eggs are in great demand for shipment to cities, poultry raising is booming, and this is the heyday of Rhode Island Reds and White Leghorns. (In my husband's childhood when he wanted an egg while the hens were vacationing in winter, he was told that eggs had become "bitter." In spring, though, surplus eggs were preserved in water glass [sodium silicate] to help raise the count of Christmas cookies—his compensation.) Thousands of hens are now captives in commercial hen houses, never seeing the light of day. No grubbing around in the barnyard or gossiping with a duck or goose. Besides providing eggs for a French omelet at the Ritz, hens are growing more and more desirable white meat from lack of exercise. Meat with an ersatz flavor.

Turkey raising seems to be an increasingly profitable venture since becoming an indoor, mechanized process, and most of the birds are sold by mid-October. From incubation on, the turkey never sees the light of day till bought for the Thanksgiving market.

Another prosperous business is cheese making in York and Lancaster counties—cup cheese, cottage, and "Swiss" especially. The farmers love their cheese—let the city people worry about cholesterol! As to butter—what is a pancake without it? Around 1800, a Lancaster County farmer's butter yield was the most lucrative except for corn. In winter he bartered his butter and eggs for goods at the local country store. In April, however, he loaded grain, eggs, and crocks of salted butter (maybe a hundred and fifty pounds) into his wagon and made his annual trip to Philadelphia. Prime butter sold for fifteen cents a pound. Though he carried his house with him like a turtle, he returned home a week later feeling rich, cosmopolitan, and exhilarated from occasional sociability at inns.

Naturally, varying soil and terrain dictated type of production. On one farm in the Great Valley near Pittsburgh where there are many Plain people, alfalfa may be the major crop; on an adjacent stony farm hugging the mountain, the emphasis is on cattle grazing. Grape growing, abandoned elsewhere, has increased in Lancaster County.

Today, the Dutch farmers, because of their desire for security and independence, are valiantly competing with the large-scale agricultural industry of the Midwest and West. Some have reduced their need for capital by renting instead of owning farmland, and working fields bought by the wealthy as a hedge against inflation. Many a farmer who either owns or rents has found the need of taking on a part-time industrial job in a neighboring town. But the soil is his real love, and he still has a cow or two for family use, as well as fowl and a vegetable garden. These are his security.

In recent years, soil management programs include cover crops, contour crops, permanent pastures on slopes or low areas not fit for cultivation, and "waste" acreage used for woodland. Drain tiles are used to make marshy land profitable. Small grains that hold water may be planted on a hillside, preventing or slowing down erosion. The farmer who insisted on buying hilly land because he got more for his money that way (the "ups" and "downs" giving him twice the area) was just born before his time.

Farms necessarily have become highly efficient. For nearly a century, The Pennsylvania State Grange has been a powerful force in bettering farm life conditions—economic, agricultural, educational, and social. There are hundreds of county branches with no restriction of membership because of political or religious beliefs. (However, there are more than forty biblical quotations in the grange ritual.) From the first, the purpose was "meeting together, talking together, working together, buying together, selling together for our mutual protection and advancement . . . We must dispense with the surplus of middlemen." This objective resulted in various grange insurance companies, a cooperative purchasing agency, banks, publications, equipment manufacturing, all projects having occasional failures before ultimate success.

The grange has been called "the farmer's door to the world," for, on the whole, his occupation is lonely. The state grange has annual meetings, and the numerous locals meet bimonthly—perhaps in a village hall, schoolhouse, or even on a farm; but most branches have their own grange halls. Women and children participate—as they do at home. The women's libber will be grateful to learn that the farm wife has always played an important role even in the national grange, and that though four offices were formed exclusively for women, she was eligible for any office—that of grand master included. At fourteen, an initiate of the junior grange learns four fundamental farm lessons based on the seasons of the year. There are higher degrees as one advances toward county, state, or national membership.

The locals sponsor dances, athletic contests, picnics, and many other social events. Humor keeps the business meetings lively too. When a visiting speaker at a grange stated that research with rats proved cigarettes conducive to cancer, a joker challenged him with "Most of us would sure like to get rid of the rats—but how do you get them to smoke?"

At local fairs there is great competition among granges for prizes for everything from grains and animals to jellies. At the Kutztown Folk Festival no less than ten grange units exhibit or supply food specialties or meals. But the original purpose of the grange is never forgotten—and members work for improved taxes and roads, better schools, rural electrification and telephones, conservation of land and forests, milk controls for dairy farmers, eradication of bovine TB, rural free delivery, help for needy members, funds for civic charities, et cetera.

Mention of the annual farm show in Harrisburg affects me like a *hitzi,* the Dutch word for a heat flash in "change of life." Years ago when I was writing a farm novel, and being "wet behind the ears" felt the farm show might be helpful, I went there to do some research. There was a crushing crowd. At one point I stopped to watch a new milking machine in action. I could barely see Daisy, chewing her cud and switching her tail, but at last a crevice opened up, and the tubes connected to Daisy's udders were plainly visible. There was no milk in the tubes, however. I was indignant. Daisy must be miserable. Soon she would be really suffering from the suction, wouldn't she? Where was the attendant? The S.P.C.A. should be phoned! I jabbed my way nearer to the outrage—and then a large family moved away and gave me the whole picture of Daisy. An automatic cow nailed to the platform!

Aside from knowing a cow when you see one, "farming" in our area has had many connotations. From the time the early settler made his gunstock and baby's cradle, the Dutch farmers have shown great versatility in their backyard shops. Originally this moonlighting wasn't a hobby but a necessity, as it may be today. The immigrant made yokes of crooked limbs or roots, and his whiffletree from virgin oak. He fashioned his harness from twisted deerskins, hemp and flax, and even used grapevines. It was only when tanning became common that the modern leather harness came into use. Often then a farmer operated a small tannery to supply his neighbors with hides. Since many of the early settlers were leather workers, there were soon tanneries in most of our trade centers producing not only harness but buckets, door hinges, coach springs, tableware, and even articles of clothing. Even now one can come upon a back-road leather shop where an artisan makes strong and beautiful items by hand, using tools often dating back to the age before industrialization. Dean Wright has called it "an age when it was a matter of pride to take your time."

In winter or in confining weather the farmer made wooden rakes, brooms from hickory, hog bristle brushes. There were always wheels to repair and barrel and tub staves to make. The more creative carved beautiful butter molds or perhaps whittled a fiddlestick from maple. As the family increased, more chairs and fireside settees were needed. Sometimes a farmer with a specialty would load his wagon and sell or trade within his area, returning home with a puppy for the boys or a new egg basket for Mom and the girls.

Though there were itinerant shoe menders, a clever farmer might repair all the family shoes in winter. Literally "re"-pair. As there were no "lefts" or "rights" then, a badly worn shoe was discarded and its mate teamed up with any other of similar size.

While his wife's spinning wheel hummed, more than one farmer wove rags into lovely patterns and color combinations. Carpet making was often a thriving family business. In the Daniel Boone Homestead, now a museum, is the loom used by Daniel's father after he had worked all day in the fields. The squire was also a blacksmith.

Over the years, backyard shops have given evidence of innumerable skills besides farming, from the artistic to the purely practical like cigar making, tinsmithing, cheese making. In the countryside today signs lead you down the farm lane to radio repairmen, cabinetmakers, electricians, basket weavers, butchers, florists. In many a rural area a farm wife raises African violets for sale or makes quilts to order. Or her specialty may be mouth-watering shoofly pies. The hardest sign for the visitor to pass is "Antiques," especially if the old barn spills out a dough tray or huge copper kettle.

In spite of secondary skills, the Dutch have clung to farming more ardently than any other group in America, fighting against all odds. Lancaster County produces more per acre than any other county in the country. (Quite a record, considering that I was told in New Holland that the best farmland costs $3,200 an acre; a fine pair of mules may bring the same; and a good buggy horse is worth $500.) Modern statistics and history lead to the same conclusion: we not only have an innate love of the soil but we work doggedly in our own way at the thing we like the best.

Fredric Klees says in his delightful book *The Pennsylvania Dutch* that we were "to a large degree the founders of the agricultural prosperity of America." What could be more auspicious for our country's future? For there's a very old Pennsylvania Dutch saying, *Tsu bluga iss tsu baeta*—"to plow is to pray."

City Smoke

Rich man, poor man, beggar man, thief,
Doctor, lawyer, merchant, chief.

WHO HASN'T CHANTED THIS "COUNTING-OUT" PRELUDE TO A CHILDHOOD GAME?
Some professions and occupations—honorable or otherwise—seem to be
perennial like those in the rhyme. Others fall into desuetude or change
complexion, like those of family doctor, shoemaker, carter, hunter, joiner, and
linen weaver.

Yet many of today's industries are directly related to skills brought here
by early settlers, and their skills were many. Still playing a part in our
economy are bricks, stone quarries, cigar factories, textiles, iron and steel—to
name a few. (If Reading and its environs are often featured in this section,
the reason isn't favoritism, but the fact that Reading is one of the oldest and
largest Pennsylvania Dutch cities and has always been noted for excellence in
both professions and business.)

The lifeblood of most industries today is the bank. Though at one time
Philadelphia was the banking center for all Dutch towns, we now have
branches of federal and state banks at every other corner. However, it seems
that a few outsiders still have the notion that the Dutch are "dumb" about
money as well as everything else. It's said that a Philadelphia counterfeiter
went upcountry with a big roll of eighteen-dollar bills to unload on the hicks.
At a village store he casually asked the proprietor if he'd change an eighteen-
dollar bill. "Vy shuah," was the answer. "What do you want—two nines or

three sixes?" The average Dutch businessman is shrewd, and many a fortune has been made in banking.

The Tobias Knoblauch Private Bank of Reading is unique in our area, and though now under state and federal regulations it has always remained in the family. It was founded by a native Austrian in 1900 for German, Italian, and Polish immigrants. The present chairman of the board, Leo Knoblauch, told me that the business began when laborers often asked his father (a housebuilder) to save for them the pay they'd need to bring relations from the old country. (Saturday night tippling was a great temptation.) Tobias Knoblauch soon licensed his banking business and developed a travel bureau as well as insurance companies. His wife was the first woman bank officer in the country. Today, Leo Knoblauch has eight other partners in banking, though he has sold the travel agency and thirty-two insurance companies. He still caters to foreigners and can speak their languages. Perhaps he's the prototype of the Dutchman in another current joke—so rich that he puts his Swiss money into American banks!

Long before workmen had anything but the sugar bowl for security, the most valued craftsman was the blacksmith, depended on by the settler for gun, ax, farm tools, andirons, and kitchen utensils. Many a smith had a seventeen-hour workday, which might include a clout from a skittish pony that "he couldn't get under," or from a mule that nearly kicked his leg off. The blacksmith had to be brawny indeed!

In the seventeenth century the Iroquois often requisitioned a smith to mend their axes, guns, hoes, and kettles. The smith who stayed at length and learned the Indian language served as interpreter too, and might become important enough to marry the chieftain's daughter. It was more expedient, of course, to carry home what he had gleaned by "keeping his ear to the ground" and learning what was brewing at the frontier. Arthur Woodward called these smiths "diplomats without portfolios."

The later blacksmith had to be ingenious when his work became more competitive. Decorative things like hinges and latches were custom made, and, since iron was scarce, had to be durable as well as artistic. Naturally, John Doe wanted a firedog different from his neighbors'. But everyone had to have horses shod, and horse shoeing was the nucleus of the business. Even today at Talmadge you can watch a blacksmith welding borium into a horseshoe so his Amish customer's horse won't slip in winter. You'll get more of a thrill too at those flying sparks than you do in passing the huge Bethlehem Steel Corporation.

The Bethlehem Iron Company was founded by a Dutchman, John Fritz, and was later headed by another Dutchman, Charles F. Schwab. Pennsylvania's huge iron industry, born of our early forges, first moved westward when a branch of the Oley Forge Spang family migrated to Juniata Valley. Finally, with state-owned canals and the railroad, Pittsburgh became the renowned iron and steel city.

No venturesome Spang or anyone else traveled westward without his Kentucky rifle, made as early as the French and Indian War. Though of Pennsylvania manufacture, it was so named because the Kentucky area was then "the frontier," opening the way to new settlements. When Daniel Boone braved the Cumberland Gap to explore midwestern valleys, he used the rifle and it soon replaced the settlers' musket, which took longer to load and used more powder.

By the time of the Revolution, gun shops in Lancaster were humming. The Kentucky rifle was a superior firearm and beautiful too, with its long octagonal barrel, curly maple stock inlaid with ornaments of brass or silver, and distinctive patch box. (The latter is of great aid to the antiquer in judging the time of the maker and his locale.) In colonial days the barrel was very long and heavy, but by the early nineteenth century was considerably shorter, and soon, with the invention of the percussion cap, became obsolete. If you happen to own one, you may be richer than you think!

The making of hardware, which once depended on forges (like the rifle), has always flourished in our area. So have foundries and machine shops. Cartech (Carpenter Technology Corporation), whose headquarters are now in Reading, is an international company distributing specialty metals. Beryllium Copper is another huge outfit. If you're just a retail shopper and want to buy handsome brass colonial candelabra, don't wait to go to Williamsburg. The trivet with satin patina I once bought there was made in Reading and rivals the skill of the early artists.

Not only forges but mills, furnaces, and many industries used Conestoga wagons. Designed by Pennsylvania craftsmen, many (though not all) were made here. On the right side of the wagon was a lazy board on which the driver often sat; as it might have been a hazard to oncoming traffic, he also drove on the right side of the road. Hence, our present custom of driving, though with no practical reason now.

The wagoners, the majority of whom were Dutch (and many from the Plain sects), were renowned for their toughness and strength. Yet, rugged as they were, they took great pride in "fancying up" their outfits. Brass bells were a must. When a wagoner bragged "I'll be there with bells on," he meant he'd rout any adversary on the way; bells were the victor's booty. Sometimes atop the bell arches were pompoms. Horses' forelocks were often braided and bedecked with ribbons of red, white, and blue. Tassels were used too, usually made of a bunch of horsehair or wool dyed blue or red (though sometimes varicolored), and dangled to the side of the horses' heads. Perhaps they helped to ward off flies, but one wonders if the beasts that were hauling two tons or more appreciated all this folderol.

Eventually the Iron Horse took over their major work. However, since many wagon features were practicable for farming, a modified type was made even into the nineteenth century and used by farmers hauling produce into Philadelphia, or by wagoners they engaged. But by 1850 the hundred-year heyday of the Conestoga wagon was over after faithfully serving the nation's needs.

A modish cousin of the wagon is the buggy. Buggy making is still a brisk business in the Dutch country since most of our Amish don't use cars. (An Old Order sect that has broadened allows ownership if the car is conservative and dark in color. Less liberal are the "Black Bumpers," who conscientiously paint all the chromium black.) The evolution of an Amish family is shown in the varying styles: the "bachelor's buggy" (an open two-seater for courting); the closed four-seater; the spring wagon, and the "six-poster," or large family carriage. When you whiz by an Amish horse clop-clopping along a country road, you somehow feel guilty as well as "gay." The leisurely Amish pace often reminds me of our being held up at times on the road, and one of our small daughters asking, "Why does the slow car always get to the head of the line?"

As collisions of cars and buggies occur much too often, repair work is a large part of the trade of the more than forty carriage-related shops in Lancaster County. Some are a one-man project with family helping in minor tasks. Others may be run in conjunction with farming or another business. For instance, Abe Zeller, a coach maker and carpenter by profession, also raises rabbits for laboratory experiments. Abe turned to coach making after making cedar chests and extension tables, and is now so swamped with orders that he's many months behind in delivery. Quite understandable, since he makes the whole coach from "scratch!"

In the carriage shop of Mr. Zook, an Amishman, the only power he uses besides muscle is from storage batteries. Sad to relate, the number of skilled workmen is waning, and so is the trade.

The Gruber Wagon Works in Berks County is of special historic interest. A hundred years ago Franklin Gruber had a small shop on his farm where he did repair work for his neighbors. To keep up with their demand he gave up farming and bought land for a more adequate shop. Here a waterwheel furnished the first power for machinery. His four sons all became master mechanics in some pertinent specialty, but apprentices were soon needed.

Business boomed. It was smart to own a Gruber wagon; only seasoned lumber was used—birch, hickory, oak, poplar, and fir. The workmanship was superior. Though business was done in the dialect, by the turn of our century the Grubers had all the latest equipment—even an elevator to heave wagons to the second floor for painting. Forty years ago a grandson became the final owner. Wagons, of course, are no longer in demand today. All that remains now is an empty picturesque, weathered, two-and-a-half-story wooden building of museum caliber. On the site of the Blue Marsh Dam, a government project, it was threatened with extinction. But happily, though, through the efforts of antiquaries, it is being moved to a safe location (if there is such a thing today!). The estimated cost of moving and restoration is close to half a million dollars.

Most of us now think of buggies as a romantic part of the past, like the bicycles of a century ago. Many a great-grandmother went about humming the wildfire song, "A Bicycle Built for Two," and many a swain must have sung it as a proposal:

> *But you'll look sweet upon the seat*
> *Of a bicycle built for two.*

The early Columbia Wheel was impressive, to say the least—fifty-two inches high, hard-tired, with a huge wheel in front and a small one in back. To ride it one must have been able to walk a tightrope or balance stilts. At a cost of a hundred and fifty dollars, it wasn't for the poor laborer who needed it most. Soon came the Star with the higher wheel in the rear (flaring into fashion with the bustle, perhaps).

When bicycles became the rage, a small Reading shop grew into a nationally known concern. William Henry Wilhelm, who had been in the paint, hat, and hardware business, turned to bicycle repairing, then manufacturing, and made the Reading, later called the Wilhelm. Irve, a sporting son, founded the city's first bicycle club, soon replaced by the Penn Wheelmen, and our most able cyclists held meets for a cheering public. By the 1890s, after the appearance of the "safety" model with smaller wheels of equal size, the Wilhelm plant turned out 37,000 bicycles annually. Irve gave up racing and became head of the business (after a broken bone or two, no doubt).

I never see a picture of an early Columbia Wheel without recalling a traumatic childhood experience. I was forbidden to own a bike—too dangerous in the city. But one day I joined some of the gang loitering at Arthur's, next door, with their bikes. Now and then one of them would make a little sortie up the street and back. I curdled with envy.

"Don't you wish you had a bike, Mildred?" taunted one.

"I don't want one."

"They're fun," taunted another.

"I know—I can ride."

"You can't either!" taunted still another.

"I *can so!*"

"Show us." This from Arthur, the prince of my dreams.

"Here, take mine."

I was seized with terror as the gang hoisted me onto the bike, which seemed higher than the water tower, and sent me flying for a dozen feet or so before I hurtled to my doom. And Arthur laughed!

Since then I have always found cars more conducive to romance. However, I suffered intensely for several years when our son entered the annual Duryea Hill Climb on Reading's Mount Penn. It was Charles Duryea who climbed Mount Penn in high gear, establishing a record. In the early

1900s he manufactured the Duryea cars here, though he and his brother Frank had made a gasoline automobile ten years earlier in New England. He turned out as many as three cars a week, some with three wheels and some with four.

Reading soon became an early center of the automobile industry. After the Duryea came the six-cylinder Acme, a famous racing car with custom-made body and brass fittings. For several years (till 1914) the S.G.V. was made by Sternbergh, Graham, and Van Tine, and ranged in price from $2,500 to $12,000. (Think of this in terms of subsequent inflation!) Models were owned by the King of England, the Czar, the Kaiser, and a smattering of Vanderbilts, Drexels, and Astors. The Reading, the Middleby, and the Daniels were made here also. Studebaker was Dutch but manufactured in Indiana. The Body Works in Fleetwood was the most prestigious in America. When General Motors bought it, it was run as a division of Fisher Body, but was moved to Detroit about twenty years ago.

Though there has been a drastic decline of vehicle manufacture, cities teem with textile workers, and nearly every Dutch town has its mill, often the heart of the village. In fact, textiles are more important than iron or steel. Made here in great quantities are dresses, underwear, shoes, and hosiery. When we asked a tenant of ours how he dared use on his sport shirts the patented alligator trademark, he shrugged and said, "Otherwise the stylish girls won't buy'em." (I might add that he isn't a Dutchman.)

Wholesale outlets in our area, such as Vanity Fair's, bring thousands of shoppers from many miles away, even those on cross-country tours. Busloads come daily, carrying off Christmas gifts of David Crystal suits "cheap at half the price." How different from the early days when there was much weaving and dyeing of linsey-woolsey and linen at home. Germantown was our first manufacturing center, producing linen and knit goods. Also, stockings were first made there on crude frames in the homes of Mennonite knitters. Over two hundred years ago the Dutch were making 720,000 pairs of stockings annually! What would the neat calves of the colonial gentlemen have done without them?

For years, our Berkshire Knitting Mills was the largest producer of seamed stockings in the world, having various foreign branches. (The affiliated Textile Machine Works built the first American full-fashioned knitting machine in 1902.) Many mills making children's socks and men's hose have also operated here. After World War II the industry began to move south where labor was cheaper and the sources of natural fibers were nearer. North Carolina has now stolen our laurels.

There was a time when my husband's hosiery plant sold a third of its output to Kresge and Woolworth who both profited by being Dutchmen: in their early days they bought much of their merchandise from other Dutchmen who accepted stock in payment (as an auslander wouldn't) and consequently all made fortunes.

Sebastian S. Kresge was born near Scranton and got his idea of a five-and-ten from Frank Woolworth whose first store was in Lancaster. Kresge, who had been a bookkeeper and then salesman, began business in Memphis in 1897. Fifty years later the S. S. Kresge syndicate operated 714 stores in the United States and Canada. Kresge was founder, sole owner, and treasurer of the Kresge foundation in Detroit, involving many millions of dollars. He was a great philanthropist.

Our area has always been full of five-and-tens, clothing shops, and department stores. John Wanamaker, another Dutchman, created a little empire of his own in Philadelphia. One of the outstanding Reading stores was the old Dives, Pomeroy and Stewart where my father-in-law was once a coat buyer. And thereby hangs a tale.

During lunch hour the young boy employees played hide-and-seek on the third floor, partly unfinished, which had a gangway with ladder at each end. It was dark here, and one mischievous boy loved to paddle his pals with a stock board when they backed down the ladder. Mr. Pomeroy also used the gangway at times, for he often chose to leave the store by an inconspicuous door only reached by a third-floor stairway. One sad day he got a horrendous whack and seized the culprit who froze with fright. The big boss demanded his name, then released him, and strode to my father-in-law's office.

"Solon, what do you know about young Billy Keim?" he asked tartly.

"He's one of the best stock boys we've ever had—has had several promotions already."

"That's all I wanted to know," said Mr. Pomeroy, and departed.

End of story.

Mr. Pomeroy was a thorough gentleman who doffed his hat to the lowliest female employee. Hats (even the nightcap) were then as vital a part of clothing as underdrawers. As a matter of fact, hat production was Reading's sole industry shortly after its founding in 1748. Of the forty thousand hats made annually most were of wool or fur and sold for a dollar. The work done by hand in the laborer's home was hard and tedious since the hat was stiff and heavy. Yet a good hatter could make eight a day. By the nineteenth century Berks County was leading the state's production for several reasons. There were great numbers of skilled workmen available here; raw material was easily obtainable; fuel was cheap; there was handy transportation by canal, railroad, and turnpike. By 1826 we were shipping large orders to the West Indies.

Among our famous hatters were Hendel Brothers who did their own fulling, dyeing, and finishing a hundred years ago, and even made their own boxes. Another, George Bollman, born in Sinking Spring in 1838, was indentured to the Levi Handel family and was given room and board, clothing and training. Eventually he went into business for himself and bought twenty-two acres at the present factory site in Adamstown. The firm, now the largest producer of wool felt hats in the country, is run by Bollman's three grandsons. Today George W. Bollman, Inc., and the Adamstown Hat Company are the only two remaining Berks County hat manufacturers. Except for the old and bald, modern man lets his own long lush ringlets keep his head warm. As for the women, who but an old granny wears a hat, even in church?

Many years ago when the cowboy hat came into vogue our son had a needling passion to own one. As the family was driving west that summer, he waited till he could buy the genuine thing. In Wyoming one day he went out on his own with his carefully hoarded allowance, and returned looking top-heavy but triumphant. When his father saw the label in the hat he grinned, winked at me, and handed it back to Jordan with "Terrific!" You guessed it, of course. The bluebird of happiness is always in your own backyard.

Frank McCloud and Son of Reading, a very small hat concern doing business till recently, was very well known for its excellent quality and making of Old Order Amish broadbrim felts. This is a specialty in our area, as many styles and sizes must meet religious specifications for both married and unmarried men.

For years the Amish have made their own straw hats. The processes are similar to those of basket weaving. There is the sizing and bleaching of the rye straw on the grass, more sizing and plaiting into braids (very fine hats have nine-straw braids), the sewing, and shaping on a wooden form. Braiding and stitching the hatband in is usually done by Amish Golden Agers.

Like hat making, basket weaving by hand is a dying art, but has continued longer than many another. Milt Lorah, living in the village of Basket in the Oley Valley, recently wove baskets in his general store, and produced a great variety with or without lids. Plain and fancy. Baskets (korrups) take on different shapes for marketing, stockings, bread, sewing, berrying, fishing, gardening, wood carrying, gathering Easter eggs, and even for diapers (*windlakorrups*). Sizes, shapes, and use vary too with the years.

Lorah grew the willows in his meadow, cut them in March, "set" them in his pond, and peeled them in April and May. (Don't go in for basket weaving thinking its many processes are simple!) Milt never wasted a moment between sales of sugar or flour scooped from a barrel. At night when he worked too late, his cronies gathering for a game of hasenpfeffer made him unpeg his basket from the lapboard and surrender it for a table. But Milt's customers came from as far away as Wisconsin.

A greater celebrity was Ollie Strausser who died in 1961, and who lived on the Oley Furnace Road. As his fame grew, Ollie exhibited at Dutch folk festivals, appeared on TV making baskets and playing gay folk tunes on his mouth organ. Eventually thousands came to see the showman at work at his modest home, and marvel at the contrast between his handiwork and the "dime a dozen" baskets in stores. Yet Ollie would never go commercial, or make more baskets than he felt lived up to his standards.

Other old Dutch industries have either died out or are growing feeble with age, yet deserve mention because of their early importance. Papermaking is one. In 1690 William Rittenhouse set up the nation's first paper mill in Roxboro, making 250 pounds of handmade paper daily. Few of the many subsequent mills remain. One is Berks County's Van Reed paper mill, in business since 1820, and once equipped to make paper by hand. A waterwheel supplied the power for chopping rags and mixing pulp. As business grew, chopped rags were taken to the nearby mill No. 2 for washing, sorting, and storing. It's said that Tom, the old horse, knew the route so well that he would wait for a loaded wagon and make the round trip alone. The old family business is now owned by a Philadelphia company.

Another lagging industry is coal mining. Anthracite was discovered in 1755 by two Dutchmen; one, a gunsmith near Nazareth, experimented with lumps of it given him by an Indian. And presto!—by the end of the century there were nearly a hundred firms engaged in coal production. Factories without waterpower needed fuel, and coal was vital for making glass, iron, and beer where "a hot fire" was needed. Legion boats carrying coal from Pottsville to Philadelphia dotted the Schuylkill River. Now you seldom even see coal rumbling down a chute into a cellar.

In the coal industry, workmen flocked to a natural resource. In most other cases, industries arose where certain kinds of artisans chose to settle—usually among earlier migrating relatives. For example, Lancaster County drew makers of musical instruments—spinets, organs, then pianos; most zithers were made in Bucks County. Artisanship often spread, of course, in relation to demand. At one time there were more than a hundred and fifty clockmakers in the Dutch area. Some workers made only a few clocks, some made dozens, and others even turned out hundreds. Suddenly, after 1800, everyone had to own a clock. And, why not, if you had to depend on nature like most of the farmers? When the rooster crowed it was 4:00 A.M. When the first bird peeped, daylight was at hand. Sometimes "the room" (parlor) had marks on the floor to indicate from shadows when it was 9:00 A.M., noon, and midafternoon. But what of cloudy days and winter? No doubt the stomach was a better criterion.

Our household is fortunate in owning one of the Daniel Oyster grandfather clocks made in Reading in the eighteenth century; it used to tick off the tedious minutes when my husband did his homework. It still plods on accurately without taking holidays and, I believe, will valiantly tick off eternity.

Our clock business, halted by the Revolutionary War, finally expired after the Industrial Revolution when Connecticut competition became too great.

The Industrial Revolution gradually seeped from English villages into America. Benjamin Franklin and his scientific coterie helped to further it; so did Tom Paine with his *Rights of Man,* declaring that "the good life must be based on material decency." The New Age concept was that energy was the "core of nature" and must be harnessed. Canals and the steam engine appeared, and machinery using nature's energy and saving man's. Towns became cities, settlements grew near the railroads, and manufacturing waxed in the Dutch country as well as everywhere else.

New industries have gradually arisen since then, some of national repute like Lancaster County's Armstrong floor covering, Trojan powerboats, Schick electric razors, Hamilton watches, New Holland farm machinery, Eshelman feeds, RCA television and electronic tubes. Isn't it interesting to note how many of these are precision products, related to skills of the early meticulous German workers? And aren't you reminded of the early production of rugs, clocks, canalboats, and wagons? The Dutch are apt to cling to their heritage in one form or another: in Lancaster today are the country's oldest tobacco shop and hardware and department stores. Each is at its original site and is operated by the same family interests founding it.

About 1860 unionism developed from the Industrial Revolution when the rapid growth of mining and business enterprise of all kinds created new problems between management and labor. Farm labor flowing into the cities brought about lower wages generally and greater competition for jobs. Also, working conditions left much to be desired. The Noble Order of the Knights of Labor (secret at first) was the first labor movement in Reading. Unlike the subsequent Federation of Labor, it included workers of any skill. By 1885, however, there were trade unions, the earliest being those of ironworkers, stonecutters, wool hatters, cigar makers, painters, and typesetters. When Berks County farmers faced a labor shortage after the last depression, the Works Progress Administration was blamed, and the Co-op resulted, operating now on a national level.

Often strikes were triggered by something seemingly trivial. In 1873 (era of the beard and moustache cup) the management of the Philadelphia and Reading Railroad demanded that all employees be clean-shaven. But who wanted to look sissy among his manly hirsute peers? The workers walked out in a body, hauling with them the couplings of all cars and the side rods of every engine. The beards triumphed. But a general Pennsylvania Railroad strike four years later resulted in twelve deaths in Reading within twenty-four hours—the most violent strike in our history.

The longest strike in our area, lasting ten months, was in 1936 at the Berkshire Knitting Mills, an open shop. Union picketers moved in to keep workers from their jobs, and even the state police were threatened. Besides one death, much violence and sabotage ensued, including the oil bombing of the mayor's home—the climax. Berkshire Knitting Mills is still nonunion, however.

A strike-which-might-have-been is suggested by an architect friend who had much experience with unions in his day. Some years ago Amish farm help were laying bricks for a school he had designed. A union leader was trying to persuade them to strike for higher wages. "We don't believe in unions," said one of the Amish ... "I know," replied the union man, "but you'd help to raise everyone's pay if you'd ask for a dollar an hour instead of eighty cents." Another Amishman doggedly laid another brick. "Then we'd lose too much when we get laid off," he huffed.

Though the public in general resents strikes and their ensuing hardships for the consumer, we must give unions their due in more ways than one. They have not only improved living conditions for the average worker but have been a boon to social welfare along other lines, such as promotion of public schools. Our Berks County tuberculosis sanatorium was a result of their interest and support.

It's heartening to turn to age-old industries that have survived not only strikes, wars, and depressions of different eras, but have greatly expanded. I suspect it's because they relate either to pleasure or security. To have a sturdy house has always been important to the Dutchman, proof being the mellow bricks of ancient barns and buildings. Clay, stone quarries, and other natural resources are close at hand. The Glen Gery Brick Company, founded in 1890, is now a leading manufacturer of bricks and concrete building materials.

The average workman (be he machine-fixer or bricklayer) has confirmed ideas about the quality of his output, and also, if he's "worldly," about relaxing at night with a foaming beer. Most are moderate drinkers, despite the old verse, a favorite of John Yoder's:

> I drink—so I stink.
> If I don't drink—still I stink.
> Better to drink and stink
> Than not to drink and still stink.

William Penn himself introduced beer here, in the seventeenth century, building a brewery near his house at Pennsbury. In 1699 when a law licensed taverns, and the quality, quantity, and prices of beer were fixed, it was an indispensable part of every meal. At Reading's first brewery in 1763, there were three kinds of brew: strong (six cents a quart); middle (three cents a quart); and small (at one cent). Half the town went daily to the brewery with kettles and buckets. Some preferred to drink on the premises with its fine fruit trees and shaded tables. Though distilleries were increasing, there was a constant demand for beer since most immigrants came from beer-drinking countries.

Soon all German communities had lager breweries. At one time there were over a hundred and twenty in the state, but with the recent closing of the Reading Brewing Company only ten of these remain. Bigger plants and automation have tolled the death knell of the small concern. Beer was even more popular after the Civil War and became a great industry a hundred years ago when primitive brewing methods were replaced. Frank Lauer of Reading was an organizer and president of the U.S. Brewers Association (and a great local philanthropist). Some of us remember when beer gardens were a respectable place to take the family for dinner, the children delighting in the prospect of chicken fricassee.

Hard liquor was in a less reputable category. But even the tirades against drunkards by Mose Dissinger, the preacher, had small effect, virulent though they were: "You have noses like red peppers, ears like doughnuts, bellies like barrels, and make faces like foxes eating wasps. You jump for the rum bottle like bullfrogs for red rags." (This profusion of metaphors would make a teetotaler tipsy!)

Whiskey has been made here since the early eighteenth century when nearly every fair-sized farm had a still or still house. Rye and corn mash were fed to pigs. Stills were taxable, some being imported from Europe; but local coppersmiths made the majority, varying greatly in size and holding from fifty to two hundred gallons. They were a large part of the coppersmith's work, as old ads attest. Since there were no commercial distilleries, farmers sold whiskey to innkeepers who lured wagoners by giving them free drinks with meals. A Conestoga wagon was designed to carry a barrel or two as part of its cargo. During the Civil War revenue was placed on whiskey, and private industry died out.

No doubt this Dutch area has always been ambivalent about liquor. An old-timer tells me that when the rich distiller's wife walked down his church aisle, the pious heard her whishing taffeta shamefully whispering, "Whiskey, whiskey, whiskey . . ." On the other hand, we have our addicts. When a wife berated her husband, "There are dozens of empty whiskey bottles in this cellar closet! Where do they all come from?" the answer was, "Don't ask *me*. I never bought an empty booze bottle in my life."

A suggested cure for leaving off schnapps is that of a shrewd Dutch farmer: "Buy a barrel of whiskey, put a faucet in it, and whenever you draw off schnapps, add an equal amount of water. The barrel is always full, but the schnapps gets weaker and weaker till you're only drinking water and have no more use for the schtuff."

For the Dutchman or anyone else who wants to "lick the habit," there is Chit-Chat Farms at Wernersville. A drying-out place, it is A.A. oriented, grows yearly, and is internationally known. It was founded by the late Richard Caron, a "recovered alcoholic," and Catherine, his wife. Previously, though having four young children, they took drink and drug addicts into their home and often worked with them there for many months. Chit-Chat guests are now "graduated" after an intensive five-week program aiming to cure body, mind, and soul. The work is a great memorial to a man who saved many lives from the hell he once battled.

However, we must never forget there are valid uses for whiskey for the average Dutchman—colds, upset stomach, cuts, and burns. For the last, "immerse white petals of lily flowers in a bottle of whiskey, put several petals on the burn, and bandage."

As with the chicken and egg enigma, it's hard to say which came first, schnapps or pretzels. One thing is certain, though most Dutchmen can live without whiskey, and many without beer, none can live happily without pretzels. Hence, our numerous factories and their renown. Bachman now packs pretzels individually so that they can be shipped internationally without breakage.

Pretzels are fattening, of course, but candy is worse. And we love our candy too. It stands to reason that two world-famous candy factories were started here by Dutchmen. The products of both are cheap. But it's said that "if you make for the classes, you eat with the masses; if you make for the masses, you eat with the classes." A whole town commemorates Milton S. Hershey, founder of the chocolate factory and the school for orphan boys (now coed), who live on its surrounding, prosperous farms. Daily tours through the immaculate factory; hockey games or the Ice Follies at the huge arena; the treasures of the museum and the fun in the amusement park and zoo—all these put one in awe of what one Dutchman can do for the benefit of others. Long live the Hershey bar with almonds!

Luden's Incorporated in Reading, though now producing many kinds of candy, was first known for its cough drops. William Luden began his business modestly in the family kitchen. It seems that one post-holiday season he had many clear toys left (clear-colored candies of various shapes, now outmoded, but beloved by children of earlier days and often hung on Christmas trees). Billy melted them down to make smaller candies of different flavors. By mistake he used menthol instead of oil of cloves—and thereby made his fortune.

I never hear his name but what I think of one of his shad fishing trips on which my husband was invited. He left home in old khaki pants and sneakers to board the Luden yacht near Philadelphia and sail to the Chesapeake. The other guests were dressed fit for an admiral's caucus. My husband's chagrin

and perplexity increased after an elegant luncheon was served—and still no sign of shad nets. Finally the yacht docked at a pier in the Chesapeake and two of the well-groomed crew hauled aboard a barrel of shad. The fishing trip was over. This is the sangfroid a candy king can afford!

Candy can make a tremendous fortune but also can thwart a promising career. Years ago I found our small grandson prowling around our house one day, furtively opening closets and cupboards.

"What on earth are you doing, Lee?" I asked.

"Playing detective."

"Is that what you'd like to be someday?"

"Yep," he reflected. "But sometimes I'm afraid the baddies'll hear the jujubes rattling around in my pocket."

With our mania for sweets, it's not surprising that our doctors here are legion. Yet you must make an appointment months in advance. One October day my husband said blithely to his lawyer, "Oh, I want to add a codicil to my will. I'm leaving my May appointment with Dr.—— to my beloved son, Jordan." But we shouldn't grex, I suppose, as many of our medical men are carrying on the high ideals of our early Dutch practitioners.

Dr. Casper Wistar was one of the founders of the University of Pennsylvania Medical School. A man of versatility, he was chemist, anatomist, author, and amateur botanist. (The lovely, showy "wistaria" was named for him, and his intellectual "Wistar parties" were famous.)

Dr. Samuel Gross of Easton, an internationally known surgeon, was president of the American Medical Association and author of the first manual of military surgery.

The famous Dr. Bodo Otto, raised in Hanover, Germany, became a Reading citizen in middle age and at sixty-five volunteered his services for the continental army. For seven years he was senior surgeon at Valley Forge and Yellow Springs. On resuming practice he was not only mentally and physically fit, with a record of immunity to all diseases and no leaves of absence, but forthwith left for Germany for new surgical instruments. How fortunate that in the medical field there is still no enforced retirement!

A Reading contemporary of Dr. Otto's was Dr. Jonathan Potts, son of Pottstown's founder. Though highly trusted, he failed to promote among his patients the idea of vaccine for smallpox. During the Revolution he was appointed director of hospitals in Canada, yet never reached it, blocked by the fortress of Quebec and the hardships of bitter winter. However (with no evidence of permission from Congress), he did use inoculation and eradicated smallpox as a major disease in the north. Forced by poor health to return to Reading, he died at thirty-six, never seeing his country's independence.

The service of doctors is only one of our numerous and varied contributions to the battlefield. Among our illustrious Revolutionary fighters was Peter Muhlenberg, a Dutch-born minister of Virginia who was put in command of the Eighth Virginia Regiment. At his farewell sermon the congregation overflowed into the churchyard. After expounding on the duties of a Christian to his country he ended by revealing the uniform beneath his robe and crying, "There is a time for preaching and praying, but also a time for battle and such a time has now arrived!" Hundreds of German Virginia settlers then volunteered.

Some of our heroes are even nameless. Almost all of Washington's bodyguard were Pennsylvania Dutch. When he took command of the Continental troops he called for companies of Germans, having seen the effectiveness of their rifles. General Howe could only combat them by hiring Hessian mercenaries who used rifles too.

There's an amusing tale about a Fourth of July celebration early in the nineteenth century. On the speaker's platform was a doddering Revolutionary veteran. The orator turned to honor him in his address. "Venerable old fighter," he said, "you were at the harrowing Battle of Trenton?" (A grunt and a nod.) "You were at Brandywine and Yorktown?" ... "Yah." ... "You fought side by side with Washington, shielding him from enemy bayonets?" ... "Nein, nein," chuckled the veteran. "Mein Gott, I was with the Hessians."

Several of our women left their mark in martial history. Charlotte Este risked her life to warn Washington of an enemy attack. Molly Pitcher (Maria Ludwig) challenged enemy fire by carrying well water to our thirsting troops. During the Slavery Rebellion, Barbara Frietchie flaunted her Union flag before Stonewall Jackson, and, according to Whittier, said, "Shoot if you must this old gray head, but spare your country's flag." And her courage was respected.

Our list of "big brass" is impressive. General George Custer, after many Civil War victories, was annihilated with his men by the Sioux Indians, leaving us the maxim, "Custer's last stand." Later distinguished Dutch military leaders have been General John J. Pershing, head of the American Army in World War I; Boyertown's General Carl Spaatz, chief of Air Force Combat Command in World War II; and General Dwight D. Eisenhower ("the one who strokes with iron"), whose great-great-grandfather settled in York before 1750 and whose father was born in Elizabethville. Since Ike's mother was a member of a Plain sect, condoning neither war nor political activity, it's ironical that he was our most distinguished military man, and politician to boot.

The Dutch, having an iron streak like Eisenhower, are independent in politics as well as in everything else. As a farm woman said, "I don't believe what them politicians say—they do like they please anyhow." The Dutch area is strongly Democratic. The country's first Democratic Club was in Reading. This was one of the three cities in the nation called "islands of socialist strength" until the national organization suffered general defeat at the polls. The socialist party was formed here in 1901, but before then many voters had deserted the two major parties in one way or another. Darlington Hoopes, Sr., Reading attorney, was the socialist presidential candidate in 1952 and 1956. Local socialists, though considered radical, accomplished much good for the community, for instance, a better sewage system, playgrounds, and recreation centers.

We've had political rebels throughout our history. Major General Thomas Mifflin, on the War Board in 1777, was involved in the Conway Cabal, which conspired to replace General Washington. Later Mifflin became first governor of Pennsylvania. James Buchanan, fifteenth president, declared against the power of right of government to interfere with slavery. When seceding states armed without government intervention, Buchanan was accused of precipitating the Civil War. Though he supported the Union before he died, the stigma remained.

Among more conventional politicians was Frederick Augustus Conrad Muhlenberg, speaker of the first and third congressional congresses. His great-great-great-grandson, Frederick Muhlenberg, a Reading architect, also served in Congress. (A recent Dutchman now in the state legislature said he'd supposed he'd find all Solomons there, but some were "bigger fools than himself.") The German Quaker background of Herbert Hoover goes back to the time of William Penn.

Though our statesmen steal the professional limelight, we have had many prominent scientists. Francis Daniel Pastorius, founder of Germantown, was considered the most learned American scholar of his day. With his vast knowledge of various sciences, law, medicine, and agriculture, he wrote the first original scientific work in America. (He also published the first school book printed in Pennsylvania—a primer—and started a night school to teach his fellow immigrants English.) Johannes Kelpius was an astronomer, and so was David Rittenhouse whose orrery calculated for the first time in history the approximate distance between sun and earth. More recently, James Lick, who had amassed a great fortune, gave the Lick Observatory to the University of California. Rittenhouse, like Pastorius, was highly accomplished: he was a noted surveyor, first director of the Mint, and followed Franklin as president of the American Philosophical Society.

Though Audubon was a native Frenchman, he lived in our area, and we have adopted him and his fame as an ornithologist and artist. Our contemporary Edward Hill, nationally known, shows the most exquisite movies of birds and flora I have ever seen. One is filled with awe and inspiration, watching a robin hatching and growing, or a bud unfolding in a series of time exposures. His narration too is sensitive and poetic.

Dr. Levi Mengel, a Reading entomologist, went with Lieutenant Peary on his polar expedition of 1891–1892. In the interior of northern Greenland Mengel found many rare and fascinating specimens, his butterflies of special beauty. The Reading Public Museum and Art Gallery has a large part of his collection.

The pursuit of science naturally leads to invention. Among our best-known inventors is Robert Fulton, born in Lancaster in 1765. Before the rich New Yorker, Robert Livingstone, enabled him to launch his steamboat in 1807, he had been a silversmith; an artist for twenty years, studying with Benjamin West in London; then a student of mechanical science.

Heading the list of our *least* known inventors are two village crackpots. One was Mike Weber, a smith near Lebanon, who loved his schnapps and performed inimitable capers during sprees. Once, after making an iron flying machine, he invited the village to a demonstration. On the roof of the smithy he fastened the wings to his body and shouted, "Flipperty flop, doe gate's ab noch der Canada shtadt." ("I'm off to Canada.") After swooping into midair, he hovered briefly, then thudded down on the garden fence. He limped away from the shambles without comment. From then on he was known as "Der Flieg Weber." Yet who knows but what he inspired the Wright brothers?

The other unsung inventor lived in Hamburg. He used to sit watching the asthmatic old iron horse puff in and out of the station, and always bemoaned "the vaste of power, vis such a enchine." Thence he designed a car with mammoth wheels in back and low ones in front. No matter what kind of hill it climbed, "it would always run downhill by its own force." We must admit that there's a very slim margin of chance between success and failure. Nor should we ever denigrate imagination, a vital factor of progress. Though obviously not always triumphant, the Mike Webers have their importance in our culture.

Our professions and industries throughout the years have been too numerous to mention, alas, excepting old ones that prevail today or have left their mark upon the nation. Suffice it to say that the Dutch have helped to make Pennsylvania one of the foremost industrial states of the union, as well as an outstanding farming area. This isn't due to happenstance, either, though once we were the geographical hub of colonial population and culture. The Dutchman has earned his laurels with thrift, hard work, ambition, honesty, and ingenuity.

Man's House and God's House

THE OBSESSION TO RESTORE OLD COUNTRY HOUSES GROWS YEARLY AS THE CITY rat race and muggings increase. Dutch farms are in great demand, especially near Allentown, Lancaster, Harrisburg, York, and Reading. (And especially those with old outbuildings and a brook.) Some buyers let the weeds take over the fields, and focus on repairing the old brick kitchen floor, unboarding fireplaces, and reviving the patina of walnut paneling. Others turn "gentleman farmers," hiring local workers to heave the hayfork. One man I know has gone into the business of raising sod for playing fields, town houses, and golf clubs. I can hear the original owner, an eighteenth-century farmer, exclaim, appalled, "Gott in Himmel, such waste of good land!"

The early Palatinate immigrants built log cabins, much like those of the even earlier Swedish and Finnish settlers. Thick walls, small window openings, and huge fireplaces offered great warmth, despite the cabin's crude nogging of wattle and daub. German and Swiss cabins, however, had corners neatly notched in German fashion, sharp-pitched roofs with central chimney, and a pent roof encircling the house. Most cabins were built above a spring, the cellar being reached only from without. The rich had houses with two rooms on first and second floors, surely a luxury in contrast to the earliest one-room dwelling. All is relative, of course. Years ago we knew a carpenter who bragged about the fine modern house he had built for his wife. It had all the latest "conweniences" except "electric" and running water!

Forgetting the stamina needed to brave the Indians and other dangers of a new and rugged land, we think of log cabins as romantic. Few original ones survive (often disguised now by clapboard sidings), and these are treasured. The Keim stone cabin, typically Germanic and medieval, was built by the Oley Valley's first known settler, and is in good condition. Threatened with demolition in the Blue Marsh Dam area (a government project) is a nest of log buildings two hundred years old—a dwelling, barn, springhouse, shed, and smokehouse that produced smoked ham and sausage until a few years ago. All have been purchased by the Pennsylvania Log House Society, which hopes to erect them again at Charming Forge, the historical furnace.

Extinct in the Dutch country is the later half-timbered house, typical of medieval Europe. And so cozy and picturesque! One automatically thinks of a rainbow flower garden, of smoke lazing from the chimney, and a small, muscled dog within turning the roast on a spit. But our second-generation settlers usually built thick-walled houses of fieldstone, and this and the timber used in construction helped to clear the land for farming. (As a settler, one learns ingenuity!) Later, stone from local quarries was used, then brick and sandstone. Toward the end of the colonial era stone and brick were more common in southeastern Pennsylvania than anywhere else in the country. No wonder the eighteenth- and nineteenth-century strangers raved in their journals of these "mansions" and their environs boasting prosperity "in the wilds." An 1874 traveler recorded: "Cattle stand with their four feet in two feet of clover. Every field is a park. Every barn is a cow palace. Every pigpen a porcine paradise. Pennsylvania is pre-eminently the State of barns." Even forty years earlier, the first Tyrone Power in his *Impressions of America,* written on tour, implies the same well-being but with something of a grudge, speaking of "their piggery of a residence and palace of a barn."

Our barn, indeed, has always been the more important. Though the Swiss or bank barn with its tiny windows appeared about 1760, records of 1798 show more log barns in Pennsylvania than all other kinds combined. Now the log barn is gone like the cabin, relegated to historical novels and movies, but we are famed for our bank barns, built into a bank or hillside as outbuildings often are—the springhouse, smokehouse, and others. (Even gristmills and early churches had one or more levels below the ground.)

The lower barn level houses cattle, sheep, swine, and horses, for here are fewer extremes of heat and cold. The animals must have their comfort though the farm family dashes from heated kitchen to icy beds. Lucky cows!

The second level is entered from the bank ramp by two large swinging doors, accommodating a fully loaded hay wagon. Bigger barns may have two or three pairs of doors; within one is a smaller door for the convenience of the farmer or an antisocial laying hen.

The upper level, supported by heavy logs or girders, stores straw and hay, with a granary in the rear or above the forebay. (The latter is a roof or upper story overhanging the barnyard like the projecting Swiss balcony.) The center space between mows is for threshing and large farm equipment, or perhaps a sleigh for blizzardly winters, but may be used for a rollicking square dance or a Sunday service of the House Amish who have no churches.

As with "man bites dog," it's refreshing to hear a joke by a Dutchman about a stranger. It seems that two city professors visiting our area stopped at a farm and noticed a calf that had just swished its tail into a knothole of the barnyard fence.

One of the erudites said to the other, "How on earth did that calf ever get into the knothole?" His companion answered, "It puzzles me more that he can't get the rest of him through."

Migrating Dutchmen have taken their barn type with them to Maryland, West Virginia, or wherever they settled throughout the years. Their security, it travels with them like a turtle's shell or an Arab's tent. The two-level barn is widely used in America, of course, and with many architectural deviations, but only in the Dutch country, including certain sections of the Midwest, mainly Indiana and Ohio, is found the forebay. This is our trademark.

Today, nearly all Pennsylvania barns are frame, or stone below and frame above, sometimes painted white, but traditionally red, and some unpainted as in the Great Valley east of Pittsburgh. (We Dutch do love our red—on barns, in salvia, quilts, maiden's blushes, and in every form of art.) What a joy for the early farmer to be able to combine his aesthetic sense with economy; when lumber became scarce and the wood needed a protective covering, he mixed all paint remnants, added linseed oil and a dry red pigment—and lo, a deep rich red barn coat!

However, barns weren't painted before 1840 (paint being too expensive)—and this brings up the subject of barn or hex signs that so intrigue the tourist. These are bright designs painted within circles, and usually on the forebay. The motifs seem endless: sunbursts; stars with various numbers of points; daisies; swastikas; teardrops; sun wheels—all beautifully colorful and geometric. The perennial question is whether they were meant to ward off evil spirits or were "just for fancy." If they were heathen Teutonic or Christian symbols, and believed to have protective powers, wouldn't they have been used before 1840—paint or no paint? And why would the wealth of geometric designs appear only after the turn of the century when hexerei, or witchcraft, had seen its heyday? Most people are willing to leave the solution of the enigma to scholars; if you want to simply enjoy the originality of this art and its appeal to the imagination, tour the Kutztown area where barn signs are most numerous.

Almost anywhere, though, you may come upon a barnscape—animals or other farm symbols painted on the forebay. Many barns have handsome brick-end designs used for ventilation (and made by blank spaces in the bricklaying): hearts, Maltese crosses, crescents, moons, tulips, and various geometrical patterns. More elaborate ventilators (but always practical) are a sheaf of wheat, hourglass or wineglass. One artist has even created a man astride a mule! Many brick-end barns are found in south central Pennsylvania.

Barns have grown in beauty throughout the years, though the cedar shingles and then tin, which replaced the early thatching of rye straw, are not so picturesque.

Since colonial days it has been a mystery that the Germans didn't follow the mother custom of building house and barn beneath one roof. Very few have been heard of, such as the first Moravian structure built in Bethlehem in 1741. It must have been comforting to hear the cattle thumping on the other side of the kitchen wall, or to be lulled to sleep by gentle lowing. Perhaps the reason for our separate barns are that here there was great space for expansion, and materials were cheaper. In any event, the Dutch have a proverb: "A plump wife and a big barn never did any man harm."

Farm homes as well as barns were built into a bank, with the main entrance (for funerals and so seldom used) on the bank side. Two adjacent front doors in a house, fairly common, often pique a stranger's curiosity. He is apt to be told that the farmer planned a separate side for his first married son. But research tells us that the reason is less romantic. In the nineteenth century when building materials became scarce, a big front hall often had to be dispensed with. Since the "company" room might only have access through another room, likely the kitchen, the guest must be spared this indignity with an outside entrance.

House orientation was usually to the south, like that of the forebay of barns. The crowning glory, the attic or garret (remember it?) was used for grain storage until the late 1800s, as there it was dry, and also pilferage was avoided. Grain was hoisted to an opening on one end of the attic wall and dumped into bins. (Rye bread was the usual fare, white being a luxury.) If the farm had no dryhouse or bake oven, other foods were often dried in the attic, or in shallow pans on a roof or off the ground in good weather. Today, many a country attic houses schnitz for a mouth-watering meal of schnitz un knepp. With its discarded old-fashioned clothing, gewgaws, and furniture, the attic equally fascinates children and greedy antique hunters. The Dutch know "there's a use for everything if you save it long enough," whether it's Grandmom's griddle or girdle, or Grandpop's storm boots.

The upper living level had one or more bedrooms, a parlor, and a kitchen used mainly in winter. It was the summer kitchen on the ground level that was lived in most—knew all the family's secrets, bickering, and merriment. Adjoining it was a root cellar, cold and dark beneath the earth, for storing food. (Springhouses served the same purpose, or separate caves stocked with potatoes, turnips, carrots, apples, and other foods for winter consumption.) John Yoder once told me that as a boy he was forbidden to pick an unblemished apple from the bin. Consequently, right up to the next year's harvest, he never ate one that hadn't gotten rot from its neighbor!

Later, there was often a separate summer house (indigenous to Pennsylvania) with a large first-floor room, a basement for food storage, and sometimes a second floor for other storage and for sleeping any farmhands. This was the place for hot weather duties like laundering and soapmaking, but mainly for cooking, done in the cavernous fireplace. (Nearby was a chicken or pig yard where garbage was eagerly awaited.) The main farmhouse was thus saved from heat, flies, and odors, and was used very little in the summer. The family, after its hard day of work, could trudge up to bedrooms cooled by thick stone walls and shutters closed against the day's boiling sun. Moreover, it was expected that no one disturb anything on the way.

With the coming of glass jars, canning and preserving were done in the summer house too, and every bean and cherry was stored on well-laden cellar shelves, every shred of cabbage contributing to a sauerkraut dinner. It was only when canned foods became available in stores, and modern equipment made the farm kitchens desirable, that the summer house became passé.

Strategically near the farmhouse was the *brivy,* or privy, which might be a one-holer, two-holer, or even more sociable. This was a great advance, since early necessaries only had a timber rail to support the *hindy,* and the first settlers often used the handiest weeds. Some privies were built singly and others adjoined the homestead, washhouse, workshed, or pigsty. But only at public places like churches or inns was there a "hers" (with crescent) and a "his" (with star).

Privies were often so poorly built that they were sweltering in the summer, though they might be a haven for hens and wasps and rats when it snowed. Sometimes a heart, triangle, or diamond carved in the door was the only ventilation. The more elegant had a cupola ventilator, curtains, and even stained-glass window—surely a status symbol. Pastoral and religious scenes, old mirrors and calendars adorned the walls, even if the privy was part toolhouse or dump.

As a rule privies were kept spotless with weekly washing, and liming in summer. "Moonlighters" made a business of privy cleaning after dark, and selling the refuse for fertilizer. Most privies are gone, of course, except at the rural church or schoolhouse, though one might still be used by a gardening housewife or busy farmer as much for convenience as not "to waste bathroom water," according to Lizzie Yoder.

Privies have always been ideal for storing old newspapers and dirty work clothes, for hide-and-seek, and furtive reading or smoking. More than one farmer, waking at night, has jumped from bed yelling, "Fire in the brivvy!" For it may be near the smokehouse, which it resembles. A funny story is that of a farm frau rushing up to a department store clerk and gasping, "Vere iss it?" . . . "Where's what?" the clerk inquired. . . . "Vy, I come in to go ott," huffed the woman. (Reminds me of our puppy!)

An important bank building was the springhouse, the earliest of log, then native stone, with few or no windows. Some of those remaining were the original two-story ancestral dwelling, kept as springhouse when the new home was built. Often they adjoin a pond harboring fish, ducks, and Canadian geese and shaded by weeping willows. As time went on, the functions of the springhouse differed, depending on whether or not there were other buildings for specific purposes. But with the inside temperature above freezing and seldom varying, it made the perfect dairy. The larger of the usual two rooms, for butter and cheese making, was crowded with table, bench for butter tubs, molds, bowls, and shelves for the overflow. Planks or stepping-stones on the cold earthen floor kept the hausfrau from worse "rheumatics." As the room might be used too for cooking apple butter, boiling soap, and for butchering and laundry, it usually had a fireplace; but some had this and the water trough outside.

In the adjoining room, the spring flowed over a gravel bed where crocks and cans rested safely in the water. Occasionally a fat pet trout came here to snoop around or visit. Though the old springhouse is now often used just for storage, washing, or playhouse, it is a favorite subject of artists aiming to capture the picturesque setting. Often it has the additional charm of old red tiles, once used on roofs of other outbuildings too, and made in local potteries.

The farm plan for outbuildings varied among ethnic groups, but usually the Germans placed the smokehouse to the rear of the dwelling, handy for the wife and daughters who cured and smoked the meat. (Germans are nothing if not efficient!) Some smokehouses were built in conjunction with other buildings, such as the bake oven, summer house, or springhouse. Brick or stone construction was considered safest, of course, though all had ample ventilation.

Farmers often helped each other with butchering, as well as haying, for the fall season was the busiest. (Once we were convulsed when a farm friend sent us "cocktail sausages," which proved to be as big as bologna.) In the early days, because of no refrigeration, much meat was fried and packed in lard or placed in brine at once after butchering. Superstitions warned that "meat should be taken out of the smokehouse in the dark of the moon to prevent its becoming wormy" and, for the same reason, "meats should not be taken out in a zodiacal sign in which is a living being."

If there happened to be an icehouse, remote in a cool wooded area, fresh meat like venison and wild fowl could be kept for months. The icehouse was filled with blocks of ice from the pond and was insulated with sawdust. Less accessible than a modern freezer, but certainly just as dependable—and cheaper.

How self-sufficient were our early farmers, with practically a little village of their own, often doing their own carpentering and blacksmith work, making baskets, weaving linen. Being a child in the "olden days" must have been wonderfully stimulating and exciting!

A "well-appointed" old farm had a tiny dryhouse with stove and many drawers and trays for drying fruits and vegetables for winter. Drawers could be opened from the outside too, happily convenient for hungry children. Many farmers raised enough for others' consumption also, and some still do, "standing market" in the nearest town. However many of their wares are being replaced by produce flown out of season from distant states. Our famous homegrown celery, for instance, is hard to find in market now—apt to be cached beneath the counter for favored steady customers. As little is grown, it is very expensive. But, oh, those short, crisp, curly stalks are sweet as sugarcane!

The separate toolhouse on a farm is a later luxury, sometimes serving more purpose than storing rakes and trowels. My husband's boyhood "club" was allowed to meet in his grandfather's toolhouse after dark, provided a coal oil lantern wasn't burned. One night rules were broken no doubt when some specially scary plan was afloat. A thundering voice ordered the boys to come out one at a time—slowly—about ten feet apart. Each received a memorable whacking.

Though pigs usually had the privacy of their sty in the early days, chickens fared less well. Those that couldn't find shelter in zero weather sought the hospitality of barn or pigsty or other refuge that the family tried to find for them at dusk. But there were always the introverts that roosted in the trees and got partly frozen combs or feet and had to slump along, one-legged and miserable, forever more. Rabbits were pests, not pets.

Though living in the city, we once had a traumatic experience when our yard man encouraged the children to raise bunnies. I think it was because Bill liked to carpenter, and indeed he did produce a most elegant two-storied hutch. The parents were bought at a pet store and Bill said the browner one was the male. After giving them time to breed, Bill put Pop "downstairs" to fend for himself, more or less. Mom was coddled with nesting and goodies in her boudoir up above. The children often examined her to watch her fattening. Then on a bitter cold spring morning, as my husband and I were dressing for breakfast, there came a tragic cry from our small son in the garden. "Daddy," he shrieked, "the papa had the babies, and they all got dead."

Moral: If you're city-bred, don't try to be a farmer.

And now, one last word on farms. The dwellings have always been modest, as a rule, particularly among the Plain people, though they do like their comfort and privacy. Unlike the gay Dutch farmer, many of them have a Grossdawdi house, adjoining the big house or cozily nearby. Here the old folks live independently (but lovingly watched over)—Grossdawdi happily puttering about with easy farm chores and Grossmom sewing for the family or helping with the children. How the city searcher must yearn for such a combination of farmhouse and guesthouse! Well, it's not for sale, or if it is it's kept within the "friendschaft."

An old or historic house rarely goes to an auslander—let him renovate a one-room schoolhouse if he wants to live here. Doesn't he know we value our treasures more than he does, and we'll hear by the grapevine when one is going up for sale?

For instance, the Historic Preservation Trust of Berks County bought the Mouns Jones House at Douglassville with its acre and a half of land when it was on its deathbed, having been gutted by fire. Built in 1716 by a Swedish settler, it is said to be the oldest surviving house in Berks County. Handed down from son to son, it was once a tavern called Lamb's Inn. Architects called the house "a little gem," though walls had buckled, windows and door-frames had gone, and beams and rafters hung loose as cobwebs. Only a large Swedish corner walk-in fireplace was nearly intact. The tollhouse on the other side of the river was entirely collapsed, and the caretaker's cottage was in great decay.

Were the society members discouraged? Not with a thrilling challenge like this. A flea market was organized for fund raising and all hands went to work, ignoring callouses—even the women hauling logs bought from another old building being razed. Today the Mouns Jones House is one of our greatest historic treasures and a monument to the intrepid spirit of a few dedicated people who cherish our tradition. But there is more to their story. They have also renovated the old White Horse Inn, within a few minutes stroll from the Mouns Jones House. The village, then called Morlattan, was on the main Philadelphia road. Naturally President Washington slept here en route to Reading, named as a possible temporary capital when Phila-delphia was having a fever epidemic.

The inn drew other celebrities too, perhaps because it sold not only "small drinks" like mead and ale, but kill-devil drinks such as Barbados rum, brandy, and a powerful punch known as a "Yard of Flannel." The Reverend Henry Melchior Muhlenberg wrote that he bought his driver a glass (a quart) of rum for eight dollars. The Duc de La Rochefoucauld-Liancourt complained that the innkeeper, then a Frenchman, "speaks poor French and worse English." The White Horse Inn was a mustering place for the army during the Revolutionary War, and later the militia trained there. It was also the home of the Society for Prevention of Thieves in Amity Township— members keeping fast horses in readiness for pursuit. Eating lunch there today when the Trust is raising funds for further projects, you can close your eyes and feel the mighty vibrations of the colonial great.

In our historical area there are many old mansions built by monied professional business or political people, but few are available today, especially those with acreage that have often been sold to developers. Of all the Dutch country boasting Georgian architecture, the Oley Valley is outstanding, for its dwellings (as well as its churches, mills, and even bridges) have notably withstood the ravages of time. The Hunter mansion is a fine example of the house built in T-form, and is famed for its handsome woodwork and outside carving. Other mansions are coveted for classical doorways, paneling, chair rails, built-in cupboards, and finely carved mantels. As a rule, a majestic stairway leads from a large central hall to the topmost story. The Fisher house, with its sixteen fireplaces and exquisite woodwork hand-carved by the master craftsman Gottlieb Drexel, draws tourists from around the nation. Washing those twenty-four paned windows must have been the albatross of many a servant down the years! The house was built in 1801 by the great-great-great-grandfather of the present owner. What tales it could tell of rich, swishing skirts of heavy silk and decades of merry children sliding down banisters! Stories of gaiety, but also of struggle, mourning, and even tragedy.

Depending on the racial background of the settlers, mansions vary from county to county, and within the county, but every type of rural house is at a premium these days. Having great appeal is the sturdy stone house showing German medieval influence. It has a steep roof pitch, central chimney, and a watershed or overhang above the doorways and sometimes all along one or two stories. Half-moon shingles on the roof are typical. Shutters may have long strap hinges and the iron is beautifully wrought. A rare bonus is the Christian door (a cross forming part of the frame) or a double Dutch or "Indian" door, protection from redskins. Bricks or stone above the windows are curved like musing eyebrows, and a great stone arch and opening lead from a side wall to the springhouse inside. (If there are swallows' holes in the wall that's all to the good, as this means good luck in Germany.)

Though some old houses have been weatherboarded or plastered, the realtor can't be deceptive about their age because of the built-in "date stones," or the later markers of marble. (Date "boards" are rare, as they were wont to weather, shrink, and fall from their niches.) Date stones give the name of the builder and often that of his frau, the date, and maybe a prayer or blessing, usually in German. Now and then there is even a macabre note: "Whether I go in or out, death stands and waits for me." The stone may be inserted at the second-story front between windows (like a caste jewel), above the door, or at the gable end, and there may be more than one. The earliest, of brownstone, vary in size and shape. Most are simple, but others can be ornate with a six-pointed star, wheel, or sculptured head. The shaped ones— such as a heart—are hard to find now as are those with blessings. Rarest are the eagle date boards, only found in Pennsylvania's Dutch sections, motifs being derived from the coinage of 1795–1804. Others not imitating coins date back to the first half of the nineteenth century. Some have inscriptions, but all have been repainted. They are usually found on stone houses. The corner-stone (still in style) was at the juncture of walls a few feet above the ground. Within a hollow were all pertinent information and objects commemorating the occasion. Date stones are also found on old barns, mills, and churches, and make a fascinating study, as do weather vanes.

Picasso felt that his valuable collection of weather vanes represented the finest examples of folk art in American history. Though their practical use is limited, they seem to have been important to early farmers. There's an old Dutch phrase, "How does the fish go today?" which means "What kind of day is it?"

Most common were roosters and fish—both Christian symbols—and though other rural motifs have often been used, the rooster is still "cock of the walk."

A newcomer to the weather-vane trade is Ivan Barnett of Lancaster, an art school graduate, professional illustrator, and wholesale candlemaker. "Making ten thousand landscape candles a year got boring," he claims. He now not only makes traditional weather vanes but is highly imaginative, using motifs of his own, though mostly animals. For his wooden weather vanes he whittles white or yellow pine from century-old barn siding. He uses scrap metal too, well rusted and pitted, and mounted with rustic-looking hardware on an iron pole.

Though Mr. Barnett's work is more imaginative, naturally it's the antique weather vane that is most highly prized—and priced. Thieves have found them lucrative.

Weather vanes are seldom seen in either our modest or luxurious suburbs, where the architecture varies from "What is it?" to ranch house and French provincial. And the Dutch do have some beautiful suburbs. But it's the older parts of towns that appeal to the average tourist who claims they look foreign. Where else do you find the row houses that we take for granted since the turn of our century when industry increased? Of brick, frame, or stone (the earliest), they usually have three stories with gable or mansard roof. Snuggled together like frankfurters in a pack, their common sidewalls defy the winter cold. I know of a second-story boarder, an old bachelor, who has no access to a yard for his little dog, and being lame is loath to climb the stairs. When Fido gives warning, he hops into a basket tied to a rope, and is lowered to the pavement. After doing what dogs usually do, he jumps into his funicular again, is hoisted up by his master, and is rewarded with a biscuit.

The small row house, with as little as ten-foot frontage, is flush with the sidewalk. The few steps from door to pavement are a boon when you lick a summer ice-cream cone or gossip in any weather. (According to an almanac joke, "It's no wonder that when a Dutch woman tells a doctor she's all tired out he asks first to see her tongue.") The parlow window flaunts all anniversary bouquets, as well as Valentine hearts or Halloween pumpkins, and enables you at your peephole to ignore hawkers so close that you can hear them breathe. A next-door sneeze, death moan, or TV program is no secret. Neighbors are very intimate. Yet you still have the prerogative of "home, sweet, home," which is not "where you hang your hat" but "where you can scratch yourself wherever you please."

The more pretentious row house has a porch, bay windows upstairs and down, and small front lawn. A narrow passageway between some double houses ends in the rear with gates leading to the garden of each. Here one may be surprised at the wealth of blooms and the flourishing vegetable patch, as well as at another porch or two off back rooms of first and second floors.

Porch-adding became popular from the middle to the end of the last century when the architect Andrew Jackson Downing alleged that no country house was fashionable without a veranda, arcade, or covered walk. Old houses took on the new look, which was often clumsy. But the Dutchman likes his rocker and he likes to sit and talk off a filling meal. On one country porch on a dark thundery night the conversation is said to have been:

Mom: "Ach, it aches me to think of Katie laying over there
      in the graveyard."
Pop: "Yah, but it ain't like she was dead."

It's natural that both owners of a double house should want to express their tastes, but it's discomfiting to see half a front porch cornice painted red, and the neighbor's half, yellow.

This type of house (still looking well corseted) may even stand alone but be more elaborate if a relic of the Victorian era. Having jigsaw scrolls, deeply recessed doorway with finials of vine or leaf patterns, and scalloped arch, it shows the influence of English or German migrations. (The occasional fleur-de-lis is a French Huguenot bequest.) The brick of the walls may be diamond-shaped. There is often fancy business along the cornices, gables, or eaves—motifs of tulip, rose, or acanthus carved in pine—and on any outbuildings too. Fine examples can still be found in Kutztown and Fleet-wood.

Old small towns seem to be one long main street of row houses, though some have a street or two parallel on either side before the open country begins. This is deceiving as to population. But everyone wants a box seat for watching traffic—or for sales advantage. A sign in front of a house in Churchtown advertises: "Revival Hemorrhoid Salve."

Lancaster has handsome old row houses, as well as York, West Chester, and the little Lititz. Charm is added too by crooked brick walks (better watch your step!) and tethering posts for horses.

Though Bethlehem, "the Christmas City," is known today mainly for its steelworks, many of the ancient buildings remain as proof of the Moravian's belief in communal living. Their towns were planned around an open public square surrounded by the church and dwellings of prime importance: in Bethlehem you'll see the old Chapel, the Sisters' House, the Widow's House, and the Schnitz House. The Young Ladies' Academy and church are two of the finest old buildings in the country, reflecting German medieval architec-ture. At the end of the eighteenth century the Moravians, like many others, succumbed to the English building tradition. Since early travelers were much impressed by the town's business complex, it may have influenced factory building in the Industrial Revolution.

The value an ancestor (whether rural or urban) gave to his house and belongings is shown in many early wills, about a third of which were signed with an *X*. First, the Dutchman provided for all debts and funeral expenses. Usually farms were willed to the oldest son who must take care of mother, "cleaning the stovepipe during her lifetime." In earlier days she might inherit the dough tray, weaver's loom, or "two washtubs, one churn, as many earthen pots as she wants, one psalm book, two hand baskets, one looking glass, three brass ladles, and one cake shovel." Sometimes she was privileged to go into the orchard for fruits for drying, or to cut firewood from woodland or to use the pump and milk house. She might even be allowed "to kill a fowl when she pleases." The settler's widow was likely very happy with "as much of my flax as she thinks proper" and ten bushels of wheat and ten of buckwheat annually. It must have been a model wife who was willed annually "one bushel of salt, half a pound of pepper and allspice each, and leather for two pair of shoes." Later one widow was given the right "to occupy new part of house in which we now live and have free passage to go thru other part to get upstairs."

All in all, it seems as if the bereaved woman didn't have time to think of changing her status, the only bequeathal of vainglory being the mirror. Though sometimes her son was advised to provide her with a small sum annually, such as sixty dollars, she must have really felt like an heiress when in 1867 she got "the $300 now set aside by law for a widow."

A child's inheritance might be a "cow or price of a cow," a loom, hogs, bedstead, and if female, "all kinds of linens, silverware, wearing apparel, kettles, oilcloth, and seashell boxes." The latter bequeathal is more modern as is that of money provided for the children's education. I'm in total accord with a testator who firmly declared: "Any child attempting to set aside the will shall be disinherited and shall receive only one shilling as a reward for their folly." It was expected that the child should obey the laws of the household, which were the laws of the house of God.

The church was man's rod, staff, and comforter, as it is for the true Dutchman today. It's a bit of a jolt to find a man as devious as old Schmick about playing hookey from church. He had recently bought his first TV. One Sunday a Methodist brother stopped in to see why he hadn't been "regilar" at service lately. Was it the "stones" again?

"Ach no," said Schmick. "And I'm regilar all right. I get fine sermons by such a bishop. And my seat ain't hard and I hear him good. And when he says, 'Now we'll take the collection,' Schmick ain't there."

As early as 1718 the English Friends settled in the valley of Oley and Monocacy, preceded only a few years by Swedes and Germans. The first worship services were held at the home of George Boone, Senior, and then in log cabins before the present stone building, first known as Oley Meeting and now Exeter Meeting, was erected. By then, some of the Boones and Lincolns had left the area, but the remains of their forebears are in the old burying ground. There is a beautiful peace within the little meetinghouse, as if the pioneers still wait in silence for the word of God. "Deeper than words is the presence of the Spirit."

City Quakers were reputedly less pious. Early Philadelphia Friends lived near shops and markets and must have had their temptations (they liked a good table as well as anyone else). A more "worldly" Quaker group found on the door of their meetinghouse one Sunday:

Market without and Meeting within,
And when Meeting is out, markets begin.

Many pre-Revolutionary meetinghouses are used today and look like dwellings. Architects and artists consider them beautiful because they are so well proportioned and every part is functional. They all had a definite plan, being rectangular, twice as long as broad, with two doors on the long side, one for men and one for women. Within, the unpainted benches faced away from the doors and toward the elders' benches. During the business sessions the women's part could be separated from the men's by means of shutters. No ornamentation either inside or out to distract one from listening for the "small, silent voice."

Once, at least, it wasn't the voice of inspiration. When our son was a small tot the family attended a Quaker meeting one Sunday. In the midst of a deep, sweet calm he began to hiccup—likely from boredom—much to our chagrin and the delight of his siblings. As their giggles became even more embarrassing, we had to leave. (I hesitate to tell family stories, knowing that others "either have children of their own—or they don't.")

Meetinghouses, like everything else, have known evolution. Originally there were only hoods over the doors, then small pedimental porticos, and finally porches. Simplicity was always the keynote, however, and even their Victorian porches were homespun. Practicality has been the basis for change. A modern meetinghouse may have kitchens or classrooms.

The early churches of the Plain sects not worshiping in homes bear a marked resemblance to the Quaker meetinghouse, simple within and without. On the grounds of an Old Order Mennonite Church there is a buzz of activity before Sunday service. "I see your silo's full, Samuel." . . . "Soon comes butchering." Farm talk mingles with neighing and whinnying, for the horses are being unhitched to do their own visiting in the sheds while their masters worship. It is a heartwarming sight: the simple garbed people, the numerous red-cheeked children, shining horses and buggies—all seemingly out of a peaceful past.

Before horse sheds and stables, horses were tied to fences and trees, and one may still see hitching posts or an "uppingblock" (stone steps for a carriage) like that at Upper Dublin Meeting. There is still evidence of stables from the end of the seventeenth century, when man and woman alike rode horseback through the wilds to worship together.

When stables couldn't accommodate the later buggies, sheds were built, but last of all by the "worldly" churches, and for several reasons. Sheds, like churches, were costly to build. Also, a pastor had to be supported, whereas the Quakers had none and the Amish and Mennonites chose one by lot who both farmed and preached for the love of God. Consequently, the church congregation, except for pastor and organist, had to pay stall rent.

There were occasional thefts during service. In spite of the wooden windows for ventilation, sheds were hot and horses became restless. No objection from the tramps, though, who camped there and only slipped off before they'd be ousted on Sunday. Where the tramps worshiped is not in the records, but reputedly they weren't as good tenants as the horses, unable to write obscenities on the walls.

It's not uncommon to see an ancient wee mother church (once a log cabin) with its nearby descendant, which may have had several renovations. There is something cozy and comforting in the sight—the old and feeble guarding the young and energetic. One such is the Augustus Lutheran Church at Trappe, founded in 1743. Though the quaint little old sanctuary is outshadowed by a stately red brick daughter church, it's the former that captivates you with its Bavarian shingled roof, original flag floor, charming pulpit, and gallery. The oddly painted marbleized columns were hewn from solid logs; the choir loft has simple carving painted blue. It all smells of ancient dust. Back of the pulpit in the graveyard are buried the famed Henry Melchior Muhlenberg and his son, Major General Peter Muhlenberg. This oldest unaltered Lutheran church in America is a National Historic Landmark.

Because of our proximity to Philadelphia, our early churches often showed the Wren influence, though few can boast an exquisite Wren-type spire like that of Reading's Trinity Lutheran (replica of the original wrecked in the 1933 hurricane). Its Sixth Street colonial doorway, often copied, is considered one of the country's finest. The church has an enviable history too. Conrad Weiser was a founder. Members have included signers of the Declaration of Independence. Sick and wounded were brought here after the Battle of Brandywine. Dr. Henry Augustus Muhlenberg resigned as pastor when he was elected to Congress in 1828.

There was much renovation and rebuilding of churches in the nineteenth century and many of the old stone buildings found their doom, giving way to an ugly Victorian. It's a thrill to find the combined beauty of architecture and religious feeling at some wayside stop, especially at dusk. Near James Creek we were privileged to peek through the old paned windows of the miniature Saint Mathews Lutheran Church. All is simple and pure within, though with "modern" coal oil lamps. One almost forgets that all the moments here weren't solemn, that they might have been lightened by the devilry of the kind of young man who arrived at service late and found the church filled. He sat on the lap of a man in the last pew, but at once began scratching himself all over. Soon he was attracting more attention than the pastor.

"What's the matter?" whispered his unwilling host.

"I got the gretz [seven-year itch]," groaned the youth.

In a matter of seconds he had the whole pew to himself.

Infinite time could be given to visiting our numerous old churches if you want to study details. One of special distinction attracting tourists is Lancaster's Old Trinity, famed for its tower and steeple and the four disciples who guard it—Matthew, Mark, Luke, and John. Its organ is one of the handsomest I have ever seen, fit for Saint Peter's in Rome. The German Lutheran Church of Potts Grove (now Pottstown) has a bell tower that was a rarity a century and a half ago. Near Hershey, beautiful colonial architecture modeled after the classic Greek is seen at Bindnagle's Church: the altar in the center is enclosed by a railing. At North Heidelberg Church near Bernville you will find the original old German locks with six-inch keys.

If history interests you more than architecture, visit the old Bethlehem cemetery where are the remains of early Christian Indians, for the Moravians were the first Protestants to convert the redskins. At the Old Warwick Church at Brickerville, baptisms are recorded since 1731. In the graveyard of the Episcopal Bangor Church of Churchtown lie soldiers of every era since the French and Indian War. At the charming Donegal Presbyterian Church, founded in 1721 in Lancaster County, there is "the witness Tree." Here the members, though formerly loyal to England, pledged support to American troops when hearing of Pennsylvania's invasion. Also, you will want to go to Zion's Reformed Church in Allentown, where the Liberty Bell was hidden during the British occupation of Philadelphia.

Man's house and God's house—the foundations of the Pennsylvania Dutchman's culture. Their architecture reflects our basic qualities, as does the architecture of any community the world over. It took strength to build cabins in the wilderness. It took ingenuity and sacrifice to house the cattle warmly. Thrift was evident in the use of local fieldstone and bricks from local clay, as well as respect for the durable rather than ephemeral. Beauty was valued too; the strong German hands that could plow the earth could also lovingly carve the most delicate woodwork or forge an immortal iron hinge. We have much to live up to and we don't always succeed. After all, we're human. But there are so many simple churches on hilltops, their spires reaching up into the blue. Don't they indicate that we try?

Round about the Countryside

WANDERING ABOUT THE COUNTRYSIDE, YOU WILL DELIGHT IN MANY A LANDMARK besides an old house or church, all linking the past with the present. There are covered bridges; moss-stoned mills (now spacious dwellings a bit too close to the road), remnants of mighty forges that were once the heart of a whole little village and produced the formidable firing shell known as the "Pennsylvania Dutch oven"; overgrown canal beds where once boatmen lustily sang:

> *Way down deep in the diving bell*
> *At the bottom of the deep blue sea,*
> *Pretty little mermaids,*
> *Pretty little mermaids*
> *All come courting me.*

If you're very lucky you may find an old store in some drowsy little village. It will have only a hint of its former glory, of course, of the days when it had its cracker, molasses, and pickle barrels, potbellied stove, and spittoon. Then coffee was ground to your need in the huge red coffee grinder; butter was scooped from a tub; everything was sold loose and put in a "tut," even garden seeds from their glass jars on the shelf. The "baker's dozen" (thirteen) was the rule. While Mom was being waited on, the rustchy child would be given a piece of sausage, a penny candy, or perhaps an apple, unless "the old ones is all and the new ones ain't yet," as Lizzie Yoder puts it.

Farmers came twice a year for their staples, and sat to chat on planks laid across nail kegs. As time went on, there might be two dozen neighborhood loiterers in the store, maybe shooting dice by the light of a coal oil lamp. Eventually, the store might furnish the silver plates for their caskets or those of their families (labeled "Father," "Mother," et cetera). Anything could be bought there except the Kohinoor diamond. An intrigued commercial salesman recently asked a village store owner, "Why don't you advertise?" The answer was, "I tried it once and people came from all over the place and bought near all the stuff I had. I felt like the hole in a doughnut."

Sucking on a twist of licorice, you'll leave the store oddly happy to continue round about the countryside.

An old inn, perhaps once called the Stag and Hound, may now be Schmick's Hotel, its former horse shed and stable housing a Chevy and a truck.

In the early eighteenth century, the main road inns and taverns were only a mile or mile and a half apart. But distance was guesswork, as there were no milestones until 1761. When dusk had shrouded farmhouse and barn, the glow of a limekiln must have been solace to the traveler, for habitation would surely be close to an inn.

Some inns evolved from the custom of strangers' stopping at the homes of the wealthy for food and shelter. A fire would be laid in the hall and a table spread with refreshments by a generous host. William Hartley of Chester County, for one, at last petitioned for a license, as "his house is continually with travelers who call for and demand necessaries, and that he has been at great charges in supplying them with bedding and their horses with provender without payment." There is evidence that tavern or inn proprietors were often men of importance and social standing. Curiously, inns changed ownership often, so the strain of business must have been as great as that of free hospitality.

Until the coming of the railroad, inns were beehives of activity. Some taverns catered only to drovers (our modern equivalent is the truck drivers' diner). The roads were full of animals being driven to eastern market cities, an important eighteenth- and nineteenth-century occupation. As a rule, wagoners slept around the fireplace in kitchen or barroom, and in milder weather under their wagons in the yard. (The two second-floor bedrooms were for gentlemen.) Meals were eaten in the barroom—it had the biggest fireplace. Much in demand was the nearby blacksmith, wagonmaker, and general store perhaps—actually till the automobile dispensed with poor old Dobbin. By then, the wagoner was only a colorful history book figure, but peddlers, tradesmen, and politicians, as well as local farmers carried on the tradition of storytelling at the bar. Today you may pick up the paper and learn that an aspiring councilman is flinging a beer party for prospective voters at some rural Hoof and Nail.

Inns were usually no bigger than a good-sized house, though no doubt Mr. Hartley's had a ballroom used by the wagoners for caper-cutting. Today, many an inn has been converted into a private dwelling. Though the tavern porch and outbuildings are missing, an old watering trough may be kept, bright with geraniums. The original cellar kitchen is now the "family room."

The era of inns and taverns seems one of romance. Even the names were provocative: Wheel Pump Inn, Rising Sun Tavern, The Death of the Fox, The Crooked Billet, The Rose Tree Inn. But not all names had appeal. As people were horrified by "The Guillotined Queen of France" (the sign had a decapitated female with bleeding head beside the body), the owner had to finally change the name to "The Silent Woman" (still headless, but erect, with no gore or hint of execution). The Golden Plough Tavern in York dates from the early 1740s even before York was briefly the nation's capital, and has been preserved by the county's historical society.

Reports of early inn meals vary considerably (no threatening Duncan Hines in those days). A traveler on the Lancaster Turnpike wrote: "Lucky to procure a few eggs with bacon. Bread heavy and sour, raised with what they call rot, hops and water boiled together." A guest on the Old York Road was luckier: "Breakfast—veal cutlets, sweetmeats, eggs and ham liberally given. Dinner little more than a repetition of breakfast, with spirits instead of coffee. Rum, whiskey and brandy placed on the table." Mrs. Elizabeth Drinker, a Philadelphia Quaker who often traveled with her husband, a wealthy merchant, and was an ardent diarist, wrote: "Dined on hearty supper of beefsteak and chocolate," and again, "With our two servants cooking, we supped pretty well."

Travel had its amusements. The Black Horse Inn exhibited two live porpoises and a learned horse, "Spotie." At one time there were also two royal tigers from Asia and a living seadog. Mrs. Drinker sometimes furnished her own amusement. At one inn the landlady was reluctant to change very dirty sheets for clean ones. Though she finally pretended to comply, the shrewd Mrs. Drinker was aware that the sheets had only been sprinkled, pressed, and dried before the fire. The Drinkers used their cloaks instead. However, the next morning before leaving, Mrs. Drinker had the final word— gleefully folding the sheets "nutmeg fashion." (I wonder if this is what we called "pi-bed" as children when we folded the upper sheet in half so that the unwary climbing into bed suddenly found himself jackknifed.)

En route to the next night's lodging, the Drinkers' equipage must have rumbled over many a graceful fieldstone bridge. As these were expensive to build, the Swiss-type covered bridges became more common in the nine-teenth century. The ravages of time have decayed many; others have been destroyed by floods throughout the years, since they were usually built at a shallows or ferry site. The Colemanville bridge, spanning a hundred and seventy feet, recently was washed from its foundations by the angry swirling Agnes, but has been restored.

The average covered bridge, made of long seasoned wood cut from ancient trees, was fifteen feet wide and high enough for a hay wagon to clear nesting birds in the eaves. Footpaths were rare, not needed by adventuresome cows or pigs nor sweethearts snatching kisses. Even now, long-dead lovers' names carved in beams, old plank floors, and bouquets of sunlight from beneath the eaves give one nostalgia for the "olden days," and a bit of guilt for desecrating the bridge by rattling through in a car.

The duty of the caretaker was to keep the bridge clean of dung, and to sweep snow into it for the runners of milk sleighs. At dark he hung a lighted lantern at either end.

Once a farmer who had an accident on entering a bridge after dark sued the caretaker for negligence. There was a lantern only at the far side, he claimed in court. The caretaker swore on the Bible that he had placed a lantern on either end. As both his wife and a neighbor had seen him leave the house with two lanterns, he won the case. But returning home in a nervous sweat, he confessed to his wife and God, "Harrey-yammer, I was scared the judge would ask if the damned thing was lighted."

Most of our covered bridges were erected in the middle of the last century, usually near a forge, paper mill, or other flourishing business. Like Griesemer's Mill Bridge, they were often named for a man, or else a nearby settlement. Numerous as they were in Berks County, only a few remain, such as those at Spangsville, Pleasantville, Virginville, and Douglassville. We have a great fondness for our old bridges, often featured in all kind of paintings, art and story books. No tourist of the Dutch country is happy until he has seen one and has proof of it in his camera. He may even take home from a gift shop a hot pad with the blessing, "May all the bridges you cross be covered ones."

The zealous Mrs. Drinker must have made many a note of the marvel of our furnaces too. Iron manufacture has been one of Pennsylvania's chief industries since the first forge at Colebrookdale began operation in 1716. By the time of the Revolution, the Schuylkill Valley had at least several dozen forges. Ironmasters were of various racial strains, but all supported the Continental Army, which would have been unable to survive without them. The forests had ample wood for charcoal for smelting ore, and an enormous amount was needed. Ore being twenty feet or so below the surface, depth

mining was rarely necessary at first, though Oley Furnace had a shaft mine. A good-sized furnace like Charming Forge (originally Tulpehocken Eisenhammer but renamed by Stiegel) produced about three hundred tons of bar iron annually.

Important early products were farm implements, stove plates, pots, kettles, slit iron for nails, Franklin fireplaces, and firebacks. Baron Stiegel cast some handsome scenic stove plates at Elizabeth Furnace. In 1765 Mary Ann Furnace made the first cookstoves. One can scarcely imagine the joy of the prosperous hausfrau who no longer had to wrestle with the fireplace crane.

The forge was the nucleus of a self-sufficing village. Hopewell Furnace, on an original land grant from the Penns, is a good example, having a general store, wheelwright and blacksmith shops, even a "widow seamstress"—all encircled by tenant houses. In the near distance was the Furnace farm. Since much of the labor was transient (nearby farmers who helped in the winter, and apprenticed or indentured workers—black and white), there were few permanent families. Yet these formed a loyal core spanning three or four generations. They were treated with consideration. Tutors were employed for their children until there was a public school system in Union Township in 1836. Bachelors took meals on the ground floor of the ironmaster's mansion. Part of Greater Hopewell Village were the woodcutters and colliers who lived in forest cabins, miners even farther away, and occasional help from the tenant houses along the road to Warwick where there was an even more productive furnace with a longer history.

The busy ironmaster lived in luxury with his candelabraed mansion and boxwood gardens. Life must have been generally lonely, however, for his wife and daughters, involved though they were with household and village duties. Their coach, of course, took them on protracted visits to relatives or the hospitality of other ironmasters; there was an annual visit to Philadelphia where father had business to transact, and a new mirror or bonnet must be bought. Also, friends from the big city came to the Furnace when traveling. Mrs. Drinker, if one of them, surely wasn't provoked to make a nutmeg bed *here* when leaving!

Intriguing as a blazing forge must have seemed to the traveler, it was neither safe nor easy for the worker; there were many risks and dangers. The housewife was in constant pursuit of dirt from the stack's vagrant ash and the black sticky dust from the unloading of charcoal wagons. There was an inferno of noise: the roar of the blast, the waterwheel's grinding, the clash of ore on barrow and shovel. Above this cacophony were the hoarse, lusty shouts of the laborers. A lullaby sung to the baby was of small avail, no doubt.

Yet every Hopewell villager must have been proud that its stoves were sold as far away as New Hampshire and its sash weights in New Orleans. Hopewell iron had always been rated superior, and in its last years met the exact specifications for railroad car wheels. By 1883, however, after a century of vibrant life, there was the final blast-out. For many years the struggling Hopewell and other furnaces had found the hot-blast or anthracite-fueled furnaces too great a competition. Gradually, too, their thousands of acres of timber had been depleted, and the industry began to move westward.

Hopewell has been immortalized, though, bought by the federal government for a National Historic Site delighting year-round tourists. You will see the venerable furnace, reconstructed stores and houses, and be tantalized by the aroma from the baker's shop. Lovely costumed guides will explain "how it used to be," and the museum and historic movie of the Furnace will verify all you have seen and heard. The remainder of its five thousand acres, owned by the state and surrounding the village, is now French Creek Park, a mecca for campers.

Responsible for the original construction of Hopewell Furnace was the son of William Bird of the famous Birdsboro Works, one of the largest and best equipped of its day. Reputedly, its iron was used in our ships for the War of 1812. After being run by several generations of the Brooke family, it combined in 1894 with the Diamond Drill and Machine Company, making mine tools, crushers, drills, and mining machinery. This company became the present Birdsboro Corporation, providing over a thousand jobs for Birdsboro and the surrounding community.

Now, with a few exceptions like Birdsboro and Cornwall Furnace (still operating after two centuries), there is little evidence of the mammoth colonial power of the great god, iron. A lone chimney stack, a mine hole, an ironmaster's mellow mansion—these are the remnants of a bustling industry.

Canals were constructed near the early furnaces to carry their products to Philadelphia and other ports. The Schuylkill-Union Canal, eventually joining Middletown on the Susquehanna River and Reading on the Schuylkill, was begun in 1795 but took over thirty years to complete. Diggers with picks and shovels (although several gangs were at work) could extend the ditches only at the rate of six miles a year.

People avidly bought stock in the new venture, some making fortunes by reselling the first issue, though there would be no dividends for many years. In the late eighteenth-century deflation, anyone who had bought at the upswing had a sagging purse. As Lucy Locket of the nursery rhyme said of her pocket, "Nothing in it but the binding around it."

Robert Fulton's steamboat on the Hudson in 1809 created wild hopes in stockholders. Why not steamboats on the canal? The paddle wheel for locomotion of canalboats? The use of towboats instead of mules and horses? But none of these proved practical. When the canal finally began to function, there was the threat of competition by the "Iron Horse," which had begun snorting along on its wooden rails. Fortunately, transportation of lumber, iron ore, coal, clay, and other industrial needs was cheaper by barge than by railway.

So eventually there was a network of canals in Pennsylvania. All seasons presented hazards. Thick ice in winter may have made the skaters gleeful, but often forced boatmen to remain in the locks for weeks. Spring freshets could be vengeful, filling canals to overflowing. Often the silt and mud loosened from walls would gather at canal entrances and impede the boats. On the other hand, during droughts, if the water level sank too low, traffic was at a standstill also. As waterways and turnpikes followed different routes, wagons couldn't be relied on for help. God, I suppose, had to take the blame for late delivery of cargo.

Muskrats caused another problem, chewing holes in the walls and giving the countryside unwelcome irrigation. On regular duty was the towpath walker, likely whistling and bantering with the boatmen as he watched for leaks in the banks. These he stuffed with straw or hay from his bundle, and covered with clay. If damage was great, a sort of repair boat ambulance came to the rescue, carrying more effective equipment, and having right of way over all other traffic.

Boatmen had to be rugged to face the vicissitudes and challenges. There are many tales of sirens or harpies on board, "foul play," and drunken brawls. Yet on the whole, the crew were peaceable, respectable family men, loving to sing and match wits during long hours while the mules plodded along the towpath. They were more than welcome too at the tobacco-sweetmeat shop of a busy canal lock, for they carried news or messages.

As in every métier, there were amusing or ingenious characters. One such was known as "Catfish Mouth" (obviously no beauty). He always bragged about his boots, which he'd gotten free through clever machination. After ordering a pair of boots from two different shoemakers, he would go back to each, say that his rich mother would pay, but first wanted to see the workmanship, and was given one boot by each to show her. Result, a pair of boots—gratis.

All canal systems suffered from the financial panics of 1836 and 1837, and in another ten years the Pennsylvania Railroad owned the state's western canals. Though most companies were surviving only through state subsidies, in 1863 the Schuylkill-Union was paying a dazzling annual dividend of 18 percent, for it had the advantage of being close to the newly discovered anthracite fields, and of hauling coal to the industrial cities. It operated a regular schedule between Port Clinton and Reading until 1910. Even twenty years later, boatloads of culm were brought from the coal-mining areas to Reading. But soon afterward the canal's properties were sold to the Reading Railroad, which in turn transferred all rights to the state, and canal life died after long and useful service. During the depression, dismantled boats abandoned at Reading were given to needy residents to chop up for firewood.

Life on the canalboats had had its gala moments from the first though. Charles Dickens, in his *American Notes,* gave a delightful description of an 1842 holiday aboard one. The "barge with the little house on it" carried thirty passengers, with red curtains "separating men's and ladies' " quarters. As there were three tiers of bunks on either side, sleeping must have been fairly intimate. On deck were a tin basin for washing, and dipper on a chain to scoop up canal water. There was a combination barber and table waiter. And the meals were good, with a variety of food and plentiful whiskey, brandy, gin, and rum sold at a bar. As some of the canals even had taverns at canal level along the route, there was never any threat of dehydration it seems.

Canals hauling timber were vital to most sawmills, now very rare like their old up-and-down saws. Along the stream of the Daniel Boone homestead there is a picturesque mill with an open pavilion enclosed at one end. The boss, no doubt, kept accounts in a heated room in bitter weather while his men processed the timber into lumber, and loaded wagons. How quiet the spot is now, with no sign of man or beast, no buzz but that of bees! Yet sawmills were once numerous, Pennsylvania being heavily wooded.

Often the sawmill was combined with the gristmill, of which there are only a few in operation today. For the convenience of farmers, they were only several miles apart. In earlier days, grain was brought to the mill in four- to six-horse wagons, and in two-horse sleighs in winter. The old millstone, weighing a ton at birth, was gradually worn down, only getting rest when the streams went dry in a drought or when the millrace froze over. The miller must have enjoyed the respite too, unless Mom kept dunning him with "Mose, this crane needs fixing." For in busy times he was evidently very, very busy. The aged William Shwartz, who lives on the site of a family mill over two centuries old, and built where the Wyomissing Creek joins the Schuylkill, says that when the mill was in full operation his grandfather stayed there day and night, snatching sleep on a bench.

In colonial days, our flour was hauled to Philadelphia to be shipped north and south in large quantities. Much of it was superfine, the top grade in the system of rating. The old mill at Lobachsville, with its wooden pulleys handmade in 1745, is a fine example of the many Berks County water-powered mills that once produced flour and feed. The mill is large—four stories high—and so is its overshoot wheel, the height of four tall men and run on stone bearings. (Little Pine Creek must be more powerful than it looks.) Whole-wheat and rye meals are still ground here now and then by Steve Kindig, the owner. But as his work is mainly a hobby, usually the mill has a powdery quiet, and sighs for the hum of busier days. There may even be a cobwebby ghost or two lurking in the shadows.

The miller's house at Millbach, with its high-pitched gambrel roof, is primarily Teutonic in architecture, and famed for its beauty—especially the paneled doors and staircase. Two of its original rooms, a bedroom and the kitchen-living room, are installed in the Philadelphia Museum.

Before the era of the fulling mills, people gathered for a "fulling frolic" or "kicking match." Cloth was "fulled" by kicking it in soapy water. (A definition of "full" is "to shrink and thicken woolen cloth by moistening, heating, and pressing.") When mills appeared, any fun in work must have vanished, as it has in so many phases of life. For instance, how many of us know the delight of making instead of buying wine?

I'm convinced that boredom—from disinterest in work, early retirement, or lack of hobbies—can cause as many deaths as the most dreaded disease. Yet, I'll wager that compared with others in the nation, fewer Dutchmen die of tedium.

Strolling through graveyards appeals to many tourists who enjoy studying old tombstones, like those of Saint Gabriel's Church in Douglassville, or Tulpehocken's Christ Lutheran Church. The first interment of Exeter Meeting was in 1736, but eventually the burying ground, not restricted to Friends, had to have a second tier of graves.

Few browsers are young. Perhaps it disturbs them to see the *Hier Ruhet* ("Here Rests") on the ancient headstones, and learn how short-lived were many of our ancestors, stricken by the pox or other epidemics. A common tender German inscription for a maiden taken by the Lord is "Jesus Loves her." Some markers have sad little homespun poems. One in Lancaster County reads:

> *It is so soon that I*
> *Was done for,*
> *I wonder what I*
> *Was begun for.*

Now and then there are touches of humor.

A rib-tickling German epitaph for any age group is:

> *Here rests my wife,*
> *God be praised and thanked.*
> *She lived long and quarreled much.*
> *O go away, good people, or*
> *   else she will*
> *Arise and start to pick on you.*

What bitter fate for such a woman not to have the final word!

There was a man who did, however, so says the Legend of the Ticking Tombstone. Fithian Menuit, born in the eighteenth century, was an extremely fat and ugly baby, and ate everything he could lay his hands on.

Fithian was sociable too, and, when a toddler, wandered into the tent of Charles Mason and Jeremiah Dixon, surveying near Strickersville for the Mason-Dixon line. He soon grabbed a watch from one of the men, and swallowed it. The watch kept on ticking inside of Fithian who grew up to be a noted watch and clock repairer. Even when Fithian died at sixty, the tick in his belly continued, and tirelessly ticks today. If you don't believe it, visit his grave at the London Tract Church in Chester County. And listen carefully!

Early tombstones were usually of limestone, though there are many of thin drab slate or sandstone. Often the lettering is green with moss, or worn down with age, and can be read only at night with a flashlight—a trick of the expert.

Markers that have touched me more keenly than any others are in the burial ground of Saint Paul's Lutheran Church near Hamburg. Early colonial, it was known until recently as Smoke Church. Certain carvings on the ancient small slabs of ordinary fieldstone that vary in size and shape look like the efforts of a child, especially in the Hollenbach family plot. Letters are crooked; words slant both ways; the names of Catarina or Margrait run off one line into the next; German abbreviations are illiterate. The whole effect is amateur. But one feels the deep sense of loss in the unsteady hand of a simple loving father.

Anyone finding the atmosphere too morose can supply his own humor, like the tramp who stopped near a gravestone with the famous epitaph:

> *As you are now, so once was I.*
> *As I am now, so once you'll be.*
> *Follow me.*

Before settling his head on the knapsack, he added this retort with his penknife:

> *To follow you I'm not content*
> *Until I know which way you went.*

A student of our folk art will note the evolution of tombstone motifs. The earliest came from Europe—the rose, the angel flying aloft, lambs (for children), doves and grapes, ivy and lilies. In Lebanon County one sees designs often used on early fraktur, barns, or furniture. Common are the hourglass, cherubs with sun spirals, the six- or eight-pointed star, and other geometric patterns based on the circle. Only occasionally is there a skull and crossbones. Urns with languid drapery often adorn the top of a marker. The early tree of life gave way to the baroque, then to the maudlin willow of the Victorians. Saint Peter's Church in Elizabethtown (1799) has more elaborate headstones than most Dutch country graveyards.

Crypts may be found in many old cemeteries such as Salem United Church of Christ in the Oley Valley or Old Saint Thomas's Church on the Bethlehem Road from Philadelphia. The carving often refers to the Bible: Text 2, Timothy fourth chapter and seventh verse, was a favorite. ("I have fought a good fight, I have finished my race, I have kept my faith.") At the Donegal Presbyterian Church in Lancaster County numerous gravestones record seventeenth-century births. It isn't rare to see a very old church surrounded by an ancient cemetery, with a second one across the road for newcomers.

You don't have to read to enjoy a graveyard. When we used to take our cocker spaniel, Fig Newton, for a walk in the burial ground at dusk, he loved to madly chase rabbits or squirrels. As they were apt to vanish behind a tombstone, Fig often ended with a badly bruised nose and complete bewilderment. But he was always eager the following day to continue the chase.

There are several dozen private burial grounds in the Oley Valley, where once lived many prominent settlers: Boones, Bertolets, Leshers, LeVans, Keims, Leinbachs, and others. Though the township was formed early and soon there were church and public cemeteries, the Moravian, Count Zinzendorf, urged settlers to bury their dead on their property, both because of convenience and avoiding financial or other obligation. The custom may have had a stabilizing effect, for some farms are still owned by direct descendants. Though early deeds required that the owner must leave "a wagon's width" access to burial plots, most are extant since roads have been widened or extended. Others are entirely overgrown, with broken headstones or strayed slabs leaning drunkenly against a wall. It's interesting to note how surnames have changed from the original German throughout the years, and the variation in spelling or eventual anglicization, like "Jaeger" to "Hunter." I have heard that the custom came from prosperity.

One of our bicentennial projects in Berks County is preserving and cleaning up private burial grounds. Active is George M. Meiser, IX, an ardent genealogist. In the Adam's Cemetery (dating back to 1733) vandals have broken or defaced memorial stones or painted peace signs on them, even on those of Revolutionary soldiers. Mr. Meiser not only deplores this desecration but claims that valuable sources of family history are lost, since the Bureau of Vital Statistics is comparatively new. Except on gravestones, early births and deaths were only recorded in a church ledger (lost perhaps), or in the case of private burial, in the family Bible, gone without a trace. Close to the ancient DeTurck cemetery in Oley, damaged headstones were cemented into a wall to preserve them. It's heartening to know that from within the area of the Blue Marsh Dam, two private burial grounds are being moved to Tulpehocken Park.

In your rambling you may come upon a funeral, but it won't be like that of yore when the church sexton tolled the bell to notify the community of death and later announced the day of service by tolling number of days between death and burial. Though private funerals were usually simple, mementos of church funerals give evidence of elaborate routine. There is the black-bordered eighteenth-century invitation, beginning, "You and your family are respectfully invited to the funeral of . . ." These were delivered personally by neighboring men while their wives cleaned the house of mourning and performed other loving duties.

On the day of the funeral, only in time for the service, the black-garbed family came down to the parlor where the corpse lay. In one instance, friends must have had a jolt. The casket lid was lined with a mirror, so they could see the corpse full length without moving from their seats. The deceased, a cabinetmaker, had made his own coffin. Who knows now—a hundred years later—if his eccentricity was due to vanity or consideration of others? He was the brother of the man who built our son's house, and a photograph of the spectacle is still in the possession of the Ritter family. To judge by the youthful portraits of Jacob and his wife above the casket, he "had right" to be vain.

In those early days, the church bell tolled every fifteen seconds as the hearse approached with its two black horses bedecked with black fly nets and tassels. A child's hearse was white—or the coffin might lie in the parents' carriage. The undertaker wore a long black swallow-tailed coat and high hat of silk or beaver. (Usually he was the cabinetmaker too, and had adorned the coffin with a silver plate reading "Asleep" or "At Rest.") Besides the texts or hymns, including the Twenty-third Psalm and "O death, where is thy sting?," the pastor gave a long sermon and read the obituary: name of deceased and parents; maiden name; dates of birth and baptism with names of pastor and sponsors; dates and details of confirmation and marriage; children alive or dead; history of the last illness and date of death; number of survivors; and at long last, an invitation to the home or an inn for the funeral dinner. The finale must have been very welcome, as many friends and relatives came from afar. Oh, the wonderful reward of leich-boi (raisin pie) after leaving the half-closed grave! And maybe a nip of schnapps first in wintry weather.

The eighteenth-century customs seem morbid, but it was an era of frequent mourning, when one was doubtful of raising a child beyond its second summer. Typhoid, consumption, epidemics, diphtheria, and smallpox were the greatest reapers. Those having died of contagion were put under glass. In the era when a corpse was kept from five to seven days, there were "ice caskets" with compartments around and under the corpse, the ice draining into a bucket below.

Considering the frequent losses of dear ones, it's natural that so many mementos have survived: the hair brooch; a sheaf of wheat in a shadow box; a mourning ring; the waxed bouquet from the corpse's hands; the memorial card (still customary with Catholics) often found in old family albums; or perhaps just a powdery rose pressed in a Bible. Today, though a burial is often from a church, funeral home service is increasingly popular. Here are smiles to hide the tears within, gay flowers (unless the Heart Fund gets contributions), no widow's weeds, and the briefest ceremony. (Recently I heard a minister say, "Don't be five minutes late or you'll miss it.") Everything is made easy. I sometimes wonder if we have forgotten that "Blessed is he who mourns" since we aim for cheer and brightness.

Remnants of graveyards, furnaces, mills, and canals show slow transition from one phase of our tradition to another. Old towns are another link. Many old town names are colorful, as are the names of streets. Schuylkill, Shamokin, Shenandoah are borrowed from the Indians, of course. Allegheny means "fair water." Oley comes from the Indian *olink*—kettle. The practical Germans often named settlements for their founders, Myerstown, Palmyra (for John Palm), Bowmansville. It's easy to guess the politics of those who founded Lancaster or King of Prussia. The origin of Boiling Springs or Pine Grove is obvious, as is that of Paradise or New Enterprise. Saue-Schwamm (pig's wallow) was gracefully discarded later for New Holland. Shoe-makersville (Shoey) was certainly the place for buying boots. Homesick Germans paid tribute to their birthplaces too—Hamburg, Heidelberg, and Strasburg. Fogelsville has combined the Dutch *fogel* (bird) and the French *ville* (city). Some place-names like Emmaus are biblical. Lacking imagination, a founder might name the settlement for an existing landmark like the Blue Ball Hotel (whose sign is still a large blue ball). Despite much bawdy surmise, when Cross Keys was renamed Intercourse in 1813, it was because of the crossroads—the Old Philadelphia Pike and the Old King's Highway.

In the richness of a day of wandering, of course, you will pass some Crest View Village shrieking newness with a grand desolate gate at the development's entrance. Whirlwind motorcycles may shave your car. But also there will be small Amish boys swinging their lunch pails, and gay quilts on a wash line. Breathe deeply of the fresh-cut hay or the heady, spicy chowchow cooking in a nearby farm kitchen. Bite into an apple dropped from a roadside tree, and remember your childhood.

Yet, the thing that counts is not what you have felt at any one moment here but the centuries of hard living, loving, and suffering implicit in all around you. This long-cherished countryside is reminiscent of the whole gamut of human emotions, none of which has really changed, despite superficialities. If you are lucky enough to feel this, you will have a deep sense of intimacy with the Dutch and a deep content in the continuity of our tradition.

The Green Arm

THIS IS NOT AN ESSAY ON HOW TO WIN PRIZES AT YOUR GARDEN CLUB WITH ROSES
or with your pumpkin at the county fair. Not that many a Dutch gardener
doesn't do both, but he uses less science than instinct—an ingrained
knowledge derived from his forebears' experience as well as his own. Home
gardening is mostly intuitive as it must have been for the nursery rhyme
maiden:

> *Mary, Mary, quite contrary,*
> *How does your garden grow?*
> *With silver bells and cockle shells*
> *And pretty maids all in a row.*

The farm wife doesn't have to read *The Secret Life of Plants*. Naturally she
talks to them, though maybe with her fingers and not aloud. They know she
loves them—she prefers them to most of her friends and spends more time
with them. Like Mrs. Machemer at farmer's market, she has a "whole green
arm."

The traditional country garden, being multiple and scattered, can
hardly be defined: vegetables here, blooms there, herbs handy to the kitchen,
a grape arbor to the south of the house, and likely on the outskirts lush red
and black raspberry bushes, and blackberries for pies. Currants and
gooseberries are more apt to be in a garden patch. Though Amish gardens
usually are less casual, surprise clusters of flowers may delight you anywhere

you look. Our mingling of reds and yellows may offend the aesthete but expresses our exuberance.

Most plants thrive best in an east or southern exposure. In the early years when a house was built, top consideration was given too to the availability of water and good drainage. Trekking to a stream or pump with a bucket was arduous, and gardens were the woman's domain after her man had "dug garden" and tossed the manure across the fence. (An ingenious but rare method of irrigation was using crocks with wicks—strips of woolen rags.) Understandably, though, she only irrigated in extremely dry weather. No one had to tell her not to water in the heat of the day, or not to hoe when the soil or plants were wet. But each growing thing, like her big family of children, took special understanding and treatment.

A wooden fence with one gate wide enough for a wheelbarrow barred animals and usually chickens that love to scratch in the garden. (Worms on the other side of the fence was always more desirable.) One woman who had an ornery hen with a great talent for flying was forced to put socks on its feet and tie them tight around the legs. Since ducks can't scratch they were sometimes invited into the sanctum sanctorum to devour the potato bugs.

The worst offenders were blackbirds and crows. They still are and always will be. Over the years there have been numerous devices to scare them away; fluttering strips of calico tied to stakes; garden hose snaked around trees; dead animals tied to trunks; an old mirror blinding in the sun; electrically charged wires; glittering ribbons of foil; any air disturbance like balloons, or pebbles rattling in bags. Wouldn't you think that just one of these would intimidate the thieves? But no! The strawberry patch, a mecca for birds, is always a special concern. You can camouflage one with a bright red border of geraniums of course. But are the birds more frightened or hungry? They seem even more brazen since the roar of trucks and jets has rent the quiet of the countryside.

The scarecrow (our Bootzamon or Bootzafraw) is now seen seldom— hardship for the tramp who must replenish his wardrobe. (There is evidence that it was used by the Indians even in the time of Columbus.) But it has often helped to protect newly planted grains, cherry trees, or shelters for young poultry liable to attack by crows. An old friend of mine is the John Yoders' Bootzafraw—wearing Lizzie's ancient cast-off clothing. She sports a Queen Mary hat; a black-gone-green Sunday meeting dress; a voluminous apron with rotting scorch blot (Leah had done the ironing); and disintegrating "gum boots." To me, a Bootzafraw is as gemütlich in spite of its tatters and gangling arms as the scarecrow in the Wizard of Oz.

Not everyone seems to agree with me, however, such as the farmer who returned late from town one Saturday night. His wife wakened in the morning to find that he had never been "on the bed." She accosted him as he stumbled from the barn with a hangover.

"Drunk again, you swilly," she shrilled. "Couldn't even get to bed!"

"You wouldn't leave me near the house," he whimpered. "Stood there all night in the garden waving your arms—and ready to knock me out."

She may be the scarecrow who so terrified the crows that they not only fled but returned corn they had stolen years before.

In earlier days crows were encouraged to eat moonshine mash, as they could more easily be caught or shot when tipsy. The shotgun has likely been the best repellent of all, but it's still as easy getting rid of crows as riding a greased pig or keeping squirrels out of a feeding station for birds. Nature has a way of being arbitrary, and though snails may be repelled by a garlic mixture, or, more recently, Paris green, and moles by the castor-oil plant or spurge—crows still triumph.

But oh, the triumph too for the woman who has fed her growing family with vegetables freshly picked and bursting with vitamins: scallions, asparagus, radishes, "salad," carrots, peas and sugar peas, beets, beans, cucumbers. Have you ever had cabbage boiled five minutes after cutting? Eaten raw peas? Or plucked a ripe tomato from its vine and devoured it without taint of salt or salad dressing? These are truly celestial, and so is freshly picked corn, though many Europeans still think it only fit for pigs.

Of course, we each have a right to our own opinion, as I once learned when a friend gave us a mess of peas from her garden. My three small children and I were having lunch; Jordan, then four, didn't care for peas, and was messing them around his plate. "You eat those peas," I told him, "or you don't get dessert." Disgruntled, he was quiet while the rest of us were chatting. "There's a pea on your place mat," I reminded him once, and, a minute later, out of the corner of my eye, I saw him shove it from the table. "Jordie, did you push that pea to the floor?" I charged him. He nodded sheepishly. "Shame on you! Get right down and pick it up!" He was gone so long that I almost forgot about him, but finally commanded, "You pick up that pea *at once!*" A muffled little voice quavered, "Don't know which one it is."

No waste of the smallest pea on the farm, however. Leftover vegetables come back to the table "so" or else appear in the vegetable soup. Final rejection is for the chickens or swine. Perishable surplus is now canned or frozen, though the hardier things still hibernate in the ground cellar or cave. The farm wife has worked just as hard for the meals she cooks as her man who has filled the silo. A clergyman watching a parishioner weed one day, remarked, "Wonderful what God can do!" The sweating hausfrau replied, "Ach, Reverend, you should of seen it when God had it alone."

Herbs are usually confined to the kitchen garden, which often includes horseradish, rhubarb, parsley, and chives. Anyone who really likes to cook (and eat) scorns the herbless prepared foods of today. The culinary sophisticate, of course, couldn't live without his racks of herb jars. Once a visiting New Yorker who offered to prepare our salad asked me where I kept the *oreg*ano. As I looked puzzled, he quickly added with a grin, "Oreg*ano* to you." But a rose is just as sweet by any other name. Over the centuries, our farm women have found herbs indispensable. A garden without thyme for stuffing, catnip for tea for junior's colic, or saffron for dye was unthinkable.

No dyeing on the farm now; the farm wife has it easy! Any color of dress she wants can be "boughten." Some of the dyes made by her ancestors came from mineral and animal sources, but the majority derived from seeds, stems, barks, leaves, and berries. Few good colors come from the edible vegetables. Purple cabbage, for instance, gives an anemic lavender green to wool. The usual red was from the madder plant. The only dye the colonial housewife couldn't make was indigo, extracted from tropical leaves. How she must have hoarded her pennies to buy it! Only a few teas, barks, lichens, and black walnuts had the acid to make a color set. Otherwise, some chemical had to be added—natural tannin, salt, vinegar, or perhaps chamber lye (stale urine).

Dyestuff, like marigolds (better fresh than dried), was cut up and soaked in warm water overnight. The next day it was gently simmered, and applied to wool well wetted and rinsed. More simmering then till the wool was darker than desired, for thorough washing would pale it. The main problem was whether the wool would permanently accept the dye or not. There were many tricks to this trade, involving the type of dye pot used (as nonreactive as possible), how much dye to use, the right amount of heat to set color and not destroy it, or cause shrinkage, et cetera.

As suggested throughout this book, herb teas can cure practically anything, it seems. The brewed flowers of our daisylike chamomile will ease cramps, relieve toothache or neuralgia, prevent nightmares, and reduce fevers. People have bathed in it to heighten skin color. It's an ingredient in many commerical herbal baths and shampoos. Sassafras tea, made from roots, twigs, or blossoms, will soothe sore eyes and stomach ulcers, relieve catarrh and gout, tone up the liver, and thin the blood. Best of all it simultaneously whets the appetite and sweetens the breath. A glutton's delight! The anise-flavored lovage (Liebsteckel) is considered a potent aphrodisiac. Are you thwarted in love? Brew the root of Adam and Eve and slyly add it to your hero's cider. Presto, wedding bells. (When Adam and Eve is planted in the garden it soon wanders out. One legend says it is discontent like the first sinners with their Garden of Eden; another that it is doomed to eternal exile.) Pleasantest remedy of all, no doubt, is a swig of whiskey and Saint-John's-wort—and this is a cure-all, I'm told (at least for worries).

Though the commonest form of medication was tea, some herb ingredients were heated into lard for salve. Poutices were made by crushing the leaves or seeds, heated with water to form a paste to apply on a cloth to the wound or inflammation.

Both herb use and herb-drying took special care and knowledge. Usually, herbs were picked on specific days of the year or in auspicious zodiac signs, and the method of picking was also important. Plants were gathered in the early morning, before the sun had sapped their dew and oil. The flowers of one might have the curative property, or the seeds of another. If the foliage was desired, it was picked before the blooms appeared, as the oil was then more potent. If barks or roots were used, the plants were harvested when mature. They were hung up by their tails in bunches to dry in garden trees, on the porch, behind the cook stove, from kitchen rafters, or in the attic.

I have used the past tense because few people bother with this old art today, or with any of the old-time plant remedies. Too much trouble. Who would think now of making horehound tea to battle winter colds? Or brewing elder blossoms to force the measles out? Sage and tansy have long been forgotten in favor of soda mints for upset stomach.

And yet many of those magic herbs and plants can still be found growing wild at certain times of the year. And many another thrives conveniently in our gardens—but is treated with weed killer. We still have a few local herb specialists, however. One, here in Reading, cultivated seventy-three plants in his yard, studying their medicinal values. When starting to gather wild teas he was surprised to find over two hundred effectual flowers and ferns growing in our woods and fields. Another collector, Uni Day, after retiring, lived in the forest, which he called his "garden," though he had a well-kept domestic herb patch too. Having inherited his knowledge from his mother, he was so gifted in preparing medicines that he was suspected by some folk of being a hex. (Obviously they didn't know that witches' gardens are always circular and only contain plants that are harmful in one way or another.) Snakeroot was his main interest, and pig ears (greater plantain), which he used for treating poison ivy. Only once did he find Adam and Eve in the forest. A few days after being transplanted in his garden, it escaped under a stone fence and made for the woods again. Still working out its karma? Had Uni Day been the old-time herb doctor, patients would have beaten a track to his door. If he'd been a skeppist, he'd have rubbed mint or peach leaves inside of a hive to make a new swarm stay there, and put sumac leaves in the bee-smoker when honey was extracted to confuse the bees and prevent stinging.

There is now a widespread rebirth of interest in curative herbs, which may be bought in natural food stores or herb shops in our malls. I recently heard a lecture by an herb doctor, also something of a psychic. His remedies are custom made; instinct tells him, he claims, what seems right for an individual. His herb compounds are put in small glass airtight tubes and are either placed on the problem spot or worn somewhere on the person. Since all were concocted at a particular time for particular people, if perchance they are worn by someone else, they must be laid on a linen cloth and subjected to the sun.

Some of his compounds are "unique": for arthritis—celery seed, lady's slipper, sweet basil, and mistletoe; for sinus—dried alfalfa sprouts, celery seed, and goldenrod. Not only does he treat the traditional ailments—but he has cures for jangled nerves and compounds for "raising consciousness." He considers all plants are herbs, using even birch leaves, watermelon seed, frankincense—and, for bee stings, chewed tobacco plug! His herb pillows are also effectual. One for insomnia includes lavender, rosemary, and pine (not dried). The energies of the pine tend to assist the telepathy process—the tiny needles acting as antennae.

He doesn't wash his herbs; they have more vitality if only dew-washed. Nor does he use insecticides. The drying process is important in order to preserve the plant's vibrations and its energy—very great when the plant is sprouting.

In the old days cucumber salve, glycerin, and rose water were commonly used for the skin. Today many commerical products contain herbs to ensure immediate beauty. Widely advertised, they have fancy names and fancy prices.

It's surprising that we have few plant legends, one being that of pimpernel (*Biewernell*), a genus of primrose whose flowers become their own umbrellas at sign of rain. Its medicinal value was once revealed from heaven in a time of pestilence, the "Voice" exhorting:

> *Drink tea of pimpernel*
> *And you shall all get well.*

Before the frost sears the garden, the farm wife has moved indoors her beloved potted plants (some embedded in the soil): her fuchsias, begonias, geraniums, Christmas cactus, and "colies" (all varieties of the coleus) with their Joseph's coats of many colors. And how lucky they will be in the house if they have a south or southwest exposure, and moreover can flaunt their beauty in a window for the passerby. Many a hausfrau has special benches or wooden, wire, or metal stands for these favorites. If they crowd out the family with their racks, shelves, and hanging baskets, it is all part of the coziness of winter. (Potted plants are even seen now and then in stable windows.)

It's a sad time for the soil-worn fingers that have worked in the open for so many months, but there are numerous compensations. Gardening is an inimitable teacher of life. The universal energy in the soil gives strength to body, mind, and spirit. There is great satisfaction in creating beauty. The gardener has her disappointments—there may be too much rain or drought or burning sun—but she has learned patience, knowing that nature has its reasons. She has a growing understanding too of life and death in the flow and ebb of the seasons. But there is always the promise of rebirth, giving hope. And in working with nature, like her man, the farm woman's cares are gone for the moment, or seem less significant. Her thoughts are lifted to happier, more meaningful things, and she knows the true joy of just "being."

When nature rests there is another compensation too—browsing through the seed catalogs and planning next year's garden. Ach, it would be nice to have dahlias again, such wine red ones like Mary Jaeger's that got a blue ribbon at the fair. And a great big nasturtium bed. Poppies too yet . . . them foxgloves didn't do so good toward the front near the snowball bush—too shady. A good place for a bed of impatiens maybe, carroty-color like her Grandpop's, the one who taught her the nursery rhyme:

> *Mary Dandy, Sugar Candy,*
> *Cook me carrots yellow.*
> *Little girls are nice to kiss*
> *But big ones suit this fellow!*

And though she was quite small then, she always got a buss. So many fancy kinds of lilies she'd like to try—but aye, yi, yi, how dear the bulbs were! And

yet she'd made good egg money this year . . . Annie Reifsnyder was stingy but
had promised a root cutting from that gloxinia that had twenty blooms at
once like it was crazy to show off.

Catalogs do give you fancy ideas, but using the cold frame for next year's
plants is much cheaper. The *Groot-Kootch* (cabbage coach), found on early
Dutch farms, is vital for raising cabbage seed to transplant throughout the
spring and summer months, ensuring ample kraut for all seasons. It is also
used for other seedlings or to "harden off" plants started in a hotbed, or for
urging hardy perennials to bloom in their first instead of second season. A
handy infirmary too for tender seeds that might rot if sown outdoors in a very
rainy spring, or whose seedlings can be nipped by a tardy frost. What a
blessing is the cold frame for extending the life of tomatoes! If it shelters the
fruit that blushes before frost, you may even have your own tomatoes at
Thanksgiving when those in stores are just pink mush and the price is
unforgivable. The cold frame is seldom idle. It will store your late
vegetables—celery, endive, cauliflower, Brussels sprouts, and others. And in
the dead of winter, lo—you have a potato bin.

Frames vary in size but usually are not more than six feet long, four feet
wide, and eight inches deep. They often lean against or are attached to a
house like a barnacle—hopefully with a southern exposure. Though covered
with sash glass as a rule, they can protect their seedlings from the frost or cold
with old bags or carpet strips. If built off the ground, they are much easier on
you if you have it "so in the back."

The hotbed differs mainly from the cold frame in using artificial heat as
well as sun, and in being embedded in an excavation. Fermenting manure in
a pit beneath the soil was the earliest additional heat supplied, and is still
used occasionally. A well-drained site is important so that water oozing into
the pit will not hamper fermentation. Later methods have been heating
through flus from wood or coal fires, and, more recently, electricity. (With the
latter, a cold frame may be turned into a hotbed or vice versa by merely
turning a switch on or off.) Besides having a commercial sash for protection
you may use unbleached muslin strips sewn together and weighted down at
the ends. More practical than the cold frame, the hotbed can start early
peppers, tomatoes, eggplants, and other things during the wintry months.
Whatever the method used, the farm wife strives for luxuriant vegetables and
flowers in all four seasons. I wonder how her man could get along without
her, despite the joke about the farmer talking to a stranger in the hardware
store. Said the stranger: "Wonderful growing weather. I hope it drives the
vegetables and everything else out of the ground for you." The farmer
answered, "Ach no, that I don't hope. It makes chust a week na that I buried
my wife." Yet, who else but the hausfrau loves the gifts of the soil as much as
her man? Waiting for the first snowdrops and crocuses, the golden daffodils,
"chickens and hens" shedding drab winter coats, the wee pips of lilies of the
valley? (They have such a wild desire to live that I have seen them push
through the asphalt of our driveway.)

And how many gardens of the city man or gentleman farmer would survive, either, if it weren't for his wife? Her approach will be different from the farm frau's. She has time to coddle the demanding sweet peas she planted on Saint Patrick's Day, or brighten her house with forsythia she has forced. The white poinsettia given her at Christmas and the dried lily, hyacinth, and other Easter plants are placed among her perennials in the spring. She may have an old-time garden with footpaths forming a cross, paths around the edge, and a boxwood border. (The formal garden has been called "a lesson in economy, ingenuity, and beauty.") But I doubt if she'll raise medicinal plants among the flowers of the outer beds; and it's far less likely that she'll either grow vegetables in the center or store them there in the winter in a hole under straw and boards. Though, ideally, the center plot was once planted with yucca, saffron, crocus, and pansies, it is now the sacred site of her sundial or birdbath.

Also, if she moves, she won't cart along a big load of perennials like the country wife. Naturally, she'll grieve to leave her beloved creation, but will stoically start anew with someone else's and add her individual touches of primrose, bleeding heart, stock, or periwinkle. And though she'll miss her rock garden, more acreage and a lily pond are a challenge. What she'd really like is to work in the garden from sunup to sundown, but since her family and social and community duties are pressing, she likely employs a gardener—part-time at least.

These Dutch gardeners are the source of many a laugh. We once had an old man who distorted all flower names: zinnians, pertunians, crocusers. He had a large repertoire of malapropisms, but his arm was green and tireless. A friend, Edith Douds, told me that one torrid summer day her yardman came wet with sweat from another neighborhood job. "Wouldn't you like to wash up with some cold water before you start the mowing?" she asked. "Yah," he said gratefully. "My bra [brow] is dripping somesing awful."

Edith and I call ourselves the vestal virgins. Many years ago I admired her new plant with the dangling red violetlike blooms. "It's an episcia I sent away for," she said. "I'll give you a slip." When Edith's plant gave up the ghost, mine was thriving and I rushed off to the rescue, then vice versa. To be sure neither of us will fail the other and so "outen the light," we both raise slips for crises.

I have seen some delightfully original gardens: Mart Eshelman's is featured on every historical house or garden tour in the Oley Valley. In his Munstead Wood, which rises behind the small old house near the road, you feel miles from nowhere. There is a labyrinth of paths (many boxwood bordered) and wild flowers among the eight acres of aged trees. Nearly all the bushes were grown from slips from his grandmother's garden or deserted cemeteries and historic places. Loitering in the Norway spruce grove, you feel reverent in this outdoor cathedral. Forget-me-nots are everywhere as well as mushrooms. You almost find yourself looking for "the little folk." Suddenly you come upon a patio, or William Swallow's *Country Boys with Apples,* or a piece of George Papashvily's sculpture. A new surprise is the herb garden: you crush the lemon balm in your fingers and vow never to wash away its pungence. Sunflowers supply the cardinals with seed in the winter. The waxwings consume the bright red winter berries. Nor do other birds go hungry.

One of the steep stone stairways laid by Mart and his late brother John takes you deeper into the wood. Here, winter over, you will find *Polygola* (wee orchids) and breathtaking masses of primroses grown from seed. When Hurricane Agnes raged through Berks County, many springs overflowed, which Mart Eshelman didn't even know he had; but he managed to transplant the freezing primroses to higher ground. In your wandering you will also find clusters of forsythia, cowslips, hepaticas on a shaded slope, an arbor of wisteria, flowering crab apple, and many dogwoods. All my life I've groped for words to describe the spiritual uplift of their branches and flowers. Reluctantly, you leave this enchanted wood, but when you have insomnia the memory of its beauty and prevalent odor of boxwood will waft you to sleep. It's incredible that since the twenties this Garden of Eden was created by Mart and John out of wilderness.

Another wild-flower garden is that of Fred Shenk, who has converted an acre of trees and thicket (once a community dump) in suburban Wyomissing to a fairyland of spring blooms—narcissus, flags, daffodils, laurel, dogwood, and other flowering shrubs. From the forests he has garnered lush ferns, violets of different species, lady's slippers, Solomon's seal, Mayapples, anemone, hepatica, and rarities such as jack-in-the-pulpit. (The forest is welcome to keep its skunk cabbage, typical as it may be.) Fred has used his skill as an architect in designing his garden, casual though it seems. And this gem of concentration and beauty is within a giant's step of the street on one side, and his wife's greenhouse on the other!

Our average dedicated gardener is usually of Dutch descent, but Peggy Klein, a New Englander, still "talks Yankee" though she is married to a Dutchman for years. (Fred, incidentally, has planted thousands of tulip trees in his hundred acres of woodland.) As you approach the house, the banking of choice begonias near the door and the nearby luxuriant bed of white violets prepare you for the extensive flower and vegetable gardens in the rear.

Being "straw gardens," these are a novelty in the area. Covering newly planted beds with straw isn't cheap (and Peggy has already used eighty bales) but it does perform miracles. No weeds to pull, no mold, no bacteria, no bugs. Plants just happily shooting up from their warm blankets to meet the warmer sunshine. Many of the beds have low boxwood borders for shelter. How does Peggy get inside to pick beans or gather bouquets? She just says "open sesame" and finds her usual place of entry. One whole bed has trespassing foxgloves, which may have come from a nearby farm growing commercial digitalis.

Peggy first learned of straw gardening twenty years ago from a *New York Times* article by a Connecticut woman who has since written a book on the subject. The author is still going strong at ninety-two—maybe even hatching a trick that will repel crows and blackbirds! Until her straw venture, Peggy struggled with various kinds of fertilizers. She was once discussing with her shy Dutch gardener what she should use. At her every suggestion, he just shook his head. Finally she said, "Well what do you think?" He swallowed his Adam's apple, blushed, dropped his head, and stammered, "Cow."

The Kleins take great pride in the two potted lemon trees on their terrace, and no wonder. The lemons are as large as grapefruit, and make quantities of delicious marmalade. (If I were a child, I would say, "Cross my heart and hope to die.") One already-old tree was bought for twenty-five dollars at auction some years ago, and has now reached the venerable age of one hundred and twenty-five.

We Dutch love our trees, for they have always treated us kindly, giving us the wherewithal for houses, furniture, and food. Or, like the weeping willow, simply adding grace to a dreary spot. I once bought a small rubber plant (*goomy-baum*) at Woolworth's for a quarter. As the years passed it grew so enormous that it presented a worse problem than Pinocchio's nose. It dominated the patio in summer, and in winter threatened to raise the roof. The Metropolitan Edison Company finally rescued us, and my *goomy-baum* (well pruned) is now in their elegant foyer nurtured by its own incandescent light. I often quail at the thought of what Met Ed will eventually have to do with it. No other tree but "The Tree in the Middle of the Road" at Limekiln has been shown more respect. This white oak was planted by early Swedish settlers and was saved by running the road on either side of it. Now in the curve of a later road, it is a revered historical landmark. It looked sickly when I saw it last, but there's a time for everything to die. My ancient oak just crashed in a tornado: though its roots were rotten, and its time had come, I mourn it.

Yet, besides the "tree of life" there's one that may be immortal, and this is Fred Rothermel's "wrought-iron tree," which he had made by a country ironmonger. About thirteen feet high, it supports his handsome clematis. (Incidentally, Fred, being an artist, can create the most exquisite tiny arrangements, using one clematis bloom with a few forget-me-nots, or a bit of mignonette combined with buttercups or johnny-jump-ups.) Fred also has a fragrant fringe tree that is a shower of ethereal pendant lace in springtime. Being native to Virginia, it is rare in this region.

Not always being ethereal, how can we help but love our black walnut trees that provide the rich nuts for cake and candy? And the chestnuts that send a shower of nuts to the ground before frost opens the burrs? From time immemorial they have been roasted on top of the cook stove—sometimes jumping off as they escaped the heat in exploding fury. The turkeys too love to peck at them when rations are thin.

But the gnarled old apple tree is likely the best loved of all, for doesn't it provide our schnitz? There was once a farmer who made such a fetish of his famous wine-sap tree that his wife warned him he'd be punished for worshiping a false idol. One day he'd been pruning the tree and had a huge pile of cuttings. Hearing a heavy crash of thunder he realized that a storm was near and rushed to finish his work. When the sudden downpour came he burrowed into the huge mound of lopped-off branches. As the storm worsened he decided he'd better dive for the house. Just as he reached it lightning struck the cutting pile. He grinned, shook his fist at the sky, and exclaimed, "You thought I was in there yet, didn't you!"

What started this love of ours for all the growing things of both utility and beauty? Our Teutonic genes, of course, making it needful not only to supply our daily fare, but to brighten life with splashes of color. Immigrants gave practical but delightful names to strange plants and flowers. Potatoes are *grumbeere,* or groundberries; an early kind of apple is the *schofnaas,* or sheep's nose; a morning glory, being funnel shaped, is known as *drechter blume.*

While the new settlers had to be content with a few blooms, the earlier Dutch immigrants of more populated areas had thriving gardens. There are still Germantown gardens that date back to colonial days, with bulbs, roots, and tubers brought from Germany: the crocus, daffodil, poet's narcissus, flag, lemon lily, Madonna lily, chrysanthemum, and many more. Cuttings of flowering almond, eglantine, lilac, box, and mock orange among others were exchanged with Quaker friends. Their seed plants foretold the ideal garden of today: pinks, sweet william, sweet rocket, rose campion, Canterbury bells, honesty, London pride, bachelor's button, and so ad infinitum.

If you don't have the wherewithal for a tussie-mussie, you could borrow from your neighbor. The tussie-mussie was an aromatic nosegay of helio- trope, lemon verbena, dried rosebuds, and was pungent with cloves, fennel, dill, or oregano—and had a most useful purpose despite the flossy name. It was a "meeting bouquet," taken to Sunday service. During too long a sermon (over two hours) one good whiff would revive the drowsy worshiper, who may have been up half the night with the baby.

If the small city gardens seem lavish they were likely emulating those of famous Philadelphia botanists. John Bartram had the first botanical garden in America, and was called by Linnaeus "the greatest natural botanist in the world." Here appeared the first tulip tree, the silver bell, cucumber tree, a horse-chestnut tree, from seed brought from England, and the ginkgo from Japan. (Today, our Shade Tree Commissions find the last very satisfactory for city streets.) Bartram traveled thousands of miles searching for new specimens and was appointed botanist to His Majesty George the Third. He was a much beloved and charitable Quaker who built his own house of hewn stone and mortar. Often he was joined by Washington, Franklin, and Jefferson for good talk and grog under his curious jujube tree. Is it surprising that the only uniformity in Washington's ragged troops was the sprig of green in their hats?

Available to the Dutch farmer who took his produce to the city were the popular gardens of Gray's Ferry. Here were shaded walks for lovers, comfortable "boxes" for old married folk, and all the current refreshments. It was exotic with tropical plants and flowers—a labyrinth of grottoes, cascades, and chain bridges. On a floating island there was even a farmhouse with garden ablaze with light after dark. Why shouldn't the visiting Dutchman find such gardening infectious and pass his enthusiasm down through the years?

Though the modern farm wife may plunk her bouquet in a mason jar—she has absorbed its beauty. In the cities there are numerous flower-arranging classes, and every woman's club has its garden group. A well-known artist is Betty Wolfe of Birdsboro whose exquisite arrangements of dried flowers and plants she has raised herself bring big prices and extravagant praise. We enjoy a variety of books on gardening, and the daily newspaper columns offer valuable hints.

Yet most of us are just learning what the farm wife has known all along, for instance, that a garden with bugs is a garden without garlic. It not only keeps away your friends if you have eaten it but will disgust the aphids. (Onions or chives are repulsive too.) This checkpoint Charlie at your raspberry bushes or grapevines will nauseate Japanese beetles; nor do they like the smell of tansy. Rabbits can be repelled by marigolds planted near strawberries, potatoes, and various bulbs. Nasturtiums are not only glorious to look at but will protect nearby squash, melons, and cucumbers from insects. We forget that everything has its Achilles' heel, and that most of the smallest living things have noses and stomachs too.

Rue, peppermint, apple and lemon and other mints keep insect pests away from the cabbage family. There are many other old tricks we might have learned over the centuries from the farmer and his wife; potato bugs don't like horseradish; asparagus beetles say "yuck" to tomatoes. The list goes on and on.

In the last decade talk of ecology, the balance of nature, and organic gardening is sweeping the country, including the Dutch area. Home gardening has vastly increased the sale of retail seeds and fertilizers, and statistics show that it has been most prevalent among young adults, college educated, and higher income groups. Why not, if a one-acre garden can provide a family of four with a year's supply of vegetables? For the last few years the Berks County commissioners have made land available to our citizens on a first-come-first-served basis. Applicants are given a packet of brochures on gardening. Anyone can now pick fresh sugar peas to cook with his potatoes, to pickle, or serve with knepp. Take note, oh ye chain stores!

There seem to be many reasons beyond the high cost of living why vegetable growing is popular here: concern about the environment, desire to make spare time productive, enjoying the exercise, delight, and pride in eating what you raise, and that basic reason—the human need to till the soil.

Paradoxical is an ad for gardening gloves I saw in a catalog. Each finger had a painted red nail. A sickening warning. Such pseudo-sophistication as protecting long red nails will bring us our dreaded but just desert—the Revolution. We'd better beware if we can't work the soil with naked hands and from sheer joy of contact with the earth.

The world needs more gardeners, for the true gardener is a poet at heart. In his moments alone with nature, though his hands may be busy, he hears a mysterious message in the hum of the bees; the heady scent of stock reaches deep within him, begging for expression; a strange little yellow polka-dotted bug or languid butterfly creates awe at the variety of nature and its infinite surprises; he feels the healing of the hot July sun and is grateful for the soothing whiff of breeze that follows; and what a miracle is the lightning whir of hummingbirds' wings! To see miracles in small things is to grow in spirit.

There is no season that doesn't touch the senses and the soul with beauty. The rebirth of spring in the air is a thing you can actually taste. Sun-drenched oaks in autumn leave you wordless and ecstatic. While gardening (though your legs ache) you are at peace with yourself, and, consequently, with all your fellowmen. In your heart then, you write a poem about the Oneness of life that you feel—created by a "simple little garden."

Jack, the Dull Boy?

EVERYONE KNOWS THE SAYING ABOUT ALL WORK AND NO PLAY AND WHAT IT DOES to Jack. What kind of play have the Dutch enjoyed throughout the years? In the days of our early settlers when man worked from sun to sun and a woman's work was never done, who had time for recreation? The solution was to make play out of work.

Wood chopping wasn't work when your neighbors helped split and chip great mounds of wood, and you fed them a roast turkey supper and square danced with their wives. Husking frolics (or bees) on long golden autumn evenings brought both sexes together in someone's barn: while fingers flew there was joking, singing, and storytelling. A lucky girl found a rare red ear to hand her swain, who kissed her to the heckling of the rest. The louder the smack the greater the teasing. When the work was done there was dancing, or *Blumsock* ("Who's Got the Nine-tails?"), and then a reward, of course, for the "crying stomach toads."

At the apple butter boilings the young were paired off to schnitz. (Too many schnitzed apples were stored and dried for the winter.) Many a lass threw a paring over her shoulder to see what initial it formed—that of her future mate, of course. The host's daughter and her beau had the honor of stirring the boiling apples till the first jig ended, when they thumped along to the fiddle with the throng.

Over a hundred years ago the barn dance in vogue at the end of the harvesting was often combined with a wedding when each man swirled the bride around to the zither. For the honor, he dropped a coin in the box for her *Haus-stire* (household effects for the new home). No wedding was complete though, until the serenade later at the home of the newly married couple. An impromptu band "played" anything from cowbells, kettles, foghorns to saws. And the more cacophony—like that from the *sei-geike*—the better. This was a wooden packing case with resined edges over which was drawn a two-by-eight plank—groaning and wheezing. The more horrendous type had crossed wires inside and sounded like the Devil with a bellyache, almost maddening. When the newlyweds could take no more the pranksters were quelled with cider and cookies. English neighbors called the group a Callithumpian Band and the French, charivari. In Pennsylvania Dutch it was the "Bull Band" and now is known sometimes as a "belling."

But long before this the prospective bride had made her trousseau quilts at the quilting bees, where there was a merry exchange of receipts, juicy bits of gossip, or sentimental tales about old calico patches. Quilting is still a popular activity in the Dutch country, though now it is usually a church project.

Once the properly "belled" couple had gone to housekeeping, the groom had less time for the male forms of recreation such as pitching horseshoes or feats of strength. When rail pitching, a man balanced a fence rail on his shoulder, pushed it back till he could grasp the end, and propelled it as far as possible without moving his feet. The same technique applied to sledge hammer tossing. In stone pushing, the competitor toed a mark, balanced a huge stone on his chest, and pushed it from him as far as he could. There were also running and jumping races, and games of ball.

More vital was hunting in our rich Pennsylvania woodland, not solely for pleasure but to help balance the budget. Rabbits, pheasants, and squirrels made nourishing meals. Deer meat could be used for weeks. (Today nearly every town has its gun club, but it saddens me to see a fine buck strapped across the hood of a car.) In the nineteenth century, turkey-shooting matches at some tavern or gristmill were justified by being held in the farmers' off season—from September through March. Raffles were an attraction too. Contestants paid to shake a box containing seven pennies (once the large colonial type), and the man with the most "heads up" carried off the turkey or other useful prize. You still hear of local raffles occasionally.

Fishing too served a dual purpose. Our streams and lakes have always abounded with trout, pickerel, catfish, yellow perch and sunnies among other catch. Once the shad, a perennial Dutch favorite, came up our Schuylkill River.

Since all the settlers worked hard in the open, they had husky appetites for the bounty of woods, streams, and land. But today, though we still love to eat, we have long supplanted the old-time frolics with socials, except for the Plain people. Picnics were originally held by the early country churches after the labors of harvest and before the work of the fall season began. But by the end of the Civil War they were rampant: those of churches, granges, WCTU—every imaginable organization. A band might even be engaged from a nearby town. Did the old Fourth of July draw its picnic crowd because of the reading of the Declaration of Independence, four or five speeches, sham battles, fireworks, balloon ascensions? No, the lure was the tantalizing fragrance of the ox roast.

We Dutch will swarm together like flies wherever food is gathered. At church or firehall suppers you can gorge on fried oysters, chicken potpie, apple dumplings, or strawberries in season. Many of us still view life as incomplete without some group's annual picnic or clambake. At the older "clambake" everyone received a net bag of roasted clams, chicken, corn, white potato, sweet potato, carrots, and onions. The clams, of course, were the pièce de résistance. Now it may be the lobster in the hodgepodge.

Years ago I knew a politician who made a fetish of eating his way through local festivities. He was ecstatic after a banquet at Governor Pinchot's mansion, where "such a red vun" (the auburn-haired Mrs. Pinchot) presided. "Ach," he gloated, "you should have seen the platters of chicken—zis high, and no vings or necks. And the meranchie [meringue] pie—it vas so sick [thick] zat ven you bit in it, it vent up your nose."

Recreation became more sophisticated as towns grew larger and men turned to trade instead of farming. After the old velocipede, the bicycle became the rage in the 1800s and clubs were formed for long-distance riding. Belles played croquet or languished in boats and canoes. Later in the century, there were even a few steamboats on the Schuylkill River (still unsmudged by coal). Animal caravans visited the towns, and sideshows—with Siamese twins or the armless lady who did needlework with mouth and toes. Medicine shows sprang up with perhaps a black man luring buyers with funny yarns, a cakewalk, or sleight of hand. Further attractions were diseased brains or tapeworms in bottles. For the more intellectual there were lectures, maybe on phrenology or animal magnetism (hypnotism). Occasional debating societies appeared. Even the little red schoolhouse on its last day of school, besides featuring spelling bees or recitations, would have a debate such as: "Which is the greater evil, slavery or intemperance?" (As hard to determine, I imagine, as "which tastes better—peaches or pears?") The genteel female, inspired by *Godey's Lady's Book* and its new patterns and ideas, beautified herself and home with gewgaws while her man played chess. With prosperity, the trend of the whole New Republic turned to "polite social intercourse, cultural and intellectual pursuits" as well as "fads and the frivolous." And even the macabre. The hanging of the early nineteenth century drew tremendous crowds. All kinds of excitement was easy to come by.

And what can be more exciting than gambling, even to win a turkey? Gambling isn't a fetish of the average Dutchman, though he's always had zest for cards. The most popular of the old country games was hasenpfeffer, still played ardently by those who prefer plenty of action to the dull demands of bridge. Jake loves to outsmart Alvin and slaps a winning trump down with exasperating gusto. Whist was in high fashion a century ago, with dedicated evening clubs.

Today, bingo is nearly as prevalent as shoofly or pretzels, and just as addictive. I suspect that bingo fans are also generous patrons of the state lottery. All revenues go to the senior citizens' program, a worthy cause, and, hence, a good alibi. But in this day of inflation there's something to be said for winning a ham with a quarter, or fifty thousand dollars with fifty cents.

As for further excitement, there is a bit of theatre in everyone's blood, I think—whether he likes to be audience, or ham actor among his cronies. Theatre was always well attended in the larger Dutch towns from the early days of the famous Fanny Kemble and the Irish Tyrone Power. After the period of adapting foreign plays, American dramas (about 1850) often contrasted the fates of rich and poor. One sqeamish nineteenth-century writer bewailed that he could only afford the gallery, where the floor was slippery from spit and occasional use as a latrine.

Nearly a hundred years ago Gilbert and Sullivan's *Pinafore* was sung in our Dutch dialect in Reading under the sponsorship of the Philharmonic Association. Pennsylvania Dutch and English were often intermingled in the libretto. According to the following limerick, it wasn't everyone's cup of tea:

> *Said a young fellow named Mr. Cott,*
> *My wife pleases me on the spot,*
> *Though it fills me with woe,*
> *To the opera I go*
> *Whether I need the sleep or not.*

Until 1888, even the stars' dressing rooms were filthy, fetid, and unheated, only "swept out" when the season closed in spring. It was John D. Mishler, known for his original production ideas, who instigated reform at his Academy of Music in Reading, and soon actors were demanding that theatres around the country follow suit. I'll bet a shoofly that Mishler was raised by a "crazy clean" Dutch mother.

Theatre has continued popular throughout the Dutch country. Minstrel shows, stock companies, and vaudevilles have all had their vogue. The internationally famous Five Bards, high-wire and trapeze performers (named for Jim Bard, the eldest) lived in Reading, which also boasted of others. I lived next door to one of them when I was first married, but never asked for his autograph. (I once saw him in the yard in his BVDs.) The Dutch-born Clark Gable drove every smitten female to see *Gone With the Wind* at least three times. Our Marion Weaver's musical about the Amish (*Plain Betsy*) became the successful Broadway *Plain and Fancy* in 1955 and continues to be popular here. We have many summer stock companies, all-year little theatre groups, college and high school performances, drama schools, and visiting Broadway shows. Because of the motley old-world mixture among us Dutch, transient European dance groups in exquisite native folk costumes draw full houses.

Dancing has always been "in" since the earliest barn dance. But America's first native professional dancer was the Dutch John Durang, born in Lancaster in 1768. His memoirs give us a delightful history of his versatile career—he also became pantomimist, slack-wire artist, clown, equestrian hero, puppeteer, and actor (though his Dutch accent was a hindrance). As a boy he was inspired by shows at the county fair and, in later years, made use of them in his pantomime, *Harvest Festival.*

When he moved in his youth to Philadelphia the theatres were closed for the duration of the war, but he saw every amateur show he could. When John was only fifteen, Mr. Russell, a well-known dancer, lived with the Durangs and, in pay for board, taught John the hornpipe and Alamande. The pigeon wing proved beyond him, but one night he dreamed he was dancing it before a large audience, and on waking knew the step perfectly. Lewis Hallam, the younger, desperate for talent for his *Lectures* (really performances), engaged John who was a great success. He then met a three-foot-tall German dwarf who taught him to play half a dozen musical instruments. Developing a "Dwarf Dance," he wore a huge face strapped to his belt, dummy arms worked by strings below it, and an enormous turban that covered the top of his body. Once he became blinded by the turban and danced offstage into the orchestra, impaling himself on a spike. For three months he was disabled. But every artist has his pitfalls (no pun intended).

The puppet show he performed in his father's house when only eighteen proved so popular that he had to hire a hall for the crowds. During 1790 he danced before many Indians who came to the city to sign treaties and learned from them the eagle tail, war, scalp, and pipe dances, and for rum bought an Indian costume having knee bracelets of dried beans that clicked like castanets. Durang danced twice before George Washington.

While raising a family he spent several years with Rickett's Circus in New York and later organized a family company, drilling wife and children for minor roles. On tour in the Dutch country, making even more use of German, and renting any large room available—even a storeroom or brewhouse—they found great response. John claimed he was the only one who ever performed before Mennonites or Dunkards, perhaps because his private life was exemplary.

Back in Philadelphia, he operated a dancing school and also appeared now and then at the Chestnut Street Theatre. But prematurely aged at fifty, he played his last role in 1819. The Durang Company, without John, stayed on the road for another six years. Ferdinand Durang, a son, was the first person to sing "The Star Spangled Banner" in public, while another son, Charles, led the chorus. It's said that "perhaps Durang's greatest contribution was bringing the theatre to the Dutch and enriching the life of the interior, preparing for famous performers to come."

The "Strouse" dance, known here after 1800, must have been a merry affair. A woman's outfit, hung upon a pine tree, was won by some lucky girl, depending on where she danced when a lantern candle sputtered out. Our nineteenth-century towns held bachelor balls, birthday balls—George Washington's being the grandest—and cotillions. An article of a small town assembly states: "No gentleman to enter the ballroom without his breeches, or to be allowed to dance without his coat."

By the days of the one-step and fox-trot it was the vogue to dance at the Tower atop Mount Penn. At the bottom of the mountain a stylish bevy of young awaited the trolley of the Gravity Railroad with its long benches and open car (fare, five cents). Girls looked like fashion plates with their long flowered gowns, ripply blossomed hats, white pumps, and kid gloves (and white or dark blue stockings!). The youths were just as seductive in white flannels, blue serge coats, white shirts, and bow ties. As the trolley crawled up the mountain (propelled by an electric motor) the fresh green smell of the forest added to romance.

The Tower's dance floor was the largest in the city and the eight- to ten-man orchestra was led by the symphony conductor. At intermission, after "Alexander's Ragtime Band" or "The Trail of the Lonesome Pine," the more energetic climbed the eight flights to the top of the Tower to look over the twinkling city and riverboats. Or perhaps to snatch a kiss or two en route.

Today we have numerous organizational or charity dances, and, of course, the blue-jeaners have their rock 'n' roll. A farmer, recently watching teen-agers dancing, exclaimed, "If that don't bring rain nothing will!"

The square dance has ever been beloved by the young and energetic, urban and rural. Today it's gathering new momentum, and we have a square dance roundup at Gettysburg College in May. Some of our champions even go as far as Texas or California to compete internationally. The Schuch Plattlers (shoe thwackers) of the Reading Liederkranz have professional engagements around the state. Dressed in dirndls and lederhosen, they have a repertoire of Tyrolean dances, usually with some simple motif as "boy chases girl." They begin their strenuous training as children of six or seven.

As its name indicates, the Liederkranz was originally just a singing group. Singing schools were the mode in the early 1800s, attended one night a week by pupils and audience, often in a schoolhouse. A famous singing master was Stephen Saint John, a Yankee schoolteacher who settled in Marietta. There were complaints that he never taught his pupils self-reliance—to sing alone or lead a church choir—but there was always the chance that a young baritone might be smitten with a soprano's trilling, and ask to see her home.

The Plain people still have their Sunday night sings when hymns are interspersed with games or conundrums. It is remarkable that their use of leisure is nearly the same as that of their forebears. Church is not a duty but a pleasure, followed by Sunday afternoons spent together in visiting and simple diversions. Indian wrestling has always been a challenge among them, and horseshoe pitching. (Even now we have our county tournaments and state championship.) Corner ball (*Mosch Balle*) is popular for males of any age.

Players at the corners of a square try to hit those of the opposing team in the center with a hard ball of straw covered with horsehide. As it can smart like a bullet, contests are rough and fast. High-spirited lads race their horses and buggies too.

Sundays mean time for Grandpop or other rheumatic elders to play chess or checkers. The Mennonite Moms play parlor games like Parcheesi, Monopoly, or bingo with the smaller fry, or lead them in singing a round, maybe "John Brown's Body." Older children let off steam with muscles. On weekdays at recess both sexes play baseball or basketball and put the same vim into scooter or running races. However, as they are raised with strong community purpose, winning is less important than feeling alive in every cell. When breathless with tug-of-war or "upsetting the hammer," they turn to something less active. Girls are very fond of "botching," a game for two with swift clapping of hands together and then on knees. Games are often invented with a stick or bit of clothesline. They have to be more ingenious than the "worldly" with their expendable plastic toys.

Otherwise, the play of all Dutch children—Plain or gay—is similar and has varied little over the years. In the spring, leapfrog is instinctive, as are all kinds of ball games. An example is "Nipsy," played in our coal regions with bat and ball being nearly anything convertible and handy. Kiteflying has the life of Methuselah. Marble contests have become national. A few fads have been outmoded—stilt-walking, hoop-rolling, top-spinning.

The more sedentary urban children used to play old maid or collect cigar bands for ashtrays. Everyone had a postcard album. (I remember getting a Florida postcard once and thinking how impressed the mailman must be that I knew anyone so far away.) Cards of birchbark had their era. Unique was a man's shirt cuff (postmarked 1900 and starched stiff as cardboard) with a New Year's greeting. For girls, a favorite indoor pastime was playing paper dolls.

Younger children still play mumblety-peg, Boonasock (beanbag), jacks, jump rope, and pitch buttons. All children love to gather wild berries.

In summer, it's a dull rural Jack who hasn't made a tree house, Indian raided, fished and swum in the creek. Tumbling downhill in a barrel without ends makes a roller coaster ride seem sissy. In autumn there's the thrill of gathering black walnuts and cracking them with black-stained fingers between flatirons at night.

In winter, every long hill becomes a *rutschie,* or coasting ground, and if you pant at the bottom and hear the warning "Yike," you know the Injuns are coming and you'd better leap aside if you don't want to fly horizontal. The old sleds with no steering gear were mostly makeshift, a bundle of rye straw, or *rutsch* boards on which you went belly flop and jetted dangerously into space. Even today on Dutch city streets the police block off *rutschies,* and traffic must pay deference to our flying Dutchmen. Hay or sleigh rides and skating on ponds and canals were often family outings. Skating still is today. Alas for anyone of either sex who hasn't played shinny on the ice. What joys many modern children miss by being glued to a TV program!

Many of our diversions are shared with equal enthusiasm by both child and adult, a fair, for instance. (Spring and fall fairs were provided by Penn's Charter to benefit trade.) Once the Whitmonday Fair was the greatest attraction. But it soon drew only pleasure seekers and deteriorated with the emphasis on amusements: menageries with zebras, monkeys, lions—the incredible elephant; patent medicine booths; velocipede races; rope walkers; trained mice; balloon ascensions; the "flying horses" (merry-go-round). After the Civil War, even the tintype! A great heyday for vendors of peanuts, gingerbread, oyster soup, popcorn, ice cream, lemonade, whiskey, and beer. "Buy me a fairing," the girls coaxed any nearby youth, obliged to dig into his pocket and treat them to leb-cake or mead. A munching crowd awaited the puffing arrival of the great "iron horse" at the station. Farm girls hiked for miles into town carrying their shoes for the boisterous dancing at inns from morning till late at night.

A murder at the York Fair in 1815 was no surprise to the revivalists bemoaning the rampant corruption of public morals since the Revolutionary War. Whitmonday, they said, had become a profanation—the church day originally commemorating the descent of the Holy Ghost upon the Disciples, after a week devoted to prayer and worship. Reformers with their "New Measures" system banned fairs, and all sorts of worldly pleasures: drinking, dancing, circuses, theatre, gaming. The famous pastor Harbaugh preached that "the boy who loves to learn dominoes . . . will learn to love cards, and so of the rest." Even children's parties were condemned as "excellent schools of levity and fantastic flourishes . . . material for silly gossip with which they anticipated the folly of riper years." (Ironically, even the revivals where "God wasn't being neglected by his children" got out of hand, noisy, and overemotional.) By the 1850s the revivalist cause had considerably weakened, yet the holiday fair spirit died out after the Civil War. A newspaper of the period declares: "Business and money will at any time take the place of recreation and amusement." If fairs were temporarily quelled, human passions and effervescence found other outlets, of course, until fairs came into their own again.

The small country fairs still feature livestock and farm products—a giant pumpkin, sparkling jars of preserved goods, colorful needlework, and simple flower arrangements. But, as at the big county fairs, which also include these things, sneaking in is the old-time fortune-teller, the weight guesser, the sideshow, the ferris wheel. Modern county fairs make the old Whitmonday revels seem tame, but our numerous folk festivals have dignity and educational value.

"Pennsylvania Dutch Days" at Hershey is a good example. Best known, perhaps, is the annual Kutztown Folk Festival, launched twenty-five years ago with much fanfare on various TV networks, and the scintillating presence of Arlene Francis. For a week in July it draws vacationers from around the nation. All exhibitors pay 20 percent of net sales as a rental fee. There are displays of basket weaving, slaughtering and butchering, wood carving, sheep shearing, fence building, apple butter boiling, candlemaking, and other trades and crafts (historic and modern) too numerous to mention. New farm machines are in action while antique farm gear looks on enviously. Crowds flock to witness the country auction, hoedown contest, the daily mock performances of an Amish wedding and the hanging of Susanna Cox for infanticide. A revived William Penn presides at Pennsylvania's famous witchcraft trial of 1683. You can drool over the making of sauerkraut or potato candy. There are booths for all kinds of lore—snake, bee, herb, funeral, washday lore. A costumed matron operates a 1914 wash machine, the model my husband's grandparents proudly owned. (We still chuckle over Grand-pop's grexing one day while repairing it, "These damned laborsaving devices make a lot of work!") Nibbling at soft pretzels or waffles, you browse at stalls displaying old books, almanacs, letters from Heaven, or hexerei secrets. At the bandstand there is a continuous series of free programs with joking, singing, dancing, and musicals about the Amish—and here you can rest your feet!

In the huge exhibition building are hundreds of quilts of exquisite workmanship and design—eagles, stars, flowers, et cetera. The more quilts you already own, the more you want to buy. Last summer, when quilts had a ceiling price of $190, a California shop owner swooped off a dozen of our Blue Ribbon winners. Our penalty for fame.

Finally, the aroma from the many supper tents proves too tempting, and once again you rest your aching feet (though overtaxing your stomach now). The women of granges or various sects have worked for days to regale you with a true Dutch feast, and while they rush the food to the tables, their "misters" are slicing more and more hams and turkeys. When you totter to your car—mind and body nourished—you are happily filled with all things Dutch and love them all. Not everyone, however, is tempted to attend. When one Dutchman said to another, "Are you going to the fair this year?" the answer was, "Vy, I don't sink so. I guess I'm Dutch enough visout."

A specialized fair is that put on by the Amish and Mennonites in the Guernsey Pavilion on Route 30 East. Here too one sees quilting, carving, woodwork, and other crafts, and farm and kitchen exhibits. There's an hourly performance of a pageant of the Plain people by a Mennonite cast and singers. Dramas and musicals are also given. Here there are more little net caps than you've ever seen assembled before, and faces more serene or merry than those of most of the "gay"!

Are you over sixty-five? There's a senior citizen's folk festival at Kittaning. If a Duncan or Cameron tainted your German ancestry, the flouncing tartans will attract you to the Scottish Highland games. You don't have to know timothy from oats to enjoy the cornhusking or flax-scutching festivals. But it's safer watching the hot-dog contest than entering, especially if you're scrupulous as the Dutchman who bought a pizza pie and asked to have it cut into slices. "Four or eight?" asked the Italian. "Vy four, of course," returned the temperate Elam. "I can't eat eight." The opportunities to share our culture, from Groundhog Day celebrations to the calendar's end, are innumerable.

Besides our many folk and craft festivals, we have spring fairs honoring daffodils, cherry blossoms, azaleas, rhododendrons. If you're a rose lover, don't miss "Roses in Bloom" at Hershey. If autumn is your favorite season, revel in one of our foliage festivals. There are many bus tours at your disposal.

Each spring there is a rash of country auctions, more gemütlich as you wander about devouring French fries and dodging children playing tag. The homestead's old brass lamp has been polished like Aladdin's, and the mason jars might be Swedish crystal. The new gilt on the old gold picture frame is blinding. Surely dead Grandmom's spectacles will sell to someone! That Dutch chair so carefully repainted by the owner will be just as assiduously scraped down to its tulips by the buyer. The auctioneer, though always joking, doesn't miss a hiccup or eye blink within the radius of a mile, for he shares the profits. I once nodded and smiled at a distant friend and found myself owning six dozen coat hangers. The "nickel man" (once the penny man) buys all that isn't bid on and hauls it off to his barn loft, waiting for antiquers. Who knows when the old coffee mill that won't grind can be sold to make a lamp?

My husband's Uncle Will had three barns full of discards and made a cozy fortune in this business. I still have a reminder of him—a sturdy shelf clock of blistered cherry wood, its glass door gaily wreathed with apples that hide the busy pendulum. The hourly bong is like a drumbeat. A two-dollar bargain.

If you want to buy a bull or chickens among other things, you may go to the Green Dragon Farmer's Market and Auction at Ephrata, open every Friday. This is one of the best and largest of its kind. Livestock is sold in the big barn, and bidding is cryptic. In a second auction house for miscellany (open during intervening hours) the atmosphere is relaxed, and even jaunty.

Jokes go with the sale of a pair of pocketbooks for seventy-five cents, a roll of wallpaper for even less for the do-it-yourselfers, or some random doorknobs. Here too perhaps you'll buy a bushel of onions "along with" or instead.

You'll need your elbows in the huge building where there are stalls for clothing, secondhand books, cheap jewelry, needlecraft materials, records, guinea pigs, and hamsters. Beside the vacuum-cleaner stand is the country butcher. A young Mennonite son helps Pop sell shoes and potatoes. (There are few Mennonite or Amish stalls.) Though there is a special market building across the alley, here is the overflow with tempting lebkuchen and home-raised celery—and if you must eat on the spot, there is also a restaurant. Be sure to dunk, or you'll be conspicuous. Among a crowd of people there is always one sad note at least—perhaps a wheelchair cripple, begging. A small boy crying and hugging a puppy asks you where the man is who buys dogs. Forget him, if you can, while you buy a hex sign for your toolhouse. And, naturally, there are antiques. Are you looking for a china rolling pin, flower bedecked?

In the outside alley there are more stalls selling gadgets and funnel cakes and farm produce. Farmers may come from within a fifty-mile range. The one who sold me honey said he "makes sale" at all our countryside markets and auctions, one for every day in the week. One of my prize possessions is the "Crazy Fingers" I once bought at Leesport. With skillful manipulation, these wire prongs rescue a ring dropped down the garbage disposal, or a broken cork in a bottle of wine. No wonder you are pushed and pulled in all directions, for there is something here for everyone.

Flea markets, lowest in the social scale of auctions, do business all year round. If you *must* buy that old seal neckpiece—fumigate it before wearing!

More exciting than any market or auction house, even if you're past the enthrallment of childhood, is the circus. A century ago, the galloping Buffalo Bill shot at glass balls tossed upward by another—and smashed them!—and Annie Oakley was equally astounding. Gone is Barnum and Bailey with its new sensational bicycle act, "Looping the Loop." But long live Ringling Brothers! (The Plain people come to see the animals but the performance is taboo.) There are zoos too in the amusement parks of Hershey, Allentown, and other towns. At horse shows, ribbons (and tumbles) are acquired. You get a kink in your neck at the Reading Air Show and thrills at the annual Duryea hill climb on Mount Penn. Birdlovers hike on Hawk Mountain or the famed Appalachian Trail. The obese cool off in Crystal Cave.

Children are taken to Paradise (Pa.) and back on the old Strasburg Railroad founded during the first term of Andrew Jackson. Incorporated in 1832, it is the oldest public utility in the state. Steam locomotive 1223 found fame in the movie *Broadway Limited* and in *Hello, Dolly!* But the history of each car is unique, number 3556 being the oldest operating standard-gauge car in the world. The new huge Railroad Museum of Pennsylvania at Strasburg is operated by the state's Historical and Museum Commission.

Then there's the "Look, Mom!" Roadside America, the "nation's largest" miniature village covering a tremendous indoor area and complete to washing on the lines and Sears catalogs in the privies. It must be an outgrowth of our early passion for the Christmas yard.

Our Dutch country tours have much to offer the jaded: the blacksmith shop at Talmadge where an Amish farmer's horse is being shod; the Lititz pretzel factory, first in America, where you watch pretzels being hand-twisted; an Amish homestead; various museums; a carriage-making shop; the furniture factory with colonial reproductions and irresistible tiny tulip-painted rockers and stools. The one-room schoolhouse at Weavertown has automatic pupils waving two urgent fingers or reciting lessons, so convincing that you expect teacher to call on you next. I could beat a weekly path to Kauffman's Country Store (since 1779) at New Holland. The motley ware includes a rainbow of vegetable seeds, homemade pies and bread, iron frying pans, buggy lanterns, old and new Dutch china, local newssheets, and antiques (even milk bottles!). Though the large line of clothing is mainly for the Plain sects, it's surprising how many worldly males, large or small, succumb to a broadbrim.

As we map-gazed at New Holland one day trying to find the best road to Strasburg, a native appeared at the curb and laughed good-naturedly. "Only good for seeing how you got where you are," he said. Indeed, it seemed a miracle when we found our Red Caboose Lodge, and slept in one of its actual cabooses (TV hidden in a potbellied stove), and breakfasted in the Victorian dining car.

Summer here is a time too for the annual family reunions (*fersammlings*) of the genealogy-minded. (It's said they get together to see who's falling apart.) Usually they meet in July or August in a grove, if the original homestead or the home of the oldest living family member isn't available. There may be a tremendous number of descendants from one early settler, for sons were the farm's machinery. Programs are elaborate, with a big dinner or "basket meal," election of officers, and many eloquent speeches assuring you that if you're not a Schmick (or whatever) you're just nobody at all. On the lighter side, there are recitations, races, quoits, baseball games, and bands. Yet the reunion ends with a service of sacred music, prayers, Scripture readings, and remarks from the *parres* (parsons).

A true Dutchman will always remember what he owes to God, including the religious freedom found here by our ancestors. Colonial America had "enlightenment" in certain sections, but there were also Deists who wanted a "reasonable religion," and the most radical, rejecting Christ, enraged the faithful, hence the early nineteenth-century revivalism. During this Second Great Awakening, revivalists sprang up all around the country, hoping to unite the forces of the Protestant sects and convert all sinners.

One of the most famous leaders was Charles Grandison Finney, a lawyer from Adams, New York, who began after brief theological instruction to preach as traveling evangelist. Our Dutch area was one of his targets. Religion here, he claimed, had come to a tragic state, as most Dutchmen believed that baptism, catechism training, and Communion were adequate entrées to Heaven. The fiery Finney insisted on rebirth, and saved many a Dutchman from Hell around 1830.

Usually, revivals were held in the more settled regions of the East, but "in the sticks" and on the western frontier there were camp meetings sometimes lasting a week and yielding many converts. (Impromptu German spirituals were often created by a folk poet.) The more pious attended several, cooking at an outdoor fireplace and setting up tents where glowing torches in the trees and purged consciences lulled them to sleep.

In 1874 the Grange Encampment at Centre County began as a one day basket lunch picnic and had a religious motive. By 1915 it went on for ten days and included entertainment, exhibits, and political speeches. Farm families from all over Pennsylvania rented the five hundred tents for the duration of the affair.

Today, our best-known camp meetings are at Mount Gretna and Rosedale, but there are other religious gatherings. Our many spiritual retreats to some quiet, inspiring area are likely a late sequel to the Second Great Awakening. Yet the complexion of worship constantly changes according to the need of the times. Now we may even seek out a yoga ashram, but the spirit is the same wherever one reaches out for God during a peaceful and nourishing interlude in the turmoil of living.

Autumn and winter in their turn bring a bewildering assortment of activities. Farmers' grange meetings can be lively with both occupational and social aspects. Lodges get down to business again. Firehall club rooms are alive with festivity, including carnivals, hoedowns, or wedding receptions with both kinds of good spirits and lavish buffets. These are a triumph of gaiety—everyone dancing with everyone else, even children. Incidentally, Reading is said to have the nation's oldest volunteer fire company, existing since Saint Patrick's Day, 1773. As far as I know, it only has one black mark against it. Some years ago Whitner's department store burned down during the firemen's parade.

Well, some may still enjoy marching, but others find it too slow-paced, especially the skiers. Various ski clubs crown beauteous snow queens. Now that snow is being manufactured, addicts are increasing and you needn't go far from home to find a lift or break a leg, though many trek to our lovely Pocono Mountains (a mecca for hunters too). The season offers you a snow-shovel contest if you prefer to "clown it." Outdoor skating is limited by our generally temperate climate. It's true that "our winters aren't what they used to be" as our oldsters lament. But after the Ice Capades at Hershey, indoor rinks are full of aspiring Olympics contestants. In our topsy-turvy world where you can ice skate in summer and play indoor tennis in winter, even the more adventurous Golden Agers are kept limber longer. Yet, active participation in sports has never been the average Dutchman's cup of tea (or mug of beer). Many of our elders claim they get enough exercise hoeing, or stoking the furnace, and are now content to watch baseball or football on TV while their wives exercise their tongues with neighbors.

Some of our armchair athletes have had their fun at sports, however. My father-in-law, Solon Bausher, used to tell a priceless story about playing on the baseball team at an annual picnic of Dives, Pomeroy and Stewart. To begin with, they were disgracefully vanquished by a visiting team supposedly from a department store in Allentown. But it seems that a pro team of that area had been brought here as a joke. The game over, the Readingites changed in Mr. Pomeroy's bedroom for the ensuing feast. One maverick, always thirsty, spied a gallon of whiskey on the top shelf of the closet, and was dared to take a drink. Soon everyone but Solon, a teetotaler, was having a healthy swig or two. It was a merry evening.

The following day my father-in-law had a phone call from Mr. Pomeroy, while another of the team happened to be in the office. "Yes, they did," he heard Solon say. "I don't drink myself but I didn't want to put a damper on the others. It was wrong to take advantage of your hospitality and I'll see that they all apologize." At Mr. Pomeroy's reply Solon burst into hearty laughter, and his young assistant relaxed.

"The boss isn't angry then?" he asked Solon after he'd hung up.

"No, just inconvenienced. He has gout, you know, and every night he soaks his feet in that whiskey."

The young man turned green, rushed to the window, and vomited.

For the more prosperous like Mr. Pomeroy, owning cars, driving through our inimitable countryside was once a favorite outing. My husband's Uncle Nibs who loved to watch the world go by on Sunday, once told us triumphantly, "Forty-eight machines passed the farm today!" But most Dutchmen are homing pigeons. John Yoder's bachelor brother once decided he would venture alone to Virginia to visit cousins. Halfway there, he headed back for Bernville and his rocker. When asked why he'd returned so soon, he said succinctly, "Nothing but scenery." We have many old folks who like to sit and think, or sometimes "just sit" (and both have their virtues).

Reflecting on the round of our modern years, I wonder if the adage should be changed to "all play and no work makes Jack a dull boy." I doubt if a small farm boy has ever been heard to fret, "What shall I do?" like his urban brother who hasn't learned to make play out of labor. With active sports being encouraged by community playgrounds, pools, school facilities, and contests, the younger city generation shows growing enthusiasm and prowess, but may consider play their due and not a reward for work. We need both, of course, but in the right proportion.

Most of us are far afield from our ancestors who diligently earned their pleasure and savored it. But I'm glad that their old view of life is still the core of a true Pennsylvania Dutchman's thinking—exhorting Jack to keep a healthy balance.

Holidays

CHILDREN AND THE YOUNG AT HEART ANTICIPATE HOLIDAYS AND PREPARE FOR them with zest. For, like the Good Fairy, they usually grant three wishes (or one of the three, at least): escape from school or work; an Easter ham, turkey, or picnic, depending on the season; and a parade.

Parades are a holiday bonus; and being a gregarious folk, we all relish them, regardless of our age. They appeared early in our Dutch culture. In the nineteenth century, usually on New Year's morning, fantasticals or mummers paraded by wagon, foot, or sleigh in the most grotesque outfits available. It was heresy for a man's one leg to look like the other. Musical instruments were cowbells, pans, speaking trumpets, even conch shells. Mock soldiers hung their provisions—herrings or beef bones—about their necks, and rolled a "fieldpiece," perhaps an aqueduct pipe on wheels.

Fantasticals originated in the Swedish section of South Philadelphia, "The Neck." But the Germans, English, Irish, and Scottish also celebrated Christmas, then the New Year with mummery. Alfred L. Shoemaker says the Episcopalians brought it from England. It is also attributed to the Holland Dutch in New York. The Quakers, of course, vetoed buffoonery. Mummers' clubs were formed in various city sections, and visited houses indiscriminately. It was de rigueur to give the men a few pence (pooled for cakes and beer) and also ask them in for a treat. Some sang amusing songs or recited verses or jingles:

Christmas is coming, the geese are getting fat,
Please to put a penny in an old man's hat.
If you haven't got a penny, a ha'penny will do.
If you haven't got a ha'penny, God bless you.

Some performed a bit of melodrama or farce. It's said that Edwin Forrest's first performance was in a parlor. In the event that you recognized a mummer (though dressed as George Washington), it was a great breach of etiquette to mention it. When business began to thrive for mummers, a "cake wagon" gathered up donations, and a few days later there were cake-cutting parties, finally leading to New Year's fund-raising balls. These were the social highlights of the season, and provided costume money. Later, when "shooters" and "mummers" became obstreperous and a public nuisance, an antimasquerade act was passed, with a high fine and imprisonment for allowing masked balls in homes. At the end of the century when mummery persisted, the mayor advised that groups band together and march up Broad Street on New Year's Day. As an incentive, the city council gave a sum of $1,725 for prizes. Today the New Year's parade in Philadelphia rivals the New Orleans Mardi Gras in grandeur. Though mummery had spread into eastern and central Pennsylvania, its last vestige in our countryside is now on Halloween.

Closely related, though, is "Shooting in the New Year," popular up to the turn of the century, and certainly saner than "dancing it in" at a country club with paper hats and horns. A group of six or eight rural men, armed with muskets, roamed from house to house from midnight till daylight. When the master was roused to the window, a long New Year's wish was read or sung by an appointed member of the group; and each man would fire separately. They were always treated to food and drink, albeit the host was nightcapped and bleary-eyed. By daylight, the well-wisher must have waxed very poetic, and all were likely in no better shape than modern revelers, but at least legs are a safer means of transportation than cars.

In the nineteenth century, Whitmonday (Battalion Day) was the traditional time for the military parade, a big event at the fair of a county seat. (Unless in government employ, all men between eighteen and forty-five had to do military service once a year or pay a fine.) Nearly every village had its militia company with motley uniforms scrambled together from chests and attics. The official fife and drum corp was often trailed by floats, clowns, fire companies (squirting water from a hand pump at pretty maids), and drunks, dogs and ecstatic children.

There is an amusing story of a captain urged after lunching at an inn to give a special drill exhibition. He ordered his men to the open space between inn and stables. After the manual of arms, he shouted "Charge bayonets," and at double quick time the company headed for an invisible enemy, the captain facing them in the lead. When instinct warned him to look behind him, the inn wall was but a few feet away. Bellowing "Company, whoa!" he saved himself from the thirsty bayonets just in time, though surely his pride was punctured.

It was the fashion of the day to poke fun at the militia. In an 1822 news joke, a sergeant says to his company, "When I say 'Fire,' all of you with firearms must shoot. Those who only have sticks and cornstalks must aim and cry 'Boo!' "

Reading, once famous for its firemen's and political parades, still has an impressive march to the cemetary on Memorial, or Decoration, Day. Graves have been decked with spring blooms—the showy peonies especially—and veterans' graves with flags. All plots are tidied fit for an enemy's inspection. When our own children were young, they sat excitedly on their grandfather's curb with a bucket, "watering the parade," reviving some gasping old Civil War soldier. They were always in a hurry to have the parade start, and in a greater hurry to have it over so we could get to the business of potato salad and red-beet eggs.

July Fourth is probably the biggest cookout day of the year. But before that the Wyomissing youngsters have already paraded their bikes—festooned with flags and bunting, and every village worth its salt has honored the grand old union. At dark we gathered in some community playground to "oh and ah" at bursting stars, pinwheels, and the finale of a flaming, thrilling American flag. Only the oldsters find the show a poor substitute for the small drab cones that, when lighted, oozed into curling worms on the sidewalk—a miracle! And the strings of penny crackers you held a match to and ran from, shrieking with delicious apprehension. Dad, always hovering nearby, finally lighted the Roman candle at bedtime. One more Fourth of July and you had escaped losing a finger or eye!

Halloween brings its parade of schoolchildren, though a small masked ghost may be shivering despite two layers of woolen undies. Fifty years ago, gates were interchanged, haystacks crowned with harrows, or privies moved to the front porch. Only the young and weak thumped on someone's door with a cabbage stolen from his garden.

Our present "trick or treat" custom is an inspired distraction. Who wants to soap cars or windows, or steal a trash can, when he can visit neighbors and collect candy and pretzels? An amusing thing happened to one of our friends on Halloween. He was called on by a pirate, an Indian, and a most beautiful little angel—all masked, of course. There was complete silence till the host produced his bribes. (Was the angel that darling little Mary Schultz from down the road?) When he dropped a rosy apple into her proffered bag, a raucous voice accused him, "Now look what you done—broke all my cookies, you dumb son of a bitch!"

Hamburg's King Frost Carnival was begun in 1910 to provide a substitute for high jinks and vandalism. It had two small bands and a hundred dollars in prizes for costumed paraders. Among the earliest prizes were a cuckoo clock, free shoeing for the finest horse, fifty pounds of flour for the oldest man marching the whole route; and for the farmers' floats—a feed bag, fifteen pounds of cattle powder, and a plow. Though at first it was feared that "everyone would be in the parade and no one to watch," four years later the carnival drew thirty thousand people from all sections of Pennsylvania. It soon took on the glamour of the old country fairs, with bands playing dance music at hotels and taverns till after midnight. Though wars and depressions suspended the annual celebrations, today it is an event long awaited by all fun-lovers.

Many smaller towns also have a costume parade for the community on Halloween. One supposedly announced last year that no beauty prize had been awarded—"nobody won." Hardly fair to our red-cheeked lasses!

When Halloween is gone, so is our parade season, alas. Yet compared with others around the nation, we Dutch make lavish preparations for the major holidays. The first one of the year, the Easter season, has special meaning beginning with Shrove Tuesday. In Germany, it was once celebrated with carnivals and ribald plays by roving bands of amateurs, for it was "the last fling before Lent." In the early nineteenth century the Dutch held Shrove Tuesday frolics, but they were more innocuous. It could be estimated how high the flax crop would be by the height of dancing, leaping feet above the barn floor. Our celebration now is limited to various superstitions and to the eating of fastnachts at breakfast. The fat in which this delicious type of doughnut was fried was thought in olden days to have a special healing power for sores. Some farm families fed the first baked fastnachts to the chickens to protect them from hawks, and to make them lay more eggs. Wagon wheels were greased with the frying fat so that the harvest they carried wouldn't be molested by rats. If a garden spade was greased, vegetables would be free of insects. The many superstitions vary from county to county. At any rate, even today, wherever you live, it's bad luck not to eat a fastnacht (best dipped in molasses before dunking).

On Ash Wednesday, the last one out of bed is the *eschapuddel* (the ashpile)—a grave disgrace, meaning all-day ribbing by the family. At one time he had his face rubbed with ashes, and, if young and last to get to school, had to carry out the ashes for the rest of the term. Cattle were also ashed to "choke the lice to death," and some perfectionists ashed garden and fruit trees as well.

There are numerous beliefs and superstitions about health and crops on all the days of Easter week, and Maundy Thursday (Green Thursday) is no exception. This is a good day for planting and for gathering herbs to use for cures throughout the year. It's essential too to eat something green unless you want to get the itch or fever, or be lousy or mulish. In certain areas it's a tradition to eat nine kinds of greens—take your choice of cabbage, turnip tops, clover, and many others. But dandelion is the perennial favorite, though there is delicious watercress in the brooks. In my childhood in Chicago we played a game called "greens on you" with the first hint of spring. It was fatal not to have a blade of grass or leaf in your pocket when your rival challenged you, or then you had to pay the agreed-on forfeit of an ice cream soda (ten cents) or a dill pickle. Could the game have had the same source as our Dutch custom? Maundy Thursday is also a day of renewal of faith, with many Communion services in the evening.

By 1869 Good Friday was declared a legal holiday in Pennsylvania. Though still a holy day for the Amish, since industrialization few others observe it except for several hours at noon. In the old days many taboos were related to Good Friday baking as well as to other household chores, weather, and gardening. For instance, one shouldn't work in the garden from Good Friday to Easter, because Jesus was buried in the earth then (but planting was condoned).

Eggs are the symbol of life—rebirth of the earth before Christianity, and afterward, of the Resurrection. Egg decorating, an old Dutch custom, originated in China in 722 B.C. The art soon spread to many cultures. A lovely legend is that of Mary, said to have given a decorated egg to Pontius Pilate when pleading for Jesus' life. Her tears falling on it made dots of brilliant color—a decoration still seen on Ukrainian eggs.

Though giving decorated eggs is an ancient custom, few cultures have clung to it as have the Pennsylvania Dutch. For nearly two hundred years, "blown" eggs have been exchanged among family members, and once were even sold in small ornate boxes by tramp craftsmen. Naturally, white hen eggs were generally used, but turkey, goose, or duck eggs are also found. The contents of the eggs were forced through holes pierced at each end, then the shell was washed out and dried before being dyed with the juice of onions, beets, berries, barks, or herbs. (Commerical dye was advertised over a hundred years ago.) Sometimes a bit of calico, a lacy fern, or flower petals were fastened to the egg before dyeing.

Scratch carving a hard-boiled egg (*oyer schritzla*—still done today) took more skill. First applying beeswax or tallow made possible the exquisite designs etched with a sharp pocket knife or needle. Commonly used were traditional motifs—tulips, angels, distelfinks. Some rare old works of sgraffito art have just the name and date. Others are more elaborate, with perhaps a loved one's likeness, or that of the current president. An egg dated 1840 has a log cabin, cider barrel, a sheaf of wheat, buckeye tree, American flag, and mountain tulips. Another has a butterfly, and a monkey soldier fiddling for two dancing goats. Others, nonpictorial, reflect the superb artistry of the Czech, Hungarian, and Ukrainian eggs. Needless to say, the old scratch-carved eggs are rare collector's items.

Most unusual were eggs trimmed with the pith of *binsa-graws* (a meadow rush). The pith was wound around the egg and pasted on, and when the whole shell was covered, bits of calico were pasted on the pith. (*Binsa-graws* was used too in other kinds of decoration, as on the base of coal oil lamps.)

Someone with sprightly fancy must have created the "egg birds" by puncturing four holes for insertion of head, wings, and tail. The finished products, brilliantly hued tropical birds (species unknown), adorned the parlor, darting about on strings.

Eventually there had to be some place to display all this artistry. Hence, now and then, a family had an "egg tree" (often something thorny like the crab apple was used), though these table decorations were a novelty till the turn of the century. Eggs scratched by the family were hung from the branches by a fine bit of wire or bright yarn or ribbon, and kept company with toy chicks, birds or baskets, and real birds' eggs or nests found during the year by the children. At an Easter frolic for the young ones, a toy rabbit or lamb guarded his nest of gifts and favors until the magic moment of sharing.

An older custom is impaling undyed eggs on a bush or small tree in the garden, and even today a lovely egg tree may surprise you in the countryside. To me, all these homespun eggs seem far more charming than the Victorian blown glass eggs of different sizes, trimmed with flowers and greetings. Yet I well remember peeking, entranced, at some exotic paper scene within them.

The popularity of the egg tree throughout the nation can be attributed to Mrs. Carrie Palsgrove, a Reading woman, who is rightfully called the "Egg Tree Lady." For over twenty years, before she died in 1953, she had an egg tree that grew from a table decoration to a tree with more than fifteen hundred exquisite eggs. It was exhibited annually at the Berks County Historical Society and at the Kutztown Folk Festival in July, and inspired Katherine Milhous's children's book, *The Egg Tree,* which gave national fame to our custom.

That the Easter bunny lays the eggs is one of the paradoxes of life, an idea brought here by the Germans. In our earliest settlements children found the eggs in caps or bonnets they had hidden around the house, or sometimes on their breakfast plates. (Naughty children were liable to get coals or pellets instead.) Some parents made nests of flax in the garden. In Lancaster County the bunny laid eggs in a bed of saffron, which stayed green all winter. It was only in the early twentieth century, after anti-Easter church prejudice was overcome, that the Oschter Haws really flourished. He doesn't visit the Plain people, however. Regardless of religious scruples, how could even the youngest farm child believe that a rabbit lays eggs? Otherwise, children wildly hunt for nests on Easter morning, and a rural Mama or Papa may still eat an egg laid on Maundy Thursday, before breakfast, to keep the fever away. Community or organizational egg hunts abound—but only for the edible variety.

Some decorated eggs are museum pieces, for instance those made by the Walter Paul family of Reading. They even use the eggs of ostriches, rheas, and emus. One goose egg has magically become a grand piano with gold braid, pearls, and rhinestones. The keys are made of black and white bugle beads. Holding up the piano lid is a toothpick bound with gold thread. Another egg has doors that open to reveal a tiny colonial couple dancing the minuet. Still another contains a wee bassinet and music box that plays Brahms's "Lullaby."

The Pauls' work rivals that of Fabergé (jeweler to the Russian czar at the turn of the century), whose eggs were made of jewels and precious metals, and opened to reveal exquisite wonders.

Commercially, candy eggs have been made here for over a century, not to mention chocolate rabbits that sell nationwide. Large chocolate eggs with peanut butter or coconut cream filling are favorites. Name-decorated, they will grace the Easter baskets for good little boys and girls. Embedded in Kelly green paper grass, they are surrounded with jelly beans, cotton chicks, and other surprises. Easter cookies are important to children too—their Mom's and the baker's. A cake rabbit of bread dough used to lay a dyed egg from beneath his tail. Later, decorum required that the egg bulge from his middle somewhere instead. A delight in either event.

"Egg picking" was the lively contest of two children testing each other's skill by striking the ends of their hard-boiled eggs together, sometimes "butt to butt," though oftener "point to point." As the broken egg was the winner's prize, a collection was bragged about like scalps. Like many another game it could be tricky. Town bullies were known to use guinea eggs bleached with vinegar, or to fill the egg with resin and challenge anyone on the street. Sometimes a rascal surprised his opponent with the messy splash of a raw egg. On farms, where competition was limited, children often resorted to picking the eggs on their own foreheads. (The custom is said to signify the breaking open of Christ's tomb.) At Easter breakfast there was great rivalry to see who could eat the most hard-boiled eggs—without acute indigestion.

On Easter morn you may go to a dawn service on the mountain to see the sunrise usher in the joyful Resurrection Day. Members of Moravian churches assemble every night of Passion Week to read the life of Jesus. On Good Friday they use a special and beautiful liturgy, which is sung and chanted in turn by pastor, choir, and congregation. On Saturday afternoon there is a Love Feast. The roaming trombone choir of Bethlehem wakens the faithful before Easter dawn when all proceed to "God's Acre" for a ceremony to honor the dead. Then at Moravian Central, the mother church, there is a service with the Easter morning liturgy and a thrilling full orchestra of wind and string instruments. The sanctuary is massed with spring blooms.

Flower-loving Dutch wives everywhere fill their windows with gay hyacinth and tulip and lily plants. And they haven't forgotten the graves of their loved ones. Our more worldly concentrate on corsages and bonnets, I regret to say. Even as early as 1883, there is mention in a journal of an "Easter parade" on Reading's Penn Street. And the weather had better be clear, as a rainy Easter portends seven more rainy Sundays!

At one time the Dutch considered Ascension Day as holy as Good Friday. Work was strictly forbidden. As Ascension Day, forty days after Easter, was on Thursday (*Dunnerschdawg,* or thunder day), it was dangerous to sew, or lightning would strike you or your home. You didn't dare replace even the most strategic button. There are many dire stories about people ignoring this belief. However, Ascension Day was the most popular day for fishing, and is still called "fishing day" now and then, as fish jump up from the water. Likewise, since the day is not good for "things descending," it's propitious to gather herbs for dysentery as well as other health-giving herbs, flowers, and teas.

Whitsuntide, the seventh Sunday after Easter, commemorating the descent of the Holy Spirit on the Apostles, is the time for Confirmation. It used to be the day when many a gangling boy proudly wore his first long pants.

Our oldest legal holiday is Thanksgiving. Though most sects commemorate it in the previous Sunday's worship, we all have tradition in our hearts as we feast together, whoever we are.

Usually in late September, Harvest Home has already been observed in many churches. For many years it rivaled New England's Thanksgiving, a Puritan substitute for the banned Christmas celebration. Our Schwenkfelders still observe their own Thanksgiving in September on the date their ancestors docked in Philadelphia. Then, when a pastor distributed apples, it was the first fresh food the immigrants had had for months. Now, in gratitude for that safe journey and deliverance from religious intolerance, their heirs still thank God by "feasting" on water, bread, butter, and apple butter.

The rest of us are not so abstemious. Our Thanksgiving "musts" are turkey with bread, potato, or oyster filling (or all!), home-raised celery, dried corn, creamed onions, pepper cabbage or coleslaw, and mince and pumpkin pies. These are just the skeleton of our groaning board. Afterward, those who can keep awake may watch a TV football game, though the ambitious may attempt a walk.

Some Thanksgivings are memorable. We used to tease unmercifully two old maiden aunts of my husband's. Though both strict teetotalers, they naturally kept whiskey in the house for sickness and mince pies. One year, it seems, each slyly gave the mincemeat an additional dose before the Thanksgiving pie was baked. The noon meal proved highly successful except for the muscular goose bought from Schwenk, the village butcher. After the cleaning-up, the women felt compelled to nap a little. When Mamie woke up at eight, all was black, and not being able to rouse her sister, thought she was dead. The final chagrin came two weeks later when they visited a farm friend from whom they had wanted to buy their Thanksgiving goose, but "it was too old" she said. Now when they groaned about the one they'd bought from Schwenk, she howled, "That's the one I sold him."

In the early eighteenth century there was no consistent Christmas celebration, scorned by some as "Dutch popery." The pro-Christmas sects were the small group of Catholics and the Episcopalian, Moravian, Lutheran, and Reformed, whose rites had some semblance to Catholicism. The "antis" were the Scotch-Presbyterians, Baptists, Methodists, Plain sects, and the Quakers. The last, who considered all days equally holy, even referred to December 25 as "the day 'they' call Christmas." There was great dissension in the state legislature in 1814, since the "Germans were absent in the Christmas holidays (as they are foolishly called) and even shamefully accepted pay for their absence." Perhaps the dour Quakers and Presbyterians foresaw our present dilemma—that of losing the holiday's meaning in the pragmatic.

Those who celebrated went to church, and, according to the indignant, then gorged away the day with food and drink. Many prosperous country people, however, had the poor in to dinner, or delivered food to them and the aged. The basket might include metzel soup made of sausage, pudding, or spareribs! (The original metzel soup was made at butchering time. Rye bread was broken into the savory pork broth, and later liquor was added. As neighbors who came in to help with butchering often grew obstreperous, it finally became safer to deliver to them a finished product.)

In those early days the children cleaned the pork bristles after butchering, and sold them to saddlers or brush makers. Since the main purpose was to buy Christmas candy, the bristles might be bartered at the general store for perhaps the only candy they got at Christmas, "belly guts." It was named for the guts of the butchered hogs, and was molasses candy pulled until white. At home, few children were given more than a candy toy or a few small cakes or schnitz.

With candy and other treats still in mind, the children "barred out the schoolmaster" at Christmas. In the days of the one-room rural subscription schools, a day or two before the twenty-fifth, children rushed to school in the black winter dawn in order to get there before the teacher. Every possible trick was used to bar him out (and not always short of violence) until he promised them a holiday and goodies. The wise teacher came well equipped and, if the youngsters were lucky, they might even get matzabaum (marzipan).

Most of the holiday amusements were out of doors—where big crowds gathered for shooting matches or fox chases. In the evenings, spelling bees or singing-school contests were popular. But surrounding all work or play there were many Christmas superstitions: it's bad luck to take on a new task between Christmas and New Year's, or to take a bath or change your underwear unless you want to get more boils than Job; cattle can be heard talking on Christmas Eve (a belief in Brittany too); if the ground is white on Christmas it will be green on Easter, and vice versa. Some believed that water will turn to wine for three minutes on Christmas Eve—but the trick, of course, was to get there at the magic moment. Ancient peoples thought that mistletoe had power to ward off evil or cure certain ills. How is that related to kissing, I wonder?

The early German settlers revered Grischt Kindle, Kriss Kringle, the Christ child who brought the Christmas Eve gifts and was often represented by a kindly adult who advised or inspired the children. Otherwise, gifts for the little ones were left by an invisible Grischt Kindle in a hat or bread basket lined with a clean white cloth. Sometimes the gift itself was called the Grischt Kindle, and might be only clear, hard toy candies shaped like animals and left, along with oranges, on the breakfast plates. (The practice survives among the Plain people, though the gifts are from Pop and Mom.) In some sections it was a custom to put hay in the barnyard for the Grischt Kindle's donkey. In the morning the dew-laden hay was fed to the cattle to ward off sickness. A rarer custom was leaving bread out all night to be blessed with dew, then eaten by the family at breakfast. Throughout the eighteenth century, Grischt Kindle was the only gift-giver in Pennsylvania.

Besides the Grischt Kindle, Santa had another source, Saint Nicholas, the legendary fifth-century Asia Minor bishop who loved the young and was known as the gift-giver. On the night of December 6 (his feast day) he came down the chimney bearing gifts, and eventually and magically crossed the ocean with the Holland Dutch who settled on the Hudson. By 1850 the two prototypes had merged and Santa Klaus filled stockings (not a German custom) and gradually ho-hoed his way into stores, Sunday schools, office parties, and nearly every niche in America.

Our modern Santa Claus stemmed from the poem, "The Night Before Christmas," written by Dr. Clement Moore for his children in 1822. But it was Thomas Nast, cartoonist for *Harper's Illustrated Weekly* (he created the symbols of the Republican elephant and the Democratic donkey), who combined his ideas with those of Dr. Moore's and gave us our definitive image of Santa.

The horrific character, the Belsnickel (not known in all areas), had counterparts in Europe from the tenth century on, but our earliest reference to him was in 1823. He arrived at dark on Christmas Eve, with blackened face or mask, clad in furs and old crazy clothes, and clanged a bell and swished a whip around scurrying legs. Children clung to their mothers or dove for safety behind the wood box. The thundering voice demanded to know who had been bad this year, and how. Since he was usually an omniscient neighbor, he might openly accuse some quivering boy of known misdeeds. Often parents too were in the dock. Had Mom been regular at church? Had Pop broken his hoe in a fit of temper? When all were thoroughly castigated and vowed reform, he scattered over the floor the nuts and hard candies from his pocket or sack. If one was too greedy among the scramblers, the whip licked his ankles again. Sometimes a child was made to say prayers, sing, or recite for his reward. After the general tussle, the Belsnickel and everyone else unwound with refreshments.

Occasionally, there was a pair of tormenters, hardly endurable, it seems. There's a story of one small boy who grimly watched from the window on a very dark Christmas Eve, but it was he who had the triumph when two Belsnickels (after many thirst-quenching visits, no doubt) tripped and fell into an open water trough. Some mumming was also called Belsnickling in the Dutch country when youths would band together, and the two customs seem to have blended in certain parts of the Dutch country. The group visits, however, were more typical of towns and cities.

Belsnickel has many spellings. The original tyrant was Pelznickel, *pelz* meaning fur and *nickel* referring to Saint Nicholas, the gift-giver. However, I have never seen an indication that the kindly saint penalized before he rewarded. Sometimes, the Belsnickel assisted Kriss Kringle, his master. (The Germans being disciplinarians, I suppose the moral was that we must confess our sins and sacrifice or suffer for everything good in life.) The custom of the Belsnickel here ebbed around 1900.

Christmas customs changed little throughout the early part of the nineteenth century, before the advent of Santa Claus and the Christmas tree. Christmas Day brought church worship (the sermon in German, of course), the big dinner, then fantastical parades, ice skating, sleighing parties, greased pig chases, and other contests. From 1830 to the Civil War the Ladies' Fair, or Fancy Fair, drew big crowds, especially in the cities. To raise charity funds, church women solicited goods from the community and supplied the needlework and food themselves. The events were often condemned as "show charity," robbing poor seamstresses of their daily bread.

Second Christmas (the 26th) was celebrated by the Dutch to the turn of our century. (All their church holidays were followed by a secular day of pleasure.) The rural youth who didn't compete in the wheelbarrow matches or the hog shootings went "to the city," often by train, to dance, see the sights, stuff with confections, and have their pictures taken. (A more recent photographer used to say, "Come closer up and you get bigger on.") However, every form of recreation, no matter how innocent, had its objectors (even among the "gay church" clergy and congregations) who believed there was too much merrymaking. When Santa Claus became a substitute for the Christ Child and even invaded the Sunday school, consternation reached its peak.

The earliest foreign Christmas tree recorded was in Strasbourg in 1608, though scholars claim that the Druids trimmed trees, and also the pre-Christian Egyptians. Seen here by 1820, trees were rare till mid-century. Our Dutch custom derives from Germany where the Christmas tree soon became commonplace. By mid-century, it was not only popular here, but all around the nation. What Katherine Milhous's book did for the Easter egg tree, *Kriss Kringle's Christmas Tree,* published in Philadelphia in 1845, did for the early custom. *Godey's Lady's Book,* that dictator of fashion, spread the idea too, and trees, as well as ladies, had a habit of changing styles. The first ones trimmed, often small cedars hauled in by the boys of a family, were placed on tables like their Easter cousins. A specially elaborate tree might be on exhibition, with admission charged and many admirers. The new industry of raising and selling evergreens began to thrive. Though there are early records of "the all paper tree," then the "all glass ornament tree," ingenuity gained favor, as well as a six-foot giant boasting nuts, fruits, and pretzels.

The early ornaments must have been enchanting. Loving hands fashioned chains of dyed popcorn, dried schnitz, cranberries, colored paper, cotton tufts or felt rosettes, walnuts painted or gleaming with tinfoil, even gaily painted oyster shells. There were gingerbread men and animals too, and a carved wooden shepherd or angel at the apex. In towns, oranges, lemons, and even mint drops might be on the tree. Later tinsel was lavishly used, and fluted paper bells that folded flat. Gleaming red apples weighed down the branches. Imported from Austria were blown glass balls varying in size and decoration, and glass horns, fish, bells, and iridescent birds with fine spun glass tails. Imagination added to the boughs all sorts of trinkets—perhaps a child on a sled, a Santa, a cluster of holly. To make snow, a recipe reads: "sprinkle the tree with water, then flour, and dust with diamond powder." Though long before my time trees were lighted occasionally with "scores of gas jets" or electric lights, I well remember the romance of tiny candles and mamas nervously guarding our butterfly skirts as we small fry danced about the tree singing "Tannenbaum."

The revolving tree, though rare, was seen here a hundred years ago. By then, and until the turn of the century, there was great originality in decoration. Now and then someone received as a practical joke a leafless tree filled with junk—tin cans, empty cigar boxes, scraps of meat, and the like. Another example, of 1900, was the tree presented by scholars to the instructors of the University of Pennsylvania's biology school; it flaunted worms, crabs, beetles, fish, human jawbones, old boots green with mold, sinister bits of rotting wood, and other absurdities. Shades of Dali! A turn of the century innovation (and still seen now and then) was a sassafras tree covered with cotton batting—to me, as great a sacrilege as the distorted beauty of bonsais. Finally the tree evolved into an outdoor project, brilliantly lighted in private yards, or a huge community spectacle. What joyous moments when we trim the fragrant fir, and how sad when we discard it, dripping needles!

Since electricity, outside lights, perhaps with a crèche or Santa Claus in sleigh, blaze in Dutch towns and countryside. The smallest city row house may have the most lavish display, the whole dwelling as well as doors and windows being outlined by lights. Naturally, each house will have a tree within also, and ornaments that may go back to Great-Grandpop's time. All nooks of the house are crammed with decorations. Markets are filled with holly and crow's-foot and poinsettias. But it's the wise Dutch hausfrau, usually rural, who ignores them for the cerise stars of the Christmas cactus she has raised, or for the blooming of her Christmas rose in the yard (good luck). A housewife still attuned to the old-fashioned leisurely traditions.

A few of the earlier customs brought from Germany along with the tree changed here because of our Santa Claus. In Germany the tree was trimmed and lighted with the children watching or helping. Here, tree, gifts, and Santa Claus were a surprise on Christmas morning. But at first we did adhere to the foreign custom of hanging the children's gifts on the branches as well as in the stockings "hung by the chimney with care."

Well over a hundred years ago, close friends exchanged Christmas cards. They were highly colored or illuminated and some were elegantly fringed. With true Victorian sentiment, even a sachet card might be sent. Generally, though, cards were advertising devices, some combined with calendars, and were handed to customers. Today, the majority of Christmas greetings are unimaginative and fated for the wastebasket. Now and then there's a compensatory card that isn't—like the exquisite handmade work of our artist friend, Fred Rothermel, who once gave us old-fashioned cutouts of angels, stars, and hearts with which to trim our tree. Recently some of his work hung on the White House Christmas tree.

What else does our modern Dutch Christmas usually involve? Custom dictates weeks of preparation. As mentioned elsewhere, fruit cake and cookie baking are the harbingers. The sweet aroma of sugar, spices, and browning dough gladdens the soul as well as the stomach. It's a happy kitchen in which a small girl may still cut out wee circles from dough scraps with Mom's thimble for "thimble cookies." Her brother rushes in from his snow fort to lick the batter bowl. And before Pop has his hat off, he samples the first batch of date strips.

Only the Moravian and Plain sects seem to adhere to their earliest concepts of Christmas. The Moravians have always honored the Christ Child in a love feast for children on the afternoon of Christmas Eve; there is another in the evening too, when the church is filled with excited sniffling toddlers and babes in arms as well as grown-ups. The music is soul-stirring with its wind instruments, kettledrum, organ, and trumpets. Ancient chorales are sung. The love feast of Moravian buns and coffee is served in the pews. Then, at the singing of "Morning Star," led by a child, trays of handmade beeswax candles are passed to the congregation. As you lift your candle high so that His light may shine in the world, there's a reverent hush before all jubilantly join in the hymns. A tender and memorable evening.

Candle burning on Christmas Eve is a Moravian custom we all observe, likely forgetting that it commemorates the Christ light. (We have strayed too from the homely beeswax candle, buying the latest atrocity at a gift shop.) The music-loving Moravians have given us too a rich inheritance of carols, such as "Silent Night, Holy Night," now usually heard, alas, on TV or radio instead of from lusty carolers. They also gave us reverence for the putz, or crèche, often combined today with a farm scene. In the early days, fresh from Moravia, they lovingly fashioned the holy family and wise men by hand, as well as the tiny animals, and some of the Bethlehem natives still have these treasures. (A specially beloved crèche may be kept in a cold room till Easter.) Everyone in the Moravian settlements goes putzing, visiting others' works of art. Their putzes are so famous that even strangers ring their doorbells.

Our modern Christmas yard is an outgrowth of the crèche scene. At first the tiny village boasted only clumsy handmade clay sheep, or people made of nuts or wishbones. Later, if Pop had the time or talent, he would carve men and animals, but otherwise they were borrowed from imported Noah's arks or were made of cardboard. There were also collapsible cardboard houses and hills and valleys of moss brought in from the woods before frost and stored in a damp place. A mirror became a lake, and sand or sawdust marked the roads. The "trees" were of Jerusalem moss or round pine. There might even be caves made from driftwood, bark, and mossy stones. In the Victorian era when scrollwork was à la mode, millworkers often turned out a sideline of fancy carved birds or animals, afterward painted and used for Christmas yard or putz.

Our modern Christmas yard may still proclaim "necessity the mother of invention," but it is often elaborate, with a train flying about a village of tiny leaden people, music tinkling from a lighted church, a mirror pond and busy barnyard. Train and village, with all things to scale, may be imported from the most skilled German workmen, and, like the Moravian putz, draw friends from miles around.

In Bethlehem, the Moravian Advent Star—two hundred feet high—is ablaze on South Mountain from the first Sunday in Advent until Epiphany. The sixty-faceted tin Moravian star is commonly used for decoration by everyone. No wonder Bethlehem is known as the Christmas City!

The Amish celebrate Christmas simply as a day to rejoice in the holiness of the family. Though Christmas day is mainly a homecoming for which Mom has·long cooked and baked, some sects hold a worship service. They have no Santa Claus myth, no tree (it's not in the Bible), no holly or mistletoe. Said a twinkling Amishman, "The only thing you need for kissing is a girl." If gifts are given, Pop makes a scooter or sled for the boys, or dower chest for an older daughter. (A small one may be allowed a doll.) Mom's flying fingers have been secretly making shirts or suspenders for the boys, bonnets and prayer caps for the girls, and mittens for everyone. Gift-giving (originally German rather than English) isn't as meaningful as the joy of family reunions and visiting friends on Second Christmas, the twenty-sixth, a day free from labor. In some areas, frolics are held on Christmas Eve, with young folks exchanging gifts, pulling taffy, and singing carols.

Our Christmas customs like those of other holidays are an ethnic blending and vary depending on peoples' inheritance, education, age, means, and where they live. But the Christ spirit is still preserved by the truly devout, and most lovingly and faithfully by our Plain sects. I'm grateful for them, like many another "gay" Dutchman who can't condone the commercial whirlpool.

Magic, White and Black

IN OUR SMUG AGE OF SCIENCE, MANY LOOK DOWN THEIR INTELLECTUAL NOSES AT any hint of the occult, or, at least, are wary of admitting interest. Yet, who doesn't have an Achilles' heel? Most of us walk around a ladder—not under it—or have an uneasy twinge if a black cat darkens our path. Thirteen at table is widely taboo and Friday the thirteenth is anathema, even among many educated and cultured. "Do you mind three on a match?" you are politely asked in polite society. Do you? If you've ever even knocked on wood you'll have a sneaking empathy for the water-witching, folk medicine lore, and powwowing (faith healing) of the Pennsylvania Dutch.

Few Americans are more superstitious, though many of our old beliefs have died with greater education. The Reverend Thomas R. Brendle wrote: "Superstitions rise up along the border of the known and unknown. As the line of the known advances, the line of the unknown is pushed back and the dark region peopled with fantastic beings is seen in the light of the common day."

Ancient enemies of the Teutons were trolls, akin to sorcerers and witches, and an instinctive fear of them lingers among us. We have superstitions about marriage, death, new babies, weather, and almost every phase of life. Many a Dutchman expects a long, severe winter if a dog's coat is heavy in fall, or the hulls of hickory nuts are close and tight. "Oh, wind, if winter comes, can spring be far behind?" Yes, if the groundhog says so. On February 2 when we look jaundiced and long for the robin, we watch the skies with anxiety, for the groundhog comes out of hibernation that day. If he sees his shadow he will snuggle back to bed for six more weeks of cold, getting precedence in our morning news over national crises.

You may take your choice of these barometers and others, for it is common knowledge that boisterous children and animals forewarn rain, or a load of barrels or crowd of women seen on the street in the morning. Quarreling English sparrows also "want rain," or bees that work twice as hard as usual. Weather forecasts stem from the whole gamut of living things and go on ad infinitum.

Many beliefs are based on observation of nature; others seem to thrive without roots, like air plants. A crazy person will "talk to the geese" who absorb his troubles and do his squawking. Since witches won't cross water, if you have no stream on your land, an effective substitute is a dog named Wasser (water) who runs around policing. Proven too. For fifteen years we had a dog named Wasser, and nary a witch here. When a Dutchman dreams of a wedding, it portends a funeral, and vice versa. As a little girl of German background in Chicago I believed this too. (Superstition is a world-traveling Hydra.) Imminent signs of death are a picture falling from a wall, a cock crow at midnight, a bird getting into the house, or a sick person fumbling with bedding. Moving him from one room to another is fatal.

To ensure children against evil illness, small bags of asafetida (devil's dreck), were once hung about their necks, and were an antidote for anything from smallpox to stomach disorders. Children in our area wore these bags longer than those in other sections, but the custom was quite common around the nation until fifty years ago. During the flu epidemic of 1920, every patient in Wernersville Hospital was given internal dosages of asafetida (intervals unknown). It still is used as a home remedy here and also may be given to horses for colic, and to chickens for lice. Though it belongs to the parsley family, devil's dreck (devil's shit) gets its dialect name from its vile odor. One old man recollects that impish boys sometimes took devil's dreck at breakfast so they "could fart in school." It was believed by some that asafetida bags could also ward off evil spirits, and if nailed above the stable lintels would protect the animals too. One old formula included herbs, bean straw, and sweepings from behind the barn door. Today, asafetida is sometimes used for animal and fish bait, but is hard to come by now in the Dutch country.

Another famous (and pleasanter) old charm is the *himmelsbrief,* or "letter from heaven," with its warnings and blessings. Printed as early as 1725 in Magdeburg, it is said by some to have been written by Christ or the Archangel Michael, though many German towns have claimed its origin. All versions are basically the same, stressing the ten commandments and offering divine protection from fire, flood, and sword. A skeptic, however, will be "forsaken by the Lord." Though believers today are rare, more than one Pennsylvania Dutch soldier in recent years left home with a *himmelsbrief* close to his dog tag. I can't vouch for its efficacy, alas.

Another mystery, dowsing, or finding an object or substance with the aid

of a rod is at least as old as written history. The average Dutchman, wanting to locate an underground spring for a well, engages a dowser, often a moonlighting farmer or tradesman. The traditional equipment is a small forked apple or peach branch, with a hand on each end gripping it firmly before one. But the type of "wishbone" used is immaterial. One nonconformist Amishman uses pliers; an 1884 dowser knew there was water below when his leg muscles twitched. Wandering over the land, the water-witcher finally feels a strong subterranean pull, sometimes so great that the wand is twisted from the hands. When the site has been chosen, he estimates the depth of the stream. Perhaps he holds a pocket watch at waist level and counts the number of pendulum swings, indicating the depth in feet of the water. Another test is hanging a button or fifty-cent piece on a thread and suspending it in a tumbler. Here too the number of swings denotes the water's depth. Incredible, isn't it, if you don't have the power yourself? But perhaps you do. Search your palm for a *W* or an *A,* more likely to be there if you're born in the sign of Aquarius.

Because our Dutch area dowses more than any other in the country, we are thought of as balmy. Yet dowsing was used by the U.S. Marines in Vietnam to detect booby traps, mines, and other snares, and I'll bet the best performer was a Dutchman. It has been used extensively in other countries too to locate water, oils, ores, missing persons, and criminals. Russia dowses widely to find natural water resources. (Incidentally, the Soviet is ahead of us in most occult research, even supporting a famous blind seeress, a peasant woman of Petrich, Bulgaria.)

In the 1920s a priest discovered that one could dowse for geopathic zones of radiation. This has become a specialty of Fritz Rhinehart, a German physicist of Fishkill, New York, who works for IBM. His theory is that when there are cracks in the rock layer eighteen to twenty miles below the earth's surface, radiation will escape from the magnum, the soft lavalike layer beneath. This radiation, he claims, is much more powerful than what you get from the sun or X rays, and can be harmful or even fatal to people living above those cracks. If they cross, they produce double radiation, causing degenerative diseases relating to a person's inherent weaknesses. He has proved that very ill people have been cured by simply moving their beds to another room in the house. "Magic? No, simply science," says Mr. Rhinehart, who can even dowse with a coat hanger and has taught others the art. Intriguing material for a murder mystery writer!

Whether we have faith in Mr. Rhinehart or not, most of us are concerned with health. Folk medicine has always been practiced in Dutch country families who still have formulas for salves and ointments *(schmiers)*. Since doctors were hard to reach years ago (have times changed or not?) the farmer had to rely on his own experience and ingenuity or the healing art of a neighbor. Even "the pill" had its precedent for the hussy who romped in haymows: "dried cock's comb, pulverized and taken internally, destroys a freshly conceived foetus, or, if taken in time, prevents conception." Poultices and teas, the most popular remedies, had many sources, and were used for countless ills. Poultices ("plasters") were made of flaxseed, catnip, buckwheat, onions, horseradish, thistleroot, red clover blossom, et cetera. I well remember my sore throat being strangled with camphorated oil and flannel and I think I recovered so quickly to avoid asphyxiation.

There were medicinal herbs in every farm garden. Sage helped to darken graying hair and mullein to bring roses to the cheeks of pining maidens. The farmer's wife must have been a walking encyclopedia, though some had books of nostrums handed down through the generations. To make the remedy effective, it was expedient to be accurate about preparation and dosage. I learned this the hard way.

Some years ago I made my weekly trip to the market house. I was always drawn to the quaint, tiny stand of a wizened woman surrounded by herbs—in jars, in bunches, in ointments, on the counter and below, behind and above it. Decoys were home-raised asparagus, a plate of garden lettuce ("salad"), and perhaps a nosegay of bluebells or arbutus. But first and foremost she was "the herb lady," herself a withered sprig of thyme.

I had been taking medication for high blood pressure, but to no avail. I asked the herb lady for a palliative and bought a little "tut" of mixed herbs, a "sure cure." She gave me specific directions for brewing it. Cunning, I prepared it a bit stronger, as my doctor was to give me a checkup later in the day, and why not impress him with phenomenal improvement? I took my tea at noon and laid down to read for a while. At once I was out like a schoolboy fighting Ali Muhammed. For five hours I slept, through the alarm clock's tocsin—and also through my appointment! When my anxious husband finally roused me my blood pressure was practically nonexistent. The rest of the tea went down the drain.

Our most commonly used herb was snakeroot, still used in isolated sections as a snakebite cure. Supposedly, animals hunt for it when bitten. Rattlesnake oil has been perennially tooted and did a big business for the medicine shows around 1900. Are you bald? Do you have a toothache? Try snake oil. Other parts of snakes have been used in remedies. Teething in babies was eased if the gums were rubbled with a rattler, which also prevented sunstroke if worn in your hat. A treatment for consumption or epilepsy was to feed the heart of a freshly killed snake to the patient. (The heart must still contain blood, however.) Boys wore eel skins on arms and legs to avoid cramps while swimming. I still blanch at the thought of the leeches my grandfather kept in a bottle or those sucking the blood from his chest.

Cupping, of course, was a common relief in the old days, not only for humans with hypertension, but for all domestic animals, especially the horse, the "gaul." Two centuries ago it was thought to cure his lameness, organic problems, eye cancer, a mad dog's bite, jaundice, and many other ailments. Blood too was mixed with other things like vinegar, turpentine, and honey to use in poultices or internally. The "fuzz that collects in clothes" seemed to be an effective ingredient.

The one farm animal denied any mode of treatment was the loathsome rat. If resident cats failed in their duty, rats were given eviction notice by the farmer. There is a relic of this practice found on an ancient Chester County property:

"Rats, I command you forthwith to depart my house, barns & premises & go to Richard Joneses a Course Lying Between west and southwest where you will be accommodated well & not Return to this premises on pain of Death & this shall be your sufficient pass April 2nd 1805."

But, returning to people—there were many absurd means of cure, like piling sauerkraut on the head of a convulsive child. As heat is reputedly good for earache, smoke was blown into the ear. In a desperate case, it might be filled with goose dung. (An old saying is, "The more vile the drug, the better the cure.") Sugared coal oil sipped from a spoon dispensed with sore throat (or perhaps the patient). Once popular too were gunpowder and tobacco juice for both external and internal problems. When small, I was once given castor oil—in beer! Even now, the odor of beer gives me gooseflesh. I'm sure we could wipe out alcoholism in a generation by dosing fledglings with castor oil in liquor.

Many of the old wives' remedies are still current among those who live near animals and watch what roots or herbs they eat when sick. With recent learning, we know that if a child craves dirt or gnaws his crib like a beaver, likely he needs potassium. Scientists and drug firms are analyzing old home curatives and patent medicines compounded from vegetable ingredients (even Indian nostrums), discovering, as one writer put it, that "there's gold among the greens." Perhaps folk medicine has a more valid basis than we give it credit for.

Along with their folk medicine and household goods, the German and Swiss immigrants brought powwowing, locally known as *braucherei,* and sometimes considered witchcraft. Though often employing folk cures, primarily it is faith healing, calling on the power of the Almighty. The early Scotch-Irish, Quakers, and others had similar beliefs. John Wesley, founder of Methodism in the eighteenth century, is quoted as saying, "Giving up witchcraft is, in effect, giving up the Bible." However, since powwowing was officially banned by the Protestant church, the practice became sub rosa.

Powwowing got its name because the immigrant "doctor" made motions similar to the Indian medicine man's. It reached its peak in the Dutch country in the nineteenth century and still exists to a small degree today despite eastern Pennsylvania's great scientific and industrial progress. As *braucherei* ebbs, practitioners and patients tend to be old folks, and the latter are usually those whom the medical doctor has failed. To be cured, it is not essential to believe in the powwower, one's self, or even God, but it's helpful.

The *braucher* may be a housewife or a man with a job whose power has been taught him by an older person, traditionally of the opposite sex, though there are exceptions. He never asks a fee: "It's God that heals." Some only "do for" people on a friendship basis, while others expect contributions. Though they may hold regular office hours in a modest parlor, when a patient is too ill to come, they will make a house call. (No "sick by appointment" practice for *them.*) They have even cured bleeding at a distance if given the baptismal name of the injured.

As patients today often have psychological problems ("not enough hard work as in the past"—my husband's theory), the doctor may chat with them first to put them at ease and appraise their way of thinking. Heat, prayer, and massage are the basic essentials of treatment. Most ailments start with inflammation over which the doctor passes his hands, or lightly strokes or blows. One claims that he is often "knocked out" when fever passes into him from the patient. To ensure success, he invokes "The Father, Son, and Holy Ghost" three times over. The patient must be willing to repeat the Lord's Prayer and Apostles' Creed.

Powwowers are called upon to heal anything from skin cancer or glaucoma to the pesky wart (and they may have a specialty). The most common complaint used to be erysipelas or "wildfire," but now is rheumatism or "arthuritis." No wonder, since the distelfink country is the "eatingest" in America, and often natives waddle rather than walk. There seem to be many "liver-grown" fretful and restless babies too (from overeating and indigestion?). If the baby is old enough he is urged to crawl through a horse collar after the treatment. When a child has trouble teething, a bat's skull may be rubbed on his gums. Treatment for hernia is given when the moon approaches fullness.

But, obviously, faith is the magic factor. When my young granddaughter had warts that resisted medication, her father decided that anything a powwower could do, he could do too. He took her to a lonely spot along the ocean, passed his hands over hers, spit on the offenders (a powwow ritual), uttered spontaneous mumbo jumbo, and told her the warts would go. In a few days they dried up and vanished.

Many a country grandmom has healed a little one's hurt with the same procedure, though more colorful vernacular: "Heila, heila, hinkel-dreck. Bis marya frie iss olles veck." ("Heal it, heal it, chicken shit. Till tomorrow morning all will be gone.")

Depending on the nature of the case powwowers may recommend an ancient home remedy or herb tea. Some have a great knowledge of herbs and grow them. Another cure is an amulet worn around the neck or pinned to the underwear. The small muslin bag may contain a German inscription written backwards or upside down, or "Nazarenus, Iesus, Rex," and a cross or row of crosses. Included is the name of the harrowing disease. Hypnotism with prayer is often effectual. Powwowers have recorded their own special charms for years and there are hundreds of their manuscript books in existence.

Though some use only the Bible (mainly verses from James and the Psalms), there are other sources of reference, especially for removing a hex or curse on someone. Die Hexabuch, the Sixth and Seventh Books of Moses, commonly called the Seven Books of Moses, is compiled from material derived from the Egyptians, Hebrew Kabbalah, Samaritans, Essenes, and the Talmud. Some of its contents are many centuries old. Only a handful of the German edition came to this country in the late 1800s, as it was banned soon because of its hidden evil intent, despite its vouching that it was published for the good of mankind. For if the Hebrew chants, incantations, and names of angels are read backward they teach black magic, and not healing. The book contains many ancient seals used to call forth the spirits.

Other *brauchers* resort to the charms of the thirteenth-century monk Albertus Magnus, who often invoked the help of Christ, the Virgin Mary, or the Apostles. His book is not only for physical ailments. For instance, Magnus offers this procedure to make a mirror forecast the future: "Buy a mirror. Write on it: 'S.Solam S.Tattler S.Echogartner Gematar.' Bury the mirror at a crossroads after sundown with the glass facing down. On the third day in the evening, remove the mirror but don't look in it until a dog or cat has looked into it first. It will then reveal the future."

Similar books that the powwower used were *The Life of Peter as Written by John*—probably of European origin. This type of publication usually came from a private press with no identification, thus avoiding suppression from the church.

A common household book of charms was Hohman's *Long Lost Friend,* sometimes called *Egyptian Secrets.* J. G. Hohman, a German redemptioner arriving around the turn of the nineteenth century, eventually made his living by doing illumination among the Dutch, though his main interest was "studying people." By 1820 he had bought a house in Reading and published his book—in German, of course. Twenty years later, most editions appeared in English, as they do today.

Hohman, a powwower himself, acknowledged material "partly from work published by a gypsy, and secret writing and other sources all over the world at different periods." At the end of his testimony he pleads, "Do I not deserve the rewards of God for publishing this book? Where else is the physician that would cure these diseases? Besides that, I am a poor man in needy circumstances and it is a little help to me if I can make a little money with the sale of my books."

There's no doubt that he was indebted to Magnus for many of his charms. When a mad dog comes bounding, says Hohman, cast this spell upon him: "Dog, hold thy nose to the ground. God made me and thee, hound." (If you can gather enough pluck and have the time before a chunk is gouged from your thigh.) Yet, reputedly, yogis in the Himalayas face wild beasts with equanimity and are unharmed because of love for all things and their faith in oneness—but only after years of asceticism.

Hohman also prescribed the following:

"If you burn a large frog and mix the ashes with water you will obtain an ointment that will, if put on any place covered with hair, destroy the hair and prevent it from growing again."

For hysterics and colds: "This must be attended to every evening—that is, whenever you pull off your shoes and stockings, run your finger between your toes and smell it. This will certainly effect a cure."

"If someone has to settle a just claim by way of a law suit let him take some of the largest kind of sage and write the names of the apostles on the leaves and put them in his shoes before entering the court house and he shall certainly gain the suit." (Did you ever put a four-leaf clover in your shoe for good luck?)

"For rheumatism, wash the part of the body affected in the water in which potatoes have been boiled."

"To cure piles, carry a horse chestnut in your pocket."

"To cure pimples, rub on them urine from a pregnant woman."

"Rub a stye with a gold wedding ring." (Another remedy used in my Chicago childhood.) Modern chemists have discovered that the ring applied to the inside of the eyelid causes tears to dissolve minute particles of gold. Contained in new preparations for styes are gold salts, which are curative.

"All is done by the Lord," wrote Hohman, and "Who carries this book shall be safe from all enemies." It's difficult to say where folk medicine ends and powwowing begins.

Most practitioners are serious, usually loyal church members, Mennonites and Catholics among them. They deny that powwowing conflicts with medical attention—they've even treated doctors, they claim. Patients often come from considerably far afield and from every social stratum. One powwower is a lay medical man who had a license from the Commonwealth of Pennsylvania for nineteen years to manufacture and sell medicine. A practitioner is not molested by the law unless he misrepresents his status, requires fees, or is thought to be responsible for a person's death.

Most powwowers claim that no special talent is needed. Didn't Jesus say, "What I can do ye can do"? Legend has it that powwowing started with the only man Jesus healed who returned to thank him. Yet, since the tribal medicine man there have always been people with healing hands and supernatural power, and faith healing has been prevalent in some form or other since the beginning of time.

In America today we not only have Christian Scientists but healers in many churches (as well as practicing psychics). Kathryn Kuhlman, before her recent death, drew thousands to Pittsburgh where her instantaneous faith cures baffled doctors who had pronounced some of the diseases terminal. The late Edgar Cayce, while in trance at Virginia Beach, was famed for diagnosing ills at any distance and effecting cures. Spiritual Frontiers Fellowship, a national group furthering study of the paranormal, particularly stresses prayer meetings, faith healing, and personal survival. Outstanding is Mrs. Olga Worrall, but many successfully practice the laying on of hands. All these methods of faith healing, and more, are represented among the Dutch by healers or patients.

Closely allied to *braucherei* is hexerei, the local name for black magic. How can you tell if you've been *verhext?* You develop a growth or pain resisting treatment, or one of your animals grows restless and ill with a mysterious malady. (A cow's udders may wither and give no milk.) The suspected witch, usually a woman, will try to give or borrow something to increase her hold over you, though she won't cross your threshold if sprinkled with salt. One thing is certain—you must get the help of a hex doctor. When he uses a countercharm on the witch he "takes a spell off" or "fixes somebody's business."

Hohman advises that cattle be made to swallow a paper on which is inscribed:

```
S A T O R
A R E P O
T E N E T
O P E R A
R O T A S
```

For a person he prescribes carrying about a paper on which has been written:

I.

N.I.R.

I.

Sanctus Spiritus

I.

N.I.R.

I.

The letters signify: "God bless me here in time and there eternally."

As the patient mends, the witch will be stricken with the same symptoms she inflicted and usually die within a few days. Long live justice! There are innumerable folk tales of these happy-ending stories, filled with curious variations.

Most powwowers refuse to take such cases, likely feeling their practice would be degraded. Some are afraid of other consequences. One powwower insisted that most diseases are caused by witches' spells, and that a vengeful witch can ruin a doctor's power.

Several years ago, the Reading newspapers publicized the case of Walter Beam, a powwower of Robesonia, R.D.1. A neighbor woman who was teaching him black magic turned on him for some reason and hexed him, he claimed, causing him to become sleepless and ill. In retribution, he put an evil charm on her barn, which burned to the ground. She had him arrested, and he pleaded guilty. Due to his advanced age, the court suspended sentence providing he would take psychiatric treatments. He soon went into a nursing home and died.

Recently, after I had been on a local TV program and mentioned this chapter of my book, I had a phone call from a man, an "ex-hex," whom I will call H–G–. We've since had some fascinating hours of conversation. He is getting on in years—gentle in manner, well read, and well spoken. It concerns him that many of today's youth throughout the world dabble in black magic without realizing its dangers. And he speaks from experience.

Fifty years ago while HG was working on a Berks County farm for his father, he came across a German copy of the Seven Books of Moses. He became so intrigued with the power it offered that he denounced God and all forms of religion, became a devout hex, and prayed each evening to the thirteen angels of Satan. And I quote: "Living apart from my family on the farm, I removed all mirrors and destroyed pictures of myself to prevent anyone from putting a curse on me." (Pictures can be used the way a tribal voodooer uses an enemy's doll image, which is pierced with pins to cause death.) "I got even with people who had done me wrong. Once I put a hex on a farmer who took sick, but I was frightened and later lifted the hex. Then I hexed his cows. One gave bloody milk and the other one died. I put a curse on another farmer's cornfield; the corn grew runty and was smothered with weeds. The whole crop failed. I once hexed a car too and it had to be junked.

"After three years I was disillusioned with hexerei and decided to return to my family, and hid the Moses book. I knew that if you'd studied black magic and gave it up the Devil would take his revenge, but I was young and healthy and not fearful. Before long, though, I grew ill and soon was emaciated, consumed with fever. The doctor couldn't determine what was wrong, or help me. He gave me just a short time to live.

"One day an old family friend, a powwower, came in to see me. It didn't take her long to guess what was the matter. 'Where's the Seven Books of Moses?' she asked. We argued about it for quite a while, but finally she convinced me to give her its hiding place. She took it to the attic, and drove a spike through it into a rafter, and cautioned all of us that it must stay there till it rotted away. Now I would get well, she said, but if the book were ever removed I would become ill again and die.

"Released from the bondage of Satan I made a complete recovery. When my parents died, and the farm was going to be sold, I went to the attic and sheathed over the rafters with Sheetrock. I'm still frightened that some owner will discover the book before it disintegrates. I've seen in a dealer's catalog that that edition of it is worth ten thousand dollars now, and it might be a temptation for someone to hunt for and sell. But not for me!"

Is it surprising that HG wants his story to be anonymous, and the farm location to remain unknown?

He gave up farming for business but has long been retired. Well acquainted with the Bible, he sometimes powwows for erysipelas and "stilling" of blood (preventing hemorrhaging). He admits wryly that he hasn't had luck with mumps, though. Powwowing isn't as prevalent as formerly, he says, but it still is found in farm areas like those around Leesport, Bernville, Oley, and Boyertown, usually not as a business. It exists in the cities too, where older people are concentrated, such as in low income housing. HG will vouch for their cures. (By an odd coincidence he is typing this book for me and has been most helpful in contributing bits of information.)

Though powwowing may be on the wane, witchcraft has certainly increased everywhere, revived by such books as *Rosemary's Baby* and *The Exorcist* as well as by articles, movies, and other media. At long last the public is accepting the fact that mind has power over matter—that "thoughts are things." Recently I read this brief report in the newspaper:

BLACK ARTS REVIVAL

Witches' covens are on the increase, English leaders have warned, and bishops are worried about the number of demonic possession cases reported to them by the clergy.

Oddly, though science and the paranormal shake hands seldom, renewed interest in all phases of the mystic may be related to our exploration of outer space. Mysticism is as old as man and his consciousness of an unknown power. Before the caveman learned to "make fire," and on into the eras of telephone, flying ship, and television, man has searched for the ultimate and constantly evasive answer to miracles.

Yet miracles come and miracles go, unsolved. I like the definition of a miracle as "something of which we cannot yet conceive." Since we all have a latent fear of occultism, as we do of death, it might be healthier if we'd meet it in the open and examine it—the bad along with the good—without prejudice.

Treasure Stops

MY PRIVATE DEFINITION OF "MUSEUM" IS "A PLACE YOU'VE LIVED NEXT DOOR TO all your life, and never visited, but plan to go to tomorrow."

Some local history bugs, of course, can tell you where to see a certain type of bridebox or Dutch bench and who sat on it and why. They also attend all things from George Washington's Birthday Weekend at Valley Forge to Patriots' Day at the Daniel Boone Homestead, and flock to the smallest dedication of a restored colonial bridge or tavern.

But what about the visiting auslander who has heard of our many treasures and would like some guidance? As I've already noted, there are various tours, but if you've come by car it's far more satisfying to browse on your own and linger longer where you will. I suggest that you start in Reading, and devote several days at least to the Dutch country highlights.

Reading's Historical Society of Berks County, like those of other Dutch cities, has treats for both sexes and all ages. Children (and their daddies) love to clang the bell of the old streetcar or bob Pompey's head; mamas drool over a dower chest with hearts and tulips. And like other cities we have our civic museum and art gallery with a less local flavor.

The Baumstown area, southeast of Reading, has many attractions, one being the privately owned house of Mordecai Lincoln, the great-great-grandfather of the president. (The original log cabin was replaced in the eighteenth century by the present two-story stone dwelling.) Mordecai and Abraham, brothers, came here from New Jersey in 1720. Nearby is the Daniel Boone Homestead. It has been tastefully restored with reproductions of a few original Boone things such as clock, chair, and gateleg table. The property (once 250 acres) is still extensive, including a sawmill, smithy, stone smokehouse, bank barn, and restored log cabin. Daniel was born here in 1734, and roamed the surrounding wilds until he was sixteen, when the Boone clan, Quakers, moved to North Carolina for religious reasons. During my first years in Reading, I was often jolted by meeting "Daniel Boone" face to face on a city street. This balmy character was an exact replica with his coonskin hat, fringed leather outfit, and formidable rifle.

During the era of the famed Daniel Boone, this whole section teemed with Leni-Lenape (Delaware) Indians, and proof is still found in arrowheads upturned by plow, or by ardent collectors who ask permission from a rural homeowner "to dig." The thought of Indians is still a thrill to small boys who love to visit the Rifle and Indian Museum east of Baumstown on Route 422. This also has an old homestead, smithy, and a gristmill with rare up-and-down saw. Dr. Bower, who subsequently owned the property, dreamed that some day it would become a shrine for local lore. What a dream come true! The museum is now a huge Swiss barn housing thousands of guns, swords, other military items, and Indian artifacts. The specialty, of course, is the Pennsylvania (misnamed "Kentucky") rifle. The present owners have added several buildings of colonial design for local eighteenth- and nineteenth-century farm tools. Unfortunately (if you have a small dunning son with you) many items are for sale, including guns, swords, insignia, arrows, and beaded pieces. But, fortunately, Mom may find an irresistible dry sink, spinning wheel, or wooden antique bowl. (Father, in the middle, has only to foot the bill.)

There is little to buy at the Mary Merritt Doll Museum near Douglassville on Route 422, but oh, what a display of every kind of toy you ever cherished or longed for! There are charming old mechanical toys and iron penny banks, the man nodding thanks with the drop of your coin; long-forgotten games like Diablo; tin and lead soldiers; fire wagons; marbles; rocking horses; live steam engines; Noah's arks; music boxes; huggable Teddy bears. And joy of joys, Schoehut's Humpty-Dumpty circus. This is mainly the boys' department, but many a little girl once was thrilled to balance a jointed clown atop a ladder.

The miniature rooms and shops, with wee dolls, furniture, and store equipment to scale, enchant everyone as do the dollhouses. Could there really have been anything so cozy in the past as the Dutch kitchen iron stove and kettles, or fireplace with its cranes and pots? Or anything so elegant as petit-point fire screens and crystal chandeliers, when Indians were peering through the windows? (I once had a unique surprise when I was on an autographing tour and a small blushing boy came up to me and stammered, "Will you do me a favor?" I said, "Of course, what is it?" He asked me to autograph a tiny book for his sister's dollhouse. I needed a magnifying glass to see *Proud to be Amish* on the cover. And there was barely room for Mildred Jordan to be written in four syllables inside.)

Mary Merritt's collection of dolls has been her passion for over fifty

years. Among them are chic French ladies as well as humble rag dolls—all sizes and nationalities, dating from 1680. Dolls may be made of wood, bisque and leather, china, or cornhusks. Kewpie and Shirley Temple are still charmers. (And paper dolls are not neglected.) You can bring your own dilapidated childhood favorite here for orthopedic treatment, or you can buy odd heads, legs, and arms, and "do it yourself." Give this museum plenty of time or you'll regret it later. I could go there daily with lunch box and succumb to sublime nostalgia.

Boyertown, directly east of Reading, is a jog out of your way, but not for father, for here is the Auto Body Works Museum. Its collection of early horse-drawn and motor vehicles (many made in this area) is superb. A *Yacht-Schindler* (small sail fishing boat) dates from 1763, and a hand-drawn fire pumper from 1790. Junior will be intrigued too with the old pony carts and sleighs, and mother will recall pictures of *her* mother's mother sitting like Queen Mary in one of the first Duryeas. Those were the romantic days when the auto sped along at fifteen miles an hour (between punctures) and strangled gawkers with whirls of dust. For the journey all were garbed in dusters, of course, and voluminous veils protected the picture hats and complexions of the women.

In the museum is the "tour wagon" (motorized house car) our family owned and went west in twenty-five years ago. She was made by the Boyertown Body Works and we called her Connie, for Conestoga. What are politely known now as "the facilities" were negligible; except for an emergency can, these were supplied by the great outdoors. Our overnight stops were aimed for a deserted schoolhouse or church area with privy. And every few days one of us would sniff and say, "Isn't it time we rent a motel room for a few hours and take showers?" Yet, Connie was a novelty and we had so many visitors en route we hardly had time for sight-seeing. How quickly things, like people, become outmoded!

But old homesteads, like that of Pottsgrove at Pottstown, seem to have constant appeal, for the ironmasters' dwellings were mansions. Built in 1752 by John Potts, it has lovely classical features, and eighteenth-century furnishings. While Mom admires the handsome dining-room table, Junior looks at it with scorn. Always hungry, he unknowingly quotes an old Dutch proverb: "What's the use of a pretty table if there's nothing on it?" Yet, it's said that even in those early days people trekked over forty miles of frontier trails just to get a look at this wonder of a dwelling. As the Potts family was active in the Revolution, it was once General Washington's headquarters. Those two-foot-thick walls must have been immune to either Indian arrows or bullets; and what roomy windowsills for Mrs. Potts's plants!

Near Morgantown, a short jaunt from Pottstown, is Saint Peter's Village, offering a variety of interests—historical, romantic, and architectural (Victorian). The story of this and the Knauertown area are closely intertwined. In 1731 the Knauer brothers, German immigrants, bought a grant of land dated 1685, and originally bought by William Penn from the Indians. They, in turn, traded it for tobacco, strong water, guns, powder, scissors, mirrors, hoes, pewter spoons, and food staples among other things. Jacob and Johann divided the land, and the latter settled along French Creek in what later became Knauertown. After erecting flour and lumber mills the family became involved with the nearby Warwick Furnaces, which produced cannon and other supplies for the Continental Army.

Washington, then at Valley Forge, sent foraging groups to the Knauertown area throughout the spring. Leading one of these forays was Lieutenant Carrington, a Virginian. During pursuit of the British, the young man was entombed in a cave by a landslide. For over a hundred years his body lay undiscovered, until granite workers found the skeleton. Beside it was a bottle containing a note to his fiancée, telling of his entrapment, his horror, and futile attempts at escape. The note ended, "He who has created us must know what is good for us and we can only submit. To know that your heart is mine atones for all I have suffered or can suffer yet. I cannot say farewell—there is no farewell to love like ours." His remains were buried in Richmond beside those of his beloved who had died of a broken heart. But I've heard that if you listen carefully near the cave you can hear his ghost moaning.

The village of Saint Peter's came into being over a hundred years ago after the discovery of black granite in that area, when the Knauer family moved there to establish living quarters for the workers. (There was even a pretzel bakery!) At the end of the Civil War, additions of a hotel, bridges over French Creek falls, and other attractions made it a favorite resort spot. During the Great Depression it languished, but is a flourishing village again. Now restored, the once luxurious hotel, with its Bavarian beer garden and German band, serves delicious meals. The little main street has a general store and many shops making and selling local crafts such as quilting, apple dolls, and carving. You can even have your portrait sketched.

But as you've scheduled Valley Forge for tomorrow, it's high time to find a motel, if indeed you haven't stopped before this.

In springtime the Valley Forge area is vibrant with dogwood and laurel. Since you go well shod, it's hard to picture barefooted soldiers camped here in the winter of 1777–1778, suffering from bitter cold, hunger, and disease. Yet the troops' thatched huts, though not original, seem to echo their misery, as do the tiny houses where Washington and his officers lived. You will visit the forts, gun pits, and trenches too; and standing before the huge Memorial Arch, you silently thank those long-gone soldiers for their stamina, which gave you freedom.

Pop now has a struggle of his own. He wants to go on to Bethlehem, but Mom wants to detour a bit to see Pennsbury Manor near Morrisville. (Women! They can't resist big houses.) Pop tells her it's only a reconstruction of William Penn's country home—just look at the guidebook. Mom argues that Junior will surely want to say he's seen the house of the man who started Pennsylvania as a "Holy Experiment." Naturally Pop goes; this is her vacation too. And later, he grudgingly admits that the mansion was magnificent, worthy of the Father of our state.

Whenever Morrisville is mentioned, I think of a Dutch friend of ours driving to New Jersey. It had begun to rain hard and as her windshield wipers were stuck, she stopped at a gas station. "My 'spritzer' won't work," she wailed to the attendant. He looked at her in alarm. "Lady," he said, "if you're really worried, you better see a doctor." A Dutch native, out of bounds, should carry a Dutch-English dictionary.

Before you drive on to Bethlehem, the old Doylestown Inn will feed you "good and plenty." Here too are the Historical Society of Bucks County and Dr. Henry Mercer's "internationally famous fireproof castle"—Fonthill. The very word *castle* draws Mom like a magnet, and she'll revel in the turrets, the forty rooms, and thirteen baths. Why Dr. Mercer, a bachelor, who lived at first in a modest farmhouse, wanted this splendor is a riddle for a psychiatrist to solve. As a young man, Mercer studied law, then became interested in archaeology, going on digs to Europe, Yucatán, and other places. When he died in 1930 he left a valuable collection of tools from his expeditions. He was also fascinated with Moravian pottery and on his property made handsome tiles and firebacks.

"How did he ever manage to stay single?" Mom asks, starry-eyed as you leave for Bethlehem.

"Would *you* want to wash all those windows?" counters Pop.

Bethlehem is best appreciated if you know its early history. The Moravians originally settled in Georgia before coming in 1740 on the sloop of the Methodist missionary Whitefield to the barony of Nazareth. He had leased land there, and intended to build a village for poor Englishmen and a school for Negroes. When he couldn't pay for the barony the Moravian church bought it. After Count Zinzendorf's visit, building progressed fast and Bethlehem became the outstanding colonial commune, supported by the European mother church, which owned all Moravian property. In five years there were more than thirty industries, including a silk mill, and much farmland. Everyone worked for the good of the whole, prospering from sales to other communities. In less than twenty years there were nearly a hundred and fifty buildings, with five schools and two inns.

Bishop Spangenberg, who headed the group, had it well organized. Babies were taken from their mothers as soon as possible, placed in a nursery, and cared for by widows or single women who couldn't do hard work. Children of three years were put into a "choir," or boarding school. Actually, there were choirs too for all categories of adults—widows, single brethren, single sisters, and others. The schedule was highly devotional, varying with each group. Love feasts and foot washing were part of the ritual. Saturday was the Sabbath, though on Sunday there was public worship. Dress was regulated, simple and practical.

Marriage was by lot. The two sexes seldom mingled except at a schnitzing bee, perhaps, and then were well chaperoned. A man taking a fancy to a pretty girl might "put in his bid" for her, and have his choice considered by the *Schwester-Pleger,* the young woman's matron. But after that the lot system was used, and the final decision was the girl's. Fate must have been hard on a homely youth without social graces, deprived of courting time, who had to leave choice of a wife to his discerning elders.

Yet life wasn't grim. As many members were of the nobility, there was a high degree of culture. Music was everywhere; it even accompanied workers in the fields. (How many years later we've adopted their psychology by easing factory jobs and dentists' drills with music!)

Moravian-owned ships brought more and more émigrés to the colony (there were no redemptioners). Bethlehem was a boom town, with its fire company and luxurious Sun Inn. This had suites of two bedchambers and a sitting room—each suite with private attendant. The inn is said to have housed every president from Washington to Lincoln. There was a special stone tavern for Indians. (During the French and Indian War, Bethlehem was severely criticized by other colonies for harboring friendly redskins.)

Twenty years after its founding, however, communal living was abandoned by common consent. Though the farms were still controlled by church authorities, industries were sold to individuals. The town continued to prosper because the wealthy Count Zinzendorf paid the church large sums of money to acquire more land and buildings. Though only church members could become permanent residents, Moravians from different countries made this little settlement unusually cosmopolitan for its day.

In 1776 the General Hospital of the Continental Army moved to the ideal buildings of Bethlehem—General Lafayette being the most famous patient. The Moravians weren't total pacifists; they were always ready to fight for their own protection.

By 1783 there was a large influx of visitors, for English was preached in the church on Sunday (most of the inhabitants were at least bilingual); Philadelphians found the town a pleasant place in torrid weather. Yet, a certain stagnation set in since matters still had to be referred to the narrow European church for decision. Natives, affected by the American and French revolutions, wanted more independence in dress, marriage, and other customs. Soon, with a loss of church members, anyone was welcome to live here or in other Moravian towns. By 1848, American Moravians separated from the mother church, and two years later, had gained absolute independence. Yet missions were still sent out, even to Alaska. In the twentieth century, railroads, steel mills, and Lehigh University made Bethlehem a modern city.

In the core of the city you may still see the original Moravian buildings near the ancient churchyard. They have a lovely aura of peace, perhaps from the vibrations of those spiritual settlers who came here to gain freedom. But to picture the ancient life here you must have empathy, and perhaps literally close your eyes and ears to encroaching civilization.

By now Junior is howling with hunger and wants to stop at a service station that says: "Eat here—get gas." Even if your fuel supply is low—take no chances. There are other places available with schnitz un knepp, which you've always wanted to try.

If you haven't been to the Schwenkfelders' Museum at Pennsburg, a stone's throw from both Bethlehem and Boyertown, you'll enjoy learning more of this Plain sect's history. The specimens of Christopher Dock's fraktur work, alone, are well worth your time. It may be that you'd rather browse around the Kutztown area with its many colorful barn signs, and rest your feet, though you feast your eyes. You have another and even more strenuous day ahead of you.

In the freshness of morning you start out for Lancaster County, the heart of the distelfink country. Be as wary of Amish buggies as they are of you. How beautiful is the rolling farmland! On the way to Ephrata you skim past Admanstown, small but still famous for hat production.

A rare treat is awaiting you at the Ephrata Cloister with its medieval buildings and unique history. Though a communistic venture like Bethlehem, how different the atmosphere! Life here wasn't joyful, but painful as fanatical soul saving can be. The Cloister's founder and spiritual leader, Conrad Beissel, was born in Germany in 1690. An erstwhile baker, he "got religion," emigrated to the colonies, and eventually by middle age founded Ephrata. His purpose was to live "according to the esoteric teachings, practice and mystical rites, and seek for both spiritual and physical regeneration as taught by the ascetic philosophers of old."

Two distinct groups lived in the Cloister: the householders (sex not forbidden but darkly scowled on); and the monks and nuns who lived apart. Though there were never more than eighty religious at one time, the community once numbered three hundred persons. Men wore the long gown and cowl of the Capuchins, and women wore white wool or linen dresses. All had monastic names. They worked feverishly hard in the fields or at one of their mills or many crafts. The colony was famed for the beauty of its work and its unusual music.

It took a spiritual giant, indeed, to rule the earthy passions of three hundred souls who had scant food, slept in cold cells, and weekly read aloud in service a report of their souls. Beissel was Father Confessor to all. But he seemed to have a magnetic charm, especially over women, attracting many middle-aged widows to the colony.

Records say that he was a miracle worker. Once he prayed that the rains might cease, and the drought was so severe that he had to pray for rain. Again, when a constable came for him with a warrant, he vanished into his cabin; though it was thoroughly searched, he later appeared at the door, which had been guarded. He could drive the evil spirits from nearby thickets or from enemies with a murderous intent. A superman, indeed.

But the group had its share of jealousy, wrangling, and sexual shenanigans—reputedly involving even Beissel, the Perfect One. In later years, with his autonomy threatened, it's understandable that he turned to drink (if this is what made his voice thick at times and his thinking foggy). When he died, leadership fell to one of the Brethren, but with the original driving force gone, from then on the Cloister was comparatively short-lived.

There are now only two of the original buildings erected by Beissel (the rest being reproductions). Saron, the Sisters' House, and the adjoining Saal (chapel) are handsome examples of medieval German architecture. Roofs are steep; miniature windows are small-paned; and dormers, like peeping eyes. The low doorways reflect the confinement of those who lived here. Colliding with a sister nun in a narrow hall was a reminder of the straight and narrow way to be followed; cracking the head when going through a doorway was a still more painful reminder of *humility*. Each of Saron's three floors has a central kitchen flanked by a common workroom and sleeping cells with one high wee window. As members slept on planks with a wooden block for a pillow, the only furniture was a small hanging cupboard.

Iron was substituted by wood whenever possible, for Beissel followed the injunction given to Moses in Deuteronomy: "Thou shalt not lift up any iron tool upon them." (Iron was symbolic of evil.) Saal was built with wooden pegs instead of nails. Not only trenchers were wooden, but also knives and spoons and even Communion goblets. Blocks of wood were used to iron clothes. Since forcing horses to work was considered sinful too, the monks donned the harness themselves, dragging plows or hauling wood. Later when horses and oxen were used, they were treated like guests, sympathetically.

And there were frequent guests in the Almonry where the wayfarer was given free lodging for the night, and every comfort. Ladies were housed in Saron, and must have marveled at the sisters' exquisite fraktur. They not only produced *The Christian ABC Book* with its highly decorative alphabets for fraktur writers; they made large sheets of fraktur with pious sentiments or scriptural texts praising the convent life. Many of them, framed, are on the Cloister walls today.

The paper mill made paper just for this purpose, as well as for the printing press and bookbindery. Everything the community did was aimed at perfection—in the sawmill, fulling mill, bakehouse, and academy, opened in 1740 for elementary and classical instruction. Pupils came from as far away as Philadelphia and Maryland. The weaver's shop is one of the few colonial half-timbered buildings left in America. The construction is of pegged timber framework chinked with stone, and clapboarded. The interior shows the half-timbered mud-plastered walls used by German settlers.

Mom and Pop are fascinated. Junior groans, "Let's get where we're going."

You walk on to the Beissel cabin, sparsely furnished by the mystic in his day. Now it has some examples of furniture built by the Brotherhood. Of special interest is the five-plate stove, fired through a hole in the kitchen fireplace, and heating the room in which it was placed.

Householders' cabins, where celibacy was not required, were comparatively luxurious. Not far off is the Cloister graveyard in which Beissel was buried.

Despite the Cloister's isolation, it became a military hospital for patriot forces after the Battle of Brandywine. Many of the brethren died of the camp fever caught from patients. Buildings had to be burned later to wipe out the infection. Captain Hale, it's said, was tenderly nursed back to health by Sister Anna. As Lizzie Yoder claims, "Love is blind but not the neighbors."

When you leave Ephrata you should drop down to the little Moravian town of Lititz, laid out in 1757. What will you see here? The early Linden Hall for girls; interesting historic houses like that of John A. Sutter who was ruined in the California gold rush, and finally made his home here; the Lititz Pretzel House, the ancient factory where Junior can curb his hunger; and the shop of the Moravian Charles Regennas who makes the old clear toy candies. What joy those bright colored translucent sweets brought to the child of a century ago—alluring "meat, fish, and fowl" shapes of all varieties. The inherited stock of more than three hundred molds produces even greater novelties, small and large; ships, frogs on bicycles, images of famous men—Santa Claus the greatest. Junior's eyes bulge at the hollow steam locomotive weighing two pounds, and nearly a foot long. And now his appetite is completely ruined. You might as well give up the idea of lunch at the famous General Sutter Inn and move on to Lancaster.

The "Red Rose City" has many historic attractions, but one of my favorites is the Fulton Opera House, also known as "The Grand Old Lady of Prince Street." Built over a 1729 jail foundation, it is the oldest building in the nation in continuous use as a theatre. The four-story structure had many other uses in its day too: there were meeting rooms, and a large hall for lectures, political rallies, and assemblies; it once served as an armory, a shooting gallery, and, again, as a storehouse for fertilizer and tobacco. After the Battle of Gettysburg it even became a hospital. It was named for our native Robert Fulton, of steamboat fame.

Under the theatre, built to seat fifteen hundred people, is the original prison archway. Even before the Civil War, it had many star performers: John Wilkes Booth, Ole Bull (the Norwegian violinist), Adelina Patti, and Mrs. Drew, mother of the Barrymores. In 1873 Fulton Hall became the Fulton Opera House, redesigned by America's famous theatrical architect Edwin Forrest Durang. The Victorian façade was left intact, but the interior was lavish, and blessed with that mysterious gift of the gods—superb acoustics. Top performers continued to come here. There were standing lines not only for Sarah Bernhardt but for Buffalo Bill, Mark Twain, and Houdini. Though the theatre degenerated into a movie house during the depression, it was restored again about twelve years ago and now has year-round programs of concerts, symphonies, operettas, and plays. Anyone seeing its *1776!* during our bicentennial year was privileged, indeed.

Equally elegant to the Grand Old Lady is Wheatland, the nineteenth-century mansion of James Buchanan, the only president born in Pennsylvania. This is another mecca for Mom, for the authentic furnishings are a bait for antique lovers. Hostesses in period costume will guide you about (keeping a sharp eye on Junior). Mom's eyes dim at the portrait of the lovely Anne Coleman, the great love of Buchanan's youth. As he remained a bachelor, his ward, Harriet Lane, was First Lady of the White House. Mom mutters, "There were a lot of First Ladies in the White House who weren't ladies when they went there!"

There are so many treasures awaiting you north, south, east, and west of the Red Rose City that you'll want to toss a coin to decide on your next day's objectives. But the Pennsylvania Farm Museum is a "must" and a lively stop. Actually, it's a whole little village, having an eighteenth-century tavern, gunsmith shop, printshop, log barn, "Grossmutter" house, church, schoolhouse, and homesteads. The brothers George and Henry Landis began this wonderful collection of local Americana, now being developed by the Commonwealth of Pennsylvania. It seems they saved everything, be it a mousetrap or fancy birdcage. Some buildings are original and restored; others have been moved to the site. The village is surrounded by fields and farms and happy browsing chickens. Houses are "authentically furnished," but some original items date from the period between 1815 and 1850.

When you have learned everything this 100-acre complex can teach you about old-time rural life, agriculture, and crafts, you may feel as ancient as I did once. After I'd published *Proud to Be Amish* and had just spoken to a grade-school group, the teacher asked, "Are there any questions?" A small boy raised his hand. I expected him to ask, "Why do the young Amish men wear beards and the old ones don't?" Instead, he inquired, "How old are you?" When I'd caught my breath, I answered, "How old do you think?" He pondered for a minute, then said, "About ninety." Rather depressing.

Not far from the Landis Valley Museum on Route 462 is the Gay Nineties Museum. Here is a charming colorful collection of memorabilia of the late 1800s. Bareheaded women will long to be seductive in one of those exotic hats. A bit east on Route 30 is the National Wax Museum with its tableau of historical events. Wax figures can be uncannily real and convincing. My husband once asked a guard in the hall the way to the men's room and was greeted with eerie silence. But, on with the trip!

With another hop, skip, and jump, you'll reach the Amish Farm and House with its seventy acres and 1744 homestead occupied by an Amish family. Before your tour a hostess will describe the history and customs of the Plain people. The house seems austere after the mansions you have visited. Rooms are heated by stoves. As there are no closets, clothing hangs on pegs on the bedroom walls. Junior will titter at the boys' suspendered trousers and broadbrimmed black hats like their fathers'. Farm buildings house the animals; there is a tobacco shed and "stripping" room and a limestone kiln. You explain to Junior how the waterwheel furnishes water for the farm, inside and out. It's fun to examine the marketing buggy, the family buggy, and the "courting buggy"—for you have passed one or more on the road. If you happen to be there in late April, you can watch the sheepshearing. The ewe may be held firm, but there's a glazed terror of helplessness in her eyes, and you'd like to free her.

You begin to get an idea of what it means to be Amish. Work the year round. Not an easy life, but healthful and satisfying, judging by what you see. And those more than contented cows at pasture—with no thought of wandering like the one a friend of ours encountered. He had taken his bride to see the Amish country and was suddenly blocked by a cow in the middle of the road. They decided they would inform a nearby plowing farmer that his cow was playing truant. They told him in English, and he looked blank. The bride then used her best college German. Again he looked blank. But our friend whose knowledge of the dialect was limited was now inspired. *"Millich lauffa"* (milk walks), he said proudly, and pointed down the road. The farmer grinned, thanked him in sign language, and went off after Bessie.

Not far south of Lancaster is the country's oldest house, built by Hans Herr's son in 1719 as a home and meetinghouse for the Mennonites. When past seventy, the bishop came to the New World to be part of William Penn's Holy Experiment. The recent restoration has been sponsored by the Lancaster Mennonite Conference Historical Society. Near the little village of Willow Street, the house is on a gently sloping hill overlooking a fertile valley. The Anabaptists fleeing Switzerland must have felt very safe here. The steep-roofed Swiss-style dwelling has been faithfully restored: the roof is of hand-cut red oak shingles; mellow brown walls have old straw and clay insulation; and the windows have been narrowed to their original size. Rooms have been rebuilt around the mammoth fireplace, which served all three floors. An unusual feature in the main room is the *eckbank,* or corner bench, attached to the walls. I was reminded of an amusing little anecdote told us by the guide of the Springs Museum in Somerset, when she showed us a Mennonite bench with knothole once used at meetings. A small bored boy, while kneeling and praying and thinking no doubt of fishing instead of God, had worked his finger into the knothole and couldn't get it out. He had to be rescued by a bigger boy beside him who had a pocket knife. I hope that God smiled at his predicament.

Leaving the Herr House, with a good jaunt southeast, you can visit the charming old birthplace of Robert Fulton, near Quarryville. But no doubt Junior is needling you to get to Gettysburg, instead.

As the area is bewilderingly vast, you'd better take the thirty-five-mile bus tour re-creating the three days of fighting. With taped narration you hear the boom of cannon and the whine of passing shells. Junior is on the edge of his seat, no longer wanting to be a cop. Mom is moved to tears when Raymond Massey's voice gives the Lincoln address at the National Cemetery site where it was first delivered. Pop has already snapped many pictures of monuments to both the Blue and the Grey—and now he has run out of film and swears under his breath. Mom reassures him (or does she?) by saying, "You'd see much more without looking through that camera hole all day."

In the Visitors' Center the cyclorama and dioramas depicting scenes of the war refresh your knowledge. Our country's leaders quote their famous sayings in the Hall of Presidents. Junior asks, "But how can they talk if they're only wax?" In the Hall of First Ladies, miniature presidential wives wear their elegant inaugural gowns. The Civil War Museum tableaux give the whole story of the Civil War era; there are cotton-picking slaves on a plantation as well as soldiers dying in battle—and that blood looks mighty real. The "talking walls" of the little Jennie Wade House tell you the story of the young woman working bread dough when she was instantly killed by a sharpshooter's bullet penetrating two wooden doors. The house stood in the midst of the battle and was punctured hard by gunfire. Lovely Jennie was the only Gettysburg citizen killed. In Charlie Weaver's Museum his tiny soldiers hand-carved with dentist's tools show the development of military dress in America. They intrigue both Pop and Junior. Here too is a historic collection of guns and more dioramas of the war. Thrilling for everyone is the Lincoln Train Museum with its sound and color movie of the presidential party en route to Gettysburg. Junior decides that instead of being a soldier he will be president.

A stop at the Prince of Peace Museum is a restful end to your day. Here scenes from the life of Christ are depicted by Paul Cunningham's beautiful hand-carved figures. Gettysburg always reminds me of the conversation of the two Dutch women in market many years ago.

"This war is somesing awful, ain't?" said one. "Do you sink if them Nazis come over to this country they'll bomb Reading yet?"

"Vy, no, Mrs. Loose," replied the other placidly. "The battlefield's at Gettysburg."

And now you are ready for food and bed! Then suddenly it's morning again. You want to start north by way of York to see the Gates House where Lafayette made the toast quashing the Conway Cabal. York, like other old cities, has much to offer. And just northeast of York is the National Association of Watch and Clock Collectors Library and Museum. (Don't let the cumbersome name mislead you.) Here is a vast and absorbing hoard of timekeeping and measuring devices from the early sundial to the electric watch. And, ironically, you'll forget what time it is and all the other sight-seeing you have scheduled.

Yet, being Americans, we're apt to panic when we've lost track of time. An octogenarian, once a conductor on the shuttle train between Bethlehem and Bath, relates a humorous experience. One day old Dan Herman hailed his train at a flag station. "Well, hop in, Dan," said the conductor to his excited friend. "I ain't going with," panted Dan. "My clock stopped and I just want to know the time." "Summertime," called the conductor with a grin, as the train chugged off.

Summertime is the best and only time you can visit Bube's Brewery and Catacombs at Mount Joy, just a good hike away. On the two underground levels you can see how beer used to be made and since beer is one of our failings (or delights), naturally Bube's is on the National Register of Historic Places.

Since Pop has had first choice in Mount Joy, it's Mom's turn, and you go to the Donegal Mills Plantation in its fine pastoral setting. The first settler came here from Donegal, Ireland, in the early 1700s, choosing the site because of two creeks that forked. Junior yawns loudly as you investigate another mill, creamery, cider press, bakehouse, and blacksmith shop. Ownership and remodeling of the homestead gradually changed and now it is a pillared mansion. Decor ranges from Empire to Victorian. Many household activities are reflected: soup making, quilting, and polite tea taking to the tune of a Regina music box. Since a group from Millersville State College is doing the research and restoration, all is historically accurate.

If you go on by way of Lebanon, visit Cornwall Furnace. It is one of the few iron furnaces that remain intact, and though it closed down in 1883, the mines are still in operation, owned by the Bethlehem Steel Company. Charming Forge near Womelsdorf (east of Reading) has little to remind you of its former distinction; the mansion with its little complex of outbuildings and tenant houses draws you because it was once run and lived in by the glamorous Baron Stiegel, who made exquisite colored glassware. I once owned a Stiegel wineglass and kept it in the dining-room cupboard. When I missed it one day my maid claimed that the cat had smashed it. Wily puss had also put all fragments in the trash can, without even an apologetic mew.

Womelsdorf's prime attraction is the Conrad Weiser house, built in 1729, and its surrounding Memorial Park. A man who changed the course of history, Weiser seldom gets his due. A monument erected to him in the park is inscribed: "As interpreter and Indian agent he negotiated every treaty from 1732 until near the close of the French and Indian War."

There was an interim in his life when he was influenced by Beissel, was baptized in Ephrata in 1735, and became a Cloister celibate, despite his wife, Ann Eve, a large family of children, and his church. He had left the Lutheran congregation in Tulpehocken when it balked at living among anti-Lutherans. It was said that he even burned the Lutheran catechism, the Psalter, and other honored books. But as "the country could neither wage war nor make peace with the Indians without him," Governor Thomas used every wile to lure him from seclusion. No doubt, the active Weiser was tired of being saintly, for he returned to become Justice of the Peace and continue Indian negotiations.

Business was conducted in the little one-room house with its huge fireplace and bake oven; sleeping quarters were in the attic above, though later there was an addition. The large stone house now used by the caretaker was built a hundred years later. In the park is a bronze statue of Shikellamy, Iroquois representative and Weiser's close friend. One hand carries a peace pipe; the other is raised in the Indian gesture of friendship. On a small knoll are the simple graves of Weiser, his wife, and several of their children.

And now your holiday is over, and you return to Reading. Its Japanese pagoda atop Mount Penn, and lighted at night, can be seen from miles away. In the old days when we came home from a family trip the children vied with one another to singsong, "I see the 'goda!'" From then on we had a "horse to the oats" gait.

The pagoda is at one end of the three-mile Skyline Boulevard overlooking the city. Here, "on a clear night you can see forever." Though obviously not of Dutch origin, the pagoda has long distinguished Reading for the stranger. The seven-story structure was built early in the century by Reading's William Witman, Sr., and copied from a picture of Nagoya Castle in Japan. It is variously said to have been built as a luxury inn, a restaurant, a tavern—even a hideout for crooks. Whatever Billy Witman's intention, it was not as philanthropic as it may seem, however, but a panacea. He was a politician who had been quarrying stone on his Mount Penn property, and citizens were incensed at the ugly scar on the mountain. Reputedly, a liquor license was refused by authorities who doubted that patrons could manage the hairpin curves "in those newfangled horseless buggies coming into vogue."

After changing hands, the pagoda was sold to the city for a dollar. Over the years it was sadly neglected, most of the Oriental artifacts and furnishings being lost or stolen. (I understand that behind locked doors is an ancient sundial inscribed "Time Is Valuable," and an exotic hand-painted bathtub with pink china roses.) But on the top floor you can see the Japanese temple bell cast in 1739, and as long as I can remember there has been a souvenir shop on the ground floor.

Since the interest of Pagoda-Skyline, Incorporated (a civic group) four years ago, great improvement has been made and more is planned. The ground floor now has Oriental antiques for sale and a cafeteria featuring Eastern food. Other floors have exhibits of native wildlife, or historic or commercial interest. The next time you come here you may find outside a moon gate, bonsai rock garden, teahouse, and waterfall. Much depends on funds from the Pennsylvania Historic Commission.

Why not get to the pagoda before you leave for home in the morning? I can almost hear your conversation before you say good night.

Mom: Oh, dear, we never got to see the Eisenhower home at Gettysburg!
Pop: Because you had to stop at every other old mansion along the way.
Junior: And I wanted a ride on the Strasburg Railroad!
Pop: You did that last summer when we toured the Amish country.
Junior: But I want to do it *again!*

This just goes to show that you can't please all of the people all of the time. Nor is there time for all the treasures that draw people to the distelfink country or the outskirts that are related to the Dutch. One day you may even want to go as far afield as the Jordan Museum of the Twenty in Toronto. It's a long way from Dutch home base, but here is where Mennonite emigrants from Pennsylvania went as early as 1800, still fearful of threats to their faith and peace. The three buildings have old Dutch furniture, household equipment, fraktur scripts, weaving, and farm implements. And don't forget Winterthur near West Chester where some of our greatest folk art is displayed in Pennsylvania Dutch rooms: primitive paintings, fraktur work, original slipware and sgraffito plates, punched tin lanterns, wrought-iron and charming weathervanes.

Even though you're only hurrying through our lovely countryside on a different trip, you'll get the feel of how both our famous men and modest farmers lived. Markers along the road give you a bit of history. Imagination fills in details. Could Governor Mifflin be merry at the ball in his mansion when the Conway Cabal might change the fate of his country? Did the farmer worry about drought as he shod horses in his own little smithy or drove his cows home from pasture? Yet the farmer must have felt more secure than most of us today, for he had faith in the God who helped him create his own little world and preserve it.

Touring unfamiliar historical sections gives you a sense of reliving the past, of empathy with its trials and glories. It's a most rewarding experience. Try it, if you aren't already an addict.

Food for the Gods

Whoa, mule, whoa!
Can't you hear me holler?
Tie a knot in that mule's tail
Or he'll jump through his collar.

FOR OUR SETTLERS, SINGING WAS A WAY OF LETTING OUT STEAM ALONG WITH their mules. The human voice was surely the first expression of music, inspired though it may have been by rippling water or a bird's joy of living. The cave woman must have crooned to her newborn baby while her man danced his supplication to the gods for rain. Down through the ages, before we made instruments to tell what the soul was feeling, some sort of song gave vent to emotions. In the case of our early immigrants, they not only sang the ballads of ancient bards, but made heroes of workaday things like a mule. No wonder music is called the universal language.

The Dutch have a rich store of ballads. Until recently there was danger of their dying out, but the 1935 folk festival in Allentown and subsequent festivals brought a revival of interest in all our folklore. Several *Volkslied* books have since been published. The Reverend Thomas R. Brendle and William Troxell did intensive research, and, interviewing the aged, made more than two hundred recordings. They found that local songs fell into four categories: immigrants' songs describing their voyages or adjustment here; indigenous, like those of the Conestoga wagoner; translations of old German, English, American, and other ethnic songs—a good example being "Ei, du schöne Schnitzelbank" ("Carpenter's workbench"), a German favorite; and variations of all three—children's game songs, for instance. In the last, questions are often asked and answered. "Is not this a sawhorse?" ... "Yah, this is a sawhorse." Along with repetition, there is often pantomime. Sometimes new verses were added to the ballads as customs changed.

The later broadside song (the dirge, or *Drauerlied),* sung to a religious melody, was fraught with moralizing on murders and hangings, recounting the deeds of the wicked and admonishing strayers to turn to God, *now,* unless they wanted to battle eternal flames in hell.

Even more gruesome, though inspiring, are the "slow tunes" of the Old Order Amish, found in their hymnal, the Ausbund. Most were written by sixteenth-century martyrs awaiting the death sentence, and were later adapted to melodies (mostly German), Gregorian chants, folk tunes, or other music. One hymn is over a thousand years old. For many years, "slow tunes" were passed on only orally from parents to children.

They commemorate the Anabaptists of South Germany and Switzerland (imprisoned in Bavaria for their faith) and their suffering and bitter loneliness in being parted from loved ones. They don't despair, though, for God is with them. The miraculous strength of Jörg Wagner, burned at the stake, is related by a fellow Anabaptist:

> *They bound him tightly to the rack;*
> *Wood and straw were set afire;*
> *But now their laughter was costly.*
> *"Jesus, Jesus," for the fourth time*
> *Did he call loudly from the fire.*

These hymns are sung a cappella, not to fixed musical key, but to a pitch set by the leader, or *Vorsenger.*

I often wonder if naughty Amish boys don't squirm with horror during the long, solemn services. Do they find solace in their half-moon pies, or in anticipation of the "fast tunes" at the Sunday evening "hymn sing"? For the Amish can be as lively at times as they are grave at others. Songs sung at frolics, weddings, and barn dances range from "What a Friend We Have in Jesus" to folk songs like "Oh, Susanna."

There was nothing even remotely gay, however, in the Ephrata Cloister of the Seventh-Day Baptists—renowned for its singing and asceticism. Deriding the stress of regimented life under the power-drunk Conrad Beissel is the following limerick:

> *An Ephrata Cloister virgin, Bernadine,*
> *Was desperately in need of a fling.*
> *No sex, scant food,*

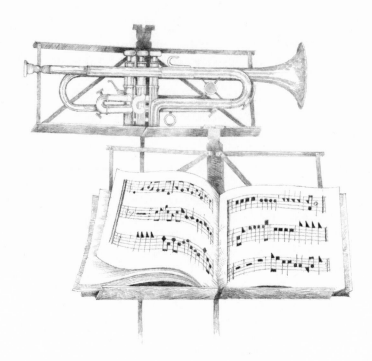

Slave's work, nun's hood—
Yet, she was forced to gird her loins
And sing.

Hymn singing was one of the Cloister's many disciplines. In addition to Beissel's voluminous output of prose and sermons, he is said to have composed over a thousand hymns and anthems, sung to well-known European Protestant tunes. The manuscript songbooks, written in literary High German, were handsomely illuminated. Music seems to have been an outlet for Beissel's mercurial temperament: members had to devote many hours a day not only to prayer but to psalms and hymns (and this after an average of five hours' sleep).

One historian wrote: "The tones issuing from the choir imitate . . . instrumental music conveying a softness and devotion almost superhuman. . . . The whole is sung on the falsetto voice, the singers scarcely moving their lips, which throws the voice up to the ceiling which is not high, and the tones . . . appear to be echoing from above and hanging over the heads of the assembly." This was in the chapel, or Saal.

Today, during summer, the vorspiel is given here when rainy weather prevents the use of the amphitheatre. The vorspiel, a musical drama, portrays early Cloister life. The well-known and long dedicated choir also presents a Christmas program in the Saal.

I was deeply moved when I attended one last December. The small candlelit chapel accommodates a very small audience who must apply for tickets months in advance. As we arrived quite early we were told we might get a glimpse of "the bride." I was astonished and gratified to learn that anyone can be married here, and that a wedding was taking place before the performance, which was memorable.

The two halves of the audience, separated by a center aisle, face one another and also an opposite balcony. Breaking the hush, a bell choir starts the program, mostly musical, except for an invocation, Scripture readings, and benediction. The choir, garbed in Capuchin robes and white nun's gowns, sings from both balconies; the audience joins them when carols are sung. The mingled perfume of greens and beeswax is somehow soporific, and we felt the reverence bequeathed by long-dead worshipers. "Oh, Tannenbaum, Wie trau sind deine Blatter!" We're more lighthearted than the ancient Brethren.

As we left the Saal to shiver through the night on our way to the museum complex for refreshments, brass instrument music peeled from Saron, the Sisters' House. En route we passed the inspiring tableau of the Annunciation, and later that of the Nativity in the Cloister's miniature stable. Real goats and sheep, and beautiful people adoring the Christ Child. The whole evening was beautiful, though the choir didn't revive the singing of Beissel's day. Perhaps his presence gave it some divine, inimitable flavor. At any rate, it was too esoteric to appeal to the outside world, and soon sank into a phase of oblivion, particularly when the Cloister disintegrated.

Not so, the singing and instrumental music of the Moravians, who founded Bethlehem in 1741. Their high level of choral and chamber music continued to grow in stature and now has world renown. The Moravian immigrants not only brought instruments with them, but imported new ones favored by European orchestras, then trained skilled workmen to reproduce them. The organs made in Bethlehem and sold to many Dutch churches were some of the finest in the colony.

Bethlehem's Trombone Choir of 1754 is the oldest musical group in the nation. (Trombones, which have been featured ever since, played death knells from the church steeple, dirges indicating sex, age, and rank of the dead.) From its earliest days, Bethlehem had a church orchestra too. The Collegium Musicum (orchestra practice), the Philharmonic with singing, and choirs for all ages were soon developed. Works by Bach, Handel, and Mozart were rendered at the many formal concerts after 1800. The Bach Choir with a chorus of thirty was organized almost a century later and gave the first presentation of Bach's Mass in B Minor in the country. As time went on, non-Moravians took part and also members of the Philadelphia Symphony Orchestra. The Bach Festival, still an annual May event, draws music lovers from everywhere.

The Moravians were as instinctively musical as birds (though by the law of averages there must have been a few who sang out of key). Count Zinzendorf, the patron father, composed over two thousand hymns, some seen in Methodist hymnals today. Moravian musicians—including those of Lititz and Nazareth—were apt to be composers too. When Franklin was in Bethlehem directing frontier defenses during the French and Indian War he wrote warmly of their superb accomplishments.

There is growing interest in research of Moravian music, which has inspired more than one doctoral dissertation. Among recordings, you can get a series of long-playing Decca discs: *Music of the Moravians in America; Six Quintets by John Frederick Peter.* (A vast relief when you've had to endure your teen-agers' blaring dance tapes!)

Musical activity in Philadelphia, antedating that of Ephrata and Bethlehem, began with Johannes Kelpius but died out early and wasn't revived until the 1760s. Though the Quakers thought music was worldly and hampered progress, the nonconforming Franklin invented the harmonica (not the mouth organ, but "improved" musical glasses). However, despite the Quaker antipathy, the religious groups were making musical history.

A new type of religious song was born in Kentucky around 1800 and was sired by the Second Awakening. Spreading first through the Deep South, it eventually came to eastern Pennsylvania and became the "white spiritual." (Contrary to belief, the Negro had taken over his master's medium and transformed it into one peculiarly his own.) The Dutch bush-meeting devotees also borrowed from their English-speaking neighbors, translated hymns into German, or reworked them and even composed originals. It was common to take a word or theme and turn it into a chorus:

> *Free grace and endless love!*
> *Free grace and endless love!*
> *Free grace and endless love!*
> *Yonder in the New Jerusalem!*

Well beloved was:

> *Jesus has been with us,*
> *And he is still with us,*
> *And he says he will be with us*
> *To the End!*

There are hymns of warning (you can't slip into heaven without conversion); softer hymns for the less wicked ("Now is the Time"); and hymns of thanksgiving. Who hasn't heard "It's that old-time religion" (thrice repeated), ending "And it's good enough for me!" The white spiritual, now called the old Dutch Chorus, was often criticized as overemotional. But it did bring more people weeping and stumbling to contrition than did the church choir with its staid director, or the contemporaneous "buckwheat music."

The latter hymns, used by various congregations, had small angular notes resembling buckwheat kernels. From them evolved the shape-note songbooks used in singing schools in the mid-1800s. Each note had a different shape (diamond, square, triangle, circle, etc.), making learning easy for the scholar. Also, there was only one staff and no key signature. The shape-note book was often considered monotonous (its ancestor was the Mennonite hymnal), and was abandoned for books of more rollicking melodies like "Bringing in the Sheaves."

But speaking of monotony, we have a story of a weary farmer who fell asleep listening to a choir on the radio after helping Daisy deliver a calf. Suddenly there was a piercing high C, which made him leap from his chair. "Mein Gott," he howled, rushing toward the barn, "Daisy gifs twins!"

Unlike the farmer, the early Germans appreciated music in any form. (Or perhaps loving music is just being American, for the Indians were fond of Jew's harps, sometimes exchanged by the white man for land.) Later singing was often accompanied by the "zitter" (not the zither as we know it today). Resembling a dulcimer, it had wire or gut strings, which were plucked by a violin bow or plectrum as it lay on the table. In its heyday a hundred years ago, it was used mainly by Mennonites to accompany hymns (but never in a meetinghouse!). Unfortunately, the hymn music they played on it has not all been collected or published. But then, little of the Mennonites' secular music has been preserved.

One had to sing more lustily to the organ in order to outdo it. No stylish parlor was without one, and many colonial churches had pipe organs. From 1776 on, John Dieffenbach and five generations of his family—wheelwrights, carpenters, and undertakers—made them as a part-time business. John D. was the first native-born American to make an organ, built for Epler's Church. (Its music has been recorded for Columbia Records.) Then deciding to make something more elaborate, he went to a church in Philadelphia installing one, and asked permission to examine it while the workmen ate lunch. Having taken measurements and made notes and drawings, he announced that he was going to build one just like it. "When you do," joked a workman, "and get it playing—invite us to hear it." He did.

John D. had had his problems with it, though; when the pipes had to be supplied he didn't know the secret of welding and there was no one to show him. The Lord helps him who helps himself, however. In talking with a tramp he had given food and shelter, John D. learned that his guest had done metalwork abroad and was happy to teach him the process. The organ, now in the Historical Society of Berks County, is made of black walnut, has a hand-carved case, and hand-wrought gold and blue pipes. A beauty, incorporating many features of the organs of Tannenburg of Lititz, colonial America's most famous builder.

Other famous Dutch manufacturers were the Krauss family, and the Kantners of Robesonia, building reed organs also. The plant of Daniel Bohler, who started business in Reading in the 1830s, became the largest and most up to date in our area, and sold to churches all over eastern Pennsylvania. Some Bohler organs, modernized or electrified, are still in use, though a bit asthmatic.

Yes, our Dutchmen loved music on every feasible occasion: weddings, funerals, church services, harvesting, barn raising, family reunions, serenades, fairs, and frolics. Most musicians were amateur. Yet, Negroes fiddling for dances could even make the old and lame kick up their heels, and still influence our style of playing and dance steps. Until 1890 there were many fiddle contests for oldsters from sixty to eighty.

Bands deserve special attention. In every village, the smallest parade or picnic was once a fiasco without its blasters. Today, Albertus Meyer's Allentown Band (not mere picnic caliber) is unequaled; yet the pride of the distelfink country has long been Reading's Ringgold Band, originating during the Civil War with the Ringgold Light Artillery. The following dialogue proves its uniqueness. Hearing music in the distance, two Dutchmen discuss it: "Das iss die Ringgold Band!" ... "How do you know?" ... "Vy, it *lissens* like the Ringgold Band."

It rose to national fame in 1932 when John Philip Sousa, "The March King," came here to conduct its eightieth anniversary concert. (Some of our local players were with Sousa's band.) At the rehearsal, the last number Sousa ever played was "The Stars and Stripes Forever"; he died suddenly before the performance.

For years, the ambition of many a teen-age boy has been to play in his high-school band. We have two friends, now elderly, who were not only musical but daring. The older one, a band member, urged his brother who studied saxophone to go to tryouts. "After only three months of lessons?" was the retort ... "Sure, just bluff your way along." ... "How?" ... "You'll find a way." And Little Brother did. Feigning great confidence, he went through all motions with flourishes, but without playing a note. When the sax section was featured, he slyly kicked over his music stand and had to fumble the sheets on the floor until the saxes had finished. He made the band.

Little Brother was born fifty years too soon. Now, lower grade schoolchildren are encouraged to play an instrument. They buy flutophones and music at cost and are given lessons. There is then a demonstration of other instruments when a child may decide to aim for band or orchestra. Charges for rental and summer class lessons is minimal, and in the fall lessons (now free) continue twice a week. In my son's family, trumpet, clarinet, sax, and flute practicing intermingle. And not to be outdone, the youngest has the French horn in mind. Few children may win a scholarship to the Juilliard School but many become knowledgeable about music, enjoying it all their lives, and others become competent players.

Consequently we Dutch have fine musicians in every medium. Our

Reading Symphony Orchestra, formed in 1913, was one of the first small city symphonies in America. It drew members of rival bands and orchestras, as well as proprietors of music shops and teachers. Salaries were fifty cents for a rehearsal and two and a half dollars for a concert. The Hippodrome Theatre donated rehearsal space; but the stage was cold and damp because the floor was scrubbed on Sunday mornings. (Butzing on any other day might be calamitous for vaudeville dancers and acrobats.) This was hard on instruments, affecting the sensitive brass especially. (Good alibi for clumsy fingers, though.) It was a minor problem, however, compared with the orchestra's struggle for survival throughout the years of depressions, wars, financial and personnel problems.

Yet, in the last half century, it has brought many famous soloists here. Its first great success was due to the appearance of the late Paul Althouse, a native, a Wagnerian tenor and member of the Metropolitan Opera. Today, Kenneth Riegel, another native, Metropolitan member and Wagnerian tenor, charms everyone not only with his rich voice but with his charisma.

Though television offers competition, many of us still prefer to be on the scene of action, which sometimes provides a human interest bonus. Several weeks ago when the symphony was featuring a group of New York City Ballet artists, the famous Jacques d'Amboise and his partner took tumbles within a minute of each other. Being professional, they recovered their poise at once and went on dancing. But before their next number, d'Amboise appeared with a can of detergent, explaining with the greatest savoir faire and humor as he went about sprinkling powder that there were trouble spots and he wanted us to get our money's worth. It's good to be reminded now and then that artists are human beings too.

By 1923 our orchestra not only employed fine musicians from out of town but some of our outstanding players were lured to college departments of music or big city orchestras. A good example is Edna Phillips, the harpist, once our neighbor, who studied with Salzedo in Philadelphia. When she was only twenty-two she became the Philadelphia Orchestra's first harpist under Stokowski—the first woman in the country to occupy a major "desk" with a symphony. She attained international fame as a soloist. Institutional teaching has never appealed to her, however; she has preferred private teaching and being consultant for master classes around the country.

I was Edna's first pupil. When she was sixteen and with our orchestra, her playing so intrigued me that I asked her if she'd teach me if I'd buy a harp. And never diffident, she agreed. With her radiant personality, I think she could make a harpist of a broomstick. Her luck with me was negligible, though, proven by my tiny daughter when I was practicing one day and let a pedal slip against the base of the harp. Phyllis looked up from her toys, frowned, and exclaimed, "Dirty racket!"

The Reading Musical Foundation, fifty years old, not only underwrites our symphony, but also an impressive list of other musical groups: Museum, Youth, and Pops concerts; Music in the Schools and musical scholarships; the

Reading Philharmonic Orchestra; the Star Series, bringing many superior artists here. And last but not least, our century-old Reading Choral Society, which sings difficult chorales and oratorios superbly. The sound of music is everywhere.

Another "universal language," appealing to the eye rather than the ear, is that of painting. Our most famous artist (if it's not hypocrisy to claim him) was Benjamin West, born in Swarthmore in 1734. He was taught by the Indians to use the reds and yellows they mixed for war paints. His mother furnished him with indigo, and hair from their cat for brushes. In his early days he was forced to paint tavern signs, as was Gilbert Stuart, his pupil later in London. The antique signboard on the King of Prussia Inn near Philadelphia reputedly was done by Stuart following an agreement that his name would not be divulged, though a square meal at the time was likely worth the ignominy.

None of our native Dutch artists have attained the fame of these giants. Two well-known nineteenth-century landscape painters were James Benade and Danny Devlan—studying under him, but mostly self-taught. Ben Austrian's forte was painting hens with little chicks—so downy that you want to squeeze them. He became famous for the chick on the Bon Ami scouring powder box with the slogan "Hasn't scratched yet!"

Christopher Shearer, a Tuckerton landscape artist I once interviewed, was lovable and wise. Though *The Faggot Gatherers* went for nearly eight thousand dollars at auction in Boston, and he once sold a painting to the German government and made "several small fortunes," he had many adversities. As his father wanted him to farm, like himself, Shearer often lived on bread and coffee in order to study with well-known European masters. For several years he was threatened with blindness. In old age he was content with a modest income from painting and raising vegetables, which he sold at market. (That must have pleased the ghost of his farmer father!)

But he'd once had a vivid dream portending that greatness was beyond him. Through a marble archway he saw a long table with glass globes of varying size under which were the busts of artists. Prominent were Michelangelo and Raphael, and far away was his own bust—under a very little glass. Beside it was that of Ben, an old schoolmate, an idiot and later a drunkard killed in a quarry. And Ben's glass was no smaller than Shearer's! "I saw myself as I really was," he told me, "and as I was meant to go down in history. Just medium." Yet, leaving his studio I was convinced that Christopher Shearer was a great human being.

Renowned for his exquisite bird paintings was Ernest Poole, curator of the Reading Museum and Art Gallery. Another bird lover, the late J. Randolph (Randy) Rowe, though hampered by arthritis, is known nationally for his wildfowl carvings and bird prints whose every feather vibrates. Yet normally he used only three colors: cadmium red medium, cadmium yellow, and ultra blue—tempered with black or white as needed. His work was represented in natural history and other museums around the country, and on nature magazine covers. His bald eagle is the official emblem of the National Rifle Association. Each year he painted the dog winners of the National Field Trial Association (sometimes from pictures but often from life), his work being presented as trophies. Versatile, as genius is prone to be, Randy recently did a series of commemorative bicentennial paintings, the first being that of a mid-eighteenth-century frontiersman.

I write affectionately of the late Ralph D. Dunkelberger who gave me my first art lesson, and was such a warm and understanding teacher. The class went into the country and I held in my trembling hand the first art tool I had used since the age of four when crayoning the wallpaper. That piece of charcoal seemed like a stick of dynamite! But Mr. Dunkelberger assured me that my clothesline with its shirts and diapers swinging in the wind was not only recognizable but "promising."

He was very patient for someone whose prints of local scenes had sold around the world. One of his best known is that of a small Dutch boy—*Pants Pockets Weather (Hösse-sock Wetter)*. As you may or may not know, this is the biting cold in which you stuff your numbed hands into your pockets for survival. In later years he painted portraits and murals. Illustrator of many books, he developed a lithographing process making his work unique in form and style.

We have had our share of perfectionists, including the picture framer to whom a friend of ours took a print of Pisa's *Leaning Miracle*. When the work was finished, Pisa was upright and adjacent buildings were on the bias.

Jack Coggins, book writer, illustrator, and landscape artist, favors boats and ships. He has lived in our area for many years and his work is highly valued along with that of many others, not native, who have made a distinctive contribution to our culture.

William Swallow came from the coal regions, but lived in Allentown most of his life and was a Dutchman among the Dutch. He was a fine, sensitive artist and teacher, doing some watercolors, but mostly ceramics, many with a modern touch. Until severely crippled with arthritis (proving fatal in middle age), he worked on large things. Afterwards, he made wall hangings of mosaic—a gorgeous butterfly being his masterpiece, I think. His work can be admired in many museums.

Practical as we Dutch are alleged to be, we have a lively interest in various media and accept with pride the auslander artists who have made their homes here. For instance, the fanciful marble sculptured animals of the late George Papashvily of Quakertown are found in many a Dutch home and garden, as well as in museums throughout the country. His work is beloved as was George, the man, for simplicity, humor, and an appeal to the child in us. (So is that of his wife, Helen, with whom he collaborated on their inimitable books of memoirs.)

Leonard Linauts, a native Latvian, is a stained glass artist who settled in our area many years ago. In his Mohnton studio he teaches his art to a few gifted apprentices. Not only our own churches but others throughout the east have been enriched by his exquisite windows, ranging from traditionally religious to abstract.

As to the art of writing, the Dutch were slow in getting started because our dialect was a deterrent for many years. But we were placid about it, like my son's schoolmate who was repeating his grade for the third time around. "You get to meet more kids this way" was his happy philosophy.

In our early days we too were satisfied with our lot. The settler had other work to do besides reading. Contributions were mainly those of spiritual leaders—dogma and hymns written in German.

After the Revolutionary war and the Compulsory Education Law of 1834, our first written dialect appeared in newspaper tales or jokes by natives. They were anonymous or with noms de plume; we Dumb Dutch had been conditioned to apologize for ourselves. But isn't it healthy that our own foibles could amuse us? In spite of our subsequent eminent scholars we continue to this day to relish dialect newspaper columns, magazine articles, and pamphlets. It's noteworthy too that most of them have been written by these very scholars, such as J. William Frey or Alfred L. Shoemaker. Preston Barba's Allentown column, "Pennsylfawnish Deitsch Eck," was a great favorite. For over thirty years Dr. Arthur D. Graeff's "Scholla" appeared in the Reading *Times* every other day and dealt with our folklore and legends. He was a serious historian also, and his work has been preserved by the Pennsylvania German Society of which he was once president, and which has published many volumes of well-researched material.

Before and after the Civil War, when auslanders began to notice us, we were still "on the inside looking out" as Dr. Earl Robacker has aptly phrased it. What seemed to intrigue strangers was stress on hexerei, superstitions, vulgarism, and so-called "struggle for riches." Unfortunately, most of us would rather hear derogatory tidbits about a person than hear of his virtues.

Within our own area, however, the bilingual reader began to be interested in literature, and educated Dutchmen felt the time had come to feature the praiseworthy in our culture and not the grotesque. The Reverend Henry Harbaugh, born in 1817, wrote short stories, novels, and poetry in both English and the dialect. His translations of *Pinafore* and *Rip Van Winkle* were an innovation. Adding to our stature was the Moravian clergyman J. Max Hart, also proving that a Pennsylvania Dutch literature could be developed, though Helen Martin, who really established the Dutch local color story, did more harm than good with her satirical writing. *Tillie, the Mennonite Maid* (1904) was a huge success (except in Pennsylvania!) and had twenty editions. However, Elsie Singmaster, her contemporary, was well beloved here for her hundreds of stories—some in national magazines—and historical novels. She is said to have idealized us "without departing from actual facts"; true, but I find her fiction two-dimensional, since she avoided our earthy and less pretty aspects. At the time, though, this was likely an advantage. Katherine Riegel Loose also dealt "fairly" with us in stories and novels. The popularity of novels (mostly by women) was on the upswing. (It's said that a novelist is a strange animal whose tail comes out of its head.)

During World War I anything German was anathema elsewhere, and this bitterness continued for years. Perhaps it was self-defense, or just the law of compensation, that made us cling to our culture. Playwrights were Clarence Iobst and Paul Weiand, who adapted English plays to the dialect and revived old folk games and dances. The Reverend Thomas R. Brendle also wrote plays and researched our folklore and customs. Debunking was still going on, of course. In 1934 Elmer Greensfelder's *Broomsticks, Amen!* about powwowers appeared on Broadway. *Papa Is All* was done by the Theatre Guild. This was the story of a family who escaped from Papa's tyranny, and both title and material were delusive. On the whole, the Dutch were still not understood and were either belittled or idealized.

In my opinion, Cornelius Weygandt's beautiful poetic books of essays did more to awaken empathy for the Dutch than any prior writing. He was born in Germantown and lived there for many years, teaching English at the University of Pennsylvania. Of his eighteen books, *The Red Hills* (1928), *The Blue Hills,* and *The Dutch Country* seem to be favorites. But all are a delight, and refreshing. "An ardent and spiritual friend of the Dutch," Weygandt claimed that the use of "Pennsylvania German" rather than "Pennsylvania Dutch" was due to pedantry or an inferiority complex.

Among other writers of this period were Ann Hark *(Hex Marks the Spot)*, Ella Maie Seiffert, Katherine Milhous, and Joseph Yoder, an Amishman whose *Rosanna of the Amish* furthered understanding of the Plain sects. The children's books of Marguerite de Angeli with her gentle prose and exquisite illustrations are classics. The library of any child, anywhere, is incomplete without at least her *Henner's Lydia* (Amish) or *Skippack School* (about Christopher Dock's era). In her eighties, she is still writing.

In the two world war eras, we produced some of the finest writing of our generation. Allentown's John Birmelin (after an early career of music) was an outstanding dialect poet and was said "to turn words into a music reflective of the Pennsylvania German soul." Being both religious and deeply human, his work had great variety. Historical material included "Regina Hartmann," "Der Paul Revere," and "Die Barbara Frietchie." He also made translations from Mother Goose rhymes and Robert Louis Stevenson's *A Child's Garden of Verses. Poems of a Reflective Nature* concern our spiritual, social, and political ills. "A Crooked World" evaluates our civilization from Adam and Eve, and on through Noah, Solomon, George Washington, Henry Ford, Hitler, Stalin, and Franklin Roosevelt, and deals with both man's virtues and failings. Birmelin was not without his sense of humor. "When I Go to the Movies" describes his vexation at a large hat in front of him and the rattling of candy papers. Then there's the homely little verse:

> *Regard once such a little mouse!*
> *It leads a domestic life.*

It lives happily in our house.
And does not strive for recognition.

A more famous poet was Wallace Stevens, also a lawyer and insurance executive. Though he was born here he lived most of his life in Hartford. He not only won the Bollingen and Pulitzer prizes in the 1950s but was a member of the National Institute of Arts and Letters, and was known internationally. The London *Times* called him the best American poet of his day, though he often mingled English and Dutch. Symbolism, abstraction, and comic irony in his work made it difficult for many to understand, but the obvious annoyed him. His unconventional use of words ("beachy" for beachlike) was intriguing, as was his sensitivity to color, sound, and texture. In "The Man with the Blue Guitar" he writes:

They said, "You have a blue guitar,
You do not play things as they are."
The man replied, "Things as they are
Are changed upon the blue guitar."

Two of his noted poems are "The Silver Ploughboy" and "Peter Quince at the Clavier." He was rightly considered "a stylist of unusual delicacy, with hypersensitive and ingenious imagination." His belief in self-searching, especially in his earlier poetry, has been called Vedantic or transcendental, but surely it is universal.

Conrad Richter, the novelist, and son of a minister, lived in eastern Pennsylvania as a youth; his books are also classics. When Donald Shenton wrote that a writer must know "the heart language of the Dutch and be able to carry across the barrier the subtlest shadings of feelings and character" he must have had Conrad Richter in mind. *The Free Man* (1943), about a German immigrant and his experiences as an indentured servant and escape to the frontier, is well worth reading. Though Pearl (Sydenstricker) Buck, daughter of missionaries, lived much of her life in China, we claim her as our most illustrious writer: she was born of German stock and finally settled in Bucks County where she lived until her death. She was the first American woman Nobel Prize winner. The Pearl Buck Foundation supports the organization she founded for Asian-American orphans who are free for adoption. For anyone attracted to our area I strongly advise that he read Fredric Klees's *The Pennsylvania Dutch* (1950); I never tire of reading it, backward or forward; it's comprehensive, warm as well as literary, and tinged with humor.

With interest on the part of others we took greater pride in our heritage. Family reunions increased. Our college students were less ashamed of their parents' earthy accent and began to research Dutch literature. Scribblers' clubs were formed and groups reviewing books, especially those with native background.

One small clique of elderly women I knew was unusually dedicated. On a blizzardy meeting day, the hostess and her valiant sister (president and secretary respectively) waited for someone else to show up. When the clock finally chimed its fatal "three," Mrs. B. briskly tapped the table and said, "The meeting will come to order. Will the secretary please read the minutes?" Her sister did. And though there was no review to be discussed, there were all those dainty sandwiches for comfort!

Due to our general literary excellence we are no longer the nation's stepchild. (Soldiers themselves may have won a few converts by sharing bologna or pretzels sent as far afield as Vietnam.) Local periodicals with a circulation beyond our area have long attracted tourists, many antiquers among them, who have discovered the charms of our crafts and way of life. Visitors buy Dutch cookbooks or specialty pamphlets like those of A. A. Aurand, and learn that all Dutch aren't Amish (or "Aim-ish," as the ignoramus calls it).

It seems, however, that everything about the Dutch can never be put on paper—the material is so rich and boundless. I recall the time when my small daughter peered seriously over my shoulder while I was writing. I said, "Lainey, would *you* like to write someday?" and, looking appalled, she answered, "Do you hafta?" But, of course, any other writer knows the answer. Writing has been called the disease for which there is no cure.

A contemporary poet (and novelist) of Dutch ancestry and international fame is Millen Brand. All his work is sensitive, but the years he lived on Crow Hill above Bally gave him the deep understanding to write his recent *Local Lives,* charming and beloved poems embracing numerous phases of Dutch life and history. A doting friend of mine keeps her copy on the bedside table along with her Bible.

The dynamic Byron Vazakas, another local poet, has written four widely published books. Many of his poems have appeared in magazines and anthologies. Byron too knows his Dutch, portraying us in a down-to-earth manner. When he hasn't been off giving readings or lecturing, I have often seen him browsing around town studying people—always keenly perceptive and feeling the deep undercurrents in what he calls "our air of permanence." I like this excerpt from his poem "Bivouac":

> *But bodies*
> *are war's numerals, a use, a*
> *tag, a disembodied act. And*
> *yet, each body, in desire,*
>
> *Is someone's wish, unique and*
> *beautiful.*

John Updike, a native Berks Countyan, is our current literary titan. Still in his prime, he continues his prolific output of novels, poetry, essays, dramas, and reviews and short stories appearing in the *New Yorker.* His first novel, *The Poorhouse Fair,* was based on our county almshouse, and was reviewed with excitement. It was variously called a sociological novel, a narrative poem in prose, and a novelist's novel, with its "multiple levels of meanings." Though some feel that Updike's work is self-conscious and contrived, it has rich imagery and sensibility, and is obviously the creation of a brilliant mind. He has just been elected to the American Academy of Arts and Letters, the greatest national honor for an artist.

How do our Dutch arts today compare with those in other parts of the country? Hard workers as we Dutch have always been, our time for "the finer things of life" has been comparatively recent. Yet we've always had a song in our hearts as we plowed, proven by our fine musical status.

Though creating lovely gardens still seems more vital to many than "fancy stuff with a brush," there is a growing number of art students. We may lean toward the graphic and not the abstract, though, like the farmer and his wife, urged to visit the museum where a granddaughter's work was being exhibited. Grandmom squinted at the painting and grunted to her man, "Vot iss it?" Grandpop: "I sink it gifs beans to ham all beat up vis eggs." Grandmom: "Ach, no vonder I got hiccups so sudden."

We may rebel too at foggy prose and pedantry. We're warm of heart and the writing that appeals is lucid, concerning home, morality, and nature. "Such wicked stuff that Leah reads—fit for the sewer," Lizzie Yoder explodes. "And it don't even haf an ending!"

It hurts that space hasn't allowed me to mention more musicians, painters, writers, and other artists whose work I either own or tremendously admire, and who deserve recognition beyond the distelfink country. For if our arts aren't always a reflection of national taste, they have supplied the needs of a small group who know that life can be rich, though simple.

Antiques-"Chust for So"

JUST WHAT IS AN ANTIQUE? IMPORTED THINGS, SAYS U.S. CUSTOMS, ARE ANTIQUES and duty-free if a century old or more.

In American antique shops, though, it seems the criterion is elastic in more ways than one. A woman examining a hammer was told that it had belonged to Thomas Jefferson.

"But it doesn't really look that old and worn," she challenged.

"Well, it's had three new heads and two new handles, madam," said the dealer, "but it's the original hammer."

The thrill of browsing in every antique shop in the countryside is that you never know what you'll come upon that, of course, you desperately need. It gets to be a hide-and-seek game, snooping through that conglomeration: shelves of glass and pewter; candle molds; paperweights; andirons; lamps and lanterns; pillow shams; coffee grinders; medals; someone's great-great-grandmother's portrait (who will know that it isn't your own?); or a down east schooner's figurehead—a bosomy, seductive Lorelei. But when you discover a candlestand with rough-hewn timber base, a water bench with low open shelves below and cupboard above, or a Brethren's love-feast bench-table, you know that you've found a real Dutch antique.

The furniture made by our rural settlers had little in common with that of the prosperous who could afford the vogues of the late sixteenth to the mid-nineteenth centuries: William and Mary, Queen Anne, Chippendale, Adam, Hepplewhite, Sheraton, Empire, and various Greek and Roman types. No four-poster beds, no mahogany desks, or grandfather clocks for the settlers. Utility was of prime importance; their work was sturdy with good materials and generous dimensions, like the heavy peasant pieces of Europe.

There's a Dutch quip about Pop saying to Mom, "Ve got to go to bed na—the company vants to go home." But the early settler, having struggled with nature all day for survival, must have collapsed on his pallet. No company for him! Even when cabins grew larger, upstairs rooms were devoid of anything but pallets for the growing family, though Mom's and Pop's bed might be built into the wall of the kitchen.

Acquiring a low, lumpy rope bed must have seemed a luxury. Along the side rails, at intervals of four or five inches, heavy rope was strung on wooden pegs to support the chaff bags (huge ticking sacks filled with straw, or perhaps leaves or cornhusks). As the rope had considerable give, Mom and Pop might collide in a valley; sitting up was sometimes the best way to get some sleep. It was an arduous task, too, to shake up and smooth out the sack each morning. The later luxury of a feather bed (comforter) brought from Europe might keep your knees warm and help your morale even if it didn't ease the spine. (When I was small I used to help my Grossmama plump up the feather bed and thought it a tremendous treat. She would always have to pant, "That's enough now.")

Until 1725, there were no bedsteads. But when beds were higher, children slept on a trundle bed pulled out from beneath the big one. Baby's hooded cradle was close beside Mom so she could easily suckle him at night. At the Springs Museum I saw a cradle so long and narrow I'm sure it must have been made for twins. No doubt howling double time when feet got tangled.

The first essential piece of kitchen furniture was the crude sawbuck table made of pine. Staunchly supported by a trestle with X ends, it often had rests running the length of the table for the feet of the weary laborer. At mealtime long benches were moved to the table from the walls or fireplace.

The settle, with arms and a high solid back, had a wood box below. The later settee was more graceful, but neither was made for long sitting. (As a Dutch woman said, "Benches are so 'near' for me because I sit so broad.") Much of the furniture besides the bed was built-in in those primitive days— benches, tables, and cupboards.

But the emigrant was always bent on bettering his new rugged life and when time and prosperity permitted, descendants of those who had learned from the Indians to make moccasins, canoes, and fishnets began to make more comfortable furniture. There were itinerant carpenters too. Many were excellent craftsmen, and though none had the finesse of Philadephia cabinetmakers, they adopted the more graceful lines of fashionable city ware. Often ingenious, they turned out some charming pieces. As sturdiness always came first, a clumsy ball foot or wooden spool-shaped knobs might give their origin away. (The Plain sects clung to the austere and bulky.)

By the early eighteenth century, the heavy Jacobean furniture lost favor, and gradually its features were simplified, influenced by William and Mary. Chairs had less height, the crest was replaced by a simple yoke, finials were discarded, carving was eliminated, and turning was simpler. However, it must have taken skill in those days to slump onto a chair and stay put!

Even by 1725, Reading and other Dutch towns were producing slat-back (ladder-back) and Windsor chairs. The former, like Chippendale, usually had rush seats but horizontal instead of upright slats. Posts, legs, and slats were gracefully curved, but as time went on, they became simpler and of lighter proportions, in Queen Anne style.

There were many adaptations of Windsor: loop-back or bow-back; fanback; comb-back; low-back; even writing armchairs. Having spindles, all were less heavy than the English type with its wide splat in the back, and were made of a combination of woods for strength. They were usually painted. By the end of the century there were even Windsors with bamboo turnings—legs, stretchers, and spindles being shaped and ridged like bamboo sticks. Turnery and joinery were of prime importance.

One can easily see why the Windsor chair, originally a peasant style and related to the German plank chair, was popular among our country folk.

The earliest rockers (nursing or sewing chairs) were made about 1738, and were slat-back. Benjamin Franklin is sometimes credited with first putting "rockers" on a chair (when did he have time for diplomacy!). Whether he added rockers to an old chair (often done later), or invented the rocker as we know it, is questionable; but the earliest are from Pennsylvania. (Personally, I think no household is complete without one. My greatest treasure has been my "rockaby" chair for children and grandchildren.)

Though rural furniture was simply made, oh, what paint could accomplish! By 1750, the Dutch gave full vent to their love of color and beauty. (After the Protestant Reformation, many must have missed the ornate richness of the churches. Then, too, homes in Germany had been dark with few windows, and if you "looked the window out" you saw the same bleakness across the way.) Large furniture was enlivened with paint and decoration (still customary in Bavaria and Austria). Most frequently used colors were the barn red (cheap and penetrating) and a soft gray blue often found on stools and wood-box settees, though also on doors, walls, and mantels. Dark brown was also popular. Paint mixed with linseed oil was thinned with turpentine or skimmed milk. Sources of dyes were primitive: reds from soil rich with iron; browns from natural or unburned earth; and blacks from lamp black, pulverized coal, or maybe peach stones. Decoration showed up best on paler shades, not used till later, however, when small things of daily use were ornamented too.

Many kinds of motifs were found. Stylized birds were often used, such as turkeys; peafowl; birds of paradise; eagles; birds shown beak to beak (usually doves); and distelfinks and parrots. (Parakeets from the Carolinas once invaded our southeastern counties.)

The heart symbolized God's eternal love (and likely that of a bridegroom for his bride). It was the tulip, though, that dominated household design. The bulb, brought to Holland by Dutch sailors in the middle of the sixteenth century, was accepted in Germany as a variation of the Holy Lily (in spite of stemming from those heathen Turks!). It soon became the symbol of conjugal love, fertility, permanence, home warmth, and peace and plenty. Used in threes, it was an emblem of the Trinity—and was even a charm against witchery. Both in realistic and stylized form, it is still the most popular Pennsylvania Dutch motif.

An artist friend of ours who has done intriguing things with Dutch designs had an amusing experience (to us, anyway!) when he joined the army. His sergeant asked one day if there were any painters in the company. Fred modestly raised his hand. He was assigned to splash gray paint on mess-hall walls. And I'll bet he did a good job of it, though he must have been tempted to add a tulip or two!

In the 1830s Jacob Maser, a cabinetmaker of the Mahontago Valley, made a limited amount of furniture of such superior quality that now nearly all is in museums. Though some pieces are massive, the smaller ones are less heavy than the farmers' work, and are distinctive as well as colorful. As a rule, on lower drawers, Maser painted tulips and angels; on shallow ones, birds and tulips. End panels had geometric designs. Daisies painted on the side of a cradle and probably heart-shaped cutouts on the ends labeled it "Mahontago."

Not long afterward, sets of six painted decorated chairs came into vogue. The most popular had a central splat or balloon back with stenciling. You may be under the illusion that all the painted furniture you see is necessarily Dutch. Many other foreign peasants decorated their furniture, and often in the same style. Though old furniture isn't often signed, the maker's name might be branded under the seat or elsewhere. But the real criterion of an authentic Dutch piece is the kind of native wood used, and not the motifs.

"Squiggling" became the fashion in the mid-nineteenth century. Though an original and unusual piece can raise the buyer's blood pressure, I'm glad one never fell to my lot. Personally, I think it's just plain "uckely" (ugly), as a Dutchman would say about a girl with a blotched complexion. The basic paint was smeared by fingers or a rag, corncob, comb, or the like, and hence dried in demented waves, rickrack lines, or whorls. This "art" was usually two-toned—brown and yellow, red and black, or, most commonly, red and yellow. Succeeding it was a comparable method called "graining." Cheap woods were used to imitate the finer grains of maple, mahogany, or rosewood in the furniture of the rich. Wood was "grained" or "marbleized" to get smoked effects with sponges, feathers, corks, or the soot of tallow candles. A shade more dignified than "squiggling," perhaps, yet often being over-yellow and brightly varnished it couldn't have looked like wood grain to the hungriest termite.

The kitchen of a monied rural settler may have had the comfort of a chair, but I doubt if it had a timepiece, though an occasional well-to-do immigrant brought one over from Germany. Pre-Revolutionary clocks were a luxury, despite their being made locally as early as 1725. The versatile Christopher Sauer made both case and works of a "superlative specimen," now in the Library Company of Philadelphia. (Often the cabinetmaker and mechanic were two different men.) In mid-century a handsome walnut tall case clock was made near Ephrata by Jacob Gorgas; it had sweet-sounding chimes and a repertoire of five hymns, one playing hourly. On the clockface were scenes of the Ephrata area. Not all good tall case clocks were of fine cabinet wood, some being of fruitwood or pine. Most soft wood clocks were originally painted, and are exceedingly rare. But usually all had metal dials, often chased with elaborate designs. The war temporarily put an end to clockmaking, however.

When clocks came into general use, dials with painted flowers or birds became so popular that brass dials lost favor. Above the dial, there were often changing moon phases, a rocking ship or other figure kept in motion by the swinging pendulum. Being custom made, no two clocks were alike. Some might be nine feet tall and have a second hand besides the hour hand. Tastes and pocketbooks varied. The dainty little grandmother clock, only forty to fifty inches tall, but built and shaped like the tall case clock, was best loved of all, though comparatively few were made here. All that most children today know of the old grandfather clock is the nursery rhyme:

> Hickory, dickory dock,
> The mouse ran up the clock.
> The clock struck one,
> And down he run,
> Hickory, dickory dock.

If you're hunting for an antique tall case clock, you'll be lucky if you find one by one of the famous Dutch makers: Daniel Rose, Christian Eby, John Bachman, Daniel Oyster, or Jacob Hostetter. And be prepared to pay plenty!

Now and then you may come across a clock with works of wood—used when metal wasn't available. But don't expect it to get you to the dentist on time: like "arthuritis," it is annoyingly sensitive to atmospheric changes.

A second category of old clocks is the shelf or mantel timepiece, a later Yankee product, but with tempting price for the frugal Dutchman who could choose between an eight-day or thirty-hour movement. It was often screwed to the wall. The reverse glass paintings on the lower panel of the door are delightful—gay with birds, historical scenes, flowers, or musical instruments. In mint condition—including decoration—it too can cost a tidy sum.

Among other kitchen wall hangings were small corner cupboards, candle sconces, and above the dry sink the mirror with shelf. There might be a spoon rack also, though this is not typically Dutch. An old Dutch proverb says, "A woman can throw out as much with a spoon as a man can bring in with a shovel."

The shovel (I hope) refers to the barn. And on your antique jaunts you will likely come across replicas of barn or hex signs. They vary greatly, and each bit of decoration within the circle, connoting eternity, is symbolic. The sun wheel (used by prehistoric man in caves in Sweden) suggests that the sun is of prime importance to life, and the average farmer will agree. A common barn sign is the pointed rosette, interesting to study. Twelve petals may indicate the months of the year, as well as resourcefulness; the two four-pointed stars, the seasons, or the four elements of the earth (as in astrology). Raindrops with their funny little tails signify abundance. And the circle's scalloped border (often seen) means smooth sailing through life. More than one barn sign is devoted to symbols of love in marriage—such as hearts, eagles, doves, distelfinks, and the tulip trinity.

If you don't believe that the barn sign is related to superstition, you'll contend that many Dutch came from Alsace where geometric designs were purely decorative; also, why would they appear only in a small Dutch area, mainly in the counties of Lehigh, Lancaster, Berks, Bucks, and Montgomery? If you do support the "hex" theory you'll counterargue: why were so many of the designs within "the witches circle" based on the number four and its multiples, a magic number in medieval and ancient mythology? You'll quote various scholars too. Didn't Dr. Cornelius Weygandt claim that a sign with seven lobes is powerful against all evil? And doesn't folklore say that a barn with six-pointed star will be protected against lightning? And that to keep the devil out, a white line should be painted around the barn door? Dr. John Joseph Stoudt (though "anti-hex") has written of other ploys that farmers used to keep the barn safe (and so why not the hex sign?). He says that as late as 1900 in the Kutztown area, domestic animals were kept from disease by small facsimiles of them placed within the barn. Moreover, in other areas, nailed to barn rafters, were triangular bits of paper with injunctions to the naughty, puckish house-spirit (Bucklich Männli) who could turn cream sour, cause the soup to boil over, or mislay a ladle you'd had in your hand just a second before. The barn warning might read: "Troll-head! I forbid you my house and cow-barn; I forbid you my bedstead" (or other things of value).

The amusing part of all today's controversy over barn signs is that if you ask a farmer why he has them, he'll just shrug and grin. Or he may volunteer, "Chust for fancy." At any rate, my guess is that you'll leave our countryside with a barn sign in your car trunk, and that it will be a conversation piece the next time you entertain.

Many quilt patterns resemble barn signs. Quilts were as much a part of the rope bed as the chaff bag, and many a Dutch Katie made what is now a precious heirloom. Though the patchwork quilts are said to have been used in India, China and Egypt before the time of Christ, the combination of patchwork and quilting is American. The crazy quilt, the earliest type, had small scraps of old material patched together. Warmth and not beauty was the goal; they were even used to keep drafts from doors and windows. Then came the appliqué quilt, with a design of one or more materials applied to a background of solid color. Homespun was rarely combined with cotton, or silk, as the effect was not only incongruous but one material wore out before the other. Sometimes, though, homespun was used as background. Quilts appliquéd with larger scraps usually had fewer patterns. A work of art kept for guests was the plain white quilt made entirely from designs finely sewn on the background: there might be as many as fifteen to twenty stitches per inch. The brick, ribbon, Roman stripe, and log designs were popular. There was also the cross-stitch quilt, stemming from early needlework days when motifs were outlined in red against a white background, as in "show" towels. Not so desirable as others, yet some are most elaborate and effective.

A freedom quilt was sometimes made for a young man coming of age, or freed of indenture or apprenticeship. In memory of a deceased woman, friends might quilt scraps of her dress materials, a touching memorial for her family. In making an album or friendship quilt, women contributed patches (often initialed) they had made to be part of the whole.

Our country's history is written not only in books, but in quilts. Betsy Ross "pieced" the red and white stripes of the first star-spangled banner together, and appliquéd the stars on their background. Frontier designs had their day with "bears' claws," turkey tracks, flying geese, tomahawks, and other designs. A common Civil War pattern was the Union quilt, with eagles appliquéd in each corner and an eight-pointed star between. In the center was a star surrounded by two circles of triangular patches. Many presidents were honored by quilt patterns like "Washington's Puzzle," Madison's "Hexagon Star," and Cleveland's "Lilies." Near the turn of this century, with more prosperity, it was the rage to use silk and velvet patches, ornately stitched together with silk floss. Certainly not so practical or enduring as their forerunners and likely used as throws on couches for madam's nap. Gay Nineties quilts featured political, operatic, or other public figures.

Quilting is complicated, as there are three planes bound together at the edges: the top with design; a bottom of muslin or other durable fabric; and a filler of cotton or wool batting between. (A worn-out quilt with good wool batting can be used as a filler.) Lizzie Yoder says it took her mother twenty-five years to make one quilt, worked on only when the children were asleep. "Mom said she sewed all her thoughts into it and fretted at what that quilt knew about her." Another woman (with fewer children, no doubt) claims to have made more than a hundred and fifty in her lifetime.

Border designs alone (and there are many varieties, including the chain, rope, and running feather) can be intricate and time consuming.

If you want to buy an authentic old Dutch quilt it's best to go to a trustworthy dealer. There are good quilts still available, many of which have never been used, though they may have slight discoloring from folding and long storage, and even a rust spot or two. But don't expect your "find" to fit your queen-sized bed; it was likely made for the era of shorter, squarer rope beds or four-posters. The price you pay will depend on the fineness of stitching and the quality of the cotton, which varied over the years. Before the cotton gin in 1792, cotton had many seeds, obvious if a quilt is held up to the light. After 1850, there were few seeds, if any.

Don't forget too that a dealer will know more about the origin of a quilt than you do, unless you're a connoisseur. Quilts were made in all the colonies. Each area had its forte. Southern belles had been taught to "sew a fine seam" as well as to capture hearts; patterns of New England maidens were more original (were bachelors scarcer?); and naturally those energetic Dutch girls made more difficult geometric designs, and if colors were more gaudy, so were their emotions. Yet they too knew how to do fine stitching, for which they were famous. Challenging were the "Rising Sun" in pieced work and "Flower Garden" in appliqué. Since book learning for women was despised, what greater bait for marriage than a dowry of many quilts?

"Katie's eighteen and feels to get *G-Heirut* [married]" must have been said as often then as now. But a hundred years ago, if she didn't have at least a dozen quilts stored away, her chances were slim. When *he* had said the magic words, the bride's quilt was begun, and since time was of the essence, neighbors were paid to help. Fingers flew; merriment abounded. There was furtive guessing as to who would be making the next bride's quilt, often the Rose of Sharon pattern. But a sure test was to have four unwed girls shake the corners of a quilt with a cat in the middle, and the girl nearest the spot from which the cat jumped out was the lucky one.

A dowry spread was a bonus. A small disk of colored material with raw edges turned over was sewn on a circular piece, then pulled into the shape of a little cup. Many disks were sewn together before the spread was given a background and lining.

Early hand-loomed coverlets of flax or wool were geometric in pattern; later ones were gay with floral patterns of striking size and brilliance. If you'd like to try one, consult one of the early pattern books (some in the archaic German of the early nineteenth century). You may get instruction on making dyes too, such as the mixing of solution of tin, indigo, tartar, and nut oil to create a lovely blue. Around the 1830s there was less home weaving, for professionals with Jacquard looms moved them from place to place, producing a greater variety of patterns.

Katie's dower chest stored not only quilts, but sheets, bolsters, show towels, and other needlework. The term "dower chest" is loosely used, only that with the bride's initials deserving the name. It is one of our earliest forms of furniture, first having the ball foot used by the Holland Dutch and no drawers. Sometimes there was a secret inner drawer and compartments at the end. Locks were simple; who would steal work so easily identified as Katie's? Of all Dutch furniture, chests are the most avidly sought for. The earliest are unpainted, usually of cherry or walnut, and are rare. Some have inlay of a

wood with contrasting color. Now and then one is seen with checkerboard design, or the smoked effect used mostly in southeastern Pennsylvania.

Having most appeal are the painted chests of pine or tulipwood, charmingly decorated like Katie's. (Backs of chests were seldom if ever painted. Once when I insisted that my small son wash the back of his neck, he grumbled, "But it doesn't show.") Front, top, and ends were embellished with stylized birds, foliage, and flowers. In reverence for the Song of Solomon's pomegranate, both its fruit and bloom were used. Except for the tulip, it is the most prevalent motif, symbolizing fertility and plenty. Despite its yellow-streaked flower, petals are often mistaken for those of the rose. On the lid of the chest may be written: "Peter Kalm made this chest on the 8th of March in the year of 1785."

Though chests vary in size, a typical one is about four feet long, two feet wide and high, and has four legs, a hinged top, and one to three drawers. With the coming of itinerant artists, some with rare skill like Heinrich Otto, the owner's initials and date might be inscribed on the back, and usually the maker's name was added, though not always. Often as good as a signature was the method of joinery, use of wooden pins, cutting of dovetails, type of hinge, and kind of motif. Typical of the nineteenth century were bracket feet, geometric designs, and greater simplicity of pattern.

Each county specialized in a different type of chest and embellishment, though tulips were used everywhere. Lancaster chests had moldings and pilasters, and three panels painted with birds, flowers, and stars. Distinctive of Lebanon chests are three drawers and arched panels supported by columns. Dauphin County was prone to use two panels designed with urns overflowing with flowers or foliage. A rare Bucks County chest has the initials of both bride and groom, and 1771. Most chests with painted decoration can be traced to southeastern Pennsylvania. Those of Berks County show more skill than most, favoring a middle panel painted with two confronting unicorns (protectors of maidenhood). Its richly painted chests had two bottom drawers. Unfortunately, as a chest was often kept at the foot of the bed and used as a chair while dressing, the lovely design may be worn and faded.

Whatever their age or condition, chests are in constant demand. I once overheard the choice conversation of some westerners in an antique shop here. Mom: "Let's get this chest for Peg—she'd adore it!" Pop: "How long do you think the money's going to last?" Mom: "But Dutch things are so much cheaper here than in Frisco—and the more we buy the more we'll save."

If Katie's bedroom boasted a hooked rug it was likely made by Mom. Materials for the rug came from her *lumba sock* (rag bag). Mom had long ago washed a burlap bag, ripped it apart, and fastened it to a rectangular wooden frame. The clamps she used were hand forged, with a tiny heart atop each screw. She was proud of her cardboard pattern, made by great-Aunt Becky. Pulling the long strips of cloth from bottom to top with the coarse crochet needle made her rheumatics jumpy; but Katie was a good girl, and she'd be sorry to lose her. And the final pattern showed up so pretty with its many, many little loops! It was even prettier when she fancied it up at both ends with tassels of yarn the same colors like those in Katie's Schrank.

Katie's Schrank (big wooden wardrobe), like her dower chest, was exuberant with tulips, distelfinks, pomegranates, and leafy tendrils on the three long drawer fronts. Someday her daughter would have a Schrank of walnut, with tulips carved on the corner stiles of the top, and perhaps between the doorheads the Teutonic double eagle bearing an American shield. This later era was partial too to carved beaded edges and detail of treatment at the corners, and maybe an original touch of brass buttons for drawer pulls. The Dutch joiner saw no shame in copying what appealed to him in Chippendale, Sheraton, or whatever, and adding what suited his fancy.

Another kind of Schrank, the kitchen dresser, was of seventeenth-century design, but had open shelves above (some with spoon rack) and drawers and a cupboard below; later when it acquired dignity as a "china cupboard," glass doors protected the teacups, small top drawers were used for cutlery, and large ones below for linens. An unusual type in the Chippendale style was a china cupboard on a chest, a number of which were made in Lebanon County. As the Dutch say, "The top of the bottom is the bottom of the top."

Thinking of the old Dutch kitchen with its Schrank, doughtray, crusted iron kettles, and cumbersome utensils recalls a lecture I once attended at the Metropolitan Edison Company. One member of the Home Economics department demonstrated all the newest electrical equipment and gadgets. Wonderschoen! But displayed at the front of the room were kitchen antiques: a glass lemon juice squeezer, a wooden rolling pin; a can opener, and many other treasures. My neighbor whispered, "What's that thing with the two big blades and handle?" ... "That's for chopping onions and nuts." ... "And that big billy club?" ... "A potato masher," I said in consternation, and when she giggled I added tartly, "Most of those things are in my kitchen now—and I use them!" I turned my attention to the newest electric stove, for which I refuse to trade in my mammoth gas dodo: it not only has two roasting ovens, but a warming oven! This marvel has made me resist the pleas of my daughters down through the years, though they make me feel I'm living in the age of the old ten-plate stove.

The early iron stove plate is much in demand (especially by those with a walk-in fireplace in which to display it). For as with most things, the German knew how to combine practicality with beauty. The plates were cast in open sand molds into which a pattern had been pressed. It might be the traditional heart and tulip design (flanked by Roman columns, oddly enough). Or it might be a depiction of Cain slaying Abel, both well girt as warriors; yet whom was there to fight except each other? (Reminiscent of the two men stranded on a desert island who made a living taking in each other's washing.)

Other biblical motifs were immensely popular too, including the Garden of Eden, which appeared on much other folk art. Naturally there were the serpent and the tree, and probably a pomegranate. In many ancient beliefs, the serpent symbolized immortality—the shedding of its skin indicating rebirth. As to Adam and Eve, they raise the perennial question: did or did not Adam have a navel? The answer could be evaded by Eve's long flowing hair, but was more difficult with Adam. With no navel, of course, he would be an imperfect human being. Yet, would God create parts without a purpose? Any theologian or painter has a right to his own opinion, and Michelangelo when painting the Sistine Chapel gave Adam a navel. Not all motifs were religious. Some stove plates had dancing scenes, animals, soldiers, and, later, classical themes.

Whether you're interested in stove plates or mirrors, you'll likely want to stop at every flea market, country auction, auction house, and antique shop you see. They are legion, and attended by all classes of people—natives and auslanders, the serious and the curious, the halt and the lame, the old and young (except perhaps for the recent collectors of beer cans). Ever since Henry Ford and Henri du Pont popularized Dutch antiques, it's been said, "Whatever is good enough for Ford and du Pont is good enough for me!"

Most flea markets are in a class with the filthy city hole-in-the-wall secondhand shops where you'll get less than you pay for. Since country farm and house auctions are usually held in February or March while farmers still have time before planting, you'll not just shiver but find only a useless milk can, battered chest, or cracked wash basin not worth a bar of soap. (Unless, of course, you can find a needle in a haystack.) Auction houses may have bargains, but it's an advantage to be native and know the reputation of the auctioneer as well as that of the collection's owner. Prices at estate sales can be surprisingly high or low, depending on publicity given, the number of interested bidders, and, oddly, on family sentiment. There may be a stop price on some seeming trifle, which a long-dead bride received from her bridegroom. Don't forget too that if anything rare is for sale, the dealers will be there full force to outbid you.

Ask yourself a few honest questions before investing in what you think is a bargain. Can you tell when a chest has been refinished or restored? If its brass drawer pulls are original? Do you know how brown the unpainted underside of a century-old chair should be? Can you distinguish between a dower chest made by one of the German immigrants in New York State, influenced by New England, from one made in Berks County? And as to that baby's high chair you yearn to buy—does it show wear, or was it one of a journeyman's samples of various types of furniture made on a small scale for children?

If you can't answer these questions and innumerable others you'd better go to the reputable antiques dealer who knows a fake when he sees one, or, if he doesn't, will express his doubt. You can rely on his long experience—his wisdom and judgment. There are many such dealers in our area, too many to recommend.

There is one place, however, too colorful to neglect, and that is Hattie Brunner's at Rheinholds, visited by thousands of people from all over the country. "Old Hattie Brunner" (since her death the place is run by her daughter-in-law, "young Hattie") began the business, and was soon known as a "character." Veteran buyers were warmed by her hearty welcome, coffee, and shoofly. (Newcomers might be offered pretzels and candy.) All visitors were so intrigued with her brusque, humorous talk (in Dutch, if you knew it) of folk art, people, politics, and random subjects that they almost forgot what they came for. In spare time, while "Mister" (Brunner) kept his store, Hattie did watercoloring. She also sang contralto in Swamp Church. But her great love was antiques, and she was never too busy to give detailed information on anything that caught your fancy. Her enthusiasm was infectious. The old house, even the bedrooms, was crammed with treasures, for Hattie never missed an important auction. Several small barns took care of the overflow—the high-seated splat-back spinning chair, the colonial loom, the three-legged stool, and all their descendants.

You asked if she might have a low-seated poplar bench such as was placed at the front of a cart for driver and passengers.

"Vy, shuah," was Hattie's quick reply. "The cane ain't in mint condition—but it's got the heart cut out on the back."

Though Hattie was kind and compassionate, she was shrewd. You couldn't talk her into a bargain. She knew the value of what she had and that in a few years you would likely get much more for your wagon seat than what you paid. "Young Hattie" carries on the tradition.

Since the antique craze is constantly growing, be wary of what you buy, and especially of *where* you get it. In more ways than one, many an amateur gloating over Pennsylvania Dutch "bargains" has "bought himself poor."

Antiques - Mainly "for Fancy"

BESIDES THE PROFESSIONAL DEALER, THERE ARE SEVERAL CATEGORIES OF collectors. Many a shrewd financier, knowing that a fine antique's value grows with age, invests in an old Dutch chest when the market is low and sells when it jumps. No heart pang involved in the parting, either. It has served its purpose.

Then there's the collector who buys because it's the "smart" social thing to do. When a friend of mine moved into a fashionable New York suburb she sold everything she owned and started from scratch to stock her new Georgian house with Georgiana. Literally—from salt cellars and inkstands to draperies (with the help of a decorator, of course). She made just one concession—electricity. But she died of a heart attack before she could enjoy her museum. As it was perfected, she likely wouldn't have enjoyed it anyway.

Her opposite is one who buys what strikes her fancy, though *where* on earth to put it? She has two settees now and still prefers sinking down into her comfortable old divan. Her house has as many periods as the page of a book. But what fun she has at auctions! At least, she isn't like the old hag beside her who buys only for the excitement of winning the bid. I class them both as "hetero-maniacs."

The monomaniac has an obsessive hobby. He may collect old keys, picture frames, or perhaps vest-pocket toothpick holders. If his wife's lucky, his mania won't take up too much space, like those stove plates of their neighbor.

Today, however, there are no more bargains, though the little Betty lamp hung on nearly every old fireplace mantel. Wrought-iron heart and tulip door latches (often taken along by a family that moved) are desirable, as well as key plates, door pulls, and cock's head hinges. Nearly impossible to find is the long-legged wrought-iron stool with a heart or other cutout on the seat. Some of the most beautifully executed tulips in iron are found in barn hardware or weighty stove plates. Cast-iron waffle irons, muffin or quick-bread pans are also scarce.

By the early 1600s copper things were made here by trained European workers. But production, compared with that of iron, was small, as the metal was hard to come by. Much "recycling" was done. A copper-framed lantern with blue glass is a treasure like the brass spirit lamp with wide candlestick base. (More common candle lanterns are of wood and glass, or glass and tin.) Though there were copper baking pans, pudding molds with the lovely sheaf of wheat or corn design, colanders, kettles, warming pans (partly brass), the best specimens of copper work, such as weather vanes, were for outdoor use.

Some of the copper apple butter kettles held as much as thirty gallons. Vessels in which food had to stand for any length of time were coated with tin because of metallic poisoning. (Once we nearly died of ptomaine after a wedding for which the chicken salad made the day before was kept in a copper pot.) You can distinguish between early foreign and American copper by the way the sheets of copper have been cut out for soldering. Americans made the "Wall of Troy" joint, similar to the slightly angled dovetailing of the cabinetmaker.

Tinware was commoner and cheaper in the first half of the nineteenth century, and better adapted to kitchen ware—kettles, dippers, nutmeg graters, and many other utensils. Moravians used tin molds for their marzipan (and tin too for their three-dimensional stars). Cottage cheese molds, usually found in the form of tulip, diamond, heart, or circle, are popular today. Cookie cutters are coveted by museums, historical societies, dealers, and private collectors. Most cutters are tin, though there are rare exceptions in the deep Dutch countryside: brass; redware pottery; whittled wood, or wood with tin cutting edges. Cutters date from 1800 to machine-made products appearing in the early 1900s. Factors determining age are design, and quality of tin and solder. Cutters of early tin, not highly refined, are heavy and badly rusted. Early solder was thick and applied in dabs. What once could be bought for a dime now costs a hundred and fifty dollars or more, especially if designs are unusual like the Victorian heart and hand. Common are tulips, birds, hearts, and animals. Earl Robacker collected a thousand cookie cutters—and no two identical!

Pierced tin was not only decorative but practical. For instance, scalded curds were poured into the cheese mold, allowing the whey to drain and the rest to make a lovely pattern. Bigger perforations were made with hammer and chisel. Others, very small, no doubt were made with hammer and nail (on pie cupboards, for example). The eagle is much favored, but found most

often is the star. Geometric designs were easiest to make, though few artists were skilled at making animals or flowers. One cupboard is even known to have George Washington's silhouette on two of its panels. Air entered the pie safe through the design and kept fresh the week's supply of baked goods. Smaller cupboards had ropes, which lowered them to and from the ceiling. Few old ones are left. These are apt to be rusty from moisture or have heavy overcoats of paint, concealing the perforations. Lids of bureau boxes, candle sconces, lanterns, mirror frames, and other things were pierced "chust for fancy." Actually, all "tin" objects were tinplate, a thin sheet of iron having been dipped into a vat of molten tin and coated. Some pieces are signed, others are dated, and a few have the location of the maker.

Toleware is the lovely but delicate little sister of the tin family. Japanning gave her a luminous look. Motifs of bold colors, even emerald green, were painted on the background—usually brown, and seldom blue, green, or yellow, so your hunt may be for red. Decoration is simple and concentrated. You find fat tomatoes (those poisonous love apples of old) on large measuring cups, coffee or tea pots; two-petaled exuberant tulips on apple or "coffin" trays (for coffee or tea pots); peaches on canisters and tea caddies; and a yellow and black distelfink on large mugs or coffeepots. Naturally, you don't ask delicate little sister to brew coffee. You shouldn't even dust her often, for her paint is apt to fleck away, and she doesn't like change of climate or handling. Yet tole was often used for things like pin trays, saltshakers, nutmeg graters, children's drinking cups, boxes with flat or trunk tops, document boxes, and tea caddies. Hence it's a thrill to find any one of these in mint condition.

There are few tinsmiths left. Alliene de Chant wrote twenty years ago about Charles Wagenhurst of Kutztown, a fourth-generation craftsman whose grandfather worked at his trade in winter and took off in spring in a covered wagon drawn by two mules to peddle his wares in the Blue Mountains. He had everything a farm wife or her man could want: cookie cutters, dish pans, sieves for cleaning lettuce, cottage cheese strainers, cone-shaped cemetery vases, coal oil lanterns, coal buckets, and pig scrapers. There were even tin initials to put on feed bags. Delayed by all the news to be shared en route, he must have felt like the little Dutch boy who said, "The hurrier I go the behinder I get."

Good old pewter, made of 80 percent tin and 20 percent copper, lost favor with all but the poor when silver cheapened. (At the cost of pewter today, you expect it to be made of silver and platinum.) It must have been a boon, though, to those whose tableware had been all of wood—used on both sides and often hacked to pieces with knife blades. Yet pewter had its failings too; being soft, it could stand only moderate heat and was sometimes cut or broken. Often a piece was melted down and replaced with a new one; during the Revolution, of course, it was made into bullets. Most pewter was imported, so there were few Dutch artisans. The twelve surviving fine pieces (verified by touchmarks) of Johann Christopher Heyne are sugar bowls, plates, whiskey flasks, and two Communion flagons in Lancaster's Trinity Lutheran Church. All authentic Dutch pieces bring big prices.

Since the British taxed American pewter, a misleading "London" may be seen in the trademark of certain pieces. There is a considerable amount of early Philadelphia pewter available with "Love London." The "Love" is thought to refer to the City of Brotherly Love. (Would that idealism could be realized!)

The following quandary was obviously that of a poor damsel with a lady's instincts:

Jeb is young and gay and good
And sends my heart a-flutter.
But all his table-wear of wood
Must spoil the taste of butter.

Sam is old he must be thirty.
Hansome strong and very clever.
Pewter tho looks pockt and dirty
And polishing takes forever.

Mose is deaf and has a crutch.
His palsy makes me quiver.
But Mose eats pap from Gaudy Dutch.
And pores his tea from silver.

Dear oh dear which one to marry?
Love is painfully contrary!

A modern pewterer of Lititz is Jay Thomas Stauffer. His touchmark is distinctive—a spread-winged eagle in a medallion with J.T.S. beneath it and stars around the border. His pieces are often mistaken for valuable antiques, as they have an old-fashioned, battered look. Though he has a simple shop at home and works alone except for an apprentice son, he's been commissioned to do limited edition plates for various institutions, and much restoration work for the state of Pennsylvania. Museums have sought him out to make unique reproductions, such as George Washington's inkstand and a key to Philadelphia's Independence Hall (he had the original key to work from). His unhurried work is beautifully done—the kind that is lasting. That's more than can be said for old nineteenth-century pewter when the alloy was so inferior that the word "pewter" was replaced by Britannia (largely tin).

Many buttons were made of pewter but all varieties seem to have a fascination for collectors, especially women. How many times our restless children were given the button box to play with! I can see them fingering with wonder and delight the discards from family suits and dresses. A hundred years from now these may be collector's items too.

During excavations of Indian villages along the Susquehanna, many metal buttons have been found, which we likely traded along with other gewgaws for furs. Back in 1750 brass buttons were advertised by Casper Wistar. As he was famed for his glassworks, no doubt he made some of the old buttons of opaque white, or the clear black, red, blue, green, or aqua of molded glass "that glow like quartz crystals in the light." Some had glass centers with tin background. Eagled brass buttons are hard to find, but so are many others of old silver, cloth, shell, or even wood. It's not unusual for a collector to ferret out any ancient clothing, hoping to find a set of twelve French buttons, worth a fortune. Another may have no desire for anything but those of historic or commemorative interest. Still another may be lured only by pictorial buttons of the nineteenth century or those of the Victorian era depicting all phases of life—events, politics, operas, poems, even legends. But lowly buttons of horn or bone were more prevalent in the Dutch country. The Crouse family of Reinholds made them for many generations until a factory fire some twenty years ago. The last horn comb and button factory in America.

I once "manufactured" a button that had innumerable collectors greedy with excitement. Having read about eighteenth-century buttons while doing research for *One Red Rose Forever,* I felt that the glamorous Baron Stiegel deserved something remarkably splendid. After publication I had a polite but suspicious letter: "I am president of the National Button Society, and having a large collection, I am curious to know where you got information on the unique button you described on page two-seventy-six." Caught, and still squirming. But reformed.

I made no deviations in describing Stiegel's glass, however, much of it typical of its day. He produced the first flint glassware for table use in the colonies, equal to Europe's finest. Pure and even in color, it was made in a variety of shades, among them green, amethyst, amber, clear white, and opaque white. Blue, obviously his favorite color, was dominant at Manheim. It's said that many Dutch thought his azure blue baptismal font would ward off whooping cough or serve as a charm against the evil eye.

Never one to do things by halves, Stiegel brought over workmen from various foreign countries, but as his glass was not made as a luxury it supplied the common trade for a dozen years or so. The rare enameled pieces so cherished by today's collectors were made by Swiss workmen. Typical designs are foliage, flowers, animals, and birds, mainly the rooster and parrot. The English made wineglasses. The specialty of the Rago Brothers from Venice were the diamond and daisy-in-the-square patterns. Individual too were styles of cream jugs, jiggers, pitchers, decanters, cruets, bottles, domed and footed urns, and vases, all sold as far away as Baltimore, New York, and Boston. (Curiously enough, Stiegel was never known to have blown a single piece of glass himself.)

As his ware was widely copied by competitors and former employees, it's exceedingly hard today to know which is genuine. Museum curators say that if a piece was in the same family before 1910 (when we imported Bohemian glass) and that if fragments from the Manheim factory compare favorably with it, it is authentic. Some experts say that it has a special "ring" when the rim is tapped, but you must have an inner ear to hear it. Others claim that they can tell by "the feel." An honest dealer will tell you that an item is "Stiegel type."

Though enameled blown glass bottles were made by Stiegel, they were also imported from Holland, filled with gin or cordials. Antique bottles (even without contents) seem to have a special appeal for many people. A real old-timer is the harvest ring (a pottery container) slipped over the arm and carried to the fields for the ersatz coffee break, the *Essich Schling* (a draft of sugar, water, and vinegar). If you enjoy acquiring things that range in size, the "chestnut" blown glass flasks of the eighteenth century can be an absorbing challenge. Their capacity varied from a gill to over five gallons. Amber pressed glass flasks were very common, with many kinds of designs, the eagle being the favorite. Vinegar, molasses, and suchlike were kept in large glass carboys, about a foot high, that held ten quarts. At the rate molasses was used, however, they must have needed frequent refilling. Wicker covers for glass bottles (to reduce breakage) often showed much artistic imagination. Collecting bottles and drinking mugs is often combined. Those of redware pottery are quite rare, as regular tipplers usually left their mugs at a tavern the way the later Victorians kept their shaving cups at the barbershop.

Redware is as typically Dutch as anything you can find, since only Pennsylvania soil had just the right amount of iron in the clay to give the pottery its distinctive red. However, as pottery made along the whole eastern seaboard had many common characteristics, Dutch redware may be hard to distinguish. Some pieces have changed hands often since colonial days. But if you buy at a country auction, you can be fairly certain you have the "real McCoy." Original pieces have been snapped up fast, and may cost you around a hundred dollars. Later redware, if made to hold liquids, was glazed inside; if merely ornamental, it was totally glazed. Colors vary: yellow, brown, green, black, cream. Many Dutch potters dug their clay on their own or nearby farms. Products of Henry Moll of Shoemakersville were not only useful but fancy—flowerpots, spittoons, bowls. One potter even operated a brickyard, and made roof tiles. Slipware is a term for redware pieces molded, but not fired with superimposed designs. These were added later over a coat of transparent glaze. A "slip cup" had openings into which quills were fitted and from which the liquid clay flowed out to ornament the pottery. An old and well-known design is the rider on the white horse, called "Faithful and True" (from Saint John's Revelation).

The pie plate *(boi-schlissel)* was of heavy clay made in a variety of sizes up to fifteen inches in diameter, and having no bottom rim. Often the edges were cogged and the whole might be plain or have slip or sgraffito decoration. (Pieces vary today from a few dollars to a four-digit figure.)

Sgraffito was usually more elaborate than slipware. The clay was given a thin white coating and designs were etched in freehand with sharp instruments deeply enough to reveal the red beneath. Further color might be added with a slip cup. Much of this early pottery had simple religious motifs. But later mugs, vases, covered jars, pie plates, and other pieces could be quite ornate, with moral or philosophical inscriptions, or a bit of humor like "I should much prefer to live as a bachelor than to give my wife the pants." Most sgraffito was made in Pennsylvania, and until the 1830s, when it passed out of favor, much was dated. It is the rarest and most expensive of Dutch pottery, and it's been said that "you may search an entire lifetime and not find a piece worth acquiring."

Stoneware, or salt glaze, soon became popular. Though made from a number of clays, it has a gray-white surface, grainy finish ("orange peel glaze"), and blue decorations. Fired at twenty-one hundred degrees, all other colors but blue (from oxide of cobalt) were baked out. Though weighty, it's usually well proportioned. Artwork may be crude, the simplest designs being flowers, plume sprays, or feathers. A rare find boasts a word or two. The potter's name doubles the price, of course, and pieces signed by Moyer, Weston, or Cowden are highly desirable.

"Gaudy Dutch" was imported from Staffordshire, but being found so seldom out of Pennsylvania, was given this misnomer. A soft-paste chinaware, with a pretension to elegance, it was sometimes called "the poor man's Crown Derby." Made for the Dutchman's taste, it was brightly decorated with peacocks, tulips, roses, et cetera. There are at least a dozen Gaudy Dutch patterns (all resembling Crown Derby), but collectors vie for the dove, oyster, vase and especially the butterfly—the rarest. Large ware like platters and vegetable dishes is the easiest to find. Small pieces were often given as Sunday-school prizes for perfect attendance, and no doubt sold for ten or fifteen cents. Many local potters couldn't meet the competition and had to give up business.

Gaudy Welsh, which had finer qualities of proportion, line, and color, and made lavish use of gilt, was often used for tea services. The best pieces resemble Royal Worcester. "Cabbage Rose" is said to be the oldest pattern, but very popular too among collectors is the strawberry and King's Rose. Roses mean elegance to many people. Many years ago, when I published *One Red Rose Forever,* I agreed to give a talk at a country Rotary Club dinner. When the committee chairman came to discuss arrangements with me he asked if I'd be willing to pass out a red rose to each wife present, "chust for fascination."

Spatterware comes still closer to being really fine pottery. Usually the center had a hand-drawn design, surrounded by dabs or spatter dots. Sponge blue is so rare that if you do find a piece you may have to pawn the family jewels to buy it.

There's an element of sleuthing in hunting for real chalkware. (This by the way is not chalk, but plaster of Paris.) Originating in Italy where figures of the Madonna and other religious objects were made, it was eventually sold in the Rhineland, and thence reached Pennsylvania in the eighteenth century. Here, however, instead of making devotional objects, we created forms from everyday life: animals, birds, bowls of fruit, buildings, busts, portrait medallions, and watchcases for the wealthy. Usually, two molds cast for front and back were cemented together (leaving the middle hollow), and painted with oil, watercolor, or whatever was handy. At the time, colors were more or less realistic, but were liable to flake off easily. Fruit pieces may only have a front and are mounted on a stand to give a bowl effect. The rare church façade is highly prized. As all chalkware is essentially fragile and susceptible to faking, dealers are reluctant to stock it.

Here are some important clues for sleuthing for chalkware. First, are you sure that adorable little poodle is hollow? The base of a top-heavy piece was often plaster-filled for stability. If you find a deer without the tip of an antler missing, are you suspicious? Much in demand, likely he'd have been grabbed up long before you see him. As a novice, you may find an especially appealing cat except for its leprous look—and be inspired to give it a face-lift. Don't try it. Chalkware is porous, and a new color can spread alarmingly, even loosening other paint near it. Better let well enough alone and be satisfied with the look of age—though this too can easily be faked. All very confusing, and if you're not a good sleuth by nature, you'll be safer to buy that whittled wooden parrot you yearn for.

Whittling was once the play of many a man when his real day's work was done. Some objects are all hand carved, some are partly lathe-turned, and others all lathe-turned—less valuable. But even these are becoming scarce. Big pieces like cigar-store Indians or merry-go-round animals seem to have vanished from the market. Small things are available at modest sums, and variety in a collection can be fun: sweet-corn grater, picture frame, bookjacks, block for pressing linen, mortar of maple and pestle of elm, puzzle toy, niddy noddy (a hand winder for skeining yarn), butter mold. The "butter-muddel" had a twofold purpose: beautifying something common and identifying the ware of a woman who sold at market. Patterns varied greatly. The cow and swan are rare, but most highly sought patterns are the usual ones of Dutch folk art. Some molds have handles. A few are initialed, but whole names and dates are exceptional. It's nearly impossible to guess the age of an undated mold, as it deteriorated from salt and water.

Boxes can teach us many a history lesson. When spices were used to preserve food, they were usually kept in the separate drawers of a box—sometimes a work of art. Candles were stored in boxes with a top that slid tightly into grooves, defeating hungry mice. The bride's box was the gift of her groom for smaller trousseau items. German-speaking émigrés of the late 1700s brought over many of these boxes, which were of shaved wood, the sides being closed by wooden pegs or thongs and pegged to heavier bottoms. Lids were elaborate with tense bride and groom, floral, and other decorations. An impassioned inscription on one declares : *Ich liebe Dich mit Lust!* Bureau or trinket boxes were copies of brides' boxes, but smaller and without the figures. Especially collectible is the nineteenth-century American "trunk box," often very tiny, with a curved top resembling that of old luggage.

Many cutlery boxes are beautiful, no doubt because the owners had means. In use as the eighteenth century advanced, they stored the precious flatware, and are miniature compared with our modern silver chests with forks for oysters and ice-cream spoons. The early traveler carried his own knife and fork to be sure of getting his share from the common pot. The fork anchored the food to his plate; the knife did the work of transportation. The earliest Dutch knives and forks (often called Welsh Mountain cutlery) were of conventional length, with handles of staghorn. The metal was of Sheffield steel, and sharp. Two long tines on the fork guaranteed your stabbing a good-sized chunk of meat—if you were quick about it. By the time of the Victorian bone handle, two-tined forks were outmoded. When spoons became common they were kept in a glass holder on the table.

If you can find a signed John Drissel box of any kind made before 1800, you're in luck. A fine artisan, he was noted for his excellent joinery and individuality. The base color was Indian red, with white, brown, and black decoration, suggesting the fraktur writing of Bucks County. Unsigned pieces often have a tulip so unique that it can serve as a signature.

Inlaid work of any wood but walnut was a rarity in boxes. The wood needed for construction was too soft for clean, concise inlay. But at the end of the nineteenth century edge-carved boxes and other objects became the fad.

Edge carving was often called "tramp work," being done by hoboes from a supply of discarded mahogany cigar boxes. The wood was ideal—thinly sawed, fine-grained, and with a smoothly finished surface that didn't splinter. The imaginative tramp with a good penknife and no pressing engagement produced, among other things, picture and mirror frames, bureau or sewing boxes, comb cases, doll furniture, and match holders. The wood was cut into small shaped pieces, and layers of these were superimposed on one another, so that there might be as many as a dozen. They were fastened together with glue and brads. (And no doubt with a prayer for dry weather till the article was paid for.) The final touch of Victorian grandeur might be brass rosette, porcelain knob, mirror insert, bits of ribbon, or sections of walnut shells.

There's as fine a distinction between whittling and carving as there is between "man" and "gentleman." Yet the work of William Schimmel (1817–1890), no gentleman, is highly prized today. A German-speaking itinerant with no tool except a sharp pocket knife, he hobbled about east-central Pennsylvania, carving animals and birds, especially eagles. Perhaps because he'd lost a leg in the Civil War, he was moody and unpredictable, fond of the bottle. Earl Robacker wrote of him: "There is a menacing ferocity in the visages of small carvings matched by no other whittler (except imitators) and his animals project in some cases an evil, dark mood." Often he was seen carving along the roadside, but farmers knew he would eventually appear, and saved blocks of wood for his visits.

He made smaller animals of one piece but for large things like eagles he carved wings separately and pegged them into the body. If the farmer had paint handy they were colored red and yellow. Though Schimmel's work is not of the earlier wood-carving period, it is primitive.

Schimmel Hall at Winterthur displays some twenty of his eagles of various sizes. Five years ago a bird listed at an auction as "Schimmel" and undated (like all his work) was declared unauthentic by a number of experienced dealers. Nevertheless, it sold for $2,400. Occasionally Schimmel produced something more fanciful like his "Garden of Eden." Adam and Eve, apple tree, serpent, and all are enclosed in a stockade mounted on a base. His human figures too have a "fierce vigor." As genius is said to be close to madness, perhaps carving was sublimation for a man who had violence in his heart.

Even Genesis wasn't so hard on Adam and Eve, as most Dutchmen can tell you. Old Bibles are treasured and at one time were kept in Bible boxes. Now and then an early family Bible may have to be sold to a dealer, but the owner with true sentiment has removed the record of numerous births, marriages, and deaths. "Engagement gifts," children born too soon after wedlock, were shamelessly inscribed, and today we often brag of their accomplishments.

In our own library are several huge, heavy old Bibles—Heilige Schrift, sturdily bound with embossed, gilded leather. One is filled with handsome engravings and numerous illustrations of weapons, animals, and even jewelry of ancient biblical countries. The Gothic type of the Gutenberg Bible (like the lettering of monks' manuscripts) was used. I handle these books reverently, as did their owners down through the generations—those whose early spidery writing gives us our family history. After two hundred years, the pages are browning and brittle. A precious and beautiful inheritance.

Perhaps someday the Revised Standard Edition of the Bible that my husband used will be as treasured by future descendants. He not only taught an adult class, but for many years was Sunday-school superintendent. Before teaching, and with Bible in hand, it was his custom to look in on various classes just to say "good-morning." Once he visited a group of preschoolers. When he left, the teacher went back to her lesson. "Now let's quiet down," she said. "Who can tell me where God is?" One little boy piped up, "He just went out the door."

The Heart of Man (Das Hertz des Menschen) was widely read in our area before 1850, mainly because it had pictures of the devil in full regalia—cloven feet, horns, pitchfork, and even wings. Engravings show a man's head with a large heart for a body, and within the heart his frame of mind. In some, Christ is depicted, in others, animals such as tigers for anger and swine for greed. Deathbed scenes of the ungodly can be harrowing.

Other rare books eagerly sought for are any from the Ephrata press, notably the *Martyr's Mirror;* ABC books or primers; buckwheat note hymnals, and scholars' copybooks. Some were illuminated. Valuable too is an original edition of Hohman's *Long Lost Friend,* so often printed since. Scrapbooks made by young ladies, a fad a hundred years ago, are also collected. If you're Dutch don't throw out any old book in your attic with hand-done work, no matter how crude it seems. It may get you for cash what you planned to buy in installments.

Though many of the Dutch are avid readers today, country folk are apt to be backward—albeit ambitious. A Reading librarian was once asked to speak at a women's club meeting in a rural nearby village. As someone had seen in the paper that she'd given an interesting talk on Liberia, she was asked to repeat it. Consternation must have quickly turned to chagrin when nary a book was mentioned!

Often a man made his own fraktur bookplate, though he might have to call "help" to an itinerant craftsman. The owner's name and perhaps his date of birth and sign of the zodiac were sometimes surrounded by a pleasing design done in tempera. It was usually the size of the book page, as were the later ones—engravings, etchings, and prints. Some have Bible quotations or moral precepts, like Bacon's "Reading maketh a full man." (When our son was reciting in high school one day he quoted the above, except that he absently said "Redding"—the way we pronounce our city—instead of "reading." There was an uproar of laughter as everyone thought of Reading Beer.)

An outstanding nineteenth-century wood engraver was George Gilbert of Philadelphia who did many things of historical interest. Most of us have seen his *Penn's Treaty*, in which the faces are amazingly individual. His excellent animal likenesses are shown in the *Union Spelling Book* and the *History of Beasts*—a Sunday-school booklet. Humor is rampant in some of his work. A full-page calendar picture shows a farmer going to a chemist for medication, and hauling along his farm door on which the doctor had written the prescription. The Temperance period inspired a bacchanalian scene of drunken pigs and people around an emptied cherry brandy flagon.

Some old books had a page or two of fraktur inserted. Fraktur indicates a "break" in early Gothic alphabet letters, but gradually came to include decorative and colorful designs. The art reached great perfection in Ephrata where it first appeared in the New World. In 1835 a traveler wrote: "The walls of all the Ephrata rooms, including meeting-room, chapels, saals, and even kammers [dormitories] are nearly covered with large sheets of elegant penmanship or ink-paintings, many of which are taken from the scriptures." Most of these (five or six feet square) have been restored, and can be seen at the cloister; others are mysteriously "lost." Most famous are the *Three Heavens* charts, and, though blurred, their original beauty can be gauged from an early photograph. Christ the Shepherd appears in the first; several hundred Capuchins with harps are in the second; and, in the third, two hundred archangels surround the throne. Framed frakturs were even placed in the rooms of departed sisters to extol their virtues.

Frakturs are highly prized today since each piece is unique, made for an individual. Probably dearest to the heart of the collector are the Geburtschein (birth certificate), the Taufschein (birth and baptismal certificate) and the Trauschein (marriage certificate), very rare now. Geburtscheine were made only by religious sects having no infant baptism, and were usually framed for walls, kept in Bibles, or pasted inside the lid of a dower chest. Some were eventually buried with the dead. Taufscheine appearing after the Revolutionary War (near the end of the fraktur period) not only had all the needful information, but embellishment by quill or watercolor on every inch of paper.

Many schoolmasters had considerable talent in fraktur schriften, and were expected to teach it to the children. The complete copybook included all alphabet letters in capitals and lower case, in print and script, plain or with flourishes, and might be illuminated. The art of Christopher Dock had widespread recognition. John Daniel Eisenbrown, an outstanding early artist, left schoolteaching to establish in Kutztown a tombstone-cutting business now located in Reading and run by his great-great-grandson. The Reverend Johann Daniel Schuhmacher was famed for his "sermon pictures," and also for his New Year's greeting cards with prayers for the welfare of his friends.

Though there were many well-known artists (and nearly half of them Schwenkfelders), there were also many mediocre itinerant scriveners. Fraktur work was found everywhere. It was mainly used for house blessings

(Haussegen), Letters from Heaven, church records, merit awards for school and Sunday school, manuscript songbooks, and such. Some fraktur artists decorated boxes and chests, like Heinrich Otto who has been called "the dean of fraktur writers."

As time went on, there were fewer religious motifs—Adam and Eve, the Last Supper, or some other biblical scene. Commoner motifs were hearts, stylized flowers, mother and child, angels, and birds. Most of these, however, had religious symbolism too.

Only seen now and then is the Geddelsbriefe, the fraktured paper in which coins were folded and presented by godparents as a baptismal gift. Rare too is the Geistliche Irrgarten, or labyrinth, representing the tortuous path of life, and usually printed. In order to make sense of the dissertation the reader might have to turn the paper a hundred times. This broadside was sometimes illuminated, no doubt by an itinerant artist. Heinrich Otto made many an Irrgarten, but hand-done ones are rare.

By 1810 there were preprinted forms for fraktur, followed by Currier and Ives lithographed productions. Oddly enough, though not legitimate fraktur, they are harder to find than originals. One of the later birth certificates was filled in by a native of Jackson County who wrote it as he would have pronounced it, "Chacksen."

There are still a few fraktur artists. Irwin Peter Mensch who died in 1952 is best known for his *Schwenkfelder Treasure Book*. It contains the records of the new Schwenkfelder Library at Pennsburg, and no two of the seventy pages are alike. The mixture of styles and motifs is fascinating. It has been said of him that "no better Gothic writing was produced by any medieval monk." Many of his designs were adapted from a duplicate of the famous Book of Kells, the oldest and most typical specimen of the sixth- and seventh-century calligraphers. Mensch used many kinds of instruments besides the quill: pins, stones, sticks, glass, nails, buckshot, rags, buttons, nutpicks, shells, and others. (Don't forget he was modern.) But his letters, birds, and flowers are handsome. And freehand, he could draw a perfect perpendicular line—no mean trick, I'm told.

He also spent over twenty-five hundred hours putting fraktur on a desk his grandfather made. It has swirls of leaves and flowers, letters and words (some of them almost microscopic) not only on the surface but in drawers and pigeonholes—the family's favorite poems or quotations.

If your walls aren't already smothered with fraktur, family portraits, daguerreotypes, pinprick work, woodcuts, engravings, paintings on silk or plush, perhaps you can squeeze in a reverse glass painting, about which there are two schools of thought. Was it all done here or was some imported? One scholar claims that the colonial fad began when a New England sea captain returned from a voyage in 1690 and brought his daughter a specimen. Being artistic, she examined the technique and devised her own system to get the same effect. At any rate, the hobby spread. Paintings must have been brought from Germany too in the early eighteenth century when the craze for all things Chinese was rampant in Europe. And what was imported was copied by aspiring females or itinerant workmen.

An 1826 New England book directs you to "set up the glass on its edge against a window, or place a lamp on the opposite side . . . and with a fine hair brush draw the outlines of your design on the glass with black. Afterwards shade it with the required colors, observing to paint that part of the work first which in others would be done last. . . . Any writing or lettering . . . must be written from right to left, contrary to the usual order." Paint that has been ground in varnish, shellac, or linseed oil is recommended.

Subjects in demand here were female portraits or those of national heroes. They were executed with much skill and directness. Most of the inscriptions were German or Pennsylvania Dutch ("Jagson" or "Waschington"). A venturesome artist might use mother-of-pearl, iridescent feathers, or shiny tea packets for the background.

Before the daguerreotype and photography, watercolor folk images were particularly popular. (Who doesn't stealthily admire his own likeness?) The outstanding artist of the early 1800s was Lewis Miller of York County. Though he was a carpenter by trade, his notebooks were filled with sketches and commentaries on his time.

The silhouettes of the same era required more skill—a keen eye and close powers of observation. It was important to capture the twist of a lip or stray lock of hair with the scissors. As professionals charged meager sums, an old silhouette is no rarity today. The well-known William Henry Brown worked so fast that "do it up brown" was invented in his honor. Master Hankes, the young Dutch prodigy, advertised that he would cut a likeness in several seconds without drawing or machine. (The latter reduced shadows cast by subjects to a desirable size.) Master Hankes charged fifty cents. (He was no Charles Willson Peale, of course.) When everyone in an artist's locality had his likeness painted, talent was turned to animals, trees, or pastoral scenes, known as cutouts.

A specialty of the cutout "pros" was the family document, resembling a family tree; these were very elaborate with arabesques and fancy scrolls, intricate leaves and flowers. Rare work was generally hand-colored like fraktur. For the best effect, the cuttings were mounted on a black background and framed. Many amateurs tried their hand at the art too, not with a sharp knife but a scissors. As paper was very expensive, bought for a specific and necessary purpose, the housewife resorted to newspaper, which "wouldn't fit the shelves." Even artificial flowers were made and attached to nonblooming plants in winter. There is a charming eighteenth-century cutout of the activities in the day of a child, from the ring of the school bell to evening prayers. All scenes were cut separately and mounted on a blue background.

Valentines healed many a broken heart in the Victorian period when laciness abounded in everything from pressed glass to furniture. Select young ladies at select schools were addicts. A brooding lover would surely brighten at:

> *As the Rose merry Grows*
> *by time (thyme) and*
> *Grapes Grows round the*
> *vine so shure*
> *you are my*
> *Valentine.*

Excepting in the Valentine season, young ladies often were busy with theorem painting, which was taught in all female seminaries. Paint was applied with "scrubs" (small stiff brushes) through stencil openings on muslin, silk, satin, or velvet. Most popular subjects were fruit and flowers, though there were also mourning pictures with tombstones and weeping people and willows.

Females did all varieties of sewing too. Little girls of even four were taught to make samplers in order to learn the alphabet and numerals, and the stitches they'd use when grown. Sewing was done on a square-meshed fabric base. Besides the personal data were embellishments of trees, flowers, birds, and inscriptions. A unique sampler declares: "I done this in my eleventh year and I hated every minute of it!"

Most wool was imported from Berlin—hence "Berlin work" meant anything sewed with wool. (Ten years ago our *keeshund,* Zuyder, could have supplied me free. Under his shiny topcoat was a thick layer of wool. We were much amused one day when he slept in his doghouse yard, and a bird swooped down for a beakful for nesting. Zuyder reacted briefly. But each time he settled down to nap again, the bird stole more.) Examples of Berlin work are headrests for chairs, bookmarks, cases for combs, needles, and cards, suspender straps, and boxes for collars, shirt studs, handkerchiefs, buttons, and the like.

A recently discovered treasure is a panel worked with Berlin wool on coarse, natural burlap. Its black folklore theme makes it unique. The monogram "MED" and the date 1876 are the only clues to its origin, but it is thought to have been done by Mary Elizabeth Drinker, a black woman of Easton, famed for her needlework. (Many black women were artists with the needle.) Its varicolored stitching depicts singing, dancing, black Punch and Judy, two children of the Civil War period with "We's free," and several white figures. There are also household motifs like a broom and sprinkling can, and various symbols—an arrow, butterfly, monkey, bear, and playing cards among them. The size is ambitious too, about two by three feet, and all sides are deeply fringed. As there is no evidence that designs were initially traced on the burlap with indelible ink or any kind of pencil, the artist must have worked directly from sketches. This sort of find is what makes antiquing so exciting.

From the variety of old needlework found, one would think that women sewed their lives away. For trousseaus—bed linen, (some dated and initialed); pincushions, some elegant with fine silks, sequins, beaded birds, tassels; crazy-quilt pillows, tobacco pouches, shoe-box covers. And, of course, the show towel, which hung atop the roller towel of coarse homespun or huck in the kitchen, or on the door of the "company room" for guests. At its best it was a masterpiece of hemstitch, cross-stitch, drawnwork, crocheting, embroidery, and fringing that amounted to bragging. Its name and date, lettering, numerals, and motifs rivaled the most elaborate sampler. Until 1840 it depended for its effect on needlework alone, with no colored threads except red perhaps. Later towels were multicolored. And woe to anyone who used them! Lizzie Yoder still displays hers for the preacher's annual Sunday dinner visit.

Much of our folk craft is thought by many to be of Dutch origin. Some of it is. But the emigrants, freed from the rigid guild system of Europe and attracted by our custom of indenture, not only copied things from the homeland (which in turn borrowed from other countries) but were inspired to create adaptations. The basis of all we think and do stems from previous generations. I remember saying to my husband about the first IBM machine, "How could anyone possibly conceive it?" He answered, "No one person did. One idea was added to others that came before it." Day by day, we Dutch are creating the Dutch antiques of tomorrow.

I expect to have many offended readers because I haven't mentioned or enlarged on hallowed collections: Moravian tiles, bird whistles, herbaria, penholders, thimbles, carved powder horns, watch charms, arrowheads, and many other fascinating items. Once again I put the blame on *space*. I apologize with a benediction from one of the old greeting cards you may collect: "May your friends be many, your troubles few—and all your sausages long."

Tell Me a Story

WHEN I USED TO HEAR MY HUSBAND AND JOHN YODER CONSUMED WITH laughter over a new dialect story, and begged for a translation, I was always told, "But it isn't nearly as funny in English." And it wasn't. It even proved pointless if the Dutch word that gave the story its zip (and might be bawdy) defied translation or needed laundering for the ladies. Any folktale is at its best in the dialect, and told orally—not in print.

Our ancient folklore with all its intriguing facets has been kept alive from the days of settlers' weddings, funerals, apple butter boilings, and parleys around the potbellied stoves of general stores. Not only Conestoga wagoners and drovers but itinerants of all kinds swarmed through the early American countryside: gypsies, tinkers, tramps, peddlers, and even school-masters. Like the almanacs, they all spread lore and legend, anecdotes, jokes, and proverbs—embellishing, distorting, enthralling. Nothing wrong with improvising too if this could hold the listener spellbound. Anyone beyond one's own farm added zest to routine. No doubt local gossip was the choicest hearsay of all, and the butcher who helped farmers in his area at butchering season must have brought a windfall.

Our oldest source of folklore is the ballad. We Dutch still sing ballads from Germany's ancient past, like "Schpinn, schpinn," in which a mother chides her listless daughter. It starts with:

"Schpinn, schpinn, meine liewe Dochder," and the first verse, translated goes:

Spin, spin, my dear daughter,
And I'll buy you a dress,
Yes, yes, my dear mother,
And one with a pocket.

The additional verses promise an apron, shoes, a cow, or other rewards. The intervening chorus, however, belies the daughter's resolve with:

I can spin no more
for my finger keeps swelling
And hurts me so much, so much.

When mother promises her a husband, cure is instantaneous:

I can spin again,
My finger swells no more,
And no longer gives me any pain, any pain.

New verses were often added to these old ballads as customs changed.

The Conestoga wagoners were fond of *zersingen*, improvising parodies of ballads in a raucous barroom contest at night. Some, too good to lose to posterity, were adopted by the countryside. Many of a political or industrial nature were influential. One ballad condemned every aspect of the cursed railroad, which was tolling the death knell of the wagoner. A verse sounds the warning:

> *The ships they will be coming with Irishmen by loads,*
> *All with their picks and shovels, to work on the rail-*
> > *roads;*
> *When they get on the railroad, it is then that they are*
> > *fixed;*
> *They'll fight just like the devil with their cudgels and*
> > *their sticks.*

Ballads fathered myths, fables, nursery rhymes, legends, and countless offspring—some illegitimate, but all with a family resemblance.

Precious to children of every land is the fairy tale, transmuting drab reality to magic. Aren't there new editions annually? Naturally the Dutch are devoted to the Brothers Grimm, especially *Little Red Riding-Hood* and *Snow White (Schneeweischen)*. Common themes are an impossible feat (climbing a glass mountain to win the princess); the apple, old as Eve; and the number "three," old as mankind and superstition.

Now and then one finds a newer folktale strongly reminiscent of some fairy-tale original. In a modern Dutch version, a farm girl tests three wooers by giving each an apple to eat. One proves wasteful, one too frugal (eating the core), and the exemplary third, of course, she marries. "Three" is still used merely for suspense in every modern parlor story and by the acrobat who has us rigid with his first two falls from the wire.

Benjamin Botkin called folklore "the stuff that travels and the stuff that sticks." Our beloved Till Eulenspiegel is a prime example of "sticking." Though seemingly mythical, he lived in Germany's Brunswick in the fourteenth century. Sometimes he's known here as Eilesschpijjel, even Eirisch Bickel, depending on where you live, but he's never so malicious as his earlier German prototype. In the countless tales of Till, caprice is his charm. A real chameleon, he was often clever, often stupid, and master of all trades in different stories—farmer, hired man, wrestler with the devil, hunter, lover, even an exasperatingly mischievous child.

One Sunday, sent by his mother over the mountain for berries, he came home with empty pail, and being asked where they were, said, "On the mountaintop. I helped them uphill. Downhill they need no help." Once Till was warned by his parents that by no means should he mention the pastor's enormous nose when he came to dinner. But as soon as grace was said and mashed potatoes dowsed with chicken gravy, Till stared at him and exploded, "Aye, yi, yi, such a pig's snout and we musn't even mention it!"

As a youth, hired by a farmer, Till was told to hitch up the wagon, "Sorrel in front and black in rear." Till's idea of tandem was unique. He hitched the sorrel span in front of the wagon, and the black behind the tailgate. Again, when the farmer told him "to grease the wagon" (not specifying the spindles) he greased it entirely.

Reputedly, when he was a tailor, he was condemned to death for numerous misdeeds. At the gallows he bargained, "Spare me and I'll show tailors how to sew and not lose the first stitch." Since all the regional tailors gathered about were avid for the secret, Till was released. "To save the first stitch you must knot the end of the thread," he told them. His advice, of course, has been followed ever since.

There are similar stories in which the protagonist has other names, yet who but Till could be so consistently eccentric and ingenious? He's often spoken of intimately: "He used to come to my Grandpop's house." Yet, by some, he's even considered to be Satan himself, though Satan was often tricked by Till in the stories.

A favorite is that of Till and the Devil, each boasting that he could stand the most heat. As a test, they both crept into a tremendous oven over a roaring fire. Finally Till could no longer bear it and crawled toward the door. "Where are you going?" demanded the Devil. "I want to add more wood to the fire," gasped Till, "I'm chilly." The Devil groaned, "I must get out—I'm burning to a crisp."

Till isn't our only wrestler with the Devil, but in recent years there are fewer tales about selling one's soul for power or riches. In those still extant, the Devil is wont to visit a barroom (sometimes in the form of a great black cat) to "buy" the soul of a gambler. He doesn't always win, though; in one tale the drinkers are holding a mock revival scene, and the Devil creates panic—and religious conversion. A story smacking of Till Eulenspiegel is that of a Dutchman who sells himself to the Devil, and lands in hell. When he begs for freedom the Devil agrees, providing the sinner can show him something new. The Dutchman asks for salt and throws it on the fire, which goes out. The Devil rants, "Get out of here as fast as you can. You're dangerous in this place."

Devil tales are related to those of hexerei or witchcraft, legion in our area. There is little mention now of Walpurgis (the witches' favorite night to be abroad), a witches' ring in fields where nothing green will grow after their dancing, or their gamboling on disputed boundary lines. Today, a witch riding her broomstick is seen only on Halloween decorations. The less obvious Dutch witch is now the one who can milk a towel, charm a gun so a man will miss his aim, or cast an evil spell on others or their domestic animals (natural in a farming section). We call a witch one who can "do more than eat bread." Since she works alone, she's not easy to ferret out. As is explained in the chapter on the occult, we get a hex doctor "to fix her" and bring about justice.

The witch isn't always a crone. Occasionally one finds a heartrending tale about "an angelic young woman" with whom some youth falls madly in love. In one such tale a mother warns her son that she has always been suspicious of the girl. His faith is slightly shaken when his sweetheart says one night the moon looks as if it has Devil's horns. But he doesn't admit this to his mother who invites the girl to dinner, and, knowing that a witch won't cross a broomstick, hides one beneath the outside stairs. The girl, arriving, pales and trembles, then draws out the broomstick, remarking lightly that someone has forgotten it. Though the evening is merry, the young man is really shocked now. The next day, his sweetheart, realizing the discovery, takes ill and dies. When the brokenhearted lover sees her she's become an old hag without teeth. When he dreams that she is crossing the moon on a broomstick, and then learns that her corpse is mysteriously missing, the poor youth is forced to face the truth at last.

A theme rivaling witchcraft in thrills is that of *Schpucherei*. The Dutch (reputedly those fond of the bottle) have often been haunted by spooks. A sleigh full of spectral revelers who were known to be killed has been seen by more than one person living near the site of the tragedy. Tales are told too of horses balking at the scene of an accident, refusing to cross a bridge perhaps. (Were *they* seeing purple elephants?) Skeptics claim that a wandering animal or some object eerie in the moonlight is mistaken for a ghost. Yet, there was one wraith that has seemingly left proof of existence. A young woman was often followed by a ghost who finally told her he had been waiting for her to receive the Holy Spirit. When he offered his hand, the terrified girl held out only the edge of her handkerchief. The part he touched "burned to crisp." The handkerchief, now two centuries old, is said to be well preserved (scorch and all) and a family heirloom.

Many ghosts, it seems, long to communicate some secret knowledge, even to birds or animals that many years later may perhaps reveal a murderer in their own mysterious fashion. Struggling for recognition, the spirit may appear as ectoplasm, a jangling of invisible chains, or only a clammy hand laid on the living.

The commonest spook tales are those of buried treasure, though few are new since 1900. Did they connote wishful thinking on the part of the impoverished immigrant? "Old Sweitzer," murdered at Penn's Creek Massacre, had buried his savings first, it seems. His restless ghost appeared each night, trying to share his secret. Neighbors claimed that they often found holes dug by people seeking money. Suddenly, it was thought that someone had found it, that Old Sweitzer had succeeded, for the haunting stopped. No ghost can find rest until his treasure is found. But the hunter must keep silent till he's touched the gold, or it will vanish.

Likely the most popular tale is *The Barber's Ghost* with its many deviations over the years. Its nucleus is this: three separate travelers, at various times when an inn is crowded, are offered a room haunted by a murdered barber. The first two flee when they hear a soft rasping voice ask, "Do you want to be shaved?" The third, with bravado, rushes toward the window to attack the ghost, and finds the voice to come from an old tree brushing the glass in the wind. In one version, the hero collects fifty dollars from the host who had bet him that he wouldn't stay the night; in another, keeping his secret, he buys the inn cheaply; in still another, he dons a sheet, sneaks down to the barroom, scares the gamblers away, and pockets the deserted winnings. The tale was told in *Baer's Almanac* in 1866, and is thought to be originally a New England story debunking spirits.

Yet even if ghosts are real, it's common knowledge that you needn't fear them. If confronted, just repeat the Lord's Prayer or a Scriptural passage, and the ghost will vanish—temporarily, at least!

In Indian stories ghosts appear occasionally at the site of a lover's leap or scalping, but most tales are straightforward—those of massacres, captivities, or encounters with other tribes or animals. It's said that the pioneers had a book teaching them to become invisible to the Indians. One settler transformed himself into a log, on which some savages sat down to rest. Later, the necromancer claimed that he felt the knife in his scalp when the Indian scraped bark from the log. Copies of the witchcraft book must have been rare indeed, considering the number of white men massacred.

The supernatural in animal folk stories usually has a moral, but in hunting stories it's purely delightful. Most of our hunting heroes were ace marksmen, of course. One was such a good shot that he never missed, and when the animals even saw him entering the woods they dropped dead from fright. Then there was the Blue Mountain hunter who ran out of ammunition, so he ate the cherries in his pocket and loaded the gun with pits. He aimed at the next buck between the eyes but it escaped: some time later he saw it with a cherry tree growing between its antlers. A butcher being pursued by a bear cut and dropped slices from the carcass he was carrying, to detain his greedy enemy. Hunting stories continue to thrive, as many farmers and Dutchmen of all trades avidly await the hunting season.

Since the hunters are often threatened by snakes, these appear often in folktales. A hunter resting on a log (snake) dozes off, and when waking finds himself a mile away, still on the back of the "log," which is drinking from a stream. There are tales of black snakes that can whistle or come when whistled to. Others can charm people, then entwine and choke them, or charm a cow and milk it. Snakes, like fish, grow gigantic in stories. It's not unusual to hear that someone killed a snake with twenty-six rattlers or "as long as a fence rail and thick as a stovepipe."

Yarns of the fabulous hoop snake improve with each refilling of the barroom glass. The hoop snake is huge, multicolored, with a stinger in its tail, which it keeps in its mouth while rolling swiftly toward a victim to attack him. Once upon a time a hoop snake missed a farmer and bit his hoe handle, which swelled to such a size that it had to be taken to a sawmill to be cut into lumber. There were boards enough for a six-room house, but alas, it's said that the wood still retained the venom. Then there were the two hoop snakes that swallowed each other up, like Eugene Field's gingham dog and calico cat.

These fall into the "tall tale" category. Nearly ever Dutch village has its Baron Münchausen, the born storyteller, maybe a no-good, but with the skill and imagination to embroider his every experience and hold his listeners spellbound. There was Old Pete, once so scared at meeting a wolf that his hair sprang up and he never saw his hat again. In the winter of 1888 it was so cold that the flame in his lantern froze and had to be broken to put out the light. Moreover, when his rooster crowed at dawn you could see its frozen breath from barn to house and his wife hung their wash on it.

Weird, indeed, is the 150-year-old tale of the Collegeville man who was buried standing up. He had willed that his grave be dug like a well, and the head part of the coffin be aboveground so that he could see what was happening on his farm. Each Saturday night—a fifth of whiskey in each pocket—he kept his vigil. Though a brick mound was built around the head part, eventually his skull emerged from the opening and at last disintegrated, being bandied about by workmen. Reputedly, he owned the land now belonging to Ursinus College.

Tramps, among other migrants, carried tales as the wind spreads seed, so it's hardly any wonder that oft-repeated details have varied. An old farmer I knew some years ago said the tramps had once regaled him for hours at night with yarns of headless ghosts, beheaded warriors, or even fairy-tale stuff about rescued maidens. My friend added with a toothless grin, "You learned a lot about your neighbors, too yet. The rich that gave the tramps rancid flitch or stale pie only fit for chickens. Or the poor that paid him good like Christians."

Tramps were given meals and shelter in the barn for random work on the farm—mending harness, umbrellas, or shoes. The more gifted were basket weavers, wood turners, fraktur artists. You might even find an astrologer or mathematician among them. A few could be vengeful if not treated right. One who was ousted for smoking in the barn returned a few nights later and cut off all the cows' tails at the rump. A certain farmer who seldom fed a tramp got his comeuppance from one he refused in a temper. The sly tramp said if he were given supper he would kill every rat on the farm with his cane. He was then taken to the kitchen, and stuffed. Beaming, he went out on the porch, sat down, and asked that the rats be brought to him so he could kill them as he'd promised.

Most tramps were German, though there was a smattering of other nationalities. Gypsies, except a few Hungarians, were of British origin. In the spring they came north, escorting their queen in her elegant van with its delicate marquetry and glittering gold mirrors. Visiting a farm in twos and threes (while one did business the others could pilfer), they mended pots and pans. However, as they'd been known to cut out the bottoms of copper kettles and substitute tin, the veteran farmer shunned them. The Balkans especially were shrewd horse dealers and doctors. A farmer might have his lame horse treated and be delighted with the quick result. But no sooner were the gypsies paid and out of the area, than the mare would limp again. There are many gypsy stories of crafty horse deals as well as more poignant ones about stolen children.

The peddlers, mostly Jews, were the most welcome of all itinerants. They not only brightened the household with news and stories on their periodic visits but brought little needs and luxuries to the farm wife starved for the outside world. The pack peddler carried his wares in a big bundle on his back, but some had wagons with a large stock from shoelaces and notions to silks and gold watches. Many had specialties—eyeglasses, pictures, tinware, lamp chimney cleaner, or even chicken delouser. "Here comes 'Whistling Joe' " would slow down the farm work, but "Here comes 'Der Bobblemoul' " (the blabbermouth) would bring all the family on the run.

One peddler had half his wagon wired off for exotic tropical birds. A farm woman who had bought a Brazilian warbler had to shop in the village two weeks later. As a storm was brewing and she had left the cage beside an open window, she soon hurried home, but not before the deluge had drenched her iridescent pet to a muddy sparrow brown. Needless to say, this peddler never visited an area twice.

In the nineteenth century one of the peddler's best-selling items was the chapbook, a pamphlet with lurid details of a capital crime or hanging—an impassioned interest of the times. This "gallows literature," accompanying the revivalist movement, stressed the moral and religious attitude of the murderer, causing heated discussions of the pros and cons of capital punishment. There were many tales about a doomed person's vowing innocence and predicting a posthumous sign to prove it, such as "a white dove will hover above my grave."

No doubt the revivalist movement, creating interest in crime, also whetted the taste for parson, or *parre*, stories. These reflect the church's stature in rural life and the Dutchman's respect for the preacher, especially if he came down to their level, threshing or butchering along with the farmer. The yarns usually recount some minister's wit, lack of fear, or naughty behavior. A common theme is that of a pastor having been drunk or involved in a scandal, then preaching "do as I say and not as I do"—yet being so obviously repentant that the congregation promptly melts. Another popular theme is that of the parre's shenanigans in raising campaign funds. Unusual, though, is an entry in George Washington's account book in 1797 acknowledging a parre's special skill: "Give my servant Christopher, to bear expenses to a parson at Lebanon in Pa. celebrated for curing persons bit by wild animals, $25.00." This was undoubtedly the Reverend Henry William Stoy, not only famed for curing victims of mad dog bites, but for his "itch salve." Stoy also had a reputation for tremendous strength. Challenged once by a neighbor, Stoy casually tossed him over a roadside fence. The whimpering man called to Stoy, "Now kindly throw my horse over to me, parson."

One minister who could preach extemporaneously on any theme suggested by his congregation looked one Sunday at the slip of paper placed on the pulpit. It was blank, and there was general tittering. "Out of nothing," he announced with spirit, "God created heaven and earth. I will take my text from Genesis." Reputedly, this was his best sermon to date. He certainly wasn't of the same ilk as the neophyte who ploddingly read his sermon with directions inserted: "Pause ... Pound ... Shake fist." Finally the church council gave him three reasons for dismissal. "One," said a deacon, "you read your sermons. Two, they're too long and dry as dust. And three—we keep right on sinning." Maybe it was the same callow parre who called on a parishioner to see why she never came to church. "Son," she said, "you just ain't old enough so you've sinned enough to preach about it."

Dr. Don Yoder tells of an eastern Pennsylvania circuit parre named Scheffrich who had inherited eleven of his father's congregations along with a barrel of sermons in the attic. After preaching the top sermon, he dropped it into an empty barrel, and when—at long last—he had exhausted the lot, he reversed the process. Since the ministry didn't solely support him (understandable), he also had a homeopathic practice, made coffins, and did stone cutting. Unique as a parre, he assisted at birth, baptized, instructed in catechism, confirmed and married, cured illness, and (if not successful), finally gave the funeral sermon and furnished the casket and gravestone.

Of all the parres, Mose Dissinger, a Lebanon County native of 1825, is the most celebrated. An unschooled carpenter "called to the ministry," he served various circuits throughout the Dutch country, drawing great crowds with his spellbinding dialect sermons. He was a fearless preacher of the truth. The Devil was real and personal to Mose, but he had his witty moments. Confronted on a street by a young loafer, taunting, "Well, Mose, how is the Devil today?" Mose quipped, "It always brings me great pleasure to meet one like you concerned with his father's welfare." When his wife came to church with a new hat bought after selling their corner cupboard, he announced from the pulpit, "Behold, here comes Mrs. Dissinger with the corner cupboard on her head." More acrid is the tale of his accepting a meal at the home of a family ostracized because of their filth. His grace was "God bless this dirty house, God bless this dirty food, and God bless poor Mose who must eat it. Amen." Parre anecdotes have been repeated throughout the decades, long after the pastor's name was forgotten or confused with another's, or his antics attributed to a different race or sect. Though details may vary, the essence is the same. Behind most of our parre stories is an attempt to better understand the man "choosen by God" whom we hold in awe—albeit with reluctance. Sometimes it's doubtful that God has done the choosing. It seems that a country bumpkin went to his minister with excitement to relate a vision. One day he had seen clouds that formed huge letters: P C, meaning Preach Christ. The parre studied the boy thoughtfully for a minute and then said, "Are you sure those letters didn't mean Plow Corn?"

The inherent humor of the Dutch is shown in our "numskull" stories too, usually featuring the clever versus the stupid. (Eulenspiegel is the classic example.) The numskull is often of a nationality new to the region. In the nineteenth century he was usually the Irishman; in the twentieth century, the Negro, then the Pole. One of the Stupid Swabian stories gives us the source of "hay foot, straw foot." A captain, exasperated at drilling yokels who didn't know left from right, had them put wisps of hay on one foot and straw on the other. The command "hay foot, straw foot" then kept them in good marching order. More subtle is the incident about the Swabian who went downhill to fetch water. To balance the full pail he carried up a sack of meal in the other hand. At the top of the hill, wanting to return the sack of meal, he carried the pail of water as balance.

If volume is a criterion, some types of folklore seem insignificant, yet reveal much of our character. *Olla Podrida* doesn't sound Pennsylvania Dutch—and isn't. (In Spanish it's a meat and vegetable stew.) But Colonel Thomas Zimmerman's *Olla Podrida* is an old collection of original Dutch poems, hymns, life sketches, tales, and so forth. If you'd like to know how to make a thief return stolen goods, this book has many methods. For instance, a wily farmer whose purse was stolen called together his ten hired men. He ordered them to go to the stable and rub the tail of the donkey, which would bray at touch of the thief. The donkey refused to cooperate. The farmer then smelled the hands of all ten men and found but one whose hands were free of donkey odor. "You are the thief," the farmer accused him. "Your hands betray you." Some thieves were made to return goods by magic incantations.

Another beloved collection is *Boonastiel,* written long ago by a news-paperman, T. H. Harter. Gottlieb Boonastiel was a merry, ingenious fellow who spent his life failing at wacky ways to make a living. He met his energetic wife, Polly, through a fluke. At the top of a hill his oxen wouldn't budge. Undaunted, Gottlieb put thorns under the tail of one. A whish of the tail, and the ox tore down like a waterfall, dragging his teammate with him and dumping Gottlieb into a bed of thistles. When he came to, he was being nursed by a pretty stranger. This was Polly. As Gottlieb was bored with farming, she managed their farm. But running for postmaster, he got but one vote—his own. He planned then to make a burglar-proof safe, which would bring him a fortune: in each safe he would put a skunk—frighten away the thief. For weeks he worked on his project—only to find that the skunk couldn't distinguish between owner and thief. Drowning disappointment with drink he tumbled into a witches' Sabbath—and barely escaped. But his new knowledge of vanquishing witches gave him an idea; he set up as a prophet, telling people how to farm or whom to marry. Before long he was considered very wise and was greeted by everyone with reverence. Honored as an oracle, Gottlieb found success at last—while Polly brought in the sheaves.

Among other less-known stories are those of bartering, a common custom in the early days of penury. Often a farm wife cut carpet rags into strips, rolled them into balls, and took a bagful to the store to trade for salt or spices. There is the story of the man whose wife gave him an egg to exchange for a bodkin. The storekeeper (also inn owner) asked the customer to the bar for a drink, and broke the man's egg into the eggnog which he ordered. What a windfall when it proved to have two yolks! "Ach Himmel," exclaimed the farmer, "you owe me another darning needle!" Bartering could be very profitable. Poor, you might swap a penknife for a buzz saw, and, after enough cunning transactions, end up rich by trading your prize bull for a farm.

Much of our humor involves farm life and reflects our sense of values. Proverbs, riddles, and aphorisms (some of European origin) are no exceptions: "As the man, so his cattle"; "The older the goat, the harder its horns." A typical riddle: Q: "What uses the largest handkerchief in the world?" A: "A hen—wipes its nose anywhere on earth." And a moron's favorite: Q: "What is the rooster doing when he stands on one foot?" A: "Holding up the other." Over a hundred years ago, a Pennsylvania Dutch sage, Abner Americanus, inscribed his sayings in sgraffito on a wooden pickle barrel top. Among others were: "When the straw leans, note the direction whence the wind bloweth," and "When a man without a flock offers you cheap lamb, tell him, 'Baa.'"

An actual happening may be the source of a common saying, as "Like Dietz's funeral—it all went to nothing." When old man Dietz lay dying, his children came from a distance to gather at his bedside. Since he took too long to die, they all agreed to go back to their farm duties (leaving funeral arrangements to the unmarried brother) and return four days later for the service. They kept their pact, swathed in black, and no doubt with an appetite for funeral pie and a nice little inheritance. However, they found the ornery old man sitting in his rocker, enjoying his meerschaum. From their indignation, you might have thought poor old Dietz was playing a practical joke.

Practical jokes can be vicious but among us Dutch are apt to be just plain fun. There's one about some youths who dressed up in sheets one night to play ghost on a courting friend. Waylaying him, one moaned, "Come, come, come with me to hell." The lover picked up some stones and retorted, "Get going or I'll stone you. . . . They don't talk Dutch in Hell." A boy asks a farmer, "If I pick the cherries from this tree can I have half?" Getting consent, he picks the fruit and is ready to leave. "Where's my half?" asks the farmer. "On the tree yet," says the wily youngster. "I only asked for half."

A choice rural trick is getting some greenhorn to hunt *Elbedritsche* (a nonexistent bird or animal) in the dead of winter. Naturally Fritz wants to know what an *Elbedritsche* is, but is warned he musn't mention it until it's caught. He's given a flashlight, "a mate-luring whistle that imitates the female cry," and a burlap bag. Then he's told not to move from some desolate spot, until the gang (supposedly chasing the bounty toward him) returns. Naturally, they've all gone back to the kitchen stove. When Fritz is more icicle than human, he crunches homeward—much the wiser. One young dupe, however, is said to have rushed back triumphant, with a rabbit in his sack, shouting, "I have it—I have it!" It was the gang who was now left "holding the bag."

Though college fraternities in our section usually subject their freshmen to this initiation stunt, the custom has been prevalent in all of Germany for generations. References to it go back to very old mythological tales indicating that the elves have "been at" some awkward, stupid fellow.

Many a personal experience, whether with *Elbedritsche* or something more factual, is destined to become folklore, I'm sure. One funny story (we say "funny" may be "funny peculiar" or "funny ha-ha") is about a couple we know whose turn it was to have their hasenpfeffer club to supper. Mrs. D. thought she'd outdo former hostesses by serving fresh lobster salad. After boiling the meat (the lobsters had been shipped from Maine) she was picking it over when the phone rang. Several minutes later, to her dismay, she found her cat munching chunks from the bowl. Angrily she tossed him out on the porch. Then since no one would know, she scooped away a bit of meat where he'd been thieving and prepared the rest.

The treat was a great success. During the card game Mrs. D. remembered that the cat had been out in the cold for hours and went to call him in. There he was on the porch floor "hard like a billy club." He had been poisoned by the same lobster all of them had eaten! She rushed to call her doctor. The only thing to do, he said, was to get the whole group to the hospital at once to have their stomachs pumped. The guests were very sporting (more sporting, no doubt, than Mr. D. who had to foot the bill and Mrs. D. who mourned her pet). They went through the ordeal merrily and merrily returned to their card game. When the party broke up late, no one seemed any the worse for the binge. And no wonder. The neighbor phoned to say, "I didn't want to distress you while your company was there so I just put your cat on the porch. He was hit by a car."

When the fund of true stories is depleted, Dutch parlor jokes enliven every party. They may seem exaggerated, but they all expose some quirk of our makeup and we enjoy poking fun at ourselves. Have you heard the one about Farmer Hinnerschitz, roused by the phone at midnight? (Wrong number; Bupplemoyer was wanted.) He's no sooner back in bed than he jumps up to answer the "three longs and two shorts." There's the same beery voice and he slams down the receiver with an oath. The third time (necessary to every joke) the farmer explodes, "Dunnervetter, I told you this is Hinnerschitz!" The drunk is even more outraged. "Ach, you dumkopf, if you're still Hinnerschitz and not Bupplemoyer (hic) then vy do you answer?"

Proving our sense of caution is the story of the farmer who asked the court for three thousand dollars in damages, though he had denied being hurt at the scene of the accident. The judge asked him to relate his grievance. A car racing down the road, the farmer said, had knocked him down (he still couldn't work) and had broken the two hind legs of Bessie, his cow. The driver had promptly put an end to the bellowing Bessie with a shotgun. "Then," huffed the farmer, "he turns to *me* and says, 'Are you hurt, too?'"

One of my husband's jokes has the Blue Ribbon for All Time Best. The disconsolate Ira confesses to his friend, Jake, at the firehall that he can't get a date with a girl more than once. Jake, the local seducer, gives him the formula: "Vy, first you gif a girl somesing good to eat, then you gif her combliments—you know, they're nice sings you say. Tell her her hair are pretty, her dress is nice, and her cheeks like peaches."

Ira leaves hopeful but is just as forlorn when they meet again.

"Didn't you do like I said?" asks Jake. "Vy shuah," wails Ira, "I fed her good at the diner. But her hair vas strubely, her dress vas schmutsich, and her cheeks vas full of pimples. I couldn't say nussing nice about any. But I did sink of a combliment. I says, 'For a fat girl you don't svett much.'"

It's been said that "culture in decay . . . is replaced by culture in the making." We still create folk stories as our customs, morals, reasoning, and sense of humor change. The culture brought here by the Palatines altered with acclimatization. Then the experiences of each new generation in contact with other ethnic groups had impact on our standards of economy, religion, and education. When new trades arose with the Industrial Revolution, all were potential sources of folktales—mills, mines, and forests.

After 1900 a great influx of immigrants brought new stories that blended with the old. Most recently our college students and GI's have made their own contributions. It seems that during the Vietnam War, a Dutch soldier offered blood for a transfusion to be given to an unconscious Chinese comrade. When he came to, the Chinese mumbled, "Ach, I sought I vasn't going to make it."

Folklore evolves from a group bound together by common social needs, from the sharing of a similar point of view if not a dialect. A people living together long enough have the same moral traditions despite variance in class, race, or its members' idiosyncrasies. Dialect like ours, in addition, unites them like epoxy glue.

From the cradle to the grave, we say expectantly, "Tell me a good Dutch story."

Fireside Yarns

ON A MORE SERIOUS LEVEL THAN TALES, THE LEGEND IS "A HISTORICAL STORY not always verifiable" though the teller usually believes it true, identifying places and persons. For didn't Grandpop Spatz get it from his own Grandpop who actually knew the person involved?

Even if such stories have no time or place, they eventually become legends if widely enough loved and repeated. Included here are a few originating beyond "the heart" of the Dutch Country proper; but these have some link with our culture and have become a popular part of an oldster's storytelling repertoire on a winter's night.

For instance, Indian legends travel as widely as did the Indians themselves; though many a Dutchman's forebears made friends with certain redskins, most encounters were fatal. These legends are numerous and usually repetitious, sometimes recounting massacres of whole families and even communities.

Typical is the tragedy of the Hochstetlers, honored by descendants with an iron marker and the rebuilding of the bake oven behind which the Indians hid. Jacob Hochstetler, 1736 immigrant, settled near the present Shartlesville in Berks County. In twenty years he had a thriving farm and family. One September night, long after a schnitzing frolic was over, a son, Jake, was awakened by their barking dog. Going to the door to investigate, he was shot in the leg by a redskin, but roused the family. The father forbade his sons to shoot at Indians: "It is not right to take the life of another even to save one's own." The house being set afire, the family sought refuge in the cellar, dashing cider on encroaching flames.

Finally, at dawn, thinking the savages had left, they crept out a small cellar window. A stealthy Indian gave the war cry. Jake and a daughter were tomahawked and scalped; the mother was stabbed through the heart with a butcher knife. Allegedly, when a redskin saw Christian's bright blue eyes he took a liking to the boy and spared him. Jacob and his sons, Christian and Joseph, were taken captives, and the barn and all outbuildings were razed by fire. Seeing they would be separated, Jacob's parting words to his sons were "If you are taken so far away and forget your German language, do not forget the Lord's Prayer."

Eventually, Jacob escaped, hid in the daytime, walked at night without rest, crossed streams and mountains, and was once so starved that he ate a dead possum full of maggots. But his murdered wife appeared in a dream to assure him he was heading for home. Finally, with a raft he'd built, he reached Fort Harris (now Harrisburg) and soon regained enough strength to travel on.

When peace was restored, Joseph left the tribe that had adopted him, and returned home also. Christian had a hard time deciding to leave the Indians but joined his family and soon married. Neither boy had forgotten the Lord's Prayer.

There is more than one legend about a white captive refusing freedom offered either by the Indians or his own conquering people. Many whites were adopted by ceremony into a tribe. Men grew to like the vigorous outdoor life and women became fond of the braves to whom they bore children. The Indians weren't always the victors in a skirmish, nor were they always the aggressors as tradition would have us believe. Many a white man could be savage too.

Two hundred years ago, Frederick Stump of Lancaster County was unable to get rid of half a dozen drunken, surly redskins (two of them squaws) who lingered near his house. Fearing injury to himself and his hired man he killed them and threw their bodies in the creek. Then, afraid the news would reach their tribe, he went further berserk, and trailing to their nearby cabins, killed three more women and a child, and set fire to the dead. There was great consternation throughout the province, for this needless cruelty could start a serious siege. Though the crazy Stump was apprehended by the law, he escaped and died in old age—repentant, I hope.

On the other hand, our famous Conrad Weiser, one of Berks County's first settlers, spent most of his life as mediator between the white men and the redskins who controlled the Indian policy in colonial Pennsylvania and the south. One winter in his youth he had lived with the Iroquois who gave him the name Terach-a-wa-gon, meaning "he who holds in his hands the reins of the universe."

In 1737, Shikellamy, the Oneida chief, had been sent by the Onondaga Council to overlook Indian affairs in Pennsylvania. He and Weiser worked together closely and became intimate friends. Shikellamy, also friendly to the Moravian missionaries, was described by Count Zinzendorf as "a truly good and excellent man, dignified, sober, prudent, refined, intelligent, and possessed of noble qualities that would do honor to many a white man." For many years he and Weiser traveled together through the wilds, keeping the western border peaceful until the French and Indian War in which Weiser served as colonel.

On one of his missions, Weiser nearly perished. With a small party of white men and Indians he was headed for Onondaga to forestall further warfare between the Iroquois and the Muskokees of Virginia. After weeks of combating blizzards and raging streams, yet only a few days away from his goal, he was so starved and exhausted that he prayed to die. It was Shikellamy who gave him courage, saying, "The good days cause men to sin, and God cannot be merciful; when it goes badly with us, God takes pity on us."

During the winter of 1748–1749 the famine near Shamokin caused the death of the aging Shikellamy. From then on Weiser's power over the Indians declined, as Shikellamy's sons never gave him the same cooperation, and opposing factions grew critical. His last years were saddened also by a growing distrust among frontiersmen, particularly those of Paxtang and the Susquehanna Valley who were determined to get the scalp bounty that Weiser opposed. It was in this area that a large mob of antagonists nearly shot him to death. He escaped when a "great smoke" suddenly arose at the foot of Tulpehocken Mountain and his enemies hurried off to explore. He lived till 1760. When visiting his grave in Womelsdorf, George Washington said, "Posterity will not forget his service."

The "Paxtang Boys," numbering over two hundred, was one of the largest nonmilitary groups protecting any community. They were organized in 1763 by a minister of Paxtang (near modern Harrisburg) by authority of the province when the governor and assembly could no longer protect the frontier from the Indians. Few inhabitants remained in the desolated land beyond the Susquehanna. The rangers, mostly church members of the Paxtang area, became the terror of the redskins. After months of bloody conflict, the Conestogas were finally massacred, except for their Moravian converts whom the Quakers sneaked to Philadelphia. The Paxtang Boys pursued them, sending the city into such a panic that it organized troops (including Quakers) to brave the onslaught of the fierce Scotch-Irish whose infamy was prodigious. However, when the latter learned of the counterattack they surprised everyone by meeting with the governor's delegation. After presenting their grievances, they returned to church and plow. Perhaps it was harvesting time. The insurrection was over, though enduring in history.

A far more tender legend is that of Indian conversion during Bethlehem's first Christmas season. In 1741 the one log cabin had a stable and chapel below and an attic room in which the settlers lived. On Christmas Eve the chapel was beautified by the holy painted wooden figures of the putz with its evergreen and moss. The comforting glow of beeswax candles eased any fear of lurking Indians. And Count Zinzendorf had come too to share the candle service and love feast, and had given the tiny settlement its name.

By the second Christmas, there was a large community building with a big tile stove and chapel. From as far away as the Pocono Mountains the Indians came to marvel at the beauty of the service and the joyful music. They confessed that they too liked to worship before "the small papoose who knows the Great Spirit's secrets." Many were converted. Even resentful Indians were curious enough to come and investigate, and left as friends, bearing gifts of ribbons and sewing materials for their squaws. For years there was peace in Bethlehem, until those who had sworn friendship were dead.

The dissatisfaction over the Walking Treaty boiled over as the white men prospered on the old hunting grounds. The fighting French Canadians were joined by the Indians who were on the rampage throughout the colonies. When Christmas came again, the redskins gathered in the woods around Bethlehem, waiting to attack at the last toll of the bell at midnight. Though alert for the war whoop they became spellbound by the sweetness and power of the music that flooded from the chapel. One by one, they began to relax, mystified by the magic of the trombone, oboe, and flute.

"The Great Spirit has spoken," they said reverently, And, humble, they vanished again into the forest.

Our best-known Indian legend is the story of the German child, Regina. When General Braddock was defeated, Indians raided the countryside, dragging young children to their caves or huts. The ten-year-old Regina, suffering from nakedness, hunger, and exhaustion in the wilderness, even had to carry a smaller girl on her back. Though placed with a cruel old squaw, Regina grew up a Christian at heart, singing German hymns and repeating the Scriptures. She was eighteen when Colonel Bouquet and his army routed the savages and brought their captives to Fort Pitt on the Ohio River, where people came to claim lost relatives. Regina's widowed mother sang an old favorite family hymn, and so identified herself to her child. Regina had formed a strong attachment to the "little sister" she had once carried on her back. The girl, now unclaimed, joyfully made her home with them.

Friend of both Indian and white man, Johnny Appleseed was a wanderer who loved his Bible and all things of God's creation. One night in a vision he had seen the Heavenly City surrounded by beautiful orchards and was told by the angels that his mission was to scatter apple seeds in the wilderness of the West. He was weird looking, with black bushy hair and beard, and dressed in an old coffee sack or cast-off clothing. As he tramped to the Pennsylvania cider mills for seed to spread in the wilds of Ohio, he made friends with all the woodland creatures from snakes to bears. When he came to an open fertile spot that someday might be settled, he stopped to plant his seeds.

The Indians trusted him: he was a different kind of paleface, with no desire to steal their land. He often lived with them for weeks, nursing the sick back to health or binding up wounds for warriors. Once, in a Shawnee village he recognized a captive child and was the only one who could comfort her.

He bought her for two dollars, and returned her to her parents. Again, when Daniel Boone had been captured by the Indians who meant to keep this famous woodsman to glorify their tribe, Johnny consoled him with Bible reading until Boone was able to escape. If Johnny knew the redmen were planning to attack a certain settlement, he left to give warning of the danger. Sometimes he made a few pennies by mending tinware at a lonely cabin. Everywhere he was welcomed and loved. He ate with horse thieves as well as with farmers; but he never failed to open his Bible and say, "Would you like a little fresh news from heaven?"

For nearly sixty years Johnny followed the trails from New York and Pennsylvania to Iowa and Missouri, always moving westward if a region's orchards were a mass of blooms in spring. Aging, he settled in Indiana. Settlers came from miles away for his little nursery trees. He was known as "the patron saint of American orchards." Is it surprising that we Dutch who so love our apples are proud that Johnny got his first seeds from Pennsylvania?

Few legendary figures are as humble and touching as Johnny Appleseed. A striking contrast was the glamorous and ambitious "Baron" Heinrich Wilhelm Stiegel, although he too was devout and created beauty. Born in Cologne, he settled in Brickerville and married the ironmaster's daughter in 1752. He soon became rich by expanding the iron business and built several mansions, elegantly furnished. One, in the town of Manheim, which he founded, had a chapel in which he preached to his workmen and neighbors. It was in Manheim that Stiegel manufactured his exquisite glassware, made by the most skilled European artists, and much treasured today. A coach-and-four could turn around in the spacious factory. Stiegel's tower near Elizabeth Furnace had several banquet halls. A cannon or buglers on the roof saluted his visitors, or announced the arrival of the baron's chariot, with its outriders and favorite pack of dogs.

For years Stiegel was one of the wealthiest men in Pennsylvania. But "pride goeth before a fall," of course; before war broke out he went bankrupt and was briefly imprisoned. During the Revolution he made a short comeback by producing cannon, shell, and shot at Elizabeth Furnace. When creditors caused his final ruin, he became pastor of the Brickerville Lutheran Church, and also taught school in one of the little tenant houses he had erected and in which he lived. During his last years he was bookkeeper for George Ege, his nephew, ironmaster of Charming Forge, which Stiegel had once owned. Not yet sixty, he died in poverty.

Charming Forge is said to be haunted by several ghosts—though not by Stiegel's. George Ege paid the government for captured Hessian soldiers whom he put to work building a millrace, and kept at night in the attic. If you listen carefully you can hear one of them pacing the floor above you. There is also said to be a "feeling" around the Forge kitchen where a servant's dress caught fire; screaming, she ran through the house and burned to death. Yet, ghosts or no ghosts, Charming Forge still carries the aura of Stiegel's romantic life and fame. Also, his bounty is still commemorated in Manheim's First Lutheran Church for which he gave the property, the rental to be "One Red Rose in June Forever." Each year his oldest descendant is presented with the most perfect rose from a Manheim garden.

Another dashing figure with a miserable end was our counterpart of Robin Hood, who stole from the rich and gave to the poor. Lewis the Robber, born in Carlisle in 1790, helped his widowed mother support the family for many years. After deserting the militia and adopting his "career" he had many escapes from jail (ironically, he married a warden's daughter and was devoted to his wife and children) and once would have been executed except for his mother's pleas. At first he preyed on county banks, then became a counterfeiter, going to Vermont to unload his clever artwork. Though essentially a highwayman, he made "personal visits" when times were hard. Once when a terrified widow sobbed that the constable was coming to take her cow for the overdue rent, Lewis gave her the needed sum, told her to get a receipt, then later stole the constable's purse, and gave her the money. His favorite victims were those in public office: he claimed that the legislature's stinting on funds for schools had denied him learning and caused him to lead an ill-spent life. Yet when he went to rob a wealthy official and heard the family praying, he sneaked away. He not only covered our countryside but spread his talents as far as New York, robbing Mrs. John Jacob Astor of a case of jewels at an auction she attended.

And herein lies a related story (though Lewis died before the tragedy of John Jacob Astor's sister). She was a Mrs. Fessler of Bainbridge (Lancaster County); a drunkard, she kept her bottle hidden in a barrel of tow. A Bainbridge man, friend of the Astor family in Germany, traveled by foot to New York to inform Mr. Astor of his sister's plight. The millionaire denied knowing him, but later sent fifty dollars a year for his sister's relief. Eventually, the payments ceased. One night Mrs. Fessler went to the barrel for her dram, and when the tow caught fire from her candle, was so badly burned that she died, leaving two poverty-stricken children, a girl and a boy. The Astors took the girl to educate, but homesick, she ran away. The simpleminded boy lived and died beneath the roots of an ancient fallen tree along the river shore—and there was buried.

Had Lewis known the Fesslers, the Astors might well have lost more than a casket of jewels. But at thirty he died in jail from a gunshot wound— he had never killed a man to protect himself. He makes perfect legend material—handsome, reckless, and charming the ladies with his gallantry and humor.

He was a hero, indeed, compared with the villainous Simon Girty, called "a wild beast in human form." After childhood in a degenerate family he lived for a while with the Senecas, adopting their dress and customs. Bitter when he failed to become a captain in the Revolution, he turned informer for the British, took part in Indian raids, and gloried in scalping and burning white captives at the stake. One raiding party murdered Lincoln's grand-father. Girty is said to have turned religious in his old age, but a Jesuit priest fled in horror after hearing only half of his confession. True to type, Girty slyly cheated the many avengers who thirsted for his life, but froze to death at seventy-seven. A pioneer could always get his children in tow by threatening, "You behave, or Simon Girty will get you!"

Another famous murderer, though pathetic, was Susanna Cox of Oley, an unwed mother who killed her child in 1809 while bound out to the Snyder family for her board and lodging. Her one romance was with Mertz, a neighboring married farmer who visited her secretly. When one of the Snyders found a dead infant in the ground cellar. Susanna confessed to bearing the child but also swore it was stillborn. She was taken to the Reading jail. In a last confession, she admitted the murder, and, in spite of skilled defense, was hung at Gallows Hill. Twenty thousand people viewed the hanging (still done in effigy at our Kutztown Fair) and many a broadside was printed—now a rare collector's item. One of the first females to get the death penalty, Susanna was the last in the state to be publicly executed.

Well over a century before her time (when more than two hundred offenses received capital punishment in England), William Penn abolished the death penalty for all crimes but willful murder. But by 1718 the Assembly of Pennsylvania was induced to adopt a criminal code with fourteen capital offenses, one being witchcraft. This was never considered by Penn to be a vice. There is a droll story about him that gives us insight into his lightness of touch as well as his power.

As early as 1683, Penn and a council of seven presided in Philadephia at the trial of Margaret Matson, a Swede, for bewitching cattle. Though she insisted that accusations came through hearsay, the jury found her guilty of having the fame of a witch if not being guilty of the indictment. Tradition says that Penn called her before him and asked, "Art thou a witch? Hast thou ridden through the air on a broomstick?" When the prisoner answered "yea," Penn said she had a perfect right to do so—that he knew of no law that forebade it—and ordered her released.

In happy contrast to the legends of Susanna Cox and Margaret Matson, that of our Mountain Mary (die Berg-Maria) is unique and beautiful. A German immigrant of the 1760s, she was orphaned when her family died of a plague en route to Philadephia. A romance having developed between Maria and a young man on board, both worked hard for several years to save money for a home (Maria in the service of the Reverend Henry Melchior Muhlenberg). On the day after their marriage her husband was called to war and fatally wounded. His employer, an Oley Valley farmer, built a log cabin for the grieving Maria and here she lived the rest of her days. Farming a few acres for her needs, she earned a small income by sending produce to market with a neighbor. As she raised many herbs and roots and studied books on their medicinal values, she soon won renown as a nurse and healer. People came from many miles away for help, or Mary trekked to their homes regardless of weather or time of night. She was buried close to the apple tree she grafted—still bearing the "Good Mary" fruit. Her sanctity has been revered throughout the years.

Mountain Mary is confused at times with "Mary Goes Over the Mountain." Some think the latter relates to the Virgin Mary's visit to her cousin Elizabeth in Judea, as told in Luke. But the Bible makes no mention of the date or weather while she traveled, and Mary Goes Over the Mountain is somehow connected with Saint Swithin's Day. She evidently traveled on that day, but no one seems to know who she was, where she was going, or why. Swithin was bishop of Winchester, and when he died on July 15, 862, was buried in the churchyard. At his canonization, the monks wanted to remove his body to the chapel, but were unable to do so because of forty days of rain. The Dutch expect a similar spell of bad weather if it rains on that date. On the other hand, a fair July 15 will bring forty days of sunshine. Perhaps, as some say, the Mary (or Maria) associated with Saint Swithin's Day is an ancient legendary figure of Germany. At any rate, there is a confusing mingling of Marys in our tradition. (Has all this anything to do with Noah's flood, I wonder?)

Most of the foregoing legends stem from persons known in their day. But all areas have colorful characters little known or remembered beyond their own environs. One such is Old Bamberger, a native of Lancaster County over two hundred years ago. Flaunting a crimson suit, white beaver hat, flowing beard, and banner, he preached the gospel and played his trumpet on the streets. Though many mocked him he had his disciples, and even carried his missionary zeal among the Northwest Indians.

A less evangical musician was Antonio Faretti, one of the organ grinders who roamed the countryside before the turn of our century. He must have had the Pied Piper touch, as it is said the entranced young farmers would drop their hoes and follow him to neighboring farms. Even in the hottest weather Antonio wore a heavy overcoat, though he was bent from the weight of his music box "as big as a trunk." Another organ grinder, growing too old for the circuit, bought a house with thirty thousand copper pennies, and settled down among his admirers.

Several peddlers won local fame too. Tommy Collins was unique, "a little tetched." In childhood, running his sled into a tree he had suffered head injuries, and later had seen his mother burn to death. Tommy would confide in his friends, "Ever since then Tommy was never quite right." However, he amazed people by reading and speaking English fluently without a Dutch accent; yet he spoke the dialect with equal ease. He sold "notions" (but never matches) and once when a woman asked for three rows of pins, Tommy answered, "Only one row. If you buy them all I won't have any for my next customer."

He had other quirks. In spite of a cordial invitation to join a family he preferred eating in the outkitchen or shed. He complained too if the soup or coffee wasn't scalding hot. Sometimes he ordered a special menu, cracker soup for instance, and saw to it that the farm wife followed his recipe. Supper over, Tommy would join the family. He might deliver a flowery political oration or simply chat. Once he described a wooden washtub he had bought for bathing. When a child said it sounded rather small, Tommy maintained, "Oh, Tommy will stand on his feet in the tub and wash as much as he can; then he'll stand on his head and wash the rest."

The homeless Tommy slept in the boiler room of the Van Reed Paper Mill, but he was neat and clean and always dressed well until his later years. Then he developed a passion for decorating himself with safety pins, buttons, badges, and premium ribbons. Small boys began to torment him. A favorite trick was to strike a match and send Tommy running off in terror. Finally, filthy in cast-off clothing, he was picked up now and then by the police who sheltered and reclothed him. But he would always lose some of his precious medals—real agony. He died when nearly eighty but had arranged for his funeral, and a few old friends saw him to his grave.

Another legendary peddler, Der Huns John (Dog John), went about the countryside for twenty-five years selling mongrels and their pups. Sometimes as many as forty of them lived with him in the wagon where he slept and cooked. When he made no sale, he begged milk and stale bread for his pets from farmers, and meat scraps and bones from butchers.

Old, sick, or unwanted hounds became part of his entourage, and he did his utmost to rejuvenate and sell them. However, those that couldn't be "repaired" he mercifully put to sleep; they were bought then for hides, or fat rendered for medications.

In the early part of this century, Der Huns John was found in an old abandoned blacksmith shop, almost starved to death along with his animals. I'll wager that they were fed first with any random food that came his way, and that they survived mostly because of love. Der Huns John was taken to the county home, but soon died. Perhaps it's better that we don't know the fate of his pets.

These mini-legends are tame compared with those of the rugged canallers who had many a vocational challenge and close escape: besides the occasional skirmish with Indians, there were battles with robbers jumping from bridges and freak accidents that maimed or caused the death of crew members.

There were also weird encounters in a class by themselves like that with Rebekah Blackfair, a young orphan, whose foster parents treated her meanly. When she disappeared from Centreville, there was insinuating talk. The craft named *The Castle Wheel* had taken on cargo at Centreville, and as it was entering a lock some miles away, the petrels, which had followed the canal from the sea, began to circle frantically above the boat. Since they were an ill omen the crew wanted to shoot them but Daddy LaGrange, the captain, argued that this would only double any bad luck. If there were a dead man aboard he had better be found. The crew tied up to the bank and removed hundreds of bags of plaster from the hold. Then the mate raised the lid of the toolbox at the bottom, and in it was the unconscious little Rebekah. When the child was revived, the petrels left in search of more promising quarry.

It seems that Rebekah had run off hoping to find relations in Harrisburg. Seeing the canalboat at the wharf she had stolen aboard to hide and had evidently fainted with fright when the cargo was dumped above and around her. She refused to return to her foster parents, so Daddy LaGrange made contact with the Overseers of the Poor and Rebekah was given a new home and grew up to tell her story gratefully.

However, life wasn't always exciting for the canallers, who often had to create diversions. Petty thieving was one of them. As canalboat food was monotonous, the men appropriated whatever they found along the way to vary their diet. It's said that farmers always planted three extra rows of corn near a canal bank for pilfering boatmen. I like the story of small David Derr, a mule driver, and his provision of a royal dinner. David was terrified of a gander that wandered with other assorted foul and animals around a shabby homestead and always viciously attacked the mule drivers with its sharp beak and flapping wings. Usually David rode past this place on his mule. But finally, tired of being molested, he vowed that he would kill the gander and approached the farm on foot. Fastening a strong fishhook to a stout piece of twine, he baited it with corn, and dangled it in wait for his enemy's charge. When the gander gobbled it up, David began to run, the gander squawking furiously behind him. Hearing the commotion the nearsighted housewife called from a distance, "Don't run, little boy. He won't bite you." But David tore along until he was out of sight, then slit the gander's throat. David was the hero at the evening banquet, but I judge that the revelers all had strong teeth and stomachs.

Many a farmer lost not only corn and fowl, but chestnut fence rails—excellent for firewood. However, at least one boatman paid for his looting. He frequently sold rope to an "odds and ends" man after soaking it to make it heavier. In later years, when he bragged of his trick to the buyer, he was told, "I didn't mind. I had my scales adjusted to take care of such little things."

One of the busiest and most earnest navigators was Tippy, a stray fox terrier. He had been found at night caught between the bow and a loose metal strip, and was nursed and kept as mascot by Charles Fortney, a young mule driver. Scaring off "wharf rats" (thieves) was Tippy's forte. But he loved any kind of authority. If the slack towrope dipped into the water, Tippy would scold and harass the mules to speed them up or fiercely pull on the rope himself. The playful Fortney sometimes gave the mules a sharp crack and the suddenly tightened rope would send Tippy somersaulting. When Tippy's eyes began to fail he often stumbled but the lead mule never stepped on his little comrade. After sixteen faithful years he was laid to rest in a coffin lined with sheepskin, covered with a sheet of glass, and was given a more ceremonious funeral than many a canaller.

Boatmen carried on an endless feud with railmen, who willed us their own brand of legend. Ephraim Jones, an engineer on the Pennsylvania Railroad, refused to obey military orders at Chambersburg one night in 1863 and saved the lives of many people. Running a munitions train, Jones was ordered by a military officer to change his run and carry a major general and his staff to Hagerstown. He refused to take orders from anyone but the military superintendent of the railroad. "How do I know what's moving between here and Hagerstown?" he demanded. The road was single-tracked and there was obvious threat of collision. Just as Jones was put under arrest and another engineer appointed, a whistle announced that an "extra" was rushing toward them. On board the unscheduled train were Governor Curtain, a Union army general, state officials, some military doctors, and wounded Federal soldiers. It's said that later when the hero visited Gettysburg, he chuckled, "General Reynolds, if I hadn't disobeyed your orders, your statue likely wouldn't be standing here today."

A less conscientious engineer, with the aid of a tree, caught a nap daily on his late run from Reading to Pottstown. Lolling in the cab with his legs dangling from the window, Bill snored away the hour until his feet brushed the fruit tree Johnny Appleseed had planted long before. This gave him ample warning that he was nearing the station. One sad day, however, his alarm had been cut down and Bill was fired before he had service enough to draw his pension.

Engineer Donnelly who ran a pay train through the dangerous Allegheny wilderness in 1909 had to be more alert than Bill to save his neck. The first car held a small safe containing bullion and newly minted coins; the second car had strongboxes from Washington filled with half a million dollars' worth of bank notes. One midnight, Donnelly "wiped the clock" (made an emergency stop) when there was a series of explosions on the track ahead. Soon a robber appeared, brandishing two guns, and ordered the crew to fill up his sack with the loot of the first car, even forcing them to haul the heavy bag up the slope before he released them. When the train sped away there must have been some gloating; the robber had taken sixty-five dollars' worth of pennies and had overlooked the half million dollars.

There were frequent train robberies, of course. One of John Yoder's firehall stories is that of a Dutch passenger in an assaulted train who quickly passed to his friend beside him the twenty dollars he owed him.

Accidents, as well as robbers, prompted many legends. In 1856 there was a frightful passenger train accident near Philadelphia, when sixty-six lives were lost in a head-on collision. Mary Benjamin Ambler, widow and proprietor of a fulling mill at Wissahickon, rushed to the wreckage with first-aid supplies and throughout the day tended the many wounded without a moment's respite. Some of the victims were later taken to her home where she continued to nurse them. In gratitude, the railroad named the station stop Ambler, a thriving Philadelphia suburb today.

Not all accidents were fatal, of course. Some were even amusing. Before the automatic coupler was invented, it was learned at the destination of a freight train that a cattle car was mysteriously missing. Hours later the car was found empty in a snowy field along the route. The cows had all swum the river and were rounded up on the other side, safe but shivering. Although there were many theories about the cause of the enigma, none seemed logical. Perhaps it was due to hexerei!

In a unique way, the railroad sired another category of legend in a class by itself. Some of our most dramatic stories derive from the days of the Underground Railroad (the organization helping fugitive slaves escape to the free states or to Canada) for there was much subversive activity here. Many a Dutch farm was the "station" to which a "conductor" (guide) brought his charges to be fed, clothed, hidden, and, hopefully, sent on to freedom. Quakers started the movement in southeastern Pennsylvania as early as the time of George Washington, who wrote a friend in 1786 about absconding slaves: "It is not easy to apprehend them because there are a great number of people who would rather facilitate the escape ... than apprehend the runaway." When pursued by the British, Washington himself is said to have found refuge in a cave at the Knauer mansion at French Creek, a cave often harboring slaves. In the next seventy-five years, thousands of people became involved either actively or financially with the movement, risking civic status if not life itself.

In the decade after the passage of the Fugitive Slave Law in 1850 hazards reached a climax. "Runaway Slave Wanted" posters infested villages and cities. Paid slave hunters with chains, whips, and guns tracked down Negroes and sent them south to their owners. Resisting blacks were shot. Even the "Free Papers" of some Negroes were publicly burned. Many an antiabolitionist made money by informing on a strange black face. A group known as the Gap Land Gang raided railway stations or wagons suspected of carrying black women and children from one underground station to another, and turned them over to the authorities for reward. A woman wanting to open a school for Negro children was imprisoned. When Thomas Garrett, a Quaker of Chester County and underground operator, was fined $8,000 he defied the court: "Judge, thee has left me with a single dollar. But I wish to say to thee and to this whole courtroom, that if anyone knows of a fugitive who needs shelter, send him to Thomas Garrett who still has a dollar." Others suspected of being operators or "shareholders" (financial supporters) were mobbed or threatened. Abolitionists were even reviled and persecuted by most churches, for the average person believed in a "gradualism" policy of freedom.

Nevertheless, the Anti-Slavery Society of Philadelphia continued to contact southern sympathizers and recruit runaways, hiding them in the Purvis mansion in a secret room built for this purpose. Messages would then be sent on to operators to expect "prime articles" or "boxes and small hams." Conductors continued to sneak slaves at night from one station to the next, usually ten miles northward.

Idealists continued to risk their lives. Among them was Hannah Gibbons. The Quaker Gibbons family of Lancaster County sheltered at least a thousand fugitives in its day. Hannah, at forty-nine, once shut herself up in a room with a Negro who had smallpox, and for six weeks nursed him back to health. By then he was able to follow the North Star by night and hide in the woods by day, taking one of the various routes to Canada. Another visionary, "Bully" Lyons, Reading town constable, locked fugitives up in the jail and boldly fed them at city expense until the underground was ready to move them on.

The Christiana riot in 1851 has been considered a major factor leading to the Emancipation Proclamation and to the Civil War itself. Warrants had been obtained for the seizure of Parker and other black fugitives who lived in a Negro colony where Parker operated a station of the underground. For some time he and his cohorts had escaped the treacheries of the Gap Land Gang. But one day Parker was warned of an invasion of kidnappers, and returning from the fields, was confronted by Klein and Gorsuch, deputies with warrants.

Parker forced them from his house, but they threatened to burn it down if he didn't peacefully concede. Mrs. Parker at an upstairs window blew the horn that signaled the underground for help. When Klein fired at her, she crouched beneath the window and continued to blow. Further shooting, not only by the deputies but by the enlisted Gap Land Gang pouring from the woods, attracted many whites of both factions: Klein read his warrant and futilely demanded their help. When Parker who had appeared at the door was wounded in the head, the first shots were fired from the house. Gorsuch was killed instantly, his son was wounded, and Klein and the Gap Land Gang fled into the woods. Infuriated Negroes rushed toward young Gorsuch to kill him too, but Parker calmed them and sent for a doctor who saved the young man's life.

By nighttime the house was filled with deputy marshals, police, U.S. commissioners, and lawyers. Parker was induced to flee with his brothers-in-law to Canada to await their families. But they were never reunited; the wives were later seized by slaveholders who sent them south.

There was so much public dissension over the riot that twenty-four U.S. Marines and eighty police were brought to Christiana to maintain peace. Several white men and nearly forty Negroes were charged with treason and levying war against the government. All were imprisoned in Philadelphia, and all but two Negroes escaping from jail were tried. The jury reached a verdict of "not guilty" but the defendants were only released after three months in jail. These and other excesses resulting from the Fugitive Slave Law turned many neutral citizens into active abolitionists, and this in turn led the angry South into secession, which precipitated war.

During the years when the underground waged its battle, new trades and professions were arising with the Industrial Revolution. The anthracite region had a large ethnic mixture: English, Welsh, Scotch, and Irish originally, then an influx of Germans, Slavs, and other races. Tales of mining disasters or strikes have a tragic sameness. The Molly Maguire legend, too long and involved to include here in toto, is unique however.

The Molly Maguire terrorists (named for a secret society in Ireland and subversive here as well) were more or less harmless at first, but grew in strength and violence during the Civil War when the increasing need for coal drew many lawless Irish workers to the region. They intimidated English and German miners and threatened dunning landlords, police, and despotic superintendents especially. Sympathizers with any of these were also targets. The society was well organized to do away with coercion in all areas; if one area planned murder, it recruited members from another to do the "dirty work," making indictment harder.

Murders, burnings, and other outrages increased after the war, causing general strikes. When young, my mother-in-law lived in Girardville next to one of the leaders, John Kehoe. His household seemed normal except for strange comings and goings late at night. When a skull and crossbones appeared on a man's property, he knew he had better make a getaway—if there were still time! A butcher who found the warning on his wagon one day drove off in panic (to safety, I hope) and was never seen in town again. After twenty years the society was dissolved through the grit of an Irish Pinkerton detective who worked for two years as a miner, was a member of the terrorists, and barely escaped detection when he was assigned to murder. His evidence led to the trial and execution of the ringleaders.

Even normally, mining was hazardous and unpredictable from day to day, but so was the life of lumberjacks. It took rugged men to conquer treacherous currents and giant jutting rocks; to pilot the huge logs destined for masts of sailing vessels as far away as England. No wonder they relaxed with squirrel or tobacco whiskey! Fights were so common that the scars from an enemy's spiked boots were called "loggers' smallpox."

Much of their lusty fun too was at the expense of another. There was an inveterate drinker named Guthrie who believed himself injured in an accident, though a doctor said he suffered only from booze. His companions took him to a hotel room and convinced him that his leg must be amputated. Blatantly, they produced knives, saw, and bandages. More whiskey was given the raving Guthrie as an anesthetic, and several men held him on an improvised operating table, while others "got to work." Guthrie was then shown a bloody beef bone—and given more whiskey, as he "soon might die." When he bawled for a priest, another prankster played the role. The next day his pals came to get him back to work, but Guthrie wept, though half sober now, "I can't—I've lost my leg." On learning the truth, he had to be dragged to the barroom to drown his humiliation.

All these legends and many others are among the potpourri we enjoy when we have time to grow mellow and reminiscent. How old is our Dutch legendary background? By the time the Age of Reason with its pompous literary forms and philosophy caused a romantic reaction, and before England became interested in a study of its old customs and formed the Folklore Society in London, the European Germans already had their Volkskinde embracing all rural life, including dances and festivals. We Dutch too like the security of a warmer, more tangible contact with others' lives.

Though in recent years we have become more aware of our rich heritage, unfortunately many legends have never been recorded and someday may be forgotten. However, scholars are at work to preserve them, and since many are based on history and national crises, they should outlast our more trivial jokes and anecdotes, amusing though they are. The legend satisfies a deep desire for "roots"—the sense of belonging to the earth and people about us, and, even more important, to the America we are helping to build.

The Dutch Weather Vane

OUR DUTCH WEATHER VANE—WHICH WAY IS IT POINTING? TO SUNNY SKIES FOR our well-loved Dutch heritage, or to stormy weather that can destroy it? I have dwelt mainly on the past and present of our culture, but what of its future?

There's an old Dutch saying: "Everything has an end but a sausage and that has two ends." An exception seems to be this kind of book. Since I began it, there have been constant changes in statistics, trends, and events. For instance, the Gruber Wagon Works has been safely moved, and Saint Peter's Village has been sold—whether for better or worse, remains to be seen. At present things look rosy, since reputedly the nineteenth-century gingerbread atmosphere and craft shops will be maintained. The gurgling little French Creek falls will have a happy way of taking care of themselves, as always.

Why do we Dutch, like all other ethnic groups, want to preserve our folklore? The answer is simple: it represents not only our unique point of view in crafts, arts, customs, social intercourse, recreation, and holidays, but is a continuing search for our hidden deeper spirit.

Yet once more we must delve into the past to understand the present and evaluate the future. Throughout most of history, all folklore culture was practically unknown to strangers except for random travelers and students. In 1876, when the Folklore Society was formed in London, England's interest in folklore led to our own American Folklore Society and an occasional revival like that of cowboy songs in 1910. But it was nearly mid-century before the nation took serious note of its varying cultures. (Long before then,

Germany and Russia were using folklore as propaganda—the former to further the superior race concept.)

Lawrence Cahill wrote recently in the *American German Review:* "Folk art is the expression of the common people, made by them and intended for their use and enjoyment. It is not the expression of professionals made for a small cultured class and it has little to do with the fashionable art of the period. It does not come out of an academic tradition, but out of craft tradition plus the personal quality of the rare craftsman who is an artist."

I would like to add more. Folk art is an expression of the common people because its roots are in their ancient past. Many Dutch do not understand the deeper meaning of the motifs on things they see or use from day to day, yet they feel their symbolism instinctively. This is the prime reason for the "enjoyment" Lawrence Cahill mentions. Since our inheritance is rich, we're proud of those who express our folk art and the rest of our culture. Though all of us are not equally creative, of course, some of the humblest have shown their talent simply in tilling the soil or using the penknife.

Yet, what of our craftsmen? Have they seen their day? There are few left whose work is their love who can make even a meager living with painstaking skill and fine materials. Their items are usually small things that catch on as a fad, like the lovely glass window ornaments, for instance. Large things such as custom-made furniture are almost unheard of, for the price must be out of reach compared with that of manufactured furniture. Ever since the Industrial Revolution, mass production—helped along by national advertising and the glamour of store displays—has been a growing threat to the crafts. If crafts survive or revive, as they do (this is true particularly in the past decade), they still have to prevail against the times.

More and more old things like my beloved lemon juice squeezer have become passé. Modern products of "planned obsolescence," of cheap materials and assembly-line workmanship, must soon be discarded. Unless, of course, you want to pay the inflationary repair charges! For years we stored a wash machine (replaced, I must admit, for a new one with more gadgets) that we couldn't give away. Moreover, no social agency would take it either, or help us to dispose of it. And yet it was in good running condition, and when hurricane Agnes caused a flood here, many people were in dire need of any kind of household equipment. We finally paid to have it hauled to a dump pile.

Old Dutch folk are usually content with what they have. But the young want everything they see. Everyone must have a TV (more necessary than a toothbrush), a car or two, French provincial in the bedroom, and "wall-to-wall"—once known as carpeting. By "everyone" I mean a cross section of our Dutch city populations, though this now includes many auslanders such as Italians, Poles, and Puerto Ricans. And why pay cash? The installment plan is so much easier—until the first of the month comes around.

The main concern of the average modern man, the Dutch included, is not creating more beauty but making more money, and in many cases inflation has made this essential. Confined to a factory job, he goes through the same motions thousands of times a day, with no need for imagination or intelligence. But his paycheck is fat and he tells himself that he is happy. Though most of the "pure" Dutch are strong-minded, mass thinking can be contagious. If the epidemic continues, what will become not only of our creativity but of our traditional sense of thrift? Will industry obliterate them entirely?

There's one typical Dutchman, though, who wouldn't let "progress" take over without a struggle. A new state road was to be broken through Ezra's farm, and surveyors came to mark it off with red flags. That night Ezra moved them. When the foreman confronted him the next day, Ezra said firmly, "No new road ain't going through *my* hayfield." The foreman read him the authority signed by the governor. Ezra was silent. But when the men got to erecting the flags again he freed his prize bull from the barn. Naturally, it made a dash for the toreadors, who scrambled up the nearest trees. "You get that damned bull penned up," shouted the angry foreman, "or he'll soon be fresh beefsteak!" Ezra shrugged. "Vell, vy don't you read him your paper?" he suggested.

Our farmers welcome constructive agricultural changes, often having taken the initiative. They know the advantage of the newest methods and machinery, and their own importance in the country's welfare. And their creed is spreading; enrollment in the College of Agriculture of Pennsylvania State University is the fifth largest in the nation and growing annually. Curiously enough, two-thirds of the freshmen are from nonrural homes. They specialize not only in agriculture but in horticulture, husbandry, and environmental resource management. A Dutch proverb says: "Even a clever hen will lay outside the nest."

Only the Plain sects continue to go their old-fashioned way, buying the farms of the "worldly" who succumb to higher education and city jobs. Yet, paradoxically, the Amishman or Mennonite is going to keep his reputation as the area's best farmer for a long time to come. His wife too will not neglect the traditional culinary or medicinal garden for a new species of zinnia.

But, on the whole, industrial progress is strangling individuality. The progress is slow and insidious. Many a Dutch city wife works in a factory too, while her young ones are in a day care center. Fine and dandy, if her income is needed for food and shoes, or if family life doesn't suffer. But who can say what the damage will be by the time the children are grown and the reckoning comes too late? Not that I'm debunking careers for women. (I'm in a glass house myself and can't throw stones!)

We Dutch had our women's libbers long before any torch was brandished. Way back in 1798 our Anne Moore was the first woman ever appointed to an office by the federal government, taking over the post-office duties of her dead husband for thirty-one years. And this, when there were only a few respectable vocations for single women: sewing, teaching, weaving, bookbinding, and the like. Then too, a hundred years ago, though most women were cooking for the harvesters, we had ardent workers for the Christian Temperance Union.

The Pennsylvania German Harriet Lane, while hostess for Buchanan in the White House, worked to correct the abuse of Indians, and, in zealous dealing with government agents, improved medical and educational facilities. She also strove for a national art center in Washington, and, with her husband, established the Harriet Lane Hospital for Children's Diseases in Baltimore. We can boast too of our Jane Addams who founded Hull House, the Chicago settlement school, and of Amelia Earhart. These are only a few of our distinguished career women. Their number continues to grow, though the average Dutch hausfrau loves home best and is proud because "she's wearing new shoes on the baby" and has knitted them herself.

Maybe I've painted too dark a picture of what modern trends have done and may do to the Dutch. We're a strong people in many ways, and who can stifle individuality—the life force? It's like thinking you've destroyed a dandelion plant only to find that some tiny hidden root has escaped you. Though swept along with the tide of progress people need self-expression, and appreciation as well. Since history has a way of repeating itself, are we going into a cycle of seeking the intimacy of others like that which occurred after the Age of Reason? Of rebelling against the "coldness" of industrial living—too much stress on the worth of the dollar? Are we getting tired of being machines, and hunting our lost individuality?

We Dutch have one big advantage here. We have many old and rural communities in which those dandelion roots are deeply embedded.

Before the world wars, Alexis Carrel in his *Man the Unknown* was perceptive enough to make the following statement: "An individual remains a man when he belongs to a small group, inhabits a village or small town where his relative importance is greater, where he can hope to become an influential citizen." (Is this why so many city people today are seeking refuge in our area where they can find solitude, develop their potential for beauty, and be individual? In the countryside one no longer has to fight his social surroundings but can let his spirit go free.)

The Dutchman came to the New World expecting freedom, tolerance, and unity of purpose. He thought and talked naturally of his fatherland as "home," but didn't want to return there to live. (Nor does today's immigrant who is grateful for America's opportunities.) Though the Dutch settler preferred his own provincial little world to the bigger world around him, he had to be flexible to survive. Yet he adopted only the customs, foods, arts, and ideas of others that *fulfilled his purpose*. From the first, he wanted any change he made to be *voluntary*.

Holding on to tradition as long as possible is a natural trait of the stubborn Dutch. And speaking of "stubborn," I once heard of a farm girl who decided to toughen her muscles by daily lifting a newborn calf from birth to bull size. How traumatic for both, no doubt equally willful!

We still relish our sauerkraut more than golumpki or pizza, and refuse to abandon our basic thinking and dialect, especially in such areas as Blandon, Oley, Leesport, Bernville or Ephrata, Lancaster and Adamstown. And occasionally we win a convert. We were much amused when a southern family we knew moved to Oley and their high-school daughter's Georgia accent was soon being infected by the Dutch—quite a droll combination.

We have our cultural missionaries too. The many Plain people who leave our area today for the South, Midwest, and Canada definitely have an effect on the communities in which they settle, spreading our traditions and dialect.

The fate of our dialect is a vital challenge today. Will we let it and all it stands for disappear? Not if some of our scholars can prevent it! In 1949 a department of American folklore was established at Franklin and Marshall College in Lancaster, the first such venture in the nation. It was instigated by three professors, all with doctorates, and all of whom had published material on Dutch culture or the eighteenth-century emigration. Among their special interests were dialect and literature; the Amish and their customs; history of religions; German imprints and bibliography of Pennsylvania; folk songs; crafts; traditions.

These three talented men, all from different counties, were Alfred L. Shoemaker, J. William Frey, and Don Yoder. Naming their project the Pennsylvania Dutch Folklore Center, Incorporated, they began by founding a journal, *The Pennsylvania Dutchman* (now *Pennsylvania Folklife*). It had immediate appeal. As the contents were varied, much being in dialect, other scholars began to contribute too.

Pennsylvania State University added Dutch dialect classes to its curriculum. Moreover, within a few years, due to the Folklore Center, thousands of recipes were tested and standardized for modern cookbooks, and sold to tourists. (Our cooking is not distinctive because we use different foods from the rest of America, but because of our Germanic preference and preparation.) Due to three dedicated men at Franklin and Marshall, interest in all things Dutch flamed like brush fire.

But there were a few other scholars who had "jumped the gun" alone and must have helped lay the brush pile. In 1935, Paul R. Wieand, teacher, artist, and lecturer on folklore, was the first to appear on radio. Invisible and with a falsetto voice he became "Sabina," a hilarious Dutch woman who enslaved all fun-lovers. In 1940, Gilbert Snyder, a school supervisor, first enthralled listeners of WEEU as "Die Wunnernaws," and was popular for years.

Dr. Frey has said, "The dialect may eventually die out but it's doubtful that its effect on the English language will ever die."

In 1950 the Folklore Center organized the Pennsylvania Dutch Folk

Festival at Kutztown. Two years later at Bynden Wood in Berks County the first annual seminar of Pennsylvania Dutch culture drew outstanding scholars in many fields as leaders. Folk festivals increased. Flocks of people from around the nation who had never been to our area came to learn about the Dutch. There was a growing demand for Dutch antiques and crafts that amounted to a craze. In a few random verses of "The Country Sale," William J. Meter wrote:

> *The people come from far away*
> *In big machines and small,*
> *Some dressed so fancy like*
> *It wonders me they call.*
>
> *I seen them buy a butter-mold*
> *For fifty cents or more*
> *That we could get for twenty cents*
> *Down at Chon Grumber's store.*
>
> *Yes well, the country sale makes good*
> *For auctioneers and all,*
> *Enough old stuff gets redd away*
> *To fill the fire hall.*

The trek to the distelfink country still continues. Our many bicentennial attractions drew great numbers of tourists, though even during the preceding year over half a million visited Lancaster County alone. At the moment, the weather vane indicates good weather, but is Dutch culture simply a passing fad? Not if we don't let it wither away from within!

And this is certainly possible. I've sadly noticed that many of my educated friends take our folklore for granted and consequently know little about it. At a recent dinner I attended, one careless guest called barn signs "hexerei." And of the ten of us, all local, no one but me had ever heard of Till Eulenspiegel. Yet what is going to replace such folktales and other fantasies and legends? What is going to satisfy the child in us that would rather make-believe with clothespins and mud pies—is it going to be TV-advertised "boughten" plastic toys?

Being an innately simple folk, we need an element of mystery to give life full satisfaction. Some of our intellectuals turn to spiritualism, philosophies like Zen, and many varieties of the paranormal. Others fantasize about life on the moon or the grotesque little UFO men from some remote planet. The farmer feels the mystic when he hopefully plants his corn, and his hausfrau when her love goes into her flowers and returns tenfold in a nameless comfort and beauty. The majority of us know the power of the mystical in the miracle of a newborn child. Mysticism is all around us and within us during the daily hours of living, if we are wise enough to sense it. Even in the compassionate touch of another's hand.

That's why our powwowing lives on from generation to generation. In ancient times it was called "the laying on of hands." Today it is more generally known as faith healing, the power of mind over matter—"mind" being the God in us. Tomorrow it may have a different name.

Here, as elsewhere, all facets of mysticism are being revived, though twentieth-century religion has drifted away from it. In most of the sects of our own areas anything that savors of the occult is taboo, even if the Devil has long been accepted as Enemy Number One. And if it isn't taboo, it's apt to be kept sub rosa so that we won't be laughed at in this age of science. But we are also in the age of Aquarius, the time for spiritual growth. Consequently, all Christian churches should be the first to confirm any kind of power of mind over matter—or why celebrate Christmas or Easter?

Yet, since over the centuries we Dutch have always sought for "the God in us," most of us still attend or support churches, feeling need for the faith and discipline around which our whole culture has been built. And the hard-core Dutchman still likes to hear a sermon in German, with no tomfoolery or rationalizing about morals.

The tomfoolery comes when church is out. Everything has its time and place in the Dutchman's life, and a bit of fun in all seven days a week is no exception. Last fall I went to the service of a little church in Oley. One of the members (who had helped with Communion) was regaling a circle of friends, and shamelessly I eavesdropped. He was telling how he had driven home in a terrible fog; when something struck his windshield and he was forced to stop, there on his fender was a big fat catfish. Then all around him he saw suckers and catfish swimming in the mist. Moreover, he even caught a nice mess for supper. At the laughter he turned solemnly to the preacher: "Ain't not, Reverend? *You* helped me and Mattie eat them." The preacher only grinned.

Wit, like God-seeking, is just one of the basic Dutch qualities stressed in this book that strengthens our culture and contributes to its longevity. Compassion is another. The Dutchman's heart is as big as a storefront Valentine. In these callous days of hurrying past a city accident for fear of legal involvement, the Dutchman—no matter how busy he may be—is ready to share another's crisis.

A month ago a fire took the lives of two small children. Neighbors gathered at the gutted Hauseman home and worked all day to clear away the debris, and will help further as they are needed. Even strangers sent gifts of food and clothing to the grief-stricken family. "It's hard to believe such friendship," wept Mr. Hauseman, "yet I always knew there were more good people than all the bad ones you read about."

Compassion, love of beauty and self-expression, obstinacy, mysticism, native wit, and strong traditionalism—where are all these long-ingrained traits going to lead us as civilization advances? The Dutchman has no intention of letting the new impair his individuality. Perhaps we have so many tourists here because we're one of the last sections of the country to be steadfast to our heritage, our folklore, customs, and morals.

Our strong conservatism, though, may be either the greatest detriment to our beneficial growth, or a major factor of cultural survival. Old times (along with our own hard work) have treated us bounteously, and we won't let them slip away without a battle. Let the city commissions raze whole blocks of buildings, including ancient midtown houses, in preparation for malls, and what happens? Groups like the Historic Preservation Trust only make greater effort to save what is historically valuable. We may have to move from our aged apartment nest with fireplace and wide windowsills to a modern one with tissue paper walls and no place for our violets. And we'll be mad as a hatter. We'll start to campaign against "progress" and its dangers, the way our ancestors did, though we know we may be forced to relent in the end, or compromise, at least.

This doesn't mean that we want to go back to the eras of Conestoga wagons, canals, and carriages. We're far past mourning the "good old days" of sleighing like the Morgantown man in 1846 who wrote: "Sleighing is not what it once was ... has lost its romance, poetry, its sentiment. In this utilitarian age folks go in sleighs on business, or make business in order to go sleighing. . . . No dashing from tavern to tavern. The young may take their sweethearts sleighing but it's a dull thing and falls far short of their daddies' doings in the same line of business."

Being conservative we may even be scared to death of flying. One Dutchman was so terrified on his first flight that the stewardess had to call the pilot to soothe him. "Don't be afraid, sir," said the pilot. "You won't die till your number comes up." . . . "But what if *your* number comes up?" chattered the Dutchman. The average Dutchman still isn't "so" for travel. Some few have their chartered trips to the Wesley or Germanic countries, or perhaps to the Holy Land. But a bus trip to Florida is safer. And still safest is remaining at home where we can comfortably read the paper, likely the *Reading Eagle* (once the *Adler,*) which hasn't changed its politics in over a century.

Yes, change is far from our liking at times. Too many oldsters can remember fifty years back when a thing was either right or wrong, when there was no thought of accepting ideas and cultures for the advancement they might have to offer. Italians, Chinese, and blacks were considered inferior, something for amusement in a book or picture show. China, for instance, was a place your child tried to reach by digging down far enough in his sand hole at the beach. But you knew he'd never get there.

Today, not only the Dutch but all Americans must become accustomed to the influx of other ethnic races. (Isn't that what America has always been about?) They should be healthful for our future too. While they cling to their own traditions, the more we guard our own. And yet, in the meantime, there is a mutual osmosis. In assimilating the best of each other's cultures, we learn to cooperate. We adjust to a variety of temperaments and customs, to being treated for some special "itis" by an Oriental doctor, to tolerating, if not condoning, mixed marriages and changing morals. Perhaps the Dutchman's saving grace is his uncanny talent of sensing the true from the false in people and things—in separating the chaff from the seed of progress.

The concept of One World is recent and hard to accept. However, we Dutch are smart enough to know that we as well as the Eurasians must grow with the times. It's a law of nature (and no one understands nature better than we do) that the withered leaf makes place for the new spring growth.

Children, being closer to their Source, know this through intuition, and willingly abandon toy animals for school days. When the teen-ager gets his driver's license, childish pranks fail to amuse him. Perhaps youth's greatest failing, as well as virture, is being absorbed in the present. The past is a bore. (You'll find few of the young, if any, working on family genealogies in the Historical Society library.) The future seems infinite. Yet, religions and philosophies have taught us down through the ages that living in the present is what counts—the living day to day successfully with others as well as with one's self.

As we mature, we may want to keep some of our former treasures (now in the attic), but actually they are only reminders of social, intellectual, and spiritual growth. Only in old age does one appraise the life picture he has painted over the years, and he is rare and blessed indeed who approves the whole, though he may blush at details. Only when we're old do we take interest in our forefathers' lives and the rich inheritance they gave us. (How often I've regretted not listening more carefully to my father's tales of his early life in the West—his friendship with Buffalo Bill and Annie Oakley, his narrow escapes from shotguns in a barroom fracas, and his triumph as first mayor of the tiny settlement of North Platte, Nebraska.)

But perhaps the youthful attitude of "today is the day" is best. Only what is most meaningful and colorful will be retained from the past. Alfred Shoemaker simply and wisely put it, "If folk belief lives on, it is filling a need in man's soul."

Though our own Dutch culture still seems to fill a great need in most of us, we too want the advantages of progress without sacrificing tradition, as I have stressed earlier in this book. And progress today leans toward unification.

Then centuries from now, as cultures blend, how will one distinguish that of the Dutch from any other? Every writer's style has a special flavor. Famous paintings don't need a signature. Hearing an old record, a good musician knows at once if he's listening to Bach, Chopin, or Debussy. A connoisseur knows the "feel" of Stiegel glass or Paul Revere silver. Have you ever dreamed of a lost loved one without actually seeing the face or form, and yet not doubted the identity for a moment because of the vibrations, the essence of the personality? This is how one will recognize our Dutch folklore in the far-off future.

What we carry in our genes and what we have created over the generations in our love of living will surely survive. Moreover, it will reflect a constant growing built upon our uniqueness of personality. It likely won't be what we now envision it, and why should it be?

We must aim for harmony—unity, not uniformity. Disparity in marriage partners can prove fulfilling, enriching, and inspiring if they look for the best in each other. One always has something to give that the other lacks. Isn't all life a matter of give and take and being wise enough to know when to do either? And nations are becoming marriage partners. John Joseph Stoudt said, "Only by discovering his home in the shared human spirit, in the Ground Being, can modern man avoid the schizoid threat of meaninglessness and despair which hangs over him."

This is a tremendous challenge, especially for the placid Dutch. Growth toward peace means suffering. It involves the curse of wars, destruction, crime, drugs, temporary annihilation of beauty and hope, and yielding the ego to the good of the whole. But only as a sacrifice to a world of eventual understanding and cooperation.

In any event, I predict that Dutch traits and folklore will outlive other American provincial cultures. My reasoning is simple. Throughout the confusing social transitions of the centuries, if anyone has remained "all of a piece" it is the Dutchman. We once laughed with John Yoder when he said, "I'm glad I don't like spinach because if I liked the damned stuff I'd be eating it all the time and I don't want to be eating something all the time I don't like."

There is something magnetizing about John and Lizzie Yoder when you feel the need to get your balance. I can understand now why I drove up there for supper just before I finished this book. I felt tense, weary, and empty of motivation, and being with the Yoders is soothing. They seem to have a halo of contentment, despite their share of sadness and ill fortune.

As I went around to the back door I knew I would leave refreshed by the very sight of the well-kept garden, the snoring old dog, John's fishing pole at the doorway, and the gleam of Lizzie's pots. Their unhurried talk or silences—both so natural—are relaxing. My own feet have always felt more comfortable when I looked at Lizzie's shoes with holes cut out for the bunions. We're all like the Yoders, I thought, behind our false façades.

They were in the kitchen, both of them being creative. John was whittling while Lizzie stirred her inimitable fried potatoes. Each was concentrating on the job of *now* as if there were no tomorrow. John had forgotten the day's factory work. Already there was a little pile of shavings on the floor. Lizzie's lips were puckered like a spider web, as when she's bent on ironing a curtain ruffle to perfection. But they were delighted to see me. I had become their *now*, despite John's embryo pig and Lizzie's frying, though they kept on with both. They always relished news of my family and Reading, especially if I'd been lucky enough to see a devastating fire. I thought, "They're as much alike as two weathered old bricks on a barnside, and just as sturdy." Yet I'd heard them have their quarrels. Once Lizzie had sputtered, "You're stubborn like a dozen bulls!"

"Chust two bulls that vant the same cow," John snorted.

"What for dirty talk is that—and at *your* aiche yet?" But Lizzie's grin was the catalyst.

"Yes, vell," John yielded, "I'll root out them peonies if you're *sure* they're froze dead."

When my news was exhausted and we had settled down to eat, I asked Lizzie, "And what have *you* been doing lately?"

"Vy, like always," she said, complacent.

"Did you finish your quilt for the new baby?"

"Yah, it's done. I show you later. They come for it Sundays."

"Mary's husband seems like a nice young man—and ambitious too."

Lizzie grunted. "Yah, he always wants to be where he ain't."

"Like that fly you're trying to swat," I teased her.

"Aye, yi, yi, it's awful. You got to clean up fly specks all over. . . . Poor Mary too. That Mike's alvays changing chobs and shirts and making more work still. It don't make sense."

"He's young yet," John defended him, digging into more coleslaw. "Anyvays, he don't change beds like some."

"Ach no, he's got it good vis Mary. She's Leah's best worker." The fly met its destiny with a whack of Lizzie's newspaper. "Yes, vell, like Mom used to say, 'It'll be all the same a hundred years from now.' "

But would it, I wondered. That's what I'd been feverishly trying to decide in the last few weeks. Perhaps I didn't understand my adopted people after all, I thought. Our contribution to the past was evident enough. The *now* presented questions. But surely our future was equivocal. A weather vane could be fickle, depending on unlooked-for high winds or storms. Wasn't it brash of me to make predictions? And yet, why was being with the Yoders so reassuring?

Lizzie passed me the rhubarb tart again. Since I'd already had one big piece, I refused, but added, "It couldn't be better."

John put another big piece on my plate. "The more you eat Lizzie's pie the better it gets."

"All right," I conceded, "to celebrate. I'm nearly finished with my writing."

Lizzie looked pleased and thoughtful. "It wonders me why you put me and Chon in that book," she said. "We're chust common."

In the moment before I answered, the whole purpose of four years of work became suddenly clear.

"That's why you're worth writing about, Lizzie. . . . You and John are—lasting!"

On one of our family holidays years ago, as we were ready to leave for home, I found our small Elaine standing in the hotel corridor gazing wistfully into her deserted room. She had fallen in love with the elevator boy and was loath to leave. I heard her saying softly, "Good-bye, Room."
And with the same nostalgia, I say now, "Good-bye, Book."

Glossary

aiche	*age*	meidung	*shunning*
ain't not?	*isn't it so?*	outen	*turn out*
auslander	*foreigner; outsider*	pannhaus	*scrapple*
braucherei	*powwowing*	Pennsylfawnish	
butzing	*cleaning up*	Deutsch Eck	*Pennsylvania Dutch corner*
common	*natural*	Plain	*referring to the religious*
company room	*guest room*		*sects (Amish, Mennonite, etc.)*
distelfink	*thistle finch*		*who wear plain clothes, ad-*
dumpkopf	*stupid person*		*here to old customs, and lead*
dunnervetter	*exclamation—"thunder weather"*		*a simple life*
fasnacht	*a kind of doughnut*	redd up	*tidy up*
ferhuddled	*confused*	rutsch	*squirm*
flieg Weber	*flying Weber*	salad	*garden lettuce*
flitch	*bacon*	schmart	*smart; wise*
frau	*wife*	schmier	*ointment*
friendschaft	*relationship; intimate group*	schmierkase	*cottage cheese*
funnel cake	*batter pressed through a funnel*	schnapps	*whiskey*
	and deep fried	schnitz	dried apple slices
gay Dutch	*those not of a Plain sect*	scholla	*echoes*
grex	*complain; grumble*	schtuff	*stuff*
grossmutter	*grandmother*	speck	*bacon*
hasenpfeffer	*stew of marinated rabbit meat;*	spritz	*spatter; sprinkle suddenly*
	a card game	tetched	*demented*
Heilige Schrift	*holy writing; Bible*	tut	*small paper bag*
hex	*a witch; to bewitch*	verhext	*bewitched*
himmel	*heaven*	wonderschöen	*wonderful*
it wonders me	*it puzzles me*	worldly	*not of the Plain sects*
leb-cake	*gingerbread*	wrenching	*wringing*
lottwarrick	*apple butter*	wunnerfitsich	*curious; nosy*

Index